HISTORICAL STUDIES
OF THE
ENGLISH PARLIAMENT

HISTORICAL STUDIES
OF THE
ENGLISH PARLIAMENT

VOLUME 1
ORIGINS TO 1399

EDITED BY

E. B. FRYDE

Reader in History, University College of Wales, Aberystwyth

AND

EDWARD MILLER

Professor of Medieval History, University of Sheffield

CAMBRIDGE
AT THE UNIVERSITY PRESS
1970

Published by the Syndics of the Cambridge University Press
Bentley House, 200 Euston Road, London, N.W.1
American Branch: 32 East 57th Street, New York, N.Y. 10022
Introduction, notes and this selection © Cambridge University Press 1970
Library of Congress Catalogue Card Number: 78-96088
Standard Book Number:
521 07613 7 clothbound
521 09610 3 paperback

Reprinted in Great Britain
by Bookprint Limited, Crawley, Sussex

In Memory of
HELEN CAM

CONTENTS

NOTES ON CONTRIBUTORS

H. M. CAM

Late Fellow of Girton College, Cambridge and subsequently Professor of History, Harvard University.

SIR GORONWY EDWARDS

Sometime Fellow of Jesus College, Oxford and subsequently Director of the Institute of Historical Research, University of London.

E. B. FRYDE

Reader in History, University College of Wales, Aberystwyth.

J. E. A. JOLLIFFE

Late Fellow of Keble College, Oxford.

F. W. MAITLAND

Late Downing Professor of Laws of England at the University of Cambridge.

T. F. T. PLUCKNETT

Late Professor of Legal History, The London School of Economics and Political Science, University of London.

T. F. TOUT

Late Professor of History, University of Manchester.

R. F. TREHARNE

Late Professor of History, University College of Wales, Aberystwyth.

B. WILKINSON

Sometime Professor of History, University of Toronto.

PREFACE

SINCE the times of the Tudors and the Stuarts, the problem of the origins
and the early history of the English parliament has engaged the attention of
publicists, politicians and historians. The very fact that parliament became
the masterpiece of the English constitution, and that it exercised the
influence it did upon constitutional development in the British Commonwealth and in lands beyond the British sphere of direct influence, has made
its development even in its earliest stages a matter of enquiry, discussion
and sometimes political mythology. In this debate it can be argued that the
publication in 1893 of F. W. Maitland's discussion of the Lenten Parliament of 1305 represented a watershed. Since that time medieval and Tudor
parliaments have been subjected to detailed and systematic scrutiny, often
in journals and transactions of learned societies not easily available to
students without access to specialized libraries. These volumes, therefore,
begin in a chronological sense with Maitland's essay and reproduce certain
of the crucial essays published since his time which have shaped the way in
which historians of the present day regard the beginnings of English
parliamentary history. For one reason and another we have been unable
to include everything we should like to have reprinted. In some cases we
were unable to obtain the necessary permission to republish and other
things had to be excluded because of the limited space at our disposal.
Even with these omissions, however, our hope is that what we have
reprinted here will provide a convenient compendium of the modern
learning about parliamentary history down to the great age of constitutional controversy which opened when a Scottish monarch became an
English king.

    As editors we have naturally accumulated a variety of obligations. We
would wish, first, to acknowledge our gratitude to the authors or their
representatives, the journals and the societies which have permitted us to
reproduce these essays. The Librarians and library staffs of the University
of Sheffield and the University College of Wales, Aberystwyth, have not
only provided copies of material but also that constant help which is too
often taken for granted by those who use their facilities. We have had every
co-operation in our dealings with the Cambridge University Press and
wish to thank especially the editorial staff of the English and American
offices. For much labour in preparing material for publication we are
grateful to Mrs Jean Wigfield and Mrs Pat Holland.

Finally, we dedicate these volumes to the memory of a scholar whose contributions to English parliamentary history find their appropriate place in this collection. Apart from that, however, Helen Cam inspired others to pursue enquiries in this field as a teacher in the Universities of London, Cambridge and Harvard; and, as President of the International Commission for the History of Representative and Parliamentary Institutions, she was one of those who enlarged the horizons of English parliamentary studies.

EDMUND B. FRYDE

EDWARD MILLER

ACKNOWLEDGEMENTS

THE editors wish to thank the authors and executors and the following publishers and journal editors for permission to reprint the articles in this volume:

The Royal Historical Society for chapter 1 which appeared in the *Transactions of the Royal Historical Society*, 4th series, XII (1940); Longmans, Green & Co Ltd and the journal editors for chapter 2 which appeared in the *English Historical Review*, LXXIV (1959); the Cambridge University Press for chapter 3 which appeared in H. M. Cam (ed.), *Selected Historical Essays of F. W. Maitland* (1957); the Clarendon Press for chapter 4 which appeared in *Oxford Essays in Medieval History presented to Herbert Edward Salter* (1934); Manchester University Press for chapter 5 which appeared in *Essays in Medieval History presented to Thomas Frederick Tout* (1925); H. M. Cam for chapter 6 which appeared in the *Proceedings of the British Academy*, XXXI (1945); the Medieval Academy of America for chapter 7 which appeared in *The English Government at Work, 1327–1336*, I (Cambridge, Mass., 1940); Toronto University Press for chapter 8 which appeared in *Essays in Medieval History presented to Bertie Wilkinson* (1969); H. M. Cam for chapter 9 which appeared in *Law-finders and Law-makers in Medieval England* (1962); the Institute of Historical Research for chapter 10 which appeared in the *Bulletin of the Institute of Historical Research*, XXVII (1954); Manchester University Press for chapter 11 which appeared in *The Collected Papers of Thomas Frederick Tout*, II (1934); Longmans, Green & Co Ltd and the journal editors for chapters 12 and 13 which appeared in the *English Historical Review*, XL (1925) and LIV (1939) respectively.

ABBREVIATIONS

A.H.R.	*American Historical Review*
B.I.H.R.	*Bulletin of the Institute of Historical Research*
Econ. H.R.	*Economic History Review*
E.H.R.	*English Historical Review*
L.Q.R.	*Law Quarterly Review*
Rot. Parl.	*Rotuli Parliamentorum*
S.I.C.	*Studies presented to the International Commission for the History of Representative and Parliamentary Institutions*
T.R.H.S.	*Transactions of the Royal Historical Society*

These are the abbreviations used in the introduction and the endnotes; some of the articles follow different conventions.

INTRODUCTION

By EDWARD MILLER

MAITLAND'S edition of the records of the parliament holden at Westminster on 28 February 1305 was published in 1893. In concluding his introduction[1] he denied 'departing very far from the paths marked out by books that are already classical'; and, although he admitted that he had trailed his coat through many fairs, we need not regard his disclaimer as 'ironical'.[2] His commentary on the records is often tentative and he made no claim to have solved, or even tackled, many of the problems raised by the early history of parliament. His essay, too, made no very immediate impact upon discussion of these problems,[3] though in retrospect it can be recognized as a turning point. McIlwain in 1910 and Pollard in 1920[4] found their point of departure in it; and these pioneers were followed by others in subjecting to critical scrutiny traditional views about the character of early parliaments which, not long before Maitland wrote, had attained a magisterial maturity in the work of William Stubbs. In this sense, the modern age of scholarly discussion about medieval English parliaments begins with Maitland's *Memoranda de Parliamento*.

PARLIAMENTARY ORIGINS

That discussion, so far as the beginnings of parliament are concerned, has had to face the preliminary question of what sort of institution we are looking for. Earlier scholars, from the seventeenth century to the nineteenth, had no problem here: their concern was with the sort of parliament which from Stuart to Victorian times had become the centrepiece of the English constitution. For Maitland, on the other hand, the nature of the records he was editing obliged him to lay stress upon the 'judicial' business done 'in or at a parliament', especially that which arose from petitions submitted by subjects; upon the doing of that business by the council or by panels which were committees of the council; and, therefore, upon the

---

[1] The material portions are printed below, ch. 3.
[2] *Letters of Frederic William Maitland*, ed. C. S. Fifoot, p. 116; H. G. Richardson and G. O. Sayles, *L.Q.R.* LXXVII (1961), 408.
[3] H. M. Cam, *Law-finders and Law-makers in Medieval England*, pp. 220–1.
[4] C. H. McIlwain, *The High Court of Parliament and its Supremacy*; A. F. Pollard, *The Evolution of Parliament* (this iconoclastic essay was virtually completed in 1915, but had to await for its finishing touches until after the end of the first world war).

I

role of the council as 'the core and essence of every *parliamentum*'. These
attributes of parliament under Edward I are now common assumptions and
they have also become the starting point for a radical reconsideration of
the origins and development of the medieval parliament. H. G. Richardson
and G. O. Sayles, in particular, have deployed an astonishing scholarship
in extending Maitland's suggestions in breadth and in depth.[1] They have
traced the judicial activity of the king's council in parliament deep into
the thirteenth century;[2] and they have established beyond all doubt the
essential part played in the development of parliament by conciliar
adjudication upon cases referred by other courts or upon the plaints and
petitions of subjects. In two respects, however, their view goes beyond that
of Maitland. He merely stressed the importance of judicial business done
in parliament; for them parliaments originally 'are of one kind only and
the essence of them is the dispensation of justice'.[3] Further, Maitland
regarded parliament as something which was still developing and unfinished in 1305, an occasion rather than an institution; for them regular,
afforced sessions of the king's council to dispense justice in the king's name
were already a normal part of administrative routine by 1258. Since
dispensing of justice was the essence of parliaments, parliament was
already a formalized institution. Here is the heart of the modern debate.

The contribution made to that debate by J. E. A. Jolliffe[4] likewise
concentrates upon this theme of 'justice', though like Maitland he evidently
allows by implication other 'factors in the beginnings of parliament'. The
importance of his essay lies, however, in his attempt to chart the stages by
which the jurisdiction of the king's court in his council in his parliament
developed towards the situation in 1305 which was revealed by Maitland.
His case that this process was gradual and complex, and that the council
was brought only slowly into that central position it occupied under
Edward I, must stand for want of any real answer to it. The first seeds seem
to have been sown when subjects petitioned the king against stringent
exchequer action; but the government of Henry III apparently found it
increasingly desirable 'to reassemble the courts of judicature with the king
and council' to deal with matters increasingly varied. Transaction of this
sort of business initially was as likely to be a matter for other tribunals

---

[1] The sheer volume of their contribution to medieval parliamentary studies is evident in
the notes to this introduction and in the select bibliography; for a recent summary of
their views, see *Parliaments and Great Councils of Medieval England*, repr. from
L.Q.R. LXXVⁿ (1961), 213–36, 401–26.

[2] Recently they have discovered a case adjourned from the king's bench to parliament
at Westminster as early as 1236: *E.H.R.* LXXXII (1967), 747–50.

[3] *B.I.H.R.* VI (1928–9), 78.

[4] Below. ch. I.

as it was for the council and only in the reign of Edward I did initial consideration of 'arduous cases' normally become a matter for the council before they were handed over to an appropriate court for 'completion of justice'. For these reasons, parliaments from the start were more than conciliar occasions. They were 'a coming together of the courts' or, as Maitland put it, occasions when 'the whole governmental force of England was brought into a focus'. They were appropriate occasions to which to refer hard cases revealed by petitions or referred by the judges; and even under Henry III and still more under Edward I such cases were numerous enough to call for regular provision to be made for dealing with them on two or three specified occasions each year. This fact, as is now generally recognized, does much to explain the regularity of the parliamentary cycle from the mid-thirteenth century onwards.

Not everything has been said about the beginnings of parliament, however, when the judicial business done therein has been fully brought into the light of day. In this connexion, as M. V. Clarke pointed out, the nature of early parliamentary records is particularly significant. At a time when 'the tradition of roll-keeping was already well established' in other courts, parliamentary records are curiously spasmodic and discontinuous, conveying an impression 'of parliament as an improvisation, something growing without a set plan or any definite centre ... The governing factor in its growth must be looked for in the miscellany of business that came before it, partly overlapping with and supplementing that of other courts and partly breaking new ground for public service ... A hard and fast theory of parliament as a high court will explain neither the facts in the records nor the failure to apply a selective principle to their make up and contents.'[1]

There is reinforcement for these negative implications of the records. Henry III in 1243 pointed to 'arduous business' which called for something more than adjudication by the king's council or the king's courts. It demanded convocation of the 'counsel of the whole realm';[2] and R. F. Treharne shows how, even before 1258, the word parliament might be used to describe occasions when earls, barons and prelates were brought together to discuss matters which were essentially 'political'.[3] He is also at one with J. G. Edwards that this notion of parliament was written into the Provisions of Oxford in 1258;[4] and it may well be that events between that date and

[1] M. V. Clarke, *Medieval Representation and Consent*, pp. 213–14; for the character of the early records of parliament, see especially H. G. Richardson and G. O. Sayles, *B.I.H.R.* VI (1928–9), 132 ff. and also T. F. Tout, *Place of the Reign of Edward II in English History*, p. 166.
[2] *Close Rolls*, 1242–7, p. 66.
[3] Below, ch. 2.
[4] Below, ch. 10.

1265 contributed to rooting this conception of parliament more deeply in English political tradition.

The use of the word then and later was doubtless often loose and un-technical, but the significant thing is that it was used to describe occasions which were a familiar and traditional feature of the constitution as well as sessions which accommodated the relatively more recent developments in judicial administration. Important in this connexion is Jolliffe's suggestion that 'the coming together of the courts' and baronial assemblies were tending to coincide in time and place by the 1250's. Important, too, is the directive of Edward I in 1280, to which J. G. Edwards draws attention,[1] in which the king sought to rationalize the ways in which both judicial and political business might be dealt with in parliaments. While some petitions, because they raised issues that were so much matters of grace, were reserved for the attention of the king and council, others were despatched to the appropriate tribunals in parliament, so that 'the king and his council can, without the burden of other business, attend to the great affairs of his realm and his foreign lands'. Such affairs, it may be added, as likely as not would call for 'common counsel', the advice and consent of those political classes capable of speaking for the whole community of the land.

In a search for the origins of parliament, then, much of recent opinion stresses the many purposes served by those occasions for which contempor-aries used this name. F. M. Powicke, in particular, points to the fact that contemporary usage of the word parliament makes it difficult for us to invest it with too much technicality, for the term was not yet a 'term of art'. The significance of parliament lay less in the particular acts done therein than 'in the concentration of them in a formal and public occasion'; as for the mystery attending the beginnings of parliament, it 'is the mystery which attends on all beginnings, when men are doing things because they are convenient and do not attach conscious significance to them'.[2] This seems to be the best explanation of the highly miscellaneous nature of the business which, in contemporary parlance, was done *in* parliament. Nor was it only the king's convenience which counted but that of all the other possible participants. The king's professional counsellors were indispens-able to him both in the audience of petitions and in treating about the great matters of his realm and foreign lands. Matters might arise in doing justice which were best settled by general remedies ordained after common counsel had been sought. At the same time, subjects whose duty it was to proffer counsel might have pleas pending before council or courts and it

---

[1] Below, p. 284.
[2] *The Thirteenth Century*, pp. 344–6; *Henry III and the Lord Edward* I, 340.

was to their advantage that they be spared two journeys where one would suffice. For a similar reason Edward I married his daughter to the Earl of Gloucester in his parliament,[1] so that his barons might at one and the same time fulfil their political obligation and attend the wedding of the season. Such practical considerations seem to explain best certain of the features of our early parliaments.

Precisely for this reason, even in the reign of Edward I, we do well to avoid exaggerating the institutional development of parliament. In the first place, the business done varied greatly between parliament and parliament. Most of Edward's taxes (and these were greater in total amount than those taken by any previous king) were obtained by some form or another of parliamentary consent, and his proceedings in this regard were rapidly hardening into custom. The tax he imposed in July 1297 with the consent only of 'the *plebs* standing around in his bedroom'[2] was widely held to be illegitimate; and when he conceded in the *Confirmatio* the same autumn that neither direct nor indirect taxes would be imposed in future 'without the common assent of the whole kingdom' we may reasonably suppose that what the king's opponents had in mind was an assembly which, in common parlance, would have been called a parliament. Again, while not all of Edward's statutes were parliamentary acts, a good deal of the quite unprecedented amount of legislation during his reign was ordained, like the Statute of Westminster I in 1275, 'by his council and by the assent of the archbishops, bishops, abbots, priors, earls, barons and the community of the land'.[3] Taxation and legislation, of course, were exceptional; justice and administration, by contrast, were constants of parliamentary business; but so, in Edward I's eyes in 1280, were the great affairs of his realm and foreign lands—war and peace, the business of Scotland and Gascony, the organization of conquered Wales, relations with Rome, projected crusades, problems of public order, the misdeeds of the king's servants. Political issues of this sort, in any particular parliament, might be many or few and more or less pressing; but it seems to have been to discuss them that prelates and magnates were summoned to a high proportion of Edward I's parliaments. Such parleys might be friendly and constructive, as at Easter 1290 when discussion produced the statute *Quia emptores* and some modification in the way the king dealt with titles to franchises. They might equally be acrimonious, as at Salisbury in February 1297, when the king's war plans led to a slanging match between himself and the Earl Marshal.

[1] Bartholomew Cotton, *Historia Anglicana* (Rolls Series), p. 174.
[2] *Flores Historiarum* (Rolls Series) III, 296.
[3] B. Wilkinson, *Constitutional History of Medieval England, 1216–1399* III, 312.

If the business of parliament was very variable, so was personnel. Some parliaments, so far as our knowledge goes, seem to have been purely administrative occasions and those who attended were presumably mainly officials (though such parliaments appear to become rarer as the reign proceeds). There was, however, right through the reign a good deal of variation from parliament to parliament, probably in response to the business the king had in view, in the size and composition of the official element and in the number of prelates and barons who were summoned. This fact underlines the extent to which, as yet, parliament was the 'child of the monarchy'.[1] The king and his intimate advisers were principally responsible for its summons, its composition, its agenda; they stage-managed the various activities which had their place in parliaments and drafted the orders, statutes and ordinances which were their product. Parliament was the means of vesting the king's government with consent, of mobilizing general support behind it and of neutralizing discontents aroused by its policies. Its administrative and judicial functions contributed to these ends, if only by ensuring that each did receive justice according to his deserts so far as was possible in an imperfect world. At the same time, the king's need for support or acquiescence also made him vulnerable, above all to pressure from the traditional political classes of medieval England. As early as 1258 the baronage had shown how parliament could be manipulated to force the king to bow to the wishes of the community; and again between 1297 and 1301, in the struggle for the charters, parliament provided one focus for political conflict. In the course of it some of the parliamentary tactics of the future were foreshadowed. Grievances were displayed in 'bills' and suggested remedies were laid out in drafts; and in 1301 the power of the purse was demonstrated when a grant of taxation was made conditional upon the king implementing promises of dis-afforestation. In the end, it is true, Pope Clement V absolved the king from promises made under duress; but what is important is that the community had discovered in parliament a means of putting pressure on the crown without recourse to revolution.[2]

BEGINNINGS OF REPRESENTATION

So far we have spoken of Edward I's parliaments as occasions which might bring together the administrative force of the king's government and some selection at least of the lay and spiritual baronage. In the reign of

[1] G. O. Sayles, *Medieval Foundations of England*, p. 449.
[2] H. Rothwell, *E.H.R.* LX (1945) and *Essays in Medieval History presented to F. M. Powicke*, pp. 319–32.

Edward I, as the table shows, this wider setting in which parliamentary business was done not infrequently extended beyond those limits. The later importance of the House of Commons has made these beginnings of

Period	Number of parliaments	Number of occasions on which were summoned		
		Knights	Burgesses	Diocesan clergy
1272–89	19	4	3	—
1290–1299	22	6	3	2
1300–1307	8	6	6	4

representation a matter of much discussion and the grounds for summoning the 'commons' has occasioned some debate. In 1295, the writs tell us,[1] knights and burgesses were to come to parliament 'with full and sufficient power on behalf of themselves' and of the community of their shire or borough 'to do whatever in the aforesaid matters may be ordained by common counsel'. This formula probably meant much the same thing as that of 1290 when the knights were to have full power to advise on and consent to those things which the earls, barons and magnates would be led to agree upon[2]—a way of putting it which suggests that their part was a subordinate and even a somewhat formal one. That fact does not mitigate the importance of J. G. Edwards's reconstruction of the history of this very deliberate demand by thirteenth-century rulers that representatives should come with plenipotentiary powers.[3] Recent investigations of its background in legal theory and practice has reinforced his view that 'formal powers of attorney' for their communities were being asked for, that in this way it was possible to ensure that 'what touches all should be approved by all', and that ultimately this power enabled the few who came to the commons (in Sir Thomas Smith's phrase) 'to bind and unbind the whole community' in many and divers matters.[4]

It does seem, however, that originally the object of summoning plenipotentiaries from the local communities was normally fiscal. As early as 1254 the lay baronage had refused to commit the lesser laity to general taxation, forcing the government to summon four knights from each shire 'to provide . . . what sort of aid they will give us in so great an emergency';[5] and, in this respect too, the period 1258–65 seems to have been something

[1] C. Stephenson and F. G. Marcham, *Sources of English Constitutional History*, pp 159–60.
[2] Wilkinson, *op. cit.*, III, 307.
[3] Below, ch. 4.
[4] See especially Gaines Post, *Studies in Medieval Legal Thought*, pp. 91 ff.
[5] For the writ of summons, see B. Wilkinson, *op. cit.*, III, 302–3.

of a watershed. It became normal in the reign of Edward I for the king to seek general consent to *general* taxes first from the representatives of the shire communities, then of the boroughs and even of the diocesan clergy; and in Easter parliament of 1290, once a decision was taken to replace a feudal aid by a comprehensive lay subsidy, knights were summoned at the very end of the parliament to complete the endorsement of this levy accorded by their betters. True, in 1290, the clergy conceded assistance to the king separately and in 1283 John of Kirkby had negotiated a tax with representatives of shires and boroughs in two distinct provincial assemblies held at York and Northampton. It was, however, evidently convenient to concentrate all the groups of consenters to taxation in one place at one time, even if not all of them contributed to taxation in precisely the same way.[1] In fact all the 'estates of the realm', the different grades or classes constituting the community, were assembled in the persons of their representatives in parliaments like those of 1295 or 1301. It is true that, in the event, the English parliament did not develop along the lines of an assembly of estates; but the fiscal motive underlying the growth of representation might easily have pushed development along those lines.

This fiscal motive also helps to explain the irregularity of the presence of the commons in Edwardian parliaments; but it will not explain quite everything even at this time. As early as 1264–5, in conditions admittedly exceptional, the 'commons' had emerged as something more than voices acclaiming a decision to vote the king money. In those years, Simon de Montfort summoned first knights from the shires, then knights and burgesses together, to parliaments held in the king's name. His action can be attributed neither to prescience of the future shape of the constitution nor to a democratic instinct, but rather to a desperate search for political backing for his unstable regime. What he did, however, was a tacit recognition that knights and burgesses were potentially political classes with their own identity and capacity. Earl Simon's tactics, it is true, created few immediately fruitful precedents even if, in 1283, Edward I summoned knights and some burgesses to 'discuss' the misdeeds of David of Wales. On the other hand, the constable and marshal in 1297, while they sought to manipulate to their own ends the grievances of the £20 landholders and the Londoners, did so without any particular parliamentary focus; and even the choice of a member for Lancashire in 1301 to present the 'bill of the prelates and nobles . . . on behalf of the whole community'[2] is an isolated

---

[1] Thus, the clergy were assessed on different principles to the laity and the towns normally contributed to lay subsidies at a higher rate than the shires and on the basis of a different list of assessable goods.

[2] Stephenson and Marcham, *op. cit.*, pp. 165–6.

occurrence and too much cannot be made of it. It is perhaps more significant that, towards the end of Edward I's reign, representatives were not infrequently summoned to parliaments from which apparently no taxes were sought. The explanation may lie in the fact that the parliaments of 1302 and 1307 met in the shadow of war with Scotland; that during the Lenten parliament of 1305 the king was evidently concerned with problems of public order;[1] and, in a more general sense, that over recent generations increased administrative burdens in their local communities had been placed upon the shoulders of knights and burgesses. If the peace was to be kept the king depended upon their co-operation as sheriffs, jurors, coroners, keepers of the peace, mayors and bailiffs; if wars were to be fought he relied upon their assistance not only as tax-payers and tax-collectors but as arrayers of troops, purveyors of supplies and the staff for the whole system of local administration which made military operations possible. It had become as essential for the king to secure at least the tacit agreement to his projects of these classes as to take the common counsel and secure the common assent of the traditional political classes of feudal England.

At least as much as fiscal needs, in fact, the administrative framework of thirteenth-century England governed the way in which the representative element in English parliaments developed. As an instrument of taxation alone parliament might have become a system of 'estates'—of separate classes separately organized within the national assembly. In this connexion, Helen Cam's discussion of the nature of the representation in parliaments is crucial.[2] From the start the commons did not represent a class or classes; they represented communities, the units of local government under the king. The shires and boroughs which were represented in parliaments, whatever intrinsic vitality they possessed, had also provided kings with a framework within which their authority could be brought to bear upon the provinces. The point was made by Maitland long ago in discussing 'the mighty forces making . . . for communalism of a certain sort' in medieval England. 'Men are drilled and regimented into communities in order that the state may be strong and the land may be at peace. Much of the communal life that we see is not spontaneous . . . The communities are far more often the bearers of duties than of rights.'[3] From one angle, the concentration of these communities in parliament in the persons of their representatives was the culmination of this process of imposing common responsibilities upon the English provinces from above.

[1] As reflected in the ordinance of trailbaston: below, p. 105–6, 358.
[2] Below, ch. 9.
[3] F. Pollock and F. W. Maitland, *History of English Law* I, 688.

Without hindsight, of course, we would make little of the commons in thirteenth-century parliaments. They were occasional and transient visitors and played a restricted part in the things done there. On the other hand, their presence from time to time is indicative of the flexibility with which the Angevin kings exploited the rights and powers inherent in their office. It was this which made variety the salient feature of early parliaments— variety of function, and therefore of appearance and composition. Their purpose was to enable the king to do what he wanted to do or what it was his duty to do or what in the circumstances he had to do. They accommodated the king's acts as the possessor of an ultimate reserve of justice and of grace, as the head of a complex administrative system, as the political chief of a relatively sophisticated political community. At the same time these kings were in no position to become successful autocrats for any length of time. Their need to secure the advice and consent of their greater subjects was a venerable tradition; and they had hardly less need for the administrative co-operation of those classes from which were drawn the representatives of the 'commonalty' of England. In different ways at different moments parliaments reflected all the diverse features of thirteenth-century political life. This explains their protean character, and also made it inevitable that there should be nothing finished about them. Edward I's parliaments were still occasions rather than the sessions of an institution. The process of definition was the work of the future.

THE REIGN OF EDWARD II

Some progress was made along that path in the ensuing decades. There was, of course, much continuity from the parliaments of Edward I. Under his son parliament was still regarded as 'a time and place for petitioning for favours and remedying wrongs';[1] and the Ordainers in 1311 even sought to increase its efficiency in this field.[2] At the same time, recurrent political crises left their mark upon parliament. That mark, it is true, should not be exaggerated and it is almost certainly going too far to suggest that it amounted to a transformation of parliament's essential nature.[3] As Tout points out,[4] it is remarkable from one angle how little parliament came into the story of opposition to Edward II. Conflict revolved principally around influence at court, the personnel and conduct of the king's ministers and the composition of the king's council; force was one of the

---

[1] H. G. Richardson and G. O. Sayles, *B.I.H.R.* VI (1928–9), 71.
[2] As J. G. Edwards points out, below p. 285–90.
[3] H. G. Richardson and G. O. Sayles, *E.H.R.* XLVII (1932), 396; H. G. Richardson, *T.R.H.S.* 4th Ser. XXVIII (1946), 27.
[4] Below, p. 299.

principal instruments used by the king's opponents to achieve their ends;
and Thomas of Lancaster apparently intended to exploit his position as
hereditary steward of England to dominate the king's household.[1] The
reign, too, saw a number of parliaments summoned which could not be
held. Deep political divisions countered the effectiveness of parliament as a
political focus of the community of the realm.

At the same time, the notion that parliament could serve this purpose
did not disappear; and naturally enough, in a time of crisis, there was a
revival of the tradition of 1258, 1300–01 and 1307 that parliament provided
an occasion for manifesting the general grievances of the community in
order to secure general remedies for them. The Ordinances of 1311 insisted
that certain matters (alienation of crown lands, the departure of the king
from the kingdom, a decision to go to war and the choice of the king's
principal ministers) required the consent of the baronage in parliament;
and a parliamentary panel was instituted to hear complaints against
ministers who contravened the Ordinances.[2] The scheme of 1311 was only
intermittently effective, but it was taken a stage further in 1318 when an
attempt was made to vest control of the king's government in a standing
council of peers and prelates. Again, in July 1321, it was in a parliament
that Edward was compelled to capitulate to the demand that he should put
away his new favourites, the Despencers, provoking one contemporary to
observe: 'it is a wonderful matter to behold how the members become
disjointed from the head when consideration is made by the magnates in
parliament without the need for the assent of the king'.[3] In these respects
parliament became one of the instruments through which a baronage,
professing that it acted for the community at large, sought to impose its
policies upon the crown. This is not to say, of course, that it set before
itself the object of achieving some new place for parliament in the constitution. How little notion of innovation there was became manifest in
1326–7 when the nobility tackled the unprecedented task of getting rid of
Edward II and replacing him by his son. The first step was military action
leading to the king's capture; the second, the convocation of a parliament
ostensibly in the king's name; but thereafter all was improvisation. The
parliament quickly developed into a 'revolutionary convention' and the
association of various 'estates' with Edward II's deposition and Edward
III's recognition has little to do with the history of parliament. It is
explicable essentially in terms of 'a nervous desire to spread responsibility

---

[1] M. McKisack, *The Fourteenth Century*, p. 55.
[2] Stephenson and Marcham, *op. cit.*, pp. 193–8.
[3] B. Wilkinson, *Constitutional History of Medieval England* ii, 155.

as widely as possible' for an act which had no justification in any past precedent.[1]

If the barons were no conscious innovators, Edward II was equally a traditionalist; and the fact that parliaments were one of the instruments of baronial political strategy compelled him to define his attitude to them, most notably in the much debated Statute of York in 1322.[2] This statute revoked the Ordinances of 1311 and forbade future attempts to constrain the king's authority after this fashion; but it concluded with a positive prescription: 'matters which are to be determined with regard to the estate of our lord the king and his heirs, or with regard to the estate of the kingdom and the people, shall be considered, granted and established in parliament by our lord the king and with the consent of the prelates, earls and barons and of the community of the kingdom, as has been accustomed in time past'.[3] It is probably too subtle to see in this clause an attempt to deflect 'the current of political dispute from the camp to a constituted organ of government'.[4] Edward's objectives were more immediate and less statesmanlike. They were governed by the situation to which the chronicler had pointed in 1321. It was for the king (not the magnates unilaterally) to consider, grant and establish provisions regulating the joint affairs of king and kingdom; and this he would do in the customary way. In other words, he is reclaiming that initiative in parliament which had belonged to his father and to those counsellors who had been his father's closest collaborators. The intention was to turn the clock back to a time when parliament was indeed the child of monarchy.[5]

Innovations, then, were achieved without conscious deliberation; yet the intensity of political conflict under Edward II did partially and insensibly modify the character of parliaments.[6] Political controversy at times threatened to crowd judicial and administrative business from the parliamentary agenda; magnates became more prominent on administrative committees like the panels of auditors of petitions; the 'great council' of magnates trenched upon the competence in parliament of the smaller,

[1] McKisack, op. cit., pp. 91–2; for these proceedings see also Wilkinson's discussion, below pp. 337–43.
[2] For a review of the extensive literature on the statute, see G. Lapsley, Crown, Community and Parliament, pp. 153 ff., and Wilkinson, op. cit., II, 134 ff.
[3] Stephenson and Marcham, op. cit., pp. 204–5.
[4] Lapsley, op. cit., pp. 227–8.
[5] Cf. McKisack, op. cit., pp. 71–3; Wilkinson also makes the point that the distinction drawn in 1308 between the king's person and his office was implicitly denied throughout and that it is here that careful drafting is most evident: Constitutional History of Medieval England II, 20, 44 and Speculum XIX (1944), 445 ff.
[6] For the nature of these changes see H. G. Richardson and G. O. Sayles, B.I.H.R. VI (1928–9), 71–88 and E.H.R. XLVII (1932), 194 ff.

official council. This growing autonomy of the magnates in parliament was one of the problems with which Edward II sought to deal in the Statute of York and there are some signs that prelates and lay baronage were showing an increasing sense of political solidarity. The term 'peers of the land' or 'peers of the realm' gained increasing currency during the reign[1] and in 1322 prelates as well as lay barons were accounted 'peers of the realm in parliament'.[2] We are some distance yet from a House of Lords, but some of the ideas which would create such a house were already in the air.

There were developments, too, in the position of the commons. The idea of parliament in the minds of the Ordainers in 1311 was a very aristocratic one. Down to that time knights and burgesses had been summoned rarely to Edward II's parliaments and the ordinances themselves were the work of barons and prelates. Representatives of shires and boroughs, however, were summoned to the August parliament of 1311, which endorsed the ordinances, and thereafter they were called to most of the remaining parliaments of the reign. There is little sign that they made any major impact upon the central political conflict of the time, but their regular presence in parliament had its own consequences. Intense controversy bred a ferment of ideas and it seems likely that the mysterious and sometimes fanciful *Modus tenendi parliamentum* reflects something of that ferment. Particularly notable is the deduction drawn in it from that 'full power' which the representatives of shires and boroughs were required to possess. 'It is proper that all things, which ought to be affirmed or rejected, granted or denied or done by parliament, should be granted by the "community" of parliament, which consists of the three grades or classes of parliament; namely, the proctors of the clergy, the knights of the counties and the burgesses who represent all the community of England; and not by the magnates, since each of them comes to parliament only for his own person.'[3] The comment may be unusually perceptive, even prophetic and it appears characteristically in that section of the document which is concerned with the granting of taxes. On a more mundane level, however, J. G. Edwards[4] has conclusively demonstrated that the supposition that the commons showed a propensity not to attend when elected is at the least

---

[1] E.g. in the proceedings against the Despencers in 1321: *Statutes of the Realm* I, 181, 184; L. O. Pike, *Constitutional History of the House of Lords*, pp. 157–8.

[2] McKisack, *op. cit.*, p. 73.

[3] For the text see M. V. Clarke, *Medieval Representation and Consent*, pp. 382–3; and for the date of the *Modus* see below, p. 370 and the references given there. The most recent discussions of this document are by J. S. Roskell, *Bulletin of the John Rylands Library* L (1968), 411–42, and by J. Taylor, *E.H.R.* LXXXIII (1968).

[4] Below, ch. 5.

a gross exaggeration and that, by this time, the regular commons man had already appeared even if he was seldom in the majority. Furthermore, once knights and burgesses came regularly to parliaments they were the natural bearers of petitions from those they represented: from the 'community of Devonshire' or the 'commonalty of the town of Lincoln' as well as from aggrieved individuals.[1] They may even have tried their hands at corporate petitioning and left the mark of this activity on the parliament roll in the form of some plaints from 'the community of England', 'the community of people of his realm' or 'the commonalty of England'.[2] Of course, the commons had no unique right to bring petitions into parliament. In 1315 the fixing of food prices was demanded by the archbishops, bishops, earls and barons; and the representatives of English communities are hardly likely to have sponsored a plaint from the merchants of Cologne.[3] On the other hand, the short roll of petitions answered by the king, prelates, earls, barons and others in the Martinmas parliament of 1325 may still be important in this connexion. Emanating from the 'liege men' of the king and 'the men of the commune of your realm', it bears many of the appearances of a primitive collection of petitions coming from or sponsored by the commons in parliament.[4]

It is even harder to determine whether such petitions gave rise to legislation. The political circumstances of the time were obviously unfavourable to the sort of programme of legislation from above carried through by Edward I in the decade after 1275; but, if the guiding hand of the king and his ministers was weakened, the most likely candidates to have stepped into the void thus created were the baronial groups which dominated the council and contemporary politics. At the same time a manifesto supposedly drawn up by the earls in 1312[5] suggests that, when the laws of the land were insufficient, they ought to be amended by the king with the prelates, earls and barons on the complaint of the people; and some statutes, especially those relating to sheriffs in 1315 and 1321, appear to show traces of such a procedure. The first was a response to the 'demonstration' of the prelates, earls, barons and other magnates in parliament and also to the grievous complaint of the people, while the second answered

[1] E.g. *Rot. Parl.* I, 289, 290.
[2] *Ibid.*, pp. 289, 290, 291, 299. We cannot, however, read too much into these phrases as is evident when we discover one petition about a certain road from the commonalty of the land and specifically from those of the east of London: *ibid.*, p. 308
[3] *Ibid.*, pp. 295, 315.
[4] *Ibid.*, p. 430; the significance A. F. Pollard (*Evolution of Parliament*, pp. 119 ff.) attributed to this roll is, however, denied by H. G. Richardson and G. O. Sayles, *B.I.H.R.* VI (1928–9), 77 n.
[5] *Chronicles of Edward I and Edward II* (Rolls Series) I, 210–14.

a 'plaint from the commune of the realm'.[1] We would be rash to make these imprecise formulae refer too explicitly to the commons, but the prehistory of the later role of common petitions as a source of legislation may still have to be sought in this period.

In spite of the muted drama of Mortimer's rule and fall the decade after Edward II was dethroned was a time of relative political calm. It affords a time for stocktaking in the history of parliamentary development and T. F. T. Plucknett has undertaken precisely this task.[2] Looked at in retrospect, as he rightly says, the period has 'a somewhat archaic air', emphasizing how incomplete and how unforeseen the changes of the preceding generation had been. Parliaments consisting of king, lords and commons were only one category of assembly convoked by Edward III; 'great councils' similar in composition to parliaments were still summoned from time to time;[3] the composition and internal organization of parliaments were only slowly settling down; the range of business with which they were concerned was still miscellaneous and variable; and the transaction of administrative and judicial business in parliament continued to be mainly a matter for the king's professional council. On the other hand some lines of development were becoming clearer by the late 1330's. The diocesan clergy had all but definitively withdrawn to convocation, thus making unlikely the emergence of an ecclesiastical 'estate' in parliament. There was increasing consistency in the specific bishops, abbots and magnate families receiving individual writs of summons, even though a clearly defined 'parliamentary peerage' still lay in the future. Representatives of shires and boroughs were summoned almost regularly. After 1327 no assembly was styled a parliament in the chancery writs of summons unless their presence was envisaged and there are some signs that the communities attached some value to being represented. When Cambridgeshire sheriffs habitually returned themselves or their cronies their action provoked protest and a demand for proper elections in the county court.[4] There were developments, too, in the role of the commons as petitioners in parliament. As early as 1327 they presented a group of petitions in the form of an 'indented bill' and repudiated any other petitions put forward in the name of the 'commons'.[5] Their petitions, moreover, appear to embrace an increasing

---

[1] *Statutes of the Realm* I, 174, 180.
[2] Below, ch. 7.
[3] The debate about the technical distinction between parliaments and great councils continues: see H. G. Richardson and G. O. Sayles, *L.Q.R.* LXXVII (1961), 233; for some of the distinctions which were beginning to be drawn, however imprecisely, see the notes below, p. 363.
[4] M. M. Taylor, *B.I.H.R.* XVIII (1940), 21 ff.
[5] *Rot. Parl.* II, 10–11; H. G. Richardson and G. O. Sayles, *B.I.H.R.* IX (1931–2), 6–12.

range of grievances and by 1339 they were being classified in a new way. 'Commune petitions' (i.e. those relating to general or public matters) were distinguished from private or singular petitions concerned only with particular or individual problems; and while the latter were dealt with by panels of auditors the former went directly to the council precisely because their subject-matter was of general import and called for general remedy.[1]

At this point, of course, the 'common petition' began to provide a basis for legislation, since one appropriate remedy for a general ill was a statute giving general and permanent redress. Almost imperceptibly the habit of the commons of presenting 'common petitions' conferred upon them a certain 'initiative' in legislation. The nature of that initiative, as Helen Cam has conclusively demonstrated,[2] needs careful scrutiny. Common petitions which were sponsored by the commons might represent their own views; alternately true initiative might lie with the king's ministers or the king's judges or with a whole range of lobbies. None the less, the petitioning techniques developed by the commons gave them a new and significant place in the procedure of parliaments; their use of it furthered the emergence of parliament as an institution representative of a common will seeking redress and betterment for the community at large. This was happening, moreover, at a strategic moment, for it coincided with the opening of the Hundred Years War. That long drawn-out conflict and the demands upon the community it occasioned created political circumstances which brought to some sort of maturity the trends of parliamentary development rooted in the preceding generation.

THE BEGINNINGS OF THE HUNDRED YEARS WAR

In many respects the middle decades of the fourteenth century were more decisive in the history of parliament than the formative years in the thirteenth century or the revolutionary years under Edward II. The composition of parliament as an assembly combining king, lay and spiritual peers, and representatives of shires and boroughs became virtually stereotyped; the prelates and lay peers summoned acquired an increasingly stable and, in the case of the latter, an increasingly hereditary character;[3] and the distinction between parliaments and great councils became clearer, so that, in 1353, it was insisted that the acts of a great council ought to be recited in the succeeding parliament and entered upon its roll since the acts of a council were not matters of record.[4] Conceivably, too, the political

---

[1] D. Rayner, *E.H.R.* LVI (1941), 198 ff., 549 ff.
[2] Below, ch. 6.
[3] Without prejudice, of course, to the king's right to summon new men at his discretion.
[4] Cam, below, p. 176; H. G. Richardson and G. O. Sayles, *B.I.H.R.* VIII (1930–1), 73–7.

stresses of the time helped to bring knights and burgesses together as a single, coherent group within parliament if only to collaborate in drawing up 'common petitions'. Of the three grades mentioned by the *Modus* the clerical proctors had withdrawn to their convocations and the shire and burghal representatives who remained were moving towards that fusion which would ultimately make them a House of Commons.

There were other significant trends of the times. The volume of judicial and administrative business transacted in parliament contracted, passing instead to council and chancery out of parliament[1] after the failure of an attempt, under a statute of 1340, to deal with individual grievances through a parliamentary commission. Increasingly, moreover, the 'justice' men sought from parliaments was less 'justice' in general than 'justice' against royal ministers who had abused their authority, a shift which culminated in the impeachment of ministers in 1376 and later years.[2] Parliamentary justice, therefore, more and more acquired political overtones. Legislation based upon 'commune petitions' endorsed by the commons also continued to grow in amount. The commons were still very often the sponsors rather than the true initiators of these petitions and the product was frequently 'ill-digested' statutes compared with the legislative programme Edward I and his expert advisers had imposed from above.[3] On the other hand, it came to be accepted that statutes made in parliament by the king with the assent of the prelates, earls and barons in response to the petition of the commons were the most authoritative way of making law and the main way permanently to change the law; further, the same authority was required for their reversal as for their initial promulgation.[4]

If the legislative authority of parliament was becoming established, progress was also being made in securing parliament's control of taxation. Its right to concede direct taxes was never seriously contested, but more controversy arose over quasi-taxes like the exercise of the king's right to requisition military supplies or to impose upon local communities an obligation to equip and pay wages to soldiers. Opposition to these burdens in parliament worked less in the direction of achieving parliamentary control than in making these rights difficult to exercise; but it is another matter entirely with the taxes on trade which assumed major importance in Edward III's war-finance. Initially he followed his grandfather's practice in 1294 and 1303 and obtained increased duties upon wool exports in

---

[1] Richardson and Sayles, *B.I.H.R.* IX (1931–2), 2–6.
[2] The matter is discussed by J. G. Edwards, below, pp. 290–6.
[3] H. M. Cam, below, ch. 6; D. Rayner, *op. cit.*, pp. 549–70; H. G. Richardson and G. O. Sayles, *B.I.H.R.* IX (1931–2), 6–13.
[4] Richardson and Sayles, *L.Q.R.* L (1934), 554–5.

particular by grants from assemblies of merchants. The merchants, however, naturally tried to mitigate the burden upon themselves of increased duties by offering lower prices to wool-growers, making it very evident that these were imposts of general incidence. By 1350 it was coming to be accepted that parliamentary consent was necessary to vary the level of the wool customs; in the following decades this assumption was extended to other imposts on trade; and in 1362 and 1370 statutory force was given to the rule that 'no imposition or charge shall be placed on wool, woolfells or hides . . . without the assent of parliament, and if any be so imposed it will be repealed and held for nought'.[1]

These changes seem to have owed little to a continuance of magnate pressure in the tradition of Edward II's time. On the whole, Edward III held the affection of the great political families and worked in substantial harmony with them in and out of parliament.[2] Before the very last years of the reign only the crisis of 1340–1 represented a rift in this lute and that a temporary one the importance of which is easily exaggerated. It was rooted in Edward's determination to deal with those officials at home whom he held responsible for the financial difficulties which had hampered his military operations, and chief among them the former chancellor, Archbishop John Stratford. The measures the king proposed were evidently summary and, in face of them, Stratford demanded and initially was denied a hearing in parliament. This denial moved notables like Arundel and Warenne to support his claim to a hearing in parliament before his peers; and when this was conceded a reconciliation was rapidly effected.[3] The matter was rounded off by the king's acceptance of a petition from the magnates that peers, even if they were ministers, were entitled to trial by their peers in parliament if any charge was laid against them. If the crisis had any lasting effect, however, it was mainly a change in a section of the higher officialdom. An older generation of ministers was replaced at the centre of affairs by a group of new men which, together with the king's friends amongst the peers, provided him with his political collaborators for much of the rest of the reign.

This, however, was not all that happened in parliament. Lords and commons in concert petitioned that breaches of the charters should be reported and dealt with there; that commissioners should be appointed in parliament to audit all accounts since the commencement of the war; and that the chief ministers of the crown should be designated in parliament and

---

[1] *Statutes of the Realm* I, 374–93.
[2] Cf. M. McKisack, *op. cit.*, p. 270.
[3] B. Wilkinson, *Constitutional History of Medieval England* II, 193–4 and *E.H.R.* XLVI (1931), 177 ff.

sworn to keep the laws of the land. The king was compelled to accede to their requests in statutory form, although he lost little time in repudiating these 'pretended' statutes when parliament disbanded. His unilateral act seems to have been accepted without demur by the lords at the next parliament in 1343 and it was left to the commons to petition that the king should keep the promises he had made. The king's answers were categorical. 'The said statute was contrary to his [coronation] oath, a blemish upon his crown and regality and contrary to the law of the land'; as for the appointment of ministers 'the king may make such ministers as he pleases and as he and his ancestors have done in all time past'.[1] What emerges from the episode is the rapidity with which differences of opinion between king and baronage were resolved, the association of the commons with the lords in the more radical demands made in 1341 and the fact that, two years later, the commons clung to the position of 1341 when the lords seem to have abandoned it. These phenomena are more comprehensible in the light of E. B. Fryde's demonstration[2] of how sharply the commons had reacted against Edward's financial measures from the very beginning of the war. As early as 1339 they had refused their adherence to the taxes proposed by the lords until they had consulted their constituents. Their independent attitude continued to develop in face of successive taxes and the economic difficulties which arose from war and plague, and was given an edge by the perennial grievances of ordinary folk about the high-handed acts of ministers of the crown at every level. The king's war-time difficulties, moreover, compelled him to remedy grievances in the hope of supply; and this general background goes far towards explaining the contemporary growth of 'common' petitioning by the commons, the basing of statutes upon their petitions and parliament's increasing control over all forms of taxation.

A salient feature of the four decades after the outbreak of the Hundred Years War, then, was the development of the part played by the commons in parliament. They were not only an indispensable element in it but a more effective interest when they arrived there. This was not a direct reflection of a spectacular increase in experienced parliament men, for re-election seems to have become little more frequent as the century proceeded, except possibly in the last years of Richard II.[3] On the other hand, men who

---

[1] *Rot. Parl.* II, 139–40 and cf. Lapsley, *Crown, Community and Parliament*, p. 258 where it is pointed out that the most Edward would allow was that, if anything good was found in the 1341 statute, it would be re-enacted and observed thenceforward. Edward's anxiety to deny any right of interference with ministerial appointments may well be connected with the changes in administrative personnel he had achieved as a by-product of the events of 1340–1.

[2] Below, ch. 8.

[3] N. B. Lewis, *E.H.R.* XLVIII (1933), 379.

served more than once did provide the greater amount of representation and there does seem to be a tendency for long-serving shire members to serve longer as the century progressed.[1] This nucleus of experienced men in parliament cannot be discounted in assessing the role of the commons, nor can the fact that so many of those who came for the communities were also men with administrative and sometimes military experience.[2] It is true that many of the shire knights especially were bound by ties of retainership and clientage to members of the higher baronage and that possibly it is 'little short of fantastic' to think of them as constituting an independent opposition to the lords in parliament.[3] On the other hand, most of them were 'self-respecting country gentlemen, of considerable administrative experience and with a standard of honour which would not permit them to be made mere tools of faction'.[4] These estimates of the commons, stressing at one and the same time their dependence and their independence, may seem to involve a paradox; and, indeed, they have given rise to some debate. The question has even been posed whether the strength of the commons as a political force was their own or that of the higher social ranks amongst which so many of them found their lords and masters.

The truth may well be that this is not a question to which an answer can be given which is valid for every period of the later middle ages. On the other hand, for the greater part of Edward III's reign the king enjoyed good relations with his nobility. Baronial factions were largely in abeyance and, therefore, there was no group of barons concerned to mobilize the interests represented by the commons against the crown. Furthermore, events in the Hilary parliament of 1348 suggest that the commons saw limits to their competence in matters of high politics, for they claimed to be too 'ignorant and simple' to offer views on the French war and professed their willingness to accept the advice given by 'the magnates and wise men of your council'.[5] .On the other hand, clearly there were many matters which the commons considered to be very much their concern. In this same parliament they did not hesitate to raise their voices against the great

[1] *Ibid.*, p. 376; K. L. Wood-Legh, *E.H.R.* XLVII (1932), 398 ff.; and for a convenient summary, J. G. Edwards, *Historians and the Medieval English Parliament*, pp. 31–3.

[2] E.g. the biographies in M. Basset, *Knights of the Shire for Bedfordshire during the Middle Ages* and A. Gooder, *Parliamentary Representation of Yorkshire*, I.

[3] H. G. Richardson, *Bulletin of the John Ryland's Library* XXII (1938), 199.

[4] *Ibid.*, p. 205; for the debate to which reference is made in what follows, see especially K. B. McFarlane and H. G. Richardson in *T.R.H.S.* 4th Ser. XXVI (1944), 53 ff. and XXVIII (1946), 21 ff.

[5] *Rot. Parl.* II, 165. M. McKisack, *The Fourteenth Century*, p. 222 stigmatizes this reply as 'awkward', but it can equally reasonably be regarded as a genuine expression of opinion by the commons that the matter lay outside their competence.

charges borne by the community, against failure to keep peace in the land, against fees taken by the king's ministers, about the need to defend the north against the Scots, about the wool staple and about the king's obligation to seek parliamentary consent for taxes.[1] Over such questions the commons, in parliament after parliament, showed an evidently independent capacity to represent the reactions of the community at large to a government which made heavy demands upon it through servants whose conduct was not always impeccable. In their concern about these matters, moreover, knights and burgesses increasingly conferred together and were consulted jointly. This growing solidarity of the commons is clear by the time of the Good Parliament of 1376. The *Anonimalle Chronicle*[2] lifts a curtain on their debates in the Chapter House at Westminster. It also tells us how, because he had shown such skill in marshalling their arguments and views, Sir Peter de la Mare was asked 'to assume the duty of expressing their will in the great parliament before the . . . lords'. This episode marks the beginning of the recorded history of the speakership, an office in which the commons found a spokesman and attorney for their collective views.[3]

The proceedings of the Good Parliament illustrate other aspects of the development of the commons. Their debates and petitions ranged over much familiar ground: the conduct of local government, the malice of labourers, the location of the staple; but a demand for a subsidy stimulated a complaint not only that the community was impoverished by taxation but that previous grants had been 'badly wasted' through the corruption of some of the king's ministers and their associates. Through their speaker the commons nominated a commission of lords with whom they might discuss this matter. There were a number of precedents for this practice of 'intercommuning' between lords and commons;[4] and, if in 1340 the initiative seemingly came from the magnates and in 1352 from Sir William Shareshull acting for the king, in 1373 the commons themselves asked for discussions and specified the peers and prelates with whom they wished to consult.[5] This, then, was not the novelty of 1376; but, while previously (and sometimes subsequently) 'intercommuning' had usually been a procedural device to reach agreement on a grant of taxation, the question

[1] *Rot. Parl.* II, 165–74.
[2] See Tout's discussion of this almost unique source, below, ch. II, and the extracts in Stephenson and Marcham, *op. cit.*, pp. 220–2.
[3] In 1406 Sir John Tiptoft was described as 'speaker and *procuratour*' for the commons: J. S. Roskell, *The Commons and their Speakers in English Parliaments*, p. 76.
[4] J. G. Edwards has investigated this practice systematically: *The Commons in Medieval English Parliaments*.
[5] *Rot. Parl.* II, 118, 237, 316.

of a subsidy on this occasion was merely the beginning of the affair. In the event the commons successfully demanded the afforcement of the king's council by nominated lords and prelates and, in pursuit of their complaints that the king's ministers were corrupt, 'on the spur of the moment stumbled upon a novel answer ... They would all maintain the accusations, in common', before the lords of parliament.[1] Impeachment, as a device for a parliamentary attack on the ministers of the crown, had thus been born.

THE REIGN OF RICHARD II

However we read the evidence, the proceedings of the Good Parliament demonstrate the advances which had been made by the commons during the fourteenth century. At the same time, their actions must also be seen in the light of changing circumstances. From the beginning of the 1370's the political harmonies of Edward III's reign were coming under strain, justifying Tout's view that parliament came to represent the 'public opinion' of all or most parts of the community in face of the king's government.[2] The commons continued to reflect popular resentment at the burden of taxation, economic difficulties and administrative corruption; but in addition a party amongst the lords were discontented with inefficient administration at home, William of Windsor's government of Ireland, John of Gaunt's increasing dominance at court and the peace policy with France with which Gaunt was associated. For the first time in the reign, in effect, there was a genuine political division within the ruling class—between Gaunt and the administration on the one side and, on the other, a group especially among the younger peers in which the Earls of March and Suffolk and Henry Percy were prominent.

We need not suppose that this group set out with forethought to manipulate the commons in 1376 to attain their ends. The co-operation of the latter with the lords arose naturally out of a mutual desire to reform an administration which both burdened and exploited the community and stood for policies which were distasteful to men of rank and influence. The initiative of the commons is documented by the unique record of the *Anonimalle Chronicle*; but if we take that at its face value it is gratuitous to deny a similar initiative to influential magnates some of whom, like March in 1373, had already voiced their criticism of Gaunt and his policies. We may also suspect that the fact that de la Mare was March's steward did something to facilitate co-operation between the two wings of opposition.[3]

[1] T. F. T. Plucknett, *T.R.H.S.*, 5th Ser. 1 (1951), 161.
[2] Below, ch. 11.
[3] Cf. Plucknett's comment that the composition of the council named and sworn in the Good Parliament suggests some competent staff-work behind the scenes: *op. cit.*, p. 157.

In this connexion Gaunt's proceedings after the parliament dispersed are not without interest. He arrested de la Mare, dismissed the counsellors thrust on the king and annulled the acts of 1376; but he also removed March and Suffolk from the marshalship and admiralty, bought over Percy and installed one of his own stewards as speaker of the docile commons in the January parliament of 1377.[1] Evidently he had some regard both for the political influence of the peers and for the power of lordship to sway opinion in the commons.

The Good Parliament, then, marks something of a parting of the ways in fourteenth-century parliamentary history. The political unanimity of king and baronage broke down in Edward III's last years in face of the king's growing incapacity; the conflict of factions thereby occasioned was prolonged into his successor's minority; and that conflict was exacerbated by Richard II's device of ruling through court nobles to whom he entrusted place and power and in whose direction he diverted the rich stream of government patronage. In these circumstances the voice of the commons, crying out as of old against the burdens and abuses of government, was in no sense stilled; but increasingly the groups of great lords excluded from Richard's favour occupied the forefront of the political scene. This fact became crushingly evident during the political crisis of 1386–8 when, as Tout has pointed out, the way was cleared by Gaunt's departure in pursuit of the crown of Castile.[2]

The crisis opened with lords and commons jointly seeking the removal of the Earl of Suffolk and Bishop Fordham from the chancellorship and treasurership.[3] Richard refused to dismiss even a scullion at their behest, whereupon they denied him financial aid in order to force him to receive a deputation. Richard agreed to receive a deputation from the commons, but instead the Duke of Gloucester and Bishop Arundel appeared on behalf both of lords and commons. The king was coerced into dismissing his ministers, agreeing to their impeachment, consenting to the nomination of their successors in parliament and accepting a council similarly nominated which would thoroughly overhaul the administration. In all this the commons played their part, no doubt enthusiastically enough since the usual charges of extravagance, waste and corruption could be hurled at Suffolk and his associates; but they are somewhat less prominent in the

---

[1] Sir Thomas Hungerford, it is true, was said to have been 'elected' by the majority of the knights; but their choice may not have been unconnected with the political situation Gaunt had striven to create and the fact that 'he contrived to place a number of his retainers in the commons': Roskell, *op. cit.*, pp. 61, 120–1.

[2] Below, p. 309.

[3] Knighton's Chronicle translated in B. Wilkinson, *Constitutional History of Medieval England* II, 242.

centre of the stage than they had been in 1376. This place was occupied by Gloucester and that most aristocratic of prelates, Bishop Arundel. Parliament, on the other hand, was still very much the principal forum of political controversy as Richard himself acknowledged in the declaration he obtained from the judges during his attempted counter-moves in 1387. The new 'statute and ordinances and commission' of 1386 were declared derogatory to the king's prerogative and regality; those who procured them and forced them on the king were declared worthy of a traitor's death; the 'king ought to have the direction of parliament', which he had the power to dissolve at will; he could dismiss his ministers at will, but the lords and commons might not impeach them; and their judgement of Suffolk in the last parliament was 'erroneous in all its parts'.[1]

This was throwing down the gauntlet with a vengeance and it was characteristic of the new times that it was picked up by the peers. In the Merciless Parliament of 1388 a small caucus of great earls led by Gloucester proceeded against the king's friends not by way of impeachment with the co-operation of the commons but initially by 'appealing' them of treason before their fellow peers in parliament. This was not something easily done, for the existing law of treason scarcely met their case; but this did not deter them from applying what they called the 'course of parliament' to convict, sentence and destroy the courtiers.[2] We need attribute no particular theoretical significance to these proceedings: the ends of the Appellants were practical and vindictive and they did not consciously set out to claim new powers for parliament. Moreover, when they imposed their own oligarchical control over the king's government, this owed little to formal arrangements made in parliament so far as our evidence goes. The Merciless Parliament had demonstrated, however, the capacity of a small group of determined and very powerful men to use parliament for their own ends; and in the course of its proceedings the commons appear to have been far less of a positive force than in 1376 or even 1386. Their first recorded intervention in 1388 was a declaration that they would have proceeded against one of the accused if the Appellants had not done so first.[3] That would hardly have satisfied de la Mare and the commons of the Good Parliament.

Richard II, on the other hand, had cause to appreciate the danger from

---

[1] *Ibid.*, pp. 249–51.

[2] *Ibid.*, pp. 250, 282.

[3] M. McKisack, *op. cit.*, p. 457, although it must be added that, after the destruction of the most prominent of the king's friends by appeal, the proceedings against the remainder took the form of impeachments involving the co-operation of the commons after the fashion of 1386: R. H. Jones, *The Royal Policy of Richard II*, p. 53.

parliament to his regality. His counter-measures in 1397–9, after he had patiently awaited a favourable moment,[1] must take account of this background. The crucial events took place in a parliament which assembled at Westminster on 17 September 1397 and which on 29 September was prorogued to Shrewsbury on 27 January 1398. Its record, for Richard, was all success. A skilful combination of appeals and impeachments accomplished the condemnation of his opponents, thus breaking the back of any possible aristocratic coalition against him. A measure of financial independence was guaranteed by a generous lay subsidy and the grant of the customs for life. A petition presented by Thomas Haxey[2] about the cost of the royal household was made the occasion to extract various concessions. Lords and commons united to declare Haxey a traitor; the lords declared it treason to move the commons to deal with any matter touching the king's person, rule or regality, thus endorsing a notion of treason propounded in the declaration of the judges in 1387; and the commons confessed that matters touching the king's person and the government of his household 'did not pertain to them at all, but solely to the king himself'.[3] Taken to its logical conclusion this last confession would have seriously circumscribed the scope of parliamentary petitions as a means of criticizing government policies.

These, perhaps, were the matters of substance transacted in this parliament, although weight has sometimes been attached to Richard's act of securing the appointment of a standing commission at the end of the Shrewsbury parliament to complete its work. Subsequently, moreover, he doctored the record in the rolls of parliament to extend the commission's mandate. In his discussion of this episode, J. G. Edwards[4] is almost certainly correct in seeing in it nothing more sinister than a desire to give the commission powers to complete the proceedings against the king's enemies. What we cannot say, of course, is how the precedent might have been applied in what looks like a deliberate programme on Richard's part or perhaps more likely of his intimate advisers and councillors to establish royal authority on a more absolutist basis. Richard had little time. The

---

[1] An alternative explanation may be that, in 1397, Richard was moved by fear of a new move against him by Gloucester and his friends: Jones, *op. cit.*, p. 71; C. M. Barron, *B.I.H.R.* XLI (1968), 17–18. On the other side it is not without interest to note that, between 1389 and 1397, Richard had made the body of retainers wearing his white hart badge 'without dispute the greatest livery in England': G. Mathew, *The Court of Richard II*, p. 151.

[2] Perhaps the most significant feature of Haxey's case is that the commons had avowed his bill amongst their common petitions, probably with a characteristic lack of scrutiny: *Rot. Parl.* III, 339.

[3] B. Wilkinson, *Constitutional History of Medieval England* II, 306–8.

[4] Below, ch. 12.

Shrewsbury parliament was dissolved on 31 January 1398 and in August 1399 he was Henry of Bolingbroke's prisoner. His brief period of un-trammelled rule was over.

The question must still be asked why Richard was so successful with the parliament of 1397–8. Something was owed to the way he played on divisions amongst the nobility, attracting some into the court circle and isolating those he wished to destroy. The latter he placed under arrest before parliament assembled, thus depriving baronial opposition of its natural leaders. A pertinent question was asked, however, by the Earl of Arundel during his trial: 'Where be those faithful commons? ... The faithful commons are not here.'[1] The charge that Richard packed the commons, made by one chronicler, cannot be supported even by the poem, *Mum and the Soothsegger*, which may well be a description of the Shrewsbury session. At best it shows careful planning by his council 'to get money for himself'. Apart from that it depicts the commons as the sort of mixed bag of men we might expect them to be. Some indeed were got at by the counsellors or were retainers of great lords or were inhibited by their hope of securing payment of money the king owed them; others, on the other hand, were merely sycophants, or demagogues easily frightened off, or men of small capacity, or inarticulate, or completely silent, sitting there 'like a nought in arithmetic, that marks a place but has no value in itself'.[2] On the other hand, Richard seems to have appreciated the need for managing the commons. If the council planned the session and got at members, a number of Richard's close supporters were in the house and one of them, Sir John Bussy, occupied the key office of speaker (as he had done in the parliaments of 1394 and January 1397). That he was imposed upon the commons, as Walsingham suggests, cannot be proven; but the way he plunged at once into an attack on the men of 1388 smacks of pre-arrangement.[3] The political significance of the commons in parliament, it would seem, had not escaped Richard II.

THE LANCASTRIAN REVOLUTION

Richard's parliamentary strategy did not save him from the consequences of his political miscalculations; and the writs in his name which convoked a parliament to meet at Westminster on 30 September 1399 were issued by his captor, Henry of Bolingbroke. These writs were the beginning of a train of events which has been much debated and which is admirably discussed

[1] M. McKisack, *op. cit.*, p. 486.
[2] H. M. Cam, *Liberties and Communities in Medieval England*, pp. 229–35.
[3] Roskell, *op. cit.*, pp. 11–12, 61.

by B. Wilkinson.[1] The situation was inevitably confused. The only precedent for getting rid of a king was that provided by Edward II's fall in 1327; but even when the fullest use was made of it there were difficulties of putting Henry in Richard's place which did not arise when Edward III had followed his father by clear hereditary right. Those difficulties were probably made worse by Henry's attempt to exploit the fable that his ancestor, Edmund of Lancaster, had been the true heir of Henry III and by Chief Justice Thirning's sharp rejection of a suggestion that he might claim the throne by right of conquest. Beyond that, there was the problem of the means by which the change of dynasty should be carried out. Lapsley a generation ago called in question Stubbs's view that the instrument used was parliament;[2] and his rejection of that notion has been reinforced by Wilkinson. Not only would such proceedings run counter to the political assumptions of the day but, with Richard's abdication or deposition, the parliament called in his name would cease to exist.

What happened in such a situation, then, was unlikely to be very tidy. A promise by Richard that he would abdicate was apparently extorted before parliament assembled; but a commission also recommended, following the precedent of 1327, that he should in addition be deposed.[3] On 30 September, according to the official record, the principal role was played by 'the estates and the people', i.e. 'the lords and the commons of parliament reinforced by others, especially Londoners'.[4] They accepted Richard's abdication; heard a lengthy rehearsal of his tyrannical acts; and, being interrogated severally and in common, declared these to be sufficient and notorious to warrant his deposition, deputing certain commissioners to bear that sentence to him. With the throne thus vacant Henry made his 'challenge' by descent from Henry III 'and through that right that God of his grace hath sent me, with the help of my kinsmen and friends, to recover it'. Thereon, as Walsingham puts it, the lords spiritual and temporal and all the estates of the realm unanimously conceded that the duke should rule over them.[5]

---

[1] Below, ch. 13 and see also his more recent treatment of this episode in *Constitutional History of Medieval England* II, 284–327.

[2] Reprinted in his *Crown, Community and Parliament*, pp. 273 ff.

[3] Wilkinson makes a good case for rejecting Lapsley's suggestion that the commission recommended Richard's deposition by parliament and that Henry refused to entertain the proposal. Adam of Usk, a member of the commission, clearly reports its decision in favour of deposition 'by the authority of the clergy and the people': *Constitutional History of Medieval England* II, 324.

[4] *Ibid.*, p. 297.

[5] Cf the official record in *Rot. Parl.* III, 423. Another chronicler says the lords gave their answers severally and the 'people' theirs by way of acclamation: Lapsley, *op. cit.*, p. 287.

Much subtlety, perhaps too much, has been applied to the interpretation of these events. Even the men of the time were anything but clear about them. The official coronation roll speaks of Richard II's cession and resignation as having taken place in parliament[1] and Adam of Usk, too, has much to say about proceedings in parliament to accomplish the Lancastrian revolution. Despite the theoretical difficulties, therefore, there is justification for Wilkinson's conclusion that 'the deposition of Richard II . . . was to be as near deposition by the High Court of Parliament as could reasonably be devised'.[2] If that much is allowed, however, Lapsley's arguments for Henry's attempts to safeguard the rights and attributes of the crown must also be allotted a certain force. The carefully drafted and widely distributed 'official' record of the events of 30 September was scrupulous in avoiding the word parliament to describe the body which accepted the abdication and deposition of Richard II and acknowledged Henry's claim to the succession; and the use of the phrase 'estates and people' seems to imply that others than the personnel of parliament participated. When it came to securing his own elevation, moreover, the closest analogy is not with proceedings in parliament but with the 'recognition' of a king in the medieval English coronation orders where 'clergy and people' or 'the people' accept their new lord by acclamation.[3] Whatever the nature of the body which deposed Richard, it is hard to see that Henry's title was a parliamentary one in any strict sense and it is possible that he very deliberately avoided having such a title thrust upon him. It is not without significance that Henry IV, almost as soon as he was on the throne, obtained a declaration from the commons that 'they wish him to be in as great liberty royal as his ancestors were before him', although at their request he prudently qualified that liberty by denying that it implied any right on his part to change ancient laws, statutes or good customs or to take anything hitherto not taken.[4] The Lancastrian revolution was a salutary warning to kings who sought excessively to stretch their prerogatives; but it is much more doubtful if it added anything specific to the accepted capacities of parliament.

Henry's first parliament, indeed, suggests a prime concern to return to

[1] H. G. Richardson, *E.H.R.* LII (1937), 39 ff.
[2] *Constitutional History of Medieval England* II, 297. On the other side, it has to be remembered that the assembly of 30 September did not follow parliamentary forms (no speaker was elected, no receivers and auditors of petitions were appointed, and outsiders seem to have been present): Mathew, *Court of Richard II*, p. 168.
[3] See the orders and 'little devices' from the twelfth century to the fifteenth in *English Coronation Records*, ed. L. G. Wickham Legg, pp. 31, 174, 219, 228 and *Liber Regie Capelle*, ed. W. Ullmann, pp. 34, 80–1.
[4] *Rot. Parl.* III, 434.

normality.[1] It was necessary, of course, to undo Richard's acts in the period 1397-9, a purpose achieved by the king with the asssent of the lord on the basis of petitions (presumably government inspired) presented by the commons. Further, the king's eldest son was made Prince of Wales, Duke of Cornwall and Earl of Chester, and acknowledged as right heir to the crown. For the rest, there was all the usual business of parliament. Receivers and auditors of petitions were appointed to deal with individual wrongs, continuing a tradition which goes back to the thirteenth century; and even a Cambridgeshire serf, in 1414, could look to parliament as a 'high court of righteousness' where justice denied him elsewhere could be got.[2] Time was also found by king and lords to discuss major political issues: the question of a Scottish expedition and the even more difficult problem of keeping safe a deposed king. Then there were financial matters, for the commons with the assent of the lords granted the king a subsidy. The commons also appeared in their fourteenth-century role as presenters of 'common' petitions. Some were presumably inspired by the court; others represented their endorsement of demands from the city of Lincoln, the burgesses of Yarmouth, the inhabitants of Shropshire, the merchants of London and other local interests. Some petitions, however, probably reflected corporate action by the commons in their role as guardians of the common interest. A request that the charters and good laws be kept, that peace be maintained and justice be dispensed to all may be regarded as common form. The king had no difficulty in assenting to it. It was another matter when they called upon the king for economy, doubtless with a view to minimizing demands for taxation. An evasive reply was offered to a request that royal grants should be made only with the advice of the council and a polite refusal to the suggestion that all alienated crown lands should be resumed. For all that, these petitions were in line with traditions which had become well established in the reigns of Edward III and Richard II.

At the same time, the commons did not push their exercise of these traditions to extremities, perhaps out of a reluctance to be held too fully responsible for the revolutionary events with which they had been associated in 1399. In this same parliament, at their request, the king through Archbishop Arundel of Canterbury defined their place in parliament. 'Since the said commons are petitioners and demanders, and the king and

[1] It assembled on 6 October 1399 and resumed, after a break for the coronation, on 13 October. New writs were issued for elections in the shires and boroughs, but most of the commons must have owed their places to their return for Richard II's last, abortive parliament: H. G. Richardson, *B.I.H.R.* xvi (1938),137 ff. For the record of Henry's first parliament, see *Rot. Parl.* III, 415-53.
[2] *Ibid.* IV, 57.

lords at all times have had and will have the judgements in parliament . . . excepting that in statutes which are to be made, or in grants and subsidies, or such matters done for the common profit of the realm, the king specially wishes to have their (i.e. the commons') advice and consent.'[1] Thus cryptically the constitutional gains made by the commons over a century were summed up. Derived initially from their full power to concede taxes on behalf of the community they had acquired a right and a duty to petition for the common advantage and to add their consent, explicit or implicit, to the remedies ordained for the common profit. There remained powers, however, which the commons did not share with the older core of the parliamentary institution: the king and lords, whose power was one not only of judgement in the narrow sense but of ultimate decision in the matters of common concern to king and kingdom. Through the control they had established over supply, and through their ability to bring the force of public opinion to bear through petitions, the commons could influence the making of decisions; but even in his first tentative beginnings Henry IV could meet petitioning with the traditional royal answer of dissent, *le roi s'avisera*.

[1] *Ibid.* III, 427, translated by B. Wilkinson, *Constitutional History of England in the Fifteenth Century*, p. 299.

SOME FACTORS IN THE BEGINNINGS OF PARLIAMENT*

by J. E. A. Jolliffe, M.A., F.R.Hist.S.

I MUST begin this paper by disclaiming any intention of entering into the detail of parliamentary procedure, a matter with which I am not qualified to deal. It has, however, occurred to me that certain changes in the administration of law, changes which begin early in the reign of Henry III, have some relevance to the origin of parliamentary jurisdiction. These changes arise from a new and more severe attitude on the part of the Crown towards franchise, and make necessary important modifications in the exchequer's methods of dealing with it. In time, I think, the many disputes between the Crown and the magnates about privilege, debt, and so forth, gave rise to a volume of petitions and subsequent trials which called for some tribunal in the nature of parliament, and these trials found a nucleus about the exchequer and the council. That is my thesis, and it is with these legal changes and their reaction upon the constitution that I propose to deal. The greater part of this paper is, therefore, concerned with the period before direct parliamentary record, and, indeed, before there is any true court of parliament. It goes very little beyond matters of law, and, if I am forced here and there to refer to the structure and procedure of parliament in later days, I do so very much subject to correction. Even for the early period with which I am concerned, I cannot attempt to assess the importance of that part of parliament which came from the *commune consilium* of

the realm. Nor can I determine how far the latter's composition and influence were separate factors in the formation
of parliament. While recognising the futility of any attempt
to set up rigid divisions between the various parts of the
thirteenth-century *curia*, I am dealing here mainly with
the forerunners of the jurisdiction and court of parliament.
Parliament as a legislature, as the grand council of the
nation, and as inheriting the providing power of the feudal
baronage, is beyond my knowledge and my present intention.

We may, perhaps, best find our way into the past by
remembering what the most cautious historians from
Madox to Maitland tell us, that the parliaments of Edward
I's day were not yet fully co-ordinated bodies; that they
drew much of their virtue from the coming together at one
time and place of courts and councils which had elsewhere
and at other times their own proper constitutions and
procedures. What unity of being parliament had was
imposed upon it by the co-ordinating and over-riding
presence of the king; otherwise its structure was still
fluid.

> If shape it might be called that shape had none
> Distinguishable in member, joint, or limb,
> . . . . . . what seemed its head
> The likeness of a kingly crown had on.

But, within this prevailing indefiniteness, one concomitant
of the Edwardian parliament is plain and can be described
in set terms, because description has to deal with ideas
and institutions which have already been worn smooth
and clear by a century of use. Those parts of the Angevin
government which have already achieved a measure of
separate identity, the courts of law, the court of the capital
justices, of the common bench, of the justices of the Jews,
and of the exchequer, have a part to play which cannot be
ignored. I believe that this part of theirs had more than
a little to do with the origin of parliamentary justice.

If we turn to the memoranda of the parliament of 1305

in Maitland's edition, we can see how a continuance into the time of session of parliament of the sessions of the courts was a part of parliament's very purpose and natural to its procedure. Trial during parliament was a twofold process in a form perhaps best defined by Hale, who tells us that the king and " the council received the petitions from the receivers, yet they rarely (if at all) exercized any decision or decisive jurisdiction upon them, but only a kind of deliberative power, or rather direction, transmitting them to the proper courts, places, or persons where they were proper to be decided ". The subject's petition, presented in the first instance to the king and his council, and, indeed, more often than Hale's words would suggest, definitively answered by them, received, in the majority of cases, a double hearing, firstly by the whole or part of the council to ascertain the reason or non-reason of the petitioner's cause and to determine what authority might best give him relief, and secondly by that one of the permanent courts to which his plea most conveniently fell, because the matter of it was akin to its normal jurisdiction : " sequatur coram Justitiariis de Banco Regis et audiatur et fiat justitia " ; [1] " adeant Cancellariam et rex vult quod justitia fiat " ; [2] " ostendat cartam coram Thesaurario et Baronibus de Scaccario et fiat justitia ".[3]*

The nature of these dual trials is well shown in the case of Roger Mortimer, who complained in 1305 that the escheator had entered upon certain of his lands in his manor of Mawardyne on the pretence that they were king's serjeanty alienated against the rules of the tenure.[4] The king and the council gave a preliminary hearing and then remitted the case to the barons of the exchequer for the second phase of its trial, the *complementum justitiae*,[5] as the phrase then went, and, from the exceptionally full

[1] *Memoranda de Parliamento* (Rolls series), ed. F. W. Maitland, p. 131.
[2] *Ibid.*, p. 129.   [3] *Ibid.*, p. 153.   [4] *Ibid.*, p. 12.
[5] *Ibid.*, p. 14. Tam regi quam praefato Rogero secundum consuetudinem regni inde fieri faciant debitum et festinum justitiae complementum.

terms of the writ to the barons, it is possible to determine precisely what was done and not done both in the council and in the exchequer. In the first, *coram rege*, hearing, Mortimer's *querela** was set forth only in outline. It consisted of a statement of his title by an original grant from Prince Edmund to his father, Roger Mortimer the elder, and also of the essential matter of charters from Henry III and Edmund with a confirmation by the former. The whole was in the abstracted form used in the first stage of answers to a *quo warranto*,** and it is evident that the king had neither examined Roger's charters nor heard the answer of the escheator. In this prima facie state of the cause, when Roger's plea may be said to have been made good only if he could substantiate his evidences and rebut any counter-pleading by the Crown, it was dismissed to the exchequer. There, in the hands of barons skilled in judgment of charters, in the rules of serjeanty, and in the history of the holdings in question, a *complementum justitiae* was made, which was the most substantial phase of the whole trial. The barons were ordered to " call before them into the exchequer the said escheator and Roger, and, having heard the reasons of the escheator for the king's right, as well as those of Roger for his, and having inspected, if necessary, such relevant charters and muniments as Roger might produce, to make speedy completion of justice, as well to the king as to Roger, according to the custom of the realm ".

It will be evident that the most real and searching stage of this and similar trials (for the majority of trials in the Edwardian parliaments were in this dual form) was fought out in the exchequer, and that the hearing before the council was of that deliberative and directive character of which Hale speaks. It would, perhaps, be most natural to our modern notions to give the name of parliamentary justice to the hearing before the council and to withhold it from that before the treasurer and the barons. We have no place for the exchequer in parliament and our idea of parliamentary trial is of one before a great council which has thrust out all other elements but the peers. Yet in the thirteenth and, indeed, in the early fourteenth century, the matter was not entirely clear. These acts of judgment of the permanent courts of justice, considered as the *complementum justitiae* to the directive decisions of the king and council, seem in Edward I's day to stand upon an uncertain verge of parliament, the exact bounds of which are not yet drawn, and about them official language is still uncertain and at times contradictory. Their position was, no doubt, itself uncertain. Contemporaries saw no formal difficulty in admitting that, though judgment was made, let us say, in the exchequer, it was none the less made in parliament. They would not always nor, perhaps, often say so, but Madox has collected instances of a use of terms which is sufficient to show that such constitutional theory as then prevailed did not rule them out of parliament.

These instances and Madox's reflections upon them are worth considering and weighing. " In the 13th year of King Edward I," he says, " the Exchequer was held (as it seems) at Westminster in the King's Parliament. And in the 26th and 27th year of the same King, Robert de Coleshull came before Walter Bishop of Coventry the Treasurer and William de Carleton a Baron of the Exchequer, in the King's Parliament, and there made Fine to the King for the cause hereunder mentioned. The Exchequer was likewise holden in the King's Parliament at Westminster (as it seems) in the 2nd year of K. Edward II." [1] Madox was conscious that this was a crucial point in parliamentary history, but he added the following words with a caution which we must still follow : " let it be considered, how these Instances are to be understood. Shall we say that the Exchequer was not holden in the same place where the Parliament was held, but only at the same time ? But the words of these Records seem to import more than that, and to mean the same Place. However, let the

[1] T. Madox, *History and Antiquities of the Exchequer*, ii. 7.

Antiquaries (who have a notion of the Communication there anciently was between the King's courts after the Division of them) determine, if they please, this matter." I doubt if Britton or Fleta could have determined it ; constitutional theory on such a matter as this can hardly be formed in a generation. Language in writ and record was not as yet precise about parliamentary justice, for the notion of a high court of parliament was only then gaining acceptance, and the novelty and indefiniteness of that court long survived its origin.[1] But let us assume no more than we need. If the *complementum justitiae* was not a judgment of parliament but only ancillary to such judgment—and this is, I imagine, a clearer definition than contemporaries could have made—it still had a vital relevance to parliament. It was still the complement of parliamentary justice, the final judgment to which the consideration of the council was preliminary.

In fact, judgment of parliament was itself not yet defined. We have writs upon the Close Roll that refer petitions to parliament or record respites until parliament shall meet, but they do not throw up a court of parliament in that high light in which, perhaps, we might expect to find it. They take little care to define the authority which will judge, or, if they do, they promise trial by judges who seem to us far short of being parliamentary in standing. Such writs, positive official statements that any given case is adjourned to parliament, are rare as late as even the early years of Edward I. When made, they seldom seem to be used advisedly to denote an unique jurisdiction of full parliament : that is remarked as an exception when it is intended. Indeed, I am not sure that any writ of the first decade of the reign promises redress of trial *by* parliament. Rather it is said that what is to be done will be

---

[1] F. W. Maitland, *Memoranda de Parliamento*, p. lxxxiv*: "It is a new thing that they should see a yet higher court above that court which is held in theory *coram ipso domino rege*. The competence of this highest court is as yet indefinite."

done *in* parliament, or *during* parliament, after trial by some court or authority specified in the writ.[1]

Under Edward I this authority is usually that of the council. The justices of the king's pleas of the market are ordered to supersede their commission in the Isle of Ely until the quindene of Michaelmas 1275. The king does not wish that the bishop's liberty in the island shall be prejudiced by their office, and what he shall cause to be provided by his council shall then be done in the parliament which he will hold at Westminster.[2] The place is the parliament, the authority is the provision of the council. Or the escheator beyond the Trent is ordered to restore the manor of Kirklaw and the park of Mitford to Hugh de Eure to be held until the coming parliament, which will be at the quindene of Michaelmas next, that the king may cause that to be done by his council in the matter which ought of right to be done.[3] The time is that of parliament, the place and the authority the council. Or again, the barons of the exchequer are told to allow William de Leybourne to hold his father's lands in Rainham until the quindene of Michaelmas next, so that at the same quindene that may be done before the king and his council which ought of right to be done.[4] The authority is the council as before, the time is that of the meeting of parliament, but in the writ parliament is not named.[5]

This is vague enough to make us doubt whether trial in parliament was already and inevitably by 1275 trial by a single high court of parliament, but at least it refers to trial by the council. But we may still meet with examples,

---

[1] *Ibid.*, p. lxvii*: " At present ' parliament ' or ' a parliament ' is not conceived as a body that can be petitioned. A parliament is rather an act than a body of persons. One cannot present a petition to a colloquy or a debate."

[2] *Calendar of Close Rolls 1272–1279*, p. 167.

[3] *Ibid.*, p. 200.   [4] *Ibid.*, p. 203.

[5] F. W. Maitland, *Memoranda de Parliamento*, p. lxvii**. " Petitions are not addressed to parliament . . . They are addressed either simply to the king or to the king and his council. The formal title for them which is in use in the chancery is ' petitiones de consilio ', ' council petitions '."

c

though they are growing rare, of a form of writ which ignores the council and specifies only what in the Edwardian parliament would be the *complementum justitiae*. Such writs warn us that trial during parliament need not involve the council at all, had sometimes been in the past, and occasionally still was, something much more restricted than trial *by* parliament, less exalted than trial *coram rege*, in fact, nothing more than trial by the exchequer. In May 1275 a writ to the sheriff of Somerset deferred demands upon the tenants of Wells and Glastonbury for divers fines and amercements until this same quindene of Michaelmas at which parliament was to meet. This was done " so that at the said quindene what shall be provided by the counsel of the treasurer and barons (of the exchequer) shall be done in this behalf ".[1] The *complementum justitiae* alone was in this case to be done during parliament. The directive judgment of the council, the first half of the dual trial, had, it must be assumed, already been done in May and out of parliament. This is a form which has a long history in the past of parliament, and if, at first thoughts, we question with Madox whether the exchequer acting judicially upon such a writ was acting parliamentarily at all, I believe that a consideration of its past use will incline us to believe that this is a doubt which has little meaning until well on into Edward's reign and none at all in that of his father. Anticipating what will, I hope, become clear later, I would dismiss it for the moment by suggesting that it cannot rightly arise until a monopoly of parliamentary justice has been asserted by a fully developed court of parliament, until that court has established a uniform direction over the action of all the courts during parliament, and reduced their decisions to the status of a *complementum justitiae* following upon its own directive judgments.

Under Henry III we find exceptionally formulae which show an Edwardian turn of language as to judgment in parliament. William de Hastincote's outlawry was revoked

[1] *Ibid.*, p. 166.

in 1248 (almost in the terms of Fleta's famous dictum),
" in curia nostra coram nobis et toto parliamento nostro ".[1]
But the reverse is far more usual : adjournments and
respites of action will be made to the time of parliament,
sometimes with an allocation of the cause to the council,[2]
but more often to the exchequer [3] or to other justices,[4]
with no hint that the council will further concern itself
or that judgment will be given in parliament in any other
sense than that of time.   It is, moreover, common as we
move back into the reign of Henry III, that all word of
parliament should be omitted from the writs, though we
may know from other sources that the day set for exchequer
justice, or judgment by other courts, is that upon which
parliament has been ordered to assemble.[5]   The laconic
indefiniteness of Edward's writs thus gives way to a precision of another kind under Henry, in which the part of
the permanent courts in time of parliament, a mere *complementum justitiae* under Edward, bears a new clarity and
importance, while the directive function of the council goes
unmentioned.   Parliament begins to appear less as a session
of a high court of the council than as a season of exchequer
judgment of a special kind, of special, freer, and more
authoritative action by the justices.

[1] *Close Rolls 1247–1251*, p. 107.

[2] *Close Rolls 1264–1268*, p. 36.   Peter of Savoy, John de Warenne,
and others summoned to appear " coram nobis et consilio nostro in
proximo parliamento nostro . . . justiciam facturi et recepturi ".*

[3] *Close Rolls 1259–1261*, p. 343.   The action for debt between John
de Berners and Cok fitz Aaron adjourned " usque ad parliamentum regis
a die Purificacionis Beate Marie in tres septimanas ut tunc coram baronibus
regis de scaccario et eis discutiatur " **

[4] *Ibid.*, p. 287.   The men of Faversham given respite from all distraints on account of their quarrel with the abbot " ad parleamentum
proximo venturum.   Et scire faciat (vicecomes) quod tunc sint coram
prefato justiciario justiciam inde recepturi ".†

[5] *Close Rolls 1264–1268*, p. 39.   The men of Brigstock and Stonor
have paid tallage and it is being exacted a second time.   They are given
respite to the quindene of Easter " ut tunc coram baronibus nostris de
scaccario eis inde plena justicia exhibeatur ibidem ".††

Close Rolls 1254–1256, p. 107.   The Prior of Northampton's claim to
immunity from tallage adjourned to the quindene of Michaelmas " ut
tunc discutiatur coram baronibus regis de scaccario ".

Our evidence for this is, of course, the Close Roll, upon which writs to officials ordering stay of action are recorded, usually in answer to petition, and with a view to trial at the time of parliament. For the parliament of the quindene of Easter 1260 we have writs in most of the forms that I have mentioned. The cause of the men of Faversham in dispute with the abbot was adjourned " ad proximum parleamentum proximo venturum . . . quod tunc sint coram . . . justiciario justiciam inde recepturi ".[1]* The sequestration of the bishop of Durham's rights in the Carlisle churches [2] and the long drawn out and important claim for the Bury St. Edmund's liberties [3] were respited *ad quindenam Pasche*** without further specification. The claim of the sheriff of Essex for allowance of expenses [4] was set for the quindene that the king might then do what was right by the counsel of the barons of the exchequer. The justices of the bench were ordered to warn John de Balliol that they would attend at the quindene to hear the appeal against Robert de Sautre and others,[5] and the new writ *de sectis* ordered all those who had exacted unwarrantable suit to appear before the capital justices at Westminster at the same term.[6]

The judgment most usually promised at the quindenes is that of the exchequer barons. In this year 1260, as in others, there were a number of cases which were simply

---

[1] *Close Rolls 1259–1261*, p. 287. [2] *Ibid.*, p. 136.

[3] " Mandatum est baronibus de scaccario quod demandas quod faciunt abbati de Sancto Edmundo de quibusdam libertatibus quas idem abbas dicit ad se pertinere, ponant in respectum usque ad quindenam Pasche, quia rex propter transfretacionem suam discussioni illius negocii ad presens non potest intendere." *Ibid.*, p. 137.†

[4] *Ibid.*, p. 32. " Ut rex tunc de consilio vestro quod justum fuerit ei fieri faciat in premissis." So, also, the executors of Henry de la Mare were given respite of debts " usque in quindenam Pasche proximo futuram ut tunc discutiatur ad scaccarium regis utrum predicti executores de predictis debitis regi respondere debeant necne."

[5] " Ponant in respectum usque in quindenam Pasche proximo sequentem : et quod idem justiciarii scire faciant predictis Roberto etc . . . quod tunc sint ibi apellum illud versus prefatos Johannem etc . . . prosecuturi si voluerint." *Ibid.*, p. 224.

[6] *Ibid.*, p. 25.

adjourned to the quindenes of Easter and Michaelmas without any statement as to which court would hear them. From the nature of many of them it is to be assumed that they would go to the exchequer. They did so because of the matter of the petitions, of the very nature of parliament justice ; for claim for franchise or for relief of debt or from official action necessarily involved exchequer record, and these were some of the commonest concerns of the parliaments of Henry. So at the quindene of Easter 1261 the widow of Solomon Bishop was ordered to appear before the justices for transgression,[1] the burgesses of Oxford were to show their charters *coram rege* to prove their claim for quittance of amercements,[2] and a Jew of Gloucester was given a day before the justices of the Jews to show his tallies and chirographs and to prove his debt against Philip Marmion.[3] But the abbot of Strata Florida had respite of Jews' debts until the quindene that his indebtedness might be examined before the barons of the exchequer,[4] and the executors of the last three bishops of Ely were also to appear before the same barons to show cause why they did not pay the king's debts.[5] Similarly, to the quindene of Michaelmas 1256 a fine owed by the prior of Bath for breach of the assize of measures was respited " ut rex tunc habeat inde consilium cum baronibus nostris de scaccario ",[6] twenty marks of debts were respited to Philip Marmion that the king might then cause what was right to be done " coram baronibus nostris de scaccario ",[7] a fine of forty shillings for neglect of suit to the honour of Peverel was placed upon inquest in the exchequer,[8] and the barons of the exchequer were ordered to give judgment upon a claim by Humphrey de Bohun for amercements of his men for certain offences of the forest.[9] All these were left to the exchequer without the council.

[1] *Ibid.*, p. 340.
[2] *Ibid.*, p. 356.   [3] *Ibid.*, p. 465.   [4] *Ibid.*, p. 370.
[5] *Ibid.*, p. 464. This was for the morrow of Clausum Pasche.
[6] *Close Rolls 1254–1256*, p. 429.
[7] *Ibid.*, p. 435.   [8] *Ibid.*, p. 440   [9] *Ibid.*, p. 414.

It would seem that at this early stage of parliamentary history the full council's intervention in pleas in time of parliament was not yet a matter of course. The exchequer, on the contrary, and, to a less degree, the benches, loom larger than the council. Edward's rule, that which gave his high court of parliament its characteristic form and function, the directive judgment of the council over all pleas and the *complementum justitiae* of the courts, both accorded during parliament, though it already existed,[1] was still only one of many expedients under Henry. In the latter's parliaments and legal councils the king's directive power was, indeed, used, but less systematically, and in ways of his own choosing. The dual trial in parliament was as yet little practised. More often Henry kept the trial wholly in the hands of the council or relegated it wholly and outright to the appropriate court. If he brought the council to add to the courts' knowledge and authority it was in other ways. He might send his councillors into the exchequer.[2] He might call the barons of the exchequer or other justices to advise with a few or the whole of the council.[3] He might commission a tribunal *ad hoc* in which several groups of justices were joined.[4] To all these and other combinations he might and did resort during parliament. The procedure of the session was even more adapt-

[1] " Johannes de Baillol venit coram . . . consilio regis et petiit considerationem baronum de Scaccario . . . et mandatum est baronibus de Scaccario quod judicium inde ei reddi faciant." *Close Rolls 1242–1247*, p. 104. In 1262 a doubtful assize is respited until the quindene of Michaelmas " ut tunc de consilio discretorum virorum fieri faciamus justicie complementum ". *Close Rolls 1261–1264*, p. 149.*

[2] So, at the quindene of Hilary 1258, the cause of the city of London against its tallagers was tried in the exchequer in the presence of the barons of the exchequer, the earls of Warwick and Gloucester, John Mansel, Henry de Bathonia, the constable of the Tower, and others of the king's council. *Liber de Antiquis Legibus*, p. 33.

[3] Respite to the quindene of Michaelmas " ut tunc eorundem baronum et aliorum fidelium regis consilio mediante jus regis et ipsius abbatis in libertatibus predictis discutiatur." *Close Rolls 1254–1256*, p. 83.**

[4] Peter de Maulay's debts respited until the quindene of Michaelmas " ut tunc per consilium baronum regis de scaccario et aliorum rex inde faciat quod de jure fuerit faciendum ". *Ibid.*, p. 132.

able than under Edward, fluctuating according to convenience from case to case and during the process of any
single case. In so far as it had worked its way towards
a rule of practice, it was one in which the council judged
within a restricted sphere ; other courts, though for exceptional causes, maintained their accustomed field of jurisdiction, and an overriding court of parliament was not yet
in regular being.

In all this, judgment *by* parliament, judgment *in* parliament, fades into judgment *during* parliament, but by the
persons and authority of the barons of the exchequer or of
the justices of the various commissions. The assumption
must, I think, be that the directive judgment of the council
was habitually accorded before parliament met and is, in
fact, reflected in the close writ itself, which thus takes
roughly the place of the writ *de cancellaria* which despatched
the causes of Edward's parliament from the council to their
complementum in the lower courts. On this ground our
own preconception might make us deny the existence of
true parliamentary jurisdiction in Henry III's parliaments,
but, since contemporaries used the term, we shall be safer
in saying that the distinction is between two kinds of
parliament. The essential difference is, indeed, clear. In
Edward's later years nearly all the petitions and pleas
which reached the subordinate courts did so after a preliminary trial before the council in parliament—the king's
court in his council in his parliament as it could be called—
and this was, perhaps, so mainly for the simple reason that
the *greater number* of them had not reached the council
before the opening day. The proclamation had called
petitioners to give in their claims within a week of the
beginning of the session ; the council, or the auditors for
them, perforce dealt with them as a single cause-sheet
within the period of parliament ; and, *for the most part,*
though not always, they were passed through the subordinate
courts and had received their final answer before or soon
after parliament's dismissal. In Henry's reign, on the

contrary, many of the pleas tried during parliament had likewise originated by petition,[1] but not *as a rule* by petition presented during parliament, rather, by casual access to the king at London, Windsor, Clarendon, or Woodstock, or upon progress, as he might most conveniently be approached throughout the year.[1] These, if he entertained them, the king already treated as petitions to receive their trial at parliament—" ostendit regi ", " monstravit regi ", " ex gravi querela audivit rex ";[1] but, in blunt contrast with the normal Edwardian usage, Henry as a rule gave them their first hearing in vacation as they came to him, and adjourned them outright to the coming session, either to the further consideration of the king and council or to the mere *complementum justitiae* of exchequer, chancellor, or justices.[2] So doing, Henry performed out of parliament, in the gap between the sessions those acts of deliberative and directive judgment which were the distinctive function of Edward's council in parliament. That conciliar judgment, which came to be the focus of parliamentary justice under Edward I, is seen under his father not yet to have moved, or not fully to have moved, into parliament. It is still unattached to any special occasion, discharged in the routine of the council's judicial function, diffused through-

---

[1] Thus writs promising enquiry at the parliament of St. Edward 1255 were issued in answer to petition on the 14th May from Ludgershall, quia abbas Sancti Edmundi regi supplicavit (*Ibid.*, p. 83), from Woodstock on 31st May for the Hospital of Oxford (*Ibid.*, p. 196), from same place on 20th June, quia abbas de Sancto Edmundo clamavit (*Ibid.*, p. 101), from Nottingham on 20th July, monstravit nobis Willelmus (*Ibid.*, p. 212), from Northampton on 30th July, quia prior Sancti Andree Norhampt' clamat (*Ibid.*, p. 107), from Nottingham on the 1st August, quia decanus et canonici ecclesie Sancti Martini London' vendicant (*Ibid.*, p. 215), from Wark on 13th September, ostensum est regi ex parte Johannis le Poer (*Ibid.*, p. 132), and from Alnwick on 23rd September, ex gravi querela venerabilis patris L. Roffensis episcopi (*Ibid.*, p. 223).

[2] The petitions granted trial at Michaelmas 1255 were variously allocated to the council, to the king himself, to the king after scrutiny of the exchequer rolls, to the counsel of Earl Richard and other magnates, to the king with further counsel, to the exchequer and other faithful men, or to the exchequer alone, cf. the preceding note.

out the year. The king, already, as always, exercising supremacy and directive judgment over all petitions for special grace, does not yet as a rule embody and exercise that supremacy in his court in his council in his parliaments.

How parliament reflected these differences in the judicial practice of the two reigns is clear, though, of course, it is a difference of degree. Under Edward, since almost all petitions came under the consideration of the king in council in parliament, that jurisdiction was beginning to emerge as the supreme co-ordinating centre of the judicial session. In his later years, at least, the high court of parliament was a visible and omnipresent reality, giving to parliament a unity and identity which we cannot mistake, though contemporaries had as yet no certain name for it. Under Henry the council had its share of justice, as it always had, and must have from the very nature of the monarchy, and to that share the most difficult causes fell and it might hear the greatest petitioners. Nor was its right to intervene at any stage of any plea ever questioned or diminished. Moreover, though for the most part in vacation of parliament, all petitions must at some time or other have been considered by the king. Yet in parliament council's jurisdiction was not yet that of a general high court. Cause after cause that would have exercised the court of Edward's parliament in that first, directive enquiry into its prima facie reasonableness fell in Henry's parliament to the sole discretion of exchequer, chancery, or benches   Henry's council probably heard *coram rege* in parliament, from beginning to end, cases that Edward would have dismissed elsewhere after the preliminaries of pleading, but the contrast in constitutional effect is by that only increased. Edward's council (or auditors) heard all justice in parliament, and, from point to point of the cause list, the attendant courts received and obeyed its direction. Its jurisdiction was at least upon the verge of becoming in itself the jurisdiction of parliament. Henry's council appeared as but one, though the greatest, of a group of courts working at one time and place each at its proper jurisdiction. Its function was chiefly a jurisdiction *in* parliament. In this juridical aspect the Henrician parliament is hardly a parliament in the Edwardian sense at all, at least it is not the session of a single high court but rather the coming together of the several courts, in part to hold *colloquium* with council, the predominant partner in their contemporaneous session, but still more to carry out their respective commissions in complement of justice under the shadow of the king's grace and in the fuller record and freedom that it conferred.

Whether I have presented this transition too abruptly it is for others to judge. For myself, I think that it enables us to see back into an earlier stage of history. For this ill-articulated session, this *colloquium* of the courts, which accompanies parliament but which has not yet been fused into a court of parliament, the raw material for such a court in time to come, does not seem to differ essentially from certain terminal sessions of the courts which were considering cases referred to them by the king at the later parliamentary terms, usually on petition, for some ten years before parliament became fixed in our constitution. It will have been noticed that, as with the later parliaments, the adjournment of petitions is not to the feasts or to their octaves but to the quindenes of the principal legal terms. Such adjournment is decisively older than parliament and after the latter appears it continues equally at regular terms whether parliament does or does not meet. The Close Rolls assume the presence at such seasons of the council, the exchequer, the capital justices, and the justices of the Jews, and, indeed, the routine of the courts had made it a practice of long standing. But in its beginning this was not yet a session of parliament nor did it synchronise with the sessions of the barons. Petitions were heard at the quindenes of Hilary, Easter, and Michaelmas with fair regularity, while great councils and parliaments were fewer and sometimes held at other terms. At first, indeed, the

association of the assembly of the barons with the quindenes was rare and accidental.   In the year 1251 Matthew
Paris speaks of a *magnum consilium* at the Purification,
but none is recorded either at Easter or Michaelmas.   Yet
at the quindenes of those two feasts the king, the justices
coram rege, and the exchequer, were in session, and a number
of causes, many from the forest eyre and some for liberties,
were heard on adjournment.   Both occasions were thoroughly " parliamentary " in their judicial business and in
the other judicial authorities present, but the barons were
absent.   This is no more than an especially striking instance
of the great and special jurisdiction of the quindenes in
action without formal recognition as parliament and without
the magnates.   It is typical of these years.   In 1248 there
were adjournments to four such legal occasions, at the
quindenes of Hilary, Easter, St. John Baptist, and Michaelmas.   The Hilary meeting was described by both treasury [1]
and chancery [2] as a parliament, the first in official record.
Matthew Paris calls the summer meeting a parliament,
though the chancery ranks it only as a *colloquium regis*.[3]
Both were attended by the magnates.   But the Michaelmas
quindene, to which also the characteristic judicial and
executive respites were accorded, was not called a parliament, and was only attended by a few prelates and barons
invited by the king to keep the feast of St. Edward with
him.[4]   Again, in 1249, the only important adjournments
by close writs were to the quindene of Michaelmas, while
the assemblies of the magnates were at the Epiphany [4]
and at the Close of Easter.[4]   In 1250 there was a council
of the magnates at Epiphany [4] and on 7th March a great
rally of the nobles to take the cross.[4]   There was nothing
of the sort at the quindene of Michaelmas, but the justice
of debt, franchise, and redress was done equally at this

[1] P.R.O., Lord Treasurer's Remembrancer's Memoranda, 20 m. 5.
(References are to the new numbering of the membranes.)

[2] *Close Rolls 1247–1251*, p. 104.

[3] *Ibid.*, p. 31.

[4] Matthew Paris, *Chronica Majora, sub anno.*

term. Not until the year 1252 does there seem to be any prospect of the legal councils and the great councils of the magnates coming together. In that year a " great parliament "[1] coincided with the quindene of Michaelmas, and there were parliaments or great councils of the barons at the quindenes of Easter 1253,[2] of Hilary[1] and Easter 1254,[3] and of Easter[4] and Michaelmas 1255.[1] The coincidence of the two institutions had by no means become a fixed rule, but it was becoming a common practice, sufficiently common, indeed, for us to have persuaded ourselves that it was necessary to a true parliament.

Beginning in 1238, reference of cases by writ close to the appropriate courts occurs after 1246 with increasing frequency at the quindenes of two or three exchequers in every year. Over a period of years this is almost always without the magnates and without the name of parliament. The occasion was royal and bureaucratic and judicial. It was, perhaps, hardly noticeable as an innovation : merely the adjournment of cases which had secured the king's interest to a fixed day from the opening of the established terms of the exchequer. Yet, since judgment by peers was seldom realised under Henry's personal rule, it embodied all the necessary resources of justice. From the legal standpoint it contained the potentiality, though it did not realise the unity, of a parliament, and it provided all that the king could gain from a supreme council of justice. It could do all that the courts were required to do " in complement of justice " in Edward's parliaments. All the courts were habitually in session. Petitions could be heard *coram rege* if they needed special authority, or referred to the exchequer if they turned on past record. The king could combine both tribunals by having charters examined critically in the exchequer and confirmed by judgment in

---

[1] *Ibid.*

[2] Matthew of Westminster, *sub anno.*

[3] *Close Rolls 1253–1254,* p. 43.

[4] *Close Rolls 1254–1256,* p. 61. Annals of Burton, in *Annales Monastici,* i. *sub anno.*

the council.   He could afforce or correct the judgments of
the king's bench or common pleas by means of a council
of which Henry de Bathonia, Henry de Bracton, Roger de
Turri, and Roger de Thurkelby were simultaneously members.[1] The knowledge of the council was completed by
that of the justices of the courts, and the council, in its
turn, strengthened and controlled the action of the standing
courts.   The records of the five or more permanent commissions of justice were brought to one place to supplement
and correct each other.   If much of the work of the quindenes went on by way of complement of justice within
each of the component courts, the occasion had a potential
unity, only intermittently realised, in the session of the
king and council.   There was in all this no sudden break
with the past.   Its full use was for the future.   As yet no
session of a single high court was recognised, still less a high
court of parliament.   But any plea could be taken up
coram rege at any stage of its trial, the council could enter
and afforce the courts of the justices, and their judgments
were made under the corrective of the king's near presence.

Though they were only a new use for old-established
sessions, these quindenal occasions were, therefore, well
qualified to deal with petition.   They were an epitome of
the personal rule upon its legal side.   Indeed, had the king
guided the regime more surely, the step of combining the
colloquium of the courts with a parliament of the magnates
might never have been taken.   When taken it was an
advance, though, perhaps, an unconscious one, towards the
revival of trial by peers.   To call a great council of the
nobles at the quindene of Hilary, Easter, or Michaelmas
was to admit the barons into the arcana of the king's legal
administration, and on more than one occasion he experienced the danger of doing so.   The Bassets and their
faction among the nobility brought the country to the
verge of civil war by their defence of Henry de Bathonia
in the magnate parliament of Purification, the quindene of

[1] *Calendar of Patent Rolls 1247–1258*, p. 451.

Hilary 1250. In that of the quindene of Michaelmas 1255 the earl of Norfolk intervened to save Robert de Rhos from the confiscation of his property as the result of a judgment *coram rege*, and this was the occasion of a personal quarrel which made the earl one of the king's bitterest enemies in 1258.

It is, indeed, remarkable that Henry allowed the *commune consilium* to meet at the same time as the special session of his courts. He did not do so as a rule until 1252. The sitting of the courts was governed by quite other considerations than was the summons to the barons. Its occasion was, as we have said, old established, judicial, bureaucratic, and royal. Its terms of meeting were fixed by the nature of the courts' business, and it did not respond to the political reasons which called together the magnates to parliament at almost any time of the year, at mid-Lent, at Ascension, or Pentecost. Nor did it meet indifferently, as the barons did, at Oxford, or Merton, or Winchester, or elsewhere. Its place of session was Westminster, and its days for considering petitions, almost without exception, the fourteenth day of one of the established legal terms. Rarely, it did such work at the quindene of Trinity, on one occasion at that of St. John. But normally, in a busy year in the 'fifties and 'sixties, those meetings which heard petitions to the king were three, and, fixed, no doubt, by the established attendance of the courts, at Hilary, Easter, and Michaelmas. By long usage the principal courts met at the feasts or their octaves, and might be expected to have made some progress in their normal routine in the first fortnight of their term. At the fourteenth day they might be ready to attend to the special jurisdiction, the petitions of the king's debtors and claimants of franchise : for, in or out of parliament, this was the matter of which the business of the quindenes upon petition, as the Close Rolls reflect it, was mainly composed.

Thus, if we take our stand in the middle 'fifties, the quindenes seem to be in process of incorporation into the

parliaments, for which they will provide a necessary afforcement of professional justiciars if parliament is to become
a general court of redress.   But only on an extreme baronial
reading of the constitution could they, for their part, need
the afforcement of the barons, and, as we trace them back,
their line of origin swings away into independence.   This
origin is seen to emerge not from the *commune consilium*
but from the permanent curia and the familiar council.
The jurisdiction makes its first appearance not long before
that of parliament, but sufficiently so for its priority to
be clear.   It is indisputably the older.   There is one group
of three respites to the quindene of Michaelmas 1238,[1] of
which one is for the exchequer [2] and another for the
exchequer of the Jews.[3]   In 1246 the bishop of Winchester
was given a day *coram rege* to prove his liberty of the
forest [4] and two disputes as to wardship [5] were adjourned
to the quindene of Michaelmas.   By 1248 we are at the
first year of a series in which the practice becomes a rule.
Henceforth the courts do this kind of justice with fair
regularity at the quindenes of Easter and Michaelmas, and
less regularly at that of Hilary, and petitions and pleas
are coming to be adjourned to them as to a routine *colloquium* of the courts.   I think we may claim that at this
stage of history we are behind parliament, which is not
named in record until 1248.[6*] We see the peculiar aggre-
gation of courts and jurisdictions which was the legal body
of Henry's later parliaments as an old, recurrent session
of the parts of the permanent curia rather than as an essential member of the intermittent baronial assemblies.   It
cannot be claimed that the witness of the Close and Patent
Rolls tells the whole story.   Petition and respite by close

---

[1] *Close Rolls 1237–1242*, pp. 86, 99, 101.
[2] The plea of the abbot of Reading for the amercements of his men.
[3] " Ut tunc inquiratur apud scaccarium Judeorum."
[4] *Close Rolls 1242–1247*, p. 444.
[5] *Ibid.*, pp. 429 and 479.
[6] I exclude the chancery's reference to parleys with the Welsh and
Scotch as parliaments, its according of the name of parliament to John's
council of Runneymede and the use of the term outside official record.

writ may have been somewhat older than 1238, though I do not think so, or the series may have been more complete from the late 'thirties than I have been able to convince myself that it was. However this may be, it represents a phase of redress on petition slightly older than parliament but already anticipating the place of the later parliaments in the subject matter with which it deals.

How shall we account for the origin of this jurisdiction ? Perhaps most easily by determining the needs and circumstances that called it into being. I would suggest that the strongest, though, of course, not the only, influence upon its development was the radical change in the Crown's attitude towards franchise which came in the middle years of Henry III. A universal movement, upon the one hand to analyse and controvert, and, upon the other, to justify, all kinds of right and obligation set in in the second quarter of the thirteenth century. The attack of the king's lawyers upon franchise, in which they began to find new methods, was minute, tireless, and prolonged, and, in my view, it had the largest share in bringing first a form of quasi-parliamentary trial and later trial in full parliament into being. The earliest hint of a systematic judicial treatment of claims for liberties comes, indeed, from a time far before parliament, when feudal rights were being roughly asserted and the government was hard put to it to keep them within bounds, that is, from the days of William Marshal's rectorship.[1] But this phase of unrest did not last, while the tension between the feudatories and the Crown became a fixed character of the reign after Henry had tested the loyalty of his vassals in 1242 and found it wanting. From 1243 we enter upon a new and more strenuous period of

---

[1] *Rotuli Litterarum Clausarum 1204–1224*, ed. T. D. Hardy, p. 383*b*. Rex Justiciariis itinerantibus in Comitatu Kancie salutem . . . Omnes autem demandas quas coram nobis fuerint quas homines exigunt de libertatibus videlicet quas dominus Cantuar' Archiepiscopus, G. comes de clara, vel alii exigunt in respectum ponatis usque in XV dies post festum Sancti Hyllarii coram consilio nostro apud Westmon'.*

At Hilary 4 Hen. III, the council was sitting in the exchequer together with the justices of the Jews, and hearing pleas of debt. *Ibid.*, p. 410.

the majority. Henry's prospects of maintaining an adequate revenue by way of gracious aid were then at an end, and he and his officials began to turn for money to the wide and untapped field of prerogative. The period of active investigation into the rights of the Crown and the usurpations of subjects had begun.

The theory which guided it was, of course, that all franchise is of its nature royal. It was hardening towards the phrase that liberties are " regalia mere domino regi spectantia".* From this flowed the consequence that no point of immunity could be established without proof of royal grant, and, with its assertion, came the need for a new means of investigation, at once more effective and more impartial. In April 1244 a general letter was issued to the sheriffs ordering them to reclaim all liberties which were not exercised by sufficient royal warrant or by ancient tenure, and which had not been used without intermission " from time immemorial until the parliament of Runney-mede ".[1] Its appearance was the warning of a new and stricter policy. From 1244 the Crown began to multiply its demands. In that year came Robert Passelew's inquest into purprestures in the forests, which yielded heavy fines, though in retrospect it was to seem light beside Geoffrey de Langley's eyre of six years later. In 1251 there began an enquiry into alienations of the king's serjeanties, of which the reign was never to hear the last,[2] and one into the franchise of weights and measures.[3] In 1253 another commission was appointed to uncover offences against the statute of the king's exchange. From 1254, at latest, a special eyre of justices *ad privata placita regis* was in action.[4] Above all, the long-drawn out, searching, and oppressive forest eyre of Geoffrey de Langley was in being by 1250. Its amercements were extravagant, as the records show, and so much was it hated and suspected that Matthew

[1] *Close Rolls 1242–1247*, p. 242.
[2] *Close Rolls 1247–1251*, p. 421.   [3] *Ibid.*, p. 446.
[4] *Close Rolls 1253–1254*, p. 8. *Ibid.*, p. 272. Henry de Bathonia and his brethren justiciarii ad privata placita regis assignati.

Paris records the belief that it was Henry's revenge upon the northern baronage for their rebellion against his father. The whole movement culminated in 1255 with that general inquisition " de juribus et libertatibus et aliis ipsum regem contingentibus"* for which six circuits of judge were commissioned and whose records have found a place in the printed edition of the Hundred Rolls.[1]

During this decade a radical change of policy took place. The spirit and much of the theory of the Edwardian statute of Gloucester already possessed the exchequer and the justices, whose successors in the next reign had little to add to the weapons which Henry's lawyers had put into their hands. More, indeed, was then attempted under the writ *quo warranto* [2] and the hated formula *non obstante* [3] than Edward ever ventured. Not only were those who petitioned for dubious liberties subjected to a far more rigorous testing of their warrants by the exchequer, before the capital justices, or the king and council, but sheriffs and justices were encouraged by the exchequer to contest privileges of long standing and to drive those who exercised them to trial. From time to time, indeed, the king was forced to rebuke the exchequer's zeal.[4] In the trials of the 'fifties,

[1] *Calendar of Patent Rolls 1247–1258*, p. 438.

[2] Especially in the unprincipled use of the *quo warranto* in claims of land by the Crown against subjects. *Abbreviatio Placitorum*, pp. 105, 107, 118. It seems to have been realised as early as 1200 that this process might be used to challenge land right and that such a use would be objectionable. Cf. the Countess of Gloucester's disclaimer of having so used it in her court. *Curia Regis Rolls of the reigns of Richard I and John*, i. 186 (Trinity Term 2 John). Henry was compelled to denounce this use of the writ when the steward of Haughley applied it to the prior of Normanbury in 1253: ab hujusmodi vexacione penitus desistens regi scire faciat si quod jus rex habeat in terra predicta ut ipsam rex per breve suum versus predictum priorem secundum consuetudinem regni petat. *Close Rolls 1251–1253*, p. 484.

[3] Sparsimque jam tales literae, in quibus inserta est haec detestabilis adjectio: non obstante antiqua libertate procedat negotium, suscitabantur. Matthew Paris, *Chronica Majora, sub anno* 1251.**

[4] The exchequer has enforced a change of usage as to the abbot of Glastonbury's immunity of return of writs: et quia hoc non pertinet ad ipsos faciendum, mandatum est eisdem baronibus ut de returno illo nichil de cetero attemptent. *Close Rolls 1247–1251*, p. 403. Rex

moreover, the exchequer was to harden its requirements and to make them more precise.   Defendants met a formula which was to become the mainstay of the Crown's case against franchise for the next century, the demand that the terms of any charter pleaded must be positive and explicit, that *verba generalia* interpreted according to the prejudice of the claimant were no answer to a *quo warranto*.[1] Thus, the onus of forcing the obscure and obsolete terms of Saxon franchise to conform to the quittances from suit, common fine and amercement, return of writs, *vetitum namium*, that were the fashion of thirteenth-century immunity, was thrust upon the claimant.   Against this new rigidity in the interpretation of charters, and especially against the requirement of express warrant for liberties, the bishops protested in their articles of grievance in 1257,[1] though their protest may never have reached the king.

This, moreover, was a period when the subject, even the great subject, was as much at the mercy of the king's justices as he had ever been.   During the twelfth century and the first half of the thirteenth the drift of Angevin government had been towards specialisation and division of powers, towards a measure of independence of the courts from the council.   It was a trend that might be carried too far.   "Lex scaccarii"[2] might well prove too good a servant of the Crown and too hard a master to

baronibus suis de scaccario.   Meminimus nos semel et secundo dedisse in mandatis quod liberos homines magistri et fratrum milicie Templi in Anglia in singulis burgis et villis Anglie quietos esse faceretis de tallagio. *Close Rolls 1251–1253*, p. 428.   Cf. *ibid.*, pp. 476 and 490.

[1] Et si praelatus compulsus comparens chartam donatoris exhibeat, licet contineatur in ea quod donator tales et tales dederit libertates . . . nil proderit ei nisi in charta de eadem libertate expresse fiat mentio. Matthew Paris, *Chronica Majora, Additamenta, sub anno 1257.*

[2] John de Ore and others " accesserunt ad nos . . . nuper querentes, cum teneant de serjeancia . . . quedam extenta facta fuit super eos . . . occasione cujus extenta exigitur ab eis per summonicionem scaccarii plus quam reddendum pertinet ad tenementa sua." The king orders the barons "quod per legem et consuetudinem scaccarii nostri, sicut expedire videritis, per inquisicionam vel novam extentam hoc faciatis emendari." *Close Rolls 1251–1253*, p. 427.

obstinate subjects, and the struggle between the Crown
and the liberties might have broken earlier into rebellion
if that trend had not been reversed. The jurisdiction of
the quindenes, beginning in the middle 'forties, thus provided a partial remedy against the centrifugal trend in the
bureaucracy. It restored to the subject his privilege of
trial, if not actually *coram rege*, at least before the exchequer
or the justices at a time when the king was at his palace
of Westminster and his council available for consultation
and appeal.

In the business of the exchequer this return to contact
with the king was made necessary not only by the interest
of subjects or the strain of occasional great causes but also
by the common course of business, by the need for constant
interchange of information and instruction between the
king and the exchequer barons and between the king and
the justices of the forests, of the Jews, and of any other of
the many special commissions that were active in these
years. The exchequer had to deal with masses of debts,
many going back to the reign of John,[1] and also with an
undergrowth of immunity and franchise which obscured
the indebtedness of every great subject in such matters
as common fine and amercement, return of writs, regard
of the forest, and the like, and it also audited the multifarious accounts of the king's debts and of his custodies and
wardships. There were debts that were clear upon the
rolls and others that were not clear. For the former the
exchequer was a sufficient court of justice, but for the latter
it might sometimes need the judgment of the king.[2]
The memoranda rolls of the treasury bear occasional marks
of this need in the minute " loquendum cum rege ".[3]* The

[1] In 1248 the abbot of Strata Florida was being distrained upon for
a tallage of the reign of John. *Close Rolls 1247–1251*, p. 48.

[2] " Si clarum fuerit debitum illud, ad judicium in eodem procedant :
si vero aliquid ambiguitatis invenerint in eodem prefatam loquelam venire
faciant certo die coram rege terminandam." *Ibid.*, p. 284.**

[3] P.R.O., Lord Treasurer's Remembrancer's Memoranda (Transcripts),
18 m. 3. Abatement of the farm of Dunwich. Loquendum cum rege.

king, upon his side, was constantly petitioned throughout the year to intervene between the debtor and the exchequer, to recognise immunity, or to pardon debt. At any time, therefore, there were petitions outstanding which could not rightly be answered from such chancery rolls as followed the king in his progress, for they needed to be checked by the enquiry of the exchequer. In addition, claimants or defendants before the eyres or the court *coram rege* were constantly seeking to rest their claims upon exchequer records.[1]

It seems, therefore, that some recurrent jurisdiction which should reassemble the courts of judicature with the king and the council was an almost inevitable need of the middle years of Henry III. If such a jurisdiction took shape it was almost certain to do so about the exchequer, since that office held most of the record necessary to the hearing of petitions of debt and franchise and its barons were on the whole the judges most familiar with the judicial issues involved. It is true that the court *coram rege* sometimes heard claims to franchise, but it had often to appeal to the treasury rolls for its evidences and the exchequer was the most proper court for such pleas. It is, therefore, natural, but none the less noteworthy, that the exchequer had anticipated the king by about a decade in separating cases which involved great persons from the mass of its *communia*, especially when they were making claims to franchise. It is of special significance that it had anticipated the terms of parliament, fastening upon the fourteenth days from the exchequers of Hilary, Easter, and Michaelmas (and less commonly that of Trinity), as days of special session for the trial of liberties. The *communia* of any term might run into several hundreds of items, and without

---

Ibid., 21 m. 1d. Tenure of manors beyond the term of their farm. Loquendum. I am indebted to Professor Julius Goebel for calling my attention to this point.

[1] *Abbreviatio Placitorum*, p. 135. Richard de la Mere before the justices *coram rege* " quod hoc sit verum trahit inde ad warantum rotulos de scaccario et petit quod rotuli videantur ".

further search into what is, after all, a very natural recasting
of agenda, I must not say for certain in what year the
practice first arose. My impression is that its adoption
was gradual, beginning about the eleventh year of the
reign, in which year the Lord Treasurer's Remembrancer
records a few important cases of debt as adjourned to the
quindene of Michaelmas.[1] By the twenty-second year concentration upon the quindenes had become a marked
feature of the rolls. At Easter in that year several great
parties, among them the countess of Warenne,[2] were respited
to the quindene of Michaelmas for claims against them,
and there was a marked tendency to adjourn cases concerning franchise to the same term. The bishop of Lincoln's claim to quittance from *murdrum* in Newark,[3] the
prior of Dunstable's claim to amercements of his men,[4] and
the objections of Warin de Monchesni and the abbot of
Chertsey to common fine in the county of Surrey,[5] were
all adjourned to that day. From this time the system
flourished, and in the twenty-fifth year it is sufficiently
established to make it worth while to put the full list of
respites and adjournments in evidence. The respites to the
quindene of Hilary in this year are for the priors of Rochester
and Wymondham, for the men of Grimsby, and for all
claimants to franchise in Essex and Hertfordshire.[6] Those
to the quindene of Easter are for William de Say, Reynold
Forester, Roger Wasthose, and the men of Hertford.[7]
Those for Michaelmas are for the prior of Brackley, Roger
de Linch, the abbot of Chertsey, claiming frankpledge and
auxilium vicecomitis, the abbot of Ramsey, William le
Breton, William de Fiennes, for arrears of scutage, John

[1] P.R.O., Lord Treasurer's Remembrancer's Memoranda Roll, 10.
[2] *Ibid.*, 12 m. 10d.
[3] *Ibid.*, 12 m. 10. " Mandatum est vicecomiti quod ponat in respectu
ad quindenam Sancti Michaelis demandam murdri quam facit . . . super
Wapentach' de Newerk quia episcopus Lincolnie clamat inde quietanciam."
[4] *Ibid.*, 12 m. 10d.
[5] *Ibid.*, 12 m. 11d.
[6] *Ibid.*, 13 m. 2d. to 13 m. 4d.
[7] *Ibid.*, 13 m. 5 to 13 m. 5d.

de Blancbuilly, Peter de Rayleigh, John de Wulurich, Humphrey de Bohun for arrears of the third penny of the earldom, the priors of Rochester, Lewisham, Dunstable, and Beaulieu, John de Tideham, Gilbert Basset, Ralf Russell, William de Tishale, and the abbot of Bec.[1]

It will be observed that the Michaelmas session is still by far the most heavily burdened, and that the persons and matters adjourned to it are almost uniformly of the kind that later engaged the king's special attention and were likely to be referred by him to the quindenes and to become the matter of future parliaments. The concentration of cases of franchise upon the Michaelmas quindene already marked out that term in 1238 and three years later it received a general sanction. Michaelmas 1241 is not only an unusually clear instance of the practice of reserving a special class of jurisdiction to the quindenes, it has the further and crucial importance that it records the acceptance of that practice as a system. In this year for the first time this day is appointed as that upon which all claimants of liberties by charter, irrespective of person, will be given judgment upon their claims.[2] The quindene of Michaelmas thus achieves an unique importance in exchequer judgment, and something like a fixed institution is brought into being within the structure of the exchequer year. Looking to the nature of this jurisdiction it is, perhaps, an allowable licence of phrase to say that, in reserving this term for judgment upon franchise, the exchequer was setting up its private " parliamentary " occasion some years before the king began to build up a similar occasion for himself. If that is too bluntly expressed, we may, I think, at least understand why, when he began to find it necessary to refer petitions as to franchise to a set term and jurisdiction, he chose the quindenes of the opening of the three principal

---

[1] *Ibid.*, 13 m. 6d. to 13 m. 11d.

[2] *Ibid.*, 13 m. 6d. " De pluribus libertatibus. Omnes qui clamant libertates per cartas habeant diem ad audiendum judicium suum de libertatibus illis . . . in quindena Sancti Michaelis.'"

exchequers of the year, and first of all that of Michaelmas. That was the day already consecrated by the barons to that kind of judgment and they were the most essential of the courts involved in any jurisdiction of petitions and appeals for special grace ; to them a majority of the petitions were expressly adjourned.

Indeed, from their initiation by the exchequer, there can have been no sudden break or acceleration in the growth of the quindenes towards their future status of parliaments. Once established as exchequer practice, the jurisdiction grew by the gradual accretion of pleas and petitions referred to it by letter close by the king. By the later 'forties the plea-list of the exchequer at the quindene of Michaelmas consisted about equally of cases adjourned by the king and by the barons themselves. The occasion engaged the king's attendance with growing regularity, and increasingly he imposed the same term upon the other commissions of justices. The justices *coram rege* also maintained their own file of the quindene of Michaelmas.[1] As the exchequer respites began sporadically in the late 'twenties and had swelled to a special but recognised jurisdiction by the 'forties, so the respites of the king began occasionally in the late 'thirties and grew until by the early 'fifties they had created a royal occasion of justice centring primarily upon the exchequer but involving other justices and soon to draw towards itself the baronial assemblies also. It was the natural order of growth, for in those days the zeal of the exchequer outran that of the king in testing and reclaiming liberties and for a number of years it was not openly questioned by subjects. It was only as this zeal was seen to be growing into a wholesale attack upon privilege, and when its victims began to petition the king in numbers against its severity, that Henry was forced to

---

[1] *Abbreviatio Placitorum*, p. 131. " Sicut continetur in cedula que est ligula brevium de quindena Sancti Michaelis anno 37." This was, however, of very old standing and its only principle was not that which prompted the exchequer. Cf. *Curia Regis Rolls*, i. 128 (Hilary Term 1 John), etc.

intervene, to find some more responsible form of trial where great issues and persons were involved, and to attend the quindenes himself with his council. The growth of this new policy, this new attention and formality on the part of the king, we may trace in outline from the Close Roll writs.

In his earlier years, until after his Gascon war, Henry was lax in his treatment of petitions when away from Westminster, and generous in pardons and recognitions of franchise. He would admit the validity of a claim upon the word of a petitioner or his friends,[1] from his own memory of past transactions, or at best from an inspection of such rolls of chancery as were itinerant with him. When disposed to severity, he showed little concern for the interests involved, for the need to be considerate had not yet been forced upon him by any dangerous outcry. As late as 1244 it was not considered that the general inquest of that year needed any form of trial more responsible than local inquest, and both enquiry and enforcement were left to the sheriffs. The two principal cases which we know to have arisen out of it, the bishop of Worcester's claim to *vetitum namium* and that of the archbishop to return of writs within the fee of Christchurch, Canterbury, were answered by orders to the sheriffs of Kent, Worcester, and Gloucester to hold inquisitions in their counties, and, if they were favourable, to allow the petitioners to enjoy their franchise.[2] Thus, petition for privilege was still thought to be adequately answered by county trial. The alternative to inquest before the sheriff, perhaps an even worse one, was trial before the exchequer, unsupported and unchecked. If Henry's sympathy were not engaged, he would remit the whole matter

---

[1] " Rex baronibus suis de scaccario, salutem. Quia protestatum est coram nobis per viros fidedignos quod quando recepimus in manum nostram castrum de Corf a fideli et dilecto nostro Petro de Malo Lacu, perdonavimus ei triginta libras . . . vobis mandamus quod predictum Petrum de omnibus denariis predictis quietum esse faciatis." *Close Rolls 1237–1242*, p. 211.

[2] *Close Rolls 1242–1247*, p. 292.

thither and leave it to inquisition,[1] to the rolls of past years,[2] or to the interpretation which the barons cared to set upon any charter of franchise that was submitted to them.[3] In so doing, he must have forfeited much of any popularity which his casual generosity could bring him, for it was a method which set too much faith in the impartiality of the exchequer and in the complaisance of parties submitted to its judgment. At best there was for some time no regular care to secure the supervision of the council over exchequer judgments.

Certain of the issues left to the exchequer during Henry's first few years of personal rule were of national importance and amply justify the jealousy with which the magnates sought the judgment of their peers. They included the Beauchamp claim to fee and inheritance in the shrievalty of Worcester [4] and the rights of the abbey of Bury St. Edmund's to its ancient liberties within the eight and a half hundreds.[5] In leaving such great persons to the exchequer, Henry was subjecting them to a one-sided reading of their charters at a time when the terms of all ancient liberties were entering upon a period of disputed interpretation. An exchequer judgment dismissed the abbot of Bury's charters as being too ambiguously ex-

---

[1] " Mandatum est baronibus de scaccario quod statim ex quo facta fuerit inquisitio de feodis militum de Fednes . . . eidem Willelmo faciant habere rationabile judicium suum secundum considerationem scaccarii regis." *Close Rolls 1237–1242*, p. 21.

[2] " Mandatum est baronibus de scaccario quod si inquirere poterint per rotulos scaccarii quod manerium de Hertford tailliatum fuit quando rex dominica sua tailliare precepit, tunc hominibus ejusdem manerii pacem faciant de tricesima." *Ibid.*, p. 64.

[3] *Ibid.*, p. 43.

[4] " Rex baronibus de scaccario, salutem. Mandamus vobis quod, inspectis diligenter rotulis de tempore Johannis regis, patris nostri et de tempore nostro, inquiratis diligenter si predecessores dilecti et fidelis nostri Willelmi de Bello Campo, vicecomitis nostri Wygornie, tenuerint comitatum illum in feodo . . . et si inveneritis quod comitatum illum sic tenuerunt permittatis predictum Willelmum eodem modo comitatum illum tenere quo predicti predecessores sui ipsum tenuerunt." *Ibid.*, p. 70.

[5] *Ibid.*, p. 404.

pressed,[1] and he did what many a lesser immunist must have longed to do also. He refused all summonses which followed upon the exchequer's judgment,[2] until, fourteen years later, he was able to force his grievance before the king.[3]

This was the stress of opposing interests and conflicting legal theories, amounting in some cases to a deadlock, which called at the end of the 'forties for a parliamentary solution. The time, indeed, was come when the king would be forced to act more deliberately alike in his own interest and in that of his petitioners, to consult the exchequer more frequently, and to bring the exchequer itself under closer supervision ; to advance, in fact, upon the road towards parliament. The quindene of Michaelmas, and to a less degree those of Hilary and Easter, were already established as the terms when the exchequer tried important cases of debt and franchise. The quindene of Michaelmas was equally the one time of the year when Henry would certainly be at Westminster of his own free will, for it coincided with the feast of the Translation of St. Edward the Confessor upon the 13th October. Throughout his life, and increasingly from 1241, the memory of the Confessor was the centre of Henry's religious cult, and he would set aside almost any business in order to come to Westminster and celebrate it with becoming secular and religious pomp. On the 13th October, then, the feast of St. Edward and quindene of Michaelmas, the king was sure to be available, and it is at least a striking coincidence that that day in 1241 was both the first full celebration of the Translation by Henry [4] and the first occasion when the

---

[1] " Propter minorem expressionem eorundem." *Close Rolls 1254–1256*, p. 83.

[2] " Demandam quam ei faciunt de xx marcis per summonicionem scaccarii . . . que xx marce jam extiterunt in demanda xv annis elapsis." *Ibid.*, p. 101.▪ 20 marks was the sum for which the barons were ready to quit the abbot of the arrears.

[3] At Michaelmas 1255. *Loc. cit.*

[4] The golden shrine of the Confessor was completed in that year.

exchequer explicitly set the quindene as its day of general judgment on franchise. At least in the later years of the reign, it was also the day when the familiar council was ordered to reassemble in full strength. This was the earliest established and, on the whole, the busiest and most regularly employed of the quindenal sessions. But Henry, though his inclination was to spend the Christmas feast at Winchester and that of Easter at Windsor or Merton, accustomed himself as pressure of business grew to remain within reach of the capital at those feasts also, and to present himself at Westminster to attend judicial business, not at the quindene of Michaelmas only, but twice or even three times a year after the other two feasts.

That these special occasions of jurisdiction were called into being by the prevailing dispute about franchise is, I think, clear both from the fact that they found their proto-type in the exchequer and from the nature of the matters they dealt with. In this the pleas of the quindenes of Easter and of Michaelmas 1251 were specially numerous but not otherwise exceptional. Of this year Matthew Paris records that a *magnum parliamentum* was held at the quindene of the Purification, but I cannot find that any *magnum consilium* or parliament met either at Easter or Michaelmas. As has already been said, the Easter session gained in importance more slowly than that of Michaelmas, but this year Henry came to Westminster two days before the quindene of Easter and remained there for over two weeks. The eyre of the forest was already making itself felt, and a number of important persons, especially ecclesi-astics, had received respites, against Geoffrey de Langley or other officials, suspending action upon judgment against them to the quindene. We may take it that in most cases respite was accorded to enable enquiry to be made through the exchequer rolls or charters to be presented.[1] Among

---

[1] As it was said in a case of the previous year : " ostensum est regi ex parte Ricardi de Grey quod G. de Langel' justiciarius foreste, ipsum et homines suos facit distringi pro quibusdam feris . . . de quibus vocat

those called to defend their forest right were the abbot of Hyde, the prior of St. Bartholomew's, and the mayor and citizens of York.[1] The inquest upon the alienated serjeanties was represented by a claim against John fitz Bernard's tenants,[2] and William of Otteringham was adjourned *coram rege* at the quindene to show his claim to a serjeanty in the king's soke of Snaith against a judgment by the justices in the previous year.[3] The bishop of Lincoln was respited for his market and fair of Biggleswade seized for default against the assize of weights and measures. The notorious criminal charge against Henry de Bathonia found its issue at the Easter quindene, and was sent thence for final judgment before the capital justices.[4]

The respites to the Michaelmas quindene, which began to be issued quite early in the year, were still more numerous than those for Easter, and they also chiefly concerned franchise and the recent judicial eyres.   Again a number of forest amercements were respited to the session and Geoffrey de Langley was himself present in the council.[5]   Among those involved were the abbots of Glastonbury, Crowland, and Netley,[6] the prior of Merton, the Knights Hospitallers, the dean and chapter of Salisbury, the city of York, and sundry laymen.   Roger Bertram joined with other Northumbrian magnates to petition for their wood rights in the forest and was promised judgment at the quindene.[7] Besides the forest, ministerial action against several other liberties was respited to the same term, for Peter of Savoy's men of the honour of Richmond for freedom from toll,[8] for Reginald de Mohun for freedom of tallage in the manor of Graywell,[9] and for the abbot of Stratford for freedom

rotulos regis ad warantum.   Et ideo mandatum est eidem G. quod eundem Ricardum . . . usque ad instans festum Beati Edwardi pacem inde faciat habere."   *Close Rolls 1247–1251*, p. 315.

[1] *Ibid.*, pp. 407, 428, 416.   [2] *Ibid.*, p. 409.
[3] *Ibid.*, pp. 261 and 421.
[4] *Ibid.*, p. 539.   [5] *Ibid.*, p. 514.   [6] *Ibid.*, p. 452.
[7] " Alii quamplures ejusdem comitatus sunt in consimili querimonia." *Ibid.*, p. 542.
[8] *Ibid.*, p. 441.   [9] *Loc. cit.*

of suit from his manor of Sudbury.[1] Another respite was for the liberty of the town of Rochester, and six days after the quindene that of Southampton was restored, presumably after judgment. Perhaps the most important cause tried was that of the men of the four cantreds of Rhos and Rhuveniog, who were resisting the introduction of English custom into the Welshry by the justiciar of Chester, and who were promised trial by the council at the quindene in the presence of the justiciar and their own representatives.[2]

I have chosen this year as typical and in no way exceptional. It is also a good year to take as our test of the nature of the jurisdiction of the quindenes, because in 1251 they were on the point of being caught up in the larger jurisdiction of parliament. For this very reason, that their independent standing is soon to be in some measure lost, it is proper to determine the nature of their justice and to see that it is already of the kind with which parliament, even the Edwardian parliament, which the statute of Gloucester, by making a general clearance, relieved of much of its justice of franchise, was to be largely concerned. The Close Rolls and the treasury Memoranda will not, it is true, tell us all the story of either quindenes or parliaments. Most Close Roll respites were issued to suspend distraints or other action by the exchequer, and their bias is almost, though not quite, as fiscal as that of the rolls of the treasury itself. But, though, from the nature of our sources, the number of pleas and petitions of exchequer provenance must be to some degree exaggerated, such pleas are still to be accepted as the staple business alike of the exchequer's Michaelmas session, of the sessions of the quindenes into which they were caught up, of the Henrician and, to a less degree, of the Edwardian parliaments. They constitute a jurisdiction common to all

[1] *Ibid.*, p. 500. " Ut tunc ostendat quietanciam quam inde habet coram baronibus de scaccario."
[2] *Ibid.*, p. 541. " Quia tunc de consilio nostro in presencia nostra et quorundam ex hominibus illis de premissis volumus habere tractatum."*

four, arising from the plain circumstances of the period and
linking successive parliamentary or quasi-parliamentary
sessions into an evident chain of common function in justice.
They tell much less than the whole story, but what they tell is
consistent, and throughout Henry's reign it does not change.
The exchequer devises its special quindenal session, the
king observes the occasion and swells its business with his
own respites and adjournments, coming himself to Westminster with his council, the parliament of barons comes at
last to afforce and to trouble the lawyers in their judicial
sessions.   But the jurisdiction, in its unknown proportion
to the full business of parliament, does not vary.

If I ventured to generalize at all about these occasions
which were called parliaments in the later years of Henry III,
it would be to deny to them precisely that single feature
which is beginning to make the parliament of the later
days of Edward I a co-ordinated judicial and constitutional
whole.   The jurisdiction of the parliaments of Edward's
maturity is that of the council acting as a supreme, directive
head of the subordinate commissions of justices and barons.
The enrolling of its records marks the uniformity and
stability of that jurisdiction.   It is coming to be a court
of parliament.   Under Henry III, as far as can be judged,
parliament is still only an occasion during which a number
of courts and jurisdictions are, for convenience, acting at
the same time and place.   There is, in so far as it can make
its standing good, the greatest court of all, a kind of *magna
curia regni*, the baronage of the realm, there is the king's
familiar council, there are the capital justices sitting, sometimes in fact, sometimes by fiction, *coram domino rege*, the
justices of the bench, the treasurer and barons of the
exchequer, the justices of the Jews.   In the absence of any
established doctrine and practice of a court of parliament,
the familiar council has no steady supremacy, no habit of
routine action over any of these bodies in parliament save
as the needs of any given case may move the king to intervene and to bring some or all of his council with him.

Judgment by peers is under the shadow of the king's dislike, but they too are still a potential Great Council in parliament. They will become so under Edward II in fact. The cause sheet of any given court for the term of parliament is, I take it, like that of the exchequer, a mixture of cases which have reached it by various routes, some by summons of the barons' own writ to parties, some by a chancery writ from the king of his sole motion, some by writ answering petition. Madox's doubts as to the standing of the exchequer in Edward's parliament can for the age of Henry III have little meaning, for the conciliar focus of parliament is not yet fixed nor the bar of parliament drawn. For any plea, at any stage of any plea, any court may lose its cognisance to the council or be afforced by councillors or by the justices of any other commission ; but that beginning of unity dissolves when its immediate purpose has been achieved. The raw stuff of a parliamentary jurisdiction is there, but with more than one possible claimant to the future status of high court of parliament. The steady routine of parliamentary trial, the fixed reality of a court of parliament, and the consistent witness of a roll of parliament are wanting.

I cannot suggest by what future stages or at what time these essentials of parliament were to come into being. Not much would be needed to form them ; perhaps some minute of an intention to submit all petitions to council during parliament before handing them down to lower courts for their *complementum justitiae* ; an adjustment no more spectacular than that which stabilised *nisi prius*,* but with even greater results. Some such slight but purposeful thrust upon the wheel would have been like Edward's handling of detail to effect radical change. The proclamation to petitioners at the opening of the session might well be an outcome of it, or even part of the means to bring it about. On the other hand, of course, it may have happened slowly. The council took a greater share of judgment during parliament under the Provisions, as it did in all other matters, and Edward may have worked upon some experience of Bigod's justiciarship.

Such speculations, however, carry me beyond the scope of this paper. I would turn in ending to the disclaimer with which I began. I lay no claim to suggest a single origin of parliament—the exchequer clearly provides only one strand—nor, indeed, to say how its jurisdiction came to the precise form it had under Edward I. Parliament takes up almost every aspect of life. It has no one origin, nor can it be comprehended in any simple formula of growth. Taking official action as I have found it in the Close and Patent rolls of chancery and in the Memoranda of the exchequer, the conclusions for which I would ask consideration are these. That the actual occasion of parliament, its terms and place of assembly, owe much, though not all, to the initiative of the exchequer. That a principal part of its judicial function arose or was greatly stimulated during the personal rule of Henry III and against the background of a challenge to feudal privilege which his justices and barons set in motion. That the special form taken by parliamentary trial under Edward I, the dual trial, was in some degree anticipated by Henry's practice of giving a preliminary hearing to petition and adjourning it to the exchequer or to some other court at the quindenes. That the association of a *magnum consilium* with the quindenal sessions to form what then went by the name of parliament was an innovation of the later years of Henry beginning from about the year 1252. Believing that these are probable conclusions from the records of Henry III's reign, I also think that they do something, though by no means everything, to explain the parliamentary institution of justice under his son. At least they seem to me to lighten the partial obscurity under which the vigorous and formative middle years of Henry III lie.

D

2

THE NATURE OF PARLIAMENT IN THE REGION OF HENRY III*

by R. F. Treharne

THE year 1272 is a convenient point at which to halt to review the growth of the English parliament over the whole period of its infancy, and to consider its origins and nature during this first stage of its development. For in that year died King Henry III, whose personal shortcomings had done so much to influence, and to allow his servants and his magnates also to influence, the initial growth of this most characteristic of English political institutions. The accession of Edward I, masterful where Henry had been weak, purposeful where he had been shiftless, and able where Henry had been incompetent, began a new and very different stage in the history of parliament, the stage of primary education, in which Edward's limited but powerful constructive genius directed its development rapidly and with enduring effect along very different lines. Down to 1272, if we except the revolutionary years 1258—65, the growth of parliament had been spontaneous and unconsidered : now it was to be planned and moulded. What we can study in the years down to 1272 is therefore the original, unforced nature of parliament in its very beginnings ; and happily the evidence, though it has many gaps and is nowhere copious, suffices to tell us what we want to know.

The double root of the English parliament, first in the Old English *witan* and the Anglo-Norman *magnum concilium*, and also in the ancient community of the shire is, of course, not in dispute. But when, beginning in the 1240s we find chroniclers, king's clerks, magnates and the king himself speaking and writing of 'the king's parliament', it slowly becomes apparent that they are thinking of something new, in the sense that the old word, ' council ', ' *conseil* ', ' *concilium* ', does not adequately express their meaning any longer. A new word is being used, if not for a totally new thing, then at least for a new way of looking at something familiar. The purpose of this enquiry is to discover as closely as possible, what those who were active in politics and in government—the king, the prelates and nobles, the officials, the king's clerks—had in mind when they used the new word ' parliament ' in any of its several forms. The result of such an investigation should prove relevant to the recent discussions of the origin and nature of parliament in England.

Mr. H. G. Richardson summarized conveniently the early history of the word in its French, Italian, Latin and English forms.[1] Before 1240 it was much better known on the Continent than in England. In its primary sense of 'conversation' or 'talk' it occurs as early as the latter half of the eleventh century, and it long kept this meaning, so that Joinville could describe as ' *leur parlement* ' the secret meetings of Louis IX and his queen on the private staircase where they sought refuge from the strict and jealous eye of Louis' mother, Blanche of Castile.[2] By a natural extension, the word came to be used for formal discussions between responsible persons or their accredited agents—'parleys', 'talks', both in war and in peace ; and this meaning took firm root, so that in 1262, Llywelyn ap Gruffydd, complaining of breaches of the truce by various Marchers, says that these occurred on the very day which both sides had agreed upon ' *ad habendum parliamentum* ', when the Welsh had assembled ' *ad dictum parliamentum* '.[3] Simultaneously, apparently beginning in Italy in the form *parlamento*, the word was also being used to describe a formal business assembly of townsmen, and during the twelfth century this meaning spread to cover the more formal meetings of the courts of kings and emperors, whether for business or for social purposes, or assemblies of his vassals called by a great baron, or a council of war held by a body of crusaders.[4] The business sessions of a craft gild, and even secret meetings of a conspiratorial character, could be styled 'parliaments' in the thirteenth century.[5]

For England, Baxter and Johnson's *Medieval Latin Word-List* notes *parliamentum*, in the sense of ' colloquy, council, parliament ', as early as 1189,* but does not give the context or the source.[6] The first use of the word in this sense in England, reported by Mr. H. G. Richardson and tentatively dated by him in 1217,[7] should be treated with the greatest reserve until we know at what date the passage he cites was in fact written. It was used in England, and particularly in the Welsh Marches, before 1220, occurring in private charters to describe meetings of a lord's court and military assemblies of his feudal service.[8] The chroniclers and the king's clerks were slower to take it up, preferring older words like *concilium* and *colloquium* until after 1240. Matthew Paris, for instance, does not use the word *parliamentum*, in the sense of an assembly of the king's

---

[1] ' The Origins of Parliament' in *Trans. Roy. Hist. Soc.*, 4th Ser., xi (1928), 137–49.**
[2] *Histoire de Saint Louis*, ed. N. de Wailly (Paris, 1867), p. 407.
[3] *Royal and other Historical Letters illustrative of the Reign of Henry III*, edit. W. W. Shirley, Rolls Series, ii (London, 1866), 219.
[4] Richardson, *op. cit.*   [5] *Ibid.*
[6] J. H. Baxter and C. Johnson, *Medieval Latin Word-List* (London, 1934), p. 294.
[7] *Op. cit.* p. 140, n. 1. The reference occurs in a continuation of William of Malmesbury's *Gesta Regum* copied into the London *Liber de Antiquis Legibus* [see *De Antiquis Legibus Liber*, ed. T. W. Stapleton (Camden Society, London, 1846), p. 202].
[8] Richardson, *op. cit.* pp. 144–5.

council or court, until 1246. He introduces the new word with an impressive magniloquence which suggests self-concious innovation, which he seeks to justify by emphasizing the importance of the assembly so described : *Edicto regio convocata, convenit ad PARLA-MENTUM generalissimum regni Anglicani totalis nobilitas Londoniis, videlicet praelatorum tam abbatum et priorum quam episcoporum, comitum quoque et baronum, ut de statu regni jam vacillantis efficaciter prout exegit urgens necessitas contrectarent.*[1]* In reprinting this passage in his *Select Charters,* Stubbs hailed this first appearance of the blessed word with a flourish of capitals.[2]   Thereafter the word, though by no means the only term now used for such assemblies, becomes rapidly more common in Matthew's chronicle, and in other contemporary works such as the *Liber de Antiquis Legibus*[3] (1254), the *Flores Historiarum*[4] (1253), and the *Annals of Burton* (1255).[5] By 1255 it was clearly accepted, even by conservative chroniclers writing in Latin, as a useful means of distinguishing specially large gatherings of the *curia regis* or the *magnum concilium,* to which the king had summoned unusually large numbers of magnates to transact important business.   But it was far from being, even at this date, the only permissible or even the commonest way of describing such an assembly, however great the attendance and however important the occasion : it was still only one of several possible terms.

But the present enquiry is directed to discovering something much more limited and precise, and therefore something more useful at this stage, than the significance attached to the word ' parliament ' by thirteenth-century chroniclers. By confining our attention for the moment to the official records, we may hope to discover what the word meant to those who summoned, took part in, or were present at these assemblies which they were beginning to call ' parliaments ', and this meaning has surely a special importance for the general enquiry into the origin and nature of parliament in England.   And as our aim is partly to assess, in a very approximate fashion, the changes in the frequency with which the word was used in official circles, and to detect, if possible, developments of meaning and of function from year to year, the unbroken series of the printed Chancery rolls for Henry III's reign provide an admirable field of evidence, enabling us to compare one short period with another, both for frequency and for meaning. A scrutiny of the comparable unbroken series of exchequer and judicial

---

[1] *Chronica Majora,* ed. H. R. Luard, Rolls Series, iv (London, 1877), 518.
[2] W. Stubbs, *Select Charters illustrative of English Constitutional History* [9th edn., edit. H. W. C. Davis (Oxford, 1913)], p. 328.
[3] *De Antiquis Legibus Liber,* pp. 20–1.
[4] *Flores Historiarum,* ed. H. R. Luard, Rolls Series, ii (London, 1890), 384.
[5] *Annales de Burton* [*Annales Monastici,* ed. H. R. Luard, Rolls Series, i (London, 1864) (= *Burton*)], 336, 360.

records of the period would obviously fill some gaps and add bulk to the detail, but would necessarily yield a heavy predominance of specialized uses of the term;* whereas the *Calendar of Patent Rolls* [1] and the *Close Rolls* [2] together yield a sufficient quantity and spread of evidence, without predetermined bias in the direction of any particular usage, to permit reliable conclusions to be drawn with reasonable assurance that the unpublished chancery material would not be likely to alter the general pattern thus obtained.**

The printed chancery rolls yield fifty-eight uses† of the word 'parliament' occurring on forty-six separate occasions in Henry III's reign : several documents use the word twice or even thrice. The first use occurs quite casually in 1242 ; the second is employed retrospectively in 1244, to refer to the meeting of King John and his barons at Runnymede in 1215††; it occurs on three occasions in 1248, and five times on three occasions in the years 1254–5. Between the early summer of 1258 and the middle of 1262, it is used thirty-one times on twenty-five occasions, and while Simon de Montfort governed England in 1264–5, it appears twelve times on eight occasions. With Henry's restoration after Evesham, it disappears for two years, but returns cautiously on five occasions between 1267 and 1269, after which it is not again employed in these records until Edward I takes it up boldly for his own deliberate purposes. It is clear that the word came into official use in the royal chancery slightly before the chroniclers began to employ it, though thereafter it was at first a little slower to take root in official usage, until the revolutionary events of the years 1258–65 firmly established it in the chancery's vocabulary during the period of constitutional experiment.

While the use of the word in these records is far too casual to allow any precise statistical interpretation of the figures, an analysis of the context in which the chancery rolls employ the word 'parliament' on these forty-six occasions nevertheless can tell us a good deal about the way in which contemporary political circles understood the word, and so throw light helpfully on the discussion of the origins and nature of parliament in England. In fact we shall find that the total resulting impression is one which we cannot mistake.

Interpreting the word 'judicial' in its widest sense we find that the word 'parliament' was employed in a judicial context in ten of the forty-six instances, and that two other uses have a quasi-judicial significance in that they are judicial in form, though administrative or political in content. The first mention of 'parliament' in the

---

[1] *Calendar of Patent Rolls; Henry III* (London, 1891–1909), 6 vols. (= C.P.R.). By the kindness of Sir David Evans, keeper of the public records, I have been able to satisfy myself that each occurrence of the word 'parliament' in the English text of this *Calendar* represents an original 'parliamentum' (or one of the alternative contemporary spellings of that word) in the Latin of the patent roll itself.

[2] *Close Rolls of the Reign of Henry III* (London, 1902–1938), 14 vols. (= C.R.).

records (30 June 1242) [1] ordering Geoffrey de Segrave, justiciar of the forest, to allow John de Neville to have his bailiwick of Shotover and Stow ' until the king's parliament which will be held at London one month after the feast of St. John the Baptist ', presumably indicates that John was to be given an opportunity of proving his right either in the exchequer or in the king's court during the forthcoming session of parliament. In ordering (4 January 1248) respite of distraint upon the archdeacon of Lincoln to enforce a judgment of the bench of common pleas against him, Henry interposed a delay ' until our parliament to be held in the octaves of the Purification, as the king has decided to consider the plea further then '.[2] On 16 February 1248 the outlawry of William de Hastincourt was quashed ' *in curia nostra coram nobis et toto parliamento nostro* '.[3] On 4 November 1258 the four knights-commissioners from various shires, who had been summoned to bring to Hugh Bigod the justiciar, in the October parliament of 1258, the records of their enquiries into personal trespasses committed in their shires, were allowed their expenses for attending ' *coram consilio nostro apud Westmonasterium in parleamento.*'[4] On 23 April 1260 the abbot of Faversham and his men were instructed to appear before the Justiciar ' in our next parliament ', to settle a lawsuit between them;[5] and later in that year (16 August) it is recorded that the Canterbury moneyers petitioned ' before the king and the council in the parliament of London ' for certain liberties which would, if granted, settle their disputed liability to tallage.[6] On 26 January 1261 the demands of John de Lymar' for several debts owed to the king's Jews were respited ' until our next parliament ',[7] and on 3 February 1261 a plea of debt was adjourned ' until the king's parliament three weeks after the Purification, so that then, before the king's barons of the exchequer and the two parties, the question may be discussed whether the disputed charter is one of damages or of debt.'[8]   The order of 12 May 1265, allowing Isabella de Fors, as an act of grace, the custody of the lands of her late brother, Baldwin de Lisle, ' until the next parliament, which will be held in London on 1 June', presumably foreshadowed proof in the king's court, during parliament, of her legal right of inheritance.[9] Another order, on 15 May 1265, required the bishop of Bangor, who had quarrelled with Llywelyn ap Gruffydd on matters ' which do not belong to ecclesiastical but only to lay jurisdiction ' and who had therefore placed Llywelyn's chapel under interdict, to postpone the interdict ' until the forthcoming parliament which we shall hold at Westminster, where

[1] *C.R. 1237–1242*, p. 447.   [2] *C.R. 1247–1251*, p. 104.
[3] *Ibid.* pp. 106–7.   [4] *C.R. 1256–1259*, p. 333.
[5] *C.R. 1259–1261*, p. 287.   [6] *C.P.R. 1258–1266*, p 90.
[7] *C.R. 1259–1261*, p. 337.   [8] *Ibid.* p. 343.
[9] *C.R. 1264–1268*, p. 118.

[the bishop] and the other prelates of our realm will be present, so that, after discussion on these matters, whatever should by right be done, shall be done to both parties'.[1] The order of 27 October 1259 requiring the report of an inquisition *ad quod damnum* to be returned 'before the next parliament'[2] is essentially administrative and fiscal, though its appearance may seem judicial: while the summonses sent on 19 March 1265 to the exiled royalist leaders 'that they should appear before us and our council in our next parliament at London on 1 June, to do and receive justice',[3] was political in purpose, though the wording might suggest an action in court.

These references to parliament in a judicial context afford adequate corroboration of Mr. Jolliffe's illuminating thesis that, in the middle years of Henry's reign it was found convenient to settle various judicial and fiscal matters at those more general assemblies of the king's council which it was becoming customary to call 'parliaments', and also that, for this reason, it was becoming usual to hold these 'parliaments' at the dates of the customary sessions of the exchequer and of the courts, so that the financial and the legal experts, the voluminous records of the exchequer and the law courts, and the great men of Church and State should all be together at the same time in one place.[4] There can be no doubt whatever that the English 'parliament', from the very first time when it was so called in any contemporary official record, was frequently used for settling both judicial and fiscal cases, whether routine or important. How greatly this growing custom affected the early development of parliament, Mr. Jolliffe has convincingly demonstrated.

But when we turn to the other thirty-four occasions when the chancery used the word 'parliament', we see at once that its judicial aspect is by no means the only, or even the most frequent or most important sense in which the word is used. We can dismiss three references[5] to preparations for forthcoming parliaments, for at most they merely show that much preparation was necessary, and in particular that large stocks of food and wine had to be transported, so that we may conclude that a large and important assembly was expected. Two other orders, which might at first sight be dismissed as mere indications of the dates from which the legality or otherwise of certain transactions in lands or liberties should be dated, have in fact a much deeper significance. The first (14 April 1244), harking back to 1215, describes the famous assembly of magnates which imposed *Magna Carta* upon King John at Runnymede as '*parleamentum de Runened*' *quod fuit inter J. regem,*

[1] *C.R. 1264–1268*, pp. 117–18.   [2] *C.P.R. 1258–1266*, pp. 47–8.
[3] *C.R. 1264–1268*, p. 36.
[4] J. E. A. Jolliffe, 'Some Factors in the Beginnings of Parliament' in *Trans. Roy. Hist. Soc.* xxii (1940), 101–39.*
[5] *C.R. 1254–1256*, p. 61 (4 April 1255) ; *C.R. 1256–1259*, p. 222 (19 May 1258) ; *ibid.* pp. 226–7.

patrem nostrum, et barones suos Anglie'.[1] The other (20 July 1262),
enforcing Pope Urban IV's recently-published condemnation of the
Provisions of Oxford, orders the resumption of all liberties ' usurped
since the Parliament of Oxford '.[2] Parliament, then, in the eyes of
Henry's clerks in 1244 and in 1262, was the occasion when the
magnates there assembled imposed upon the king the two most
famous and far-reaching restraints upon royal authority known to
the century, the Great Charter and the Provisions of Oxford.

But before we plunge into these questions of high politics, there
are some normal activities of a non-judicial character which are
indicated in certain of these references to ' parliament '. One writ
sees parliament as the convenient occasion for a muster before the
king starts out on a Welsh campaign (25 May 1258).[3] Another
(17 February 1261) actually describes as ' our forthcoming parliament
at London ' the mustering of all of Henry's supporters in anticipation of civil war, saying that ' since it is necessary that you should
come prepared to our forthcoming parliament at London, you are,
by all means in your power, to be there with horses and arms in the
aforesaid parliament '.[4] The knighting of one of Henry's *valetti*
' in our parliament of Oxford ', recorded on 6 June 1258,[5] is another
reminder that the word could have a military connotation. Foreign
policy, too, is treated in parliament: Peter de Montfort conducts
the envoys of Llywelyn ap Gruffydd ' to the parliament to be held at
Oxford one month after Whitsuntide ' (2 June 1258):[6] safe-conduct
is given to the envoys whom Llywelyn is sending ' to the present
parliament ' (8 July 1260),[7] in which the Welsh truce ' made in the
parliament of Oxford by the counsel of the magnates of the council '
was extended to allow further negotiations (25 July 1260).[8] There
are also three references to the fact that Richard de Grey was
appointed constable of Dover Castle and Chamberlain of Sandwich
' in the last parliament of Oxford, in the 42nd year of our reign,
by the counsel of the magnates of the council '.[9] (8 September and
24 October 1259; 28 November 1260).

But, if these early references to ' parliament ' in the official
records show one thing above all others, it is that, to those actively
concerned in politics and government, the purpose of parliament
was to enable the king to consult his great men—and others too if
he so desired—upon important matters of public concern. Henry
III himself took this view of parliament, as is evident from at least
nine of these writs in which he employed the word, at dates before
the revolutionary parliament of Oxford or after his recovery of

[1] *C.R. 1242–1247*, p. 242. [2] *C.R. 1261–1264*, p. 142.
[3] *C.R. 1256–1259*, pp. 223–4. [4] *C.R. 1259–1261*, p. 457.
[5] *C.R. 1256–1259*, p. 229. [6] *C.P.R. 1247–1258*, p. 632.
[7] *C.P.R. 1258–1266*, p. 81. [8] *Ibid*, p. 83.
[9] *C.P.R. 1258–1266*, pp. 42, 47 ; *C.R. 1259–1261*, p. 305.

power in 1265. On 9 March 1248 Henry instructed the bishop of Norwich not to enforce the recent papal order granting to the see of Canterbury the first-fruits of all livings in lay gift, 'since our magnates, in our last parliament which was held at London, refused absolutely to consent' and the king 'is unwilling to attempt anything further in this matter until he has again held colloquy with the said magnates.'[1] On 19 February 1255, when the determined resistance of the English clergy to Rostand's new and severe assessment for the Sicilian tenth had forced both Alexander IV and Rostand to give way, Henry instructed the papal agents to abandon all attempts to enforce the new assessment 'until the parliament which is to be held at Westminster three weeks after Easter',[2] when presumably he hoped to raise again, with the prelates who would then be present, his urgent need for more money to enable him to fulfil his crusader's vow.

A writ of 2 April 1254 shows clearly how Henry normally regarded the duty of his magnates to attend parliament when he bade them come. In this writ he excused the newly elected bishop of Lincoln from the need to attend in person 'at the parliament which will be held at Westminster a fortnight after Easter, provided he send to the said parliament someone to represent him, who, together with the other magnates, will be able to answer the king in the matters of the aid and the other things which the king has put to them, so that the king's business, which is to be dealt with in the said parliament, shall not be held up by his absence'.[3]

On 30 July 1260, at a time when Henry had regained a large measure of control over his own chancery and seal, he certified that Roger Mortimer should not be held accountable for the loss of Builth Castle to Llywelyn on 18 July, since Henry had 'commanded Roger to be with him in London a fortnight after midsummer to treat with the king and the magnates of the council on urgent affairs of the king and the realm (and) the said Roger came by the king's special precept to the said parliament at London' on the very day on which Builth fell.[4]

After Evesham, Henry still continued to regard parliament as an occasion for transacting important and public business in consultation with his great men—at his own discretion, of course. On three occasions the records show him settling both general and particular matters concerning the Disinherited and expressly mentioning that this was done in parliament. On 8 March 1267 Henry promised that he would 'be careful to ordain at the instant parliament at St. Edmunds what shall be most convenient to be done for the king and for the city of London in the matter of the state and

---

[1] *C.R. 1247-1251*, p. 109.   [2] *C.P.R. 1247-1258*, p. 399.
[3] *C.R. 1253-1254*, p. 43.   [4] *C.P.R. 1258-1266*, p. 85.

liberties of the said city '.[1] The close roll records on 13 July 1267 that the Lord Edward received the Ely rebels into the king's peace ' in the common form in which the Disinherited were received at London at the last parliament since the peace made between our lord the king and the earl of Gloucester '.[2] On 20 October 1268 it was noted that ' in the parliament of Winchester in the 49th year ' Henry had pardoned William de Saham, a clerk in the household of the rebel leader Hugh Despenser.[3]

Two other post-Evesham entries show Henry consulting his magnates on important public business in parliament *eo nomine*. In September 1268 Louis IX had invited Henry to meet him at Boulogne in October to discuss Henry's co-operation in Louis' newly-projected crusade. On 28 September Henry replied expressing deep joy at Louis' news, but saying that although he would have come gladly and without fail to Boulogne as Louis asked, he could not do so, owing to the delays in his domestic affairs caused by his own crusading problems. He had called ' a general, full and solemn parliament ' at London for the quinzaine of Michaelmas so that he might discuss these matters with his great men and make the safest provision for each of them, and then, together with those of his nobles who had taken the Cross, he would be able to make the necessary arrangements with safety.[4] And finally, the last entry of our forty-six, dated 21 June 1269, addressed ' to the archbishops and all others coming to the instant parliament at Midsummer at London ', explains that illness has prevented Henry from reaching London on the day appointed for the assembly, and asks them ' out of reverence and honour for him, to stay there and await his arrival for a little while, as on the following day he will direct his steps thither, God willing, to have treaty and colloquy with them as he had previously arranged '.[5]

If Henry, who distrusted his barons and consulted them only when he could not avoid doing so, or when he urgently wanted their help, took this view of his parliaments, we may expect the party of reform, when it was in control of the government, to make even more of it. The Provisions of Oxford themselves—not included among the forty-six references in the Chancery rolls— show best their view of parliament. ' There shall be three parliaments a year, the first at the octaves of Michaelmas, the second on the morrow of Candlemas, the third on the first day of June . . . (and) to these parliaments there shall come the elected counsellors of the king, even though they be not summoned, to review the state of the realm and to deal with the common needs of the realm and the king together; and at other times they shall come at the

[1] *C.P.R. 1266–1272*, p. 133.
[2] *C.P.R. 1266–1272*, p. 265.
[5] *C.P.R. 1266–1272*, p. 384.
[3] *C.R. 1264–1268*, p. 379.
[4] *C.R. 1264–1268*, p. 552.

king's summons, when there is need.'[1] 'The *communitas* shall elect twelve sound men to come to the parliaments and also on other occasions as need shall be, when the king or his council shall summon them, to deal with the needs of the king and of the realm.   And the *communitas* shall ratify whatever these twelve shall do.   And this shall be done to spare the cost of the community.'[2]   The Provisions of Westminster—also not included among the forty-six references to parliament in the chancery rolls—add some instructive footnotes showing the reformers' views on how parliament should be conducted.   'It is provided that no one shall come to parliament with horses, armour and weapons, unless he is specially ordered to do so by the king or by his council, or by writ, for the common needs of the land.'[3]   'Let it be arranged that two or three of the *mesne gent* of the council be always in attendance on the king from one parliament to the next, and let them be changed at each parliament, and their actions reviewed at each parliament, so that if anything they have done needs changing, it shall be changed by the council.   And if any important business arises between the parliaments, which cannot be settled by the aforesaid two or three, or cannot conveniently be held over until the next parliament, all the members of the council shall be summoned by writ to deal with the matter, and the writ shall indicate the reason for the summons unless it be secret.'[4]   And the official text of the Provisions of Westminster (again not one of the forty-six) shows very plainly their view of the function of parliament.   'These are the provisions and the establishments made at Westminster at the Michaelmas parliament by the king and his council and the twelve elected by the common counsel in the presence of the community of England, which was then at Westminster, in the 43rd year of the reign of Henry.'[5]

Legislation, the proclamation of reforms, and the transaction of other matters of general public interest, are the principal contexts of the mention of parliament in the chancery records while the reformers were in power.   The commissions appointing four knights in every shire to enquire into grievances were issued on 4 August 1258 'in pursuance of an ordinance lately made in the parliament of Oxford '.[6]   On 28 November and 4 December 1259 all who had given payments to local officials to obtain justice, or who wished to complain of trespasses done to them by local officials ' since the last parliament of Oxford ', when these offences were declared illegal, are called upon to report their complaints to the justices of the special eyre.[7]   Immediately after their victory at Lewes, the reformers summoned to the parliament of June 1264

---

[1] *Burton*, p. 452. [2] *Ibid.* [3] *Ibid.* p. 476.
[4] *Ibid.* p. 477. [5] *Ibid.* p. 479. [6] *C.P.R. 1247–1258*, pp. 645–9.
[7] *C.R. 1259–1261*, pp. 142, 145.

four knights from every shire, ' elected by the assent of the shire, [to be sent] on behalf of the whole community to the forthcoming parliament at London on the octaves of Trinity to treat with the king and with the prelates, magnates and other faithful subjects of the king concerning the business of the king and of the realm '.[1] The chief item in this business was the new constitution, the *Forma Pacis*, by which England was to be governed until a permanent settlement could be achieved by arbitration, and which ' was made in the parliament of London held about the feast of the Nativity of St. John the Baptist, with the consent, will and precept of the lord king and of the prelates, the barons, and the community there present '.[2] On 3 July the recalcitrant royalists of the Welsh March were ordered to come to this parliament of London ' to treat of the state of the realm ' and to bring with them ' to the said parliament ' the prisoners of war whom they held captive.[3]

To the next parliament, the famous assembly of January 1265, the prelates, magnates and nobles of the realm were summoned ' both for negotiating the liberation of the Lord Edward and for other matters touching the community of the realm '.[4] The government also summoned to this parliament in the same terms, four burgesses from each of a large number of boroughs, since it ' greatly needed their presence and that of other faithful subjects . . . to treat of these matters along with the king and the aforesaid magnates of the realm, and to lend counsel on these things '.[5] From every shire two knights were also summoned ' to treat with us and with our council on the release of Edward our dearest son, and to provide security in this matter, and also for other difficult business of our realm '.[6] The two knights from Yorkshire, ' who were present at the aforesaid parliament on behalf of their county ' for longer than had been initially expected, were allowed ' reasonable expenses for coming to the said parliament, staying there, and returning home again '.[7] To the next parliament, the exiled royalists Peter of Savoy, John de Warenne, Hugh Bigod and William de Valence were summoned ' to appear before us and our council in our next parliament at London on 1 June, to do and receive justice ',[8] a political ultimatum in judicial form. Of the forty-six occasions when the chancery rolls use the word ' parliament ', all have now been mentioned save three occurring early in 1260, when Henry III repeatedly forbade parliament to meet: these will more conveniently be dealt with at a later stage.[9] Enough, however, has emerged to enable us to see what ' parliament ' signified to the men who used

---

[1] *C.P.R. 1258–1266*, p. 360: Latin text in Stubbs, *Select Charters* (9th edn.) p. 400.
[2] *C.P.R. 1258–1266*, p. 365: Latin text in Stubbs, *Select Charters* (9th edn.), p. 400.
[3] *C.P.R. 1258–1266*, p. 362.   [4] *C.R. 1264–1268*, p. 89.
[5] *Ibid.* pp. 87, 89.   [6] *Ibid.* p. 96.   [7] *Ibid.*
[8] *Ibid.* p. 36.   [9] *Infra*, pp. 83–4.

the word in the chancery documents, and to the king, the nobles and prelates, and the high officials who gave them their instructions.

The first plain fact is that ' parliament ' was not, except between 1258 and 1265, a ' term of art ' with a specific and invariable meaning in its context.   It is a word used in an unconsidered and haphazard fashion, found in some documents, but not in others which might equally well have been expected to employ it.   The same assembly will be called a ' parliament ' in one letter, a ' colloquy ' in the next, while a third letter will not employ a noun to describe it at all. The same meeting is frequently called ' parliament ' and ' colloquy ' even in a single letter.   ' Parliament ', right down to the end of our period of survey, has come into competition with older, more formal words as a description of a political assembly of the whole realm, but it is as yet a long way from having gained a monopoly of the description.

Next we note that although many important and unimportant things are done ' in ' or ' during ' parliament, or even ' at ' parliament, nothing is ever done ' by ' parliament during these years.   Parliament is not yet either an institution or a body: it is an occasion. That being so, it is, strictly speaking, premature to talk of its ' functions '; we should rather say that we can observe certain things being done at, in, or during the time of parliament.   The list of these things that we can compile from our forty-six instances of the use of the word ' parliament ' in the chancery rolls could be greatly expanded if we first listed all of the assemblies which are so styled in these forty-six instances, and then noted everything that was done in all of these assemblies, whether the individual writ recording what was done used the word ' parliament ' or not.   It could be expanded much farther if we drew up a list of all the assemblies which, by the criteria which we are seeking to establish, merit the name of parliament (whether the records so style them or not), and we then listed and classified all the many things that all of these assemblies are recorded as having done.   But that is not what this paper is seeking to do: our object is to discover, not what was done in a number of assemblies which we have decided to call ' parliaments ', but simply what was in the minds of contemporary men in political circles when they actually used the word.   Accordingly we keep strictly to our forty-six instances, supplemented by a few more drawn from other contemporary official documents, and so we avoid, as far as possible, bringing our own preconceptions and our own interpretations of the evidence into the picture at all.

Let us fully agree that parliament was concerned with justice and that justice was done during the sessions of parliament or even in parliament itself; and let us in no way dispute that parliaments were being summoned to coincide with the sessions of the exchequer

in order that important fiscal matters might thus be more conveniently handled. We cannot, however, come away from a review
of these contemporary official uses of the word between 1242 and
1272 with any impression that for the men who authorized or for
those who drew up these documents, parliament was an occasion
of purely, or even of primarily, administrative convenience for the
transaction of judicial and financial business, however useful these
two aspects of parliament might be. We have seen in these letters
' parliament ' as the occasion for knighting one of the king's *valetti*,[1]
for making an important appointment,[2] for receiving envoys from
Wales and for negotiating a truce with them.[3] We have seen it
as the occasion for an assembly of the military forces of the realm,
whether to go thence against the Welsh [4] or to maintain the king's
authority against potential rebels among the king's own subjects.[5]
We have seen that it was summoned to grant an aid to the king in
1254,[6] and to discuss both the financial and the military preparations
for a crusade.[7] The magnates assembled in parliament have
debated and refused a papal demand for one year's fruits from
vacant benefices in lay patronage.[8] Of parliament as the occasion
for the discussion, approval and promulgation of laws there has
been strikingly important evidence: it was ' in pursuance of an
ordinance made in the Parliament of Oxford ' that the sweeping
enquiry into the grievances of individuals against public officials was
launched in 1258:[9] and the great collection of legal, procedural and
administrative reforms known as the Provisions and Establishments
of Westminster was adopted and proclaimed in the Parliament of
Westminster in November 1259.[10] That the Provisions of Oxford
were adopted in the Parliament of Oxford in 1258, and the *Forma
Regiminis* in the London Parliament of 1264 [11] shows that parliament
was the occasion for discussing, approving and proclaiming legislation
on the most fundamental of all matters of law—the constitution and
powers of the governing authority in the state. There is ample
material here to show that Henry and his ministers, his clerks and his
magnates too, who slowly grafted the foreign word ' parliament ' on
to English political and constitutional usage, employed it themselves
in a far wider connotation than that of mere administrative convenience in judicial and in fiscal matters.

When the committee of twenty-four proposed, in the Provisions
of Oxford, that three parliaments should be held at fixed dates every
year, to be attended, without summons, by the king's fifteen
elected councillors (with provision for emergency meetings by special
summons), ' to review the state of the realm and to deal with

[1] *Supra*, p. 76, n. 5.   [2] *Supra*. p. 76, n. 9   [3] *Supra*. p. 76, nn. 6, 7, 8.
[4] *Supra*, p. 76, n. 3.   [5] *Supra*. p. 76, n. 4.   [6] *Supra*. p. 77 n. 3.
[7] *Supra*, p. 77, n. 2, p. 78, n. 4. [8] *Supra*, p. 77, n. 1.   [9] p. 79, n. 6.
[10] *Supra*, p. 79, n. 5.   [11] *Supra*. p. 80, n. 2.

the common needs of both the realm and the king ' ; [1] and when it further recommended that, at all of these parliaments, the *communitas Angliae* should be represented by twelve other elected magnates having power to pledge the assent of the whole *communitas* to whatever the fifteen and the twelve should jointly decide ' concerning the needs of the king and of the realm ',[2] we can hardly suppose that the committee was merely regulating sessions of the exchequer or of the courts of justice. Nor was it merely judicial or fiscal gatherings which were contemplated in the Provisions of Westminster when that ordinance forbade anyone to ' come to parliament with horse, armour and weapons, unless specially required by the king and council to do so for the common needs of the realm '.[3] When the council of fifteen, in the Provisions of Westminster, decreed that the king should be attended between the meetings of parliament by two or three ' *mesne gent* ' of the council, who should be changed at each parliament and whose actions while in attendance on the king should be reviewed, and if necessary, corrected at each parliament; and that if, between parliaments, any urgent matter arose which the councillors serving their rota felt unable to settle themselves, they should summon a special session of the full council to deal with it,[4] obviously it was neither law courts nor exchequer that was intended by the references to parliament. It was not the action of either a court of law or of the exchequer when the last clause of the Provisions of Westminster declared ' these are the provisions and establishments made at Westminster at the Michaelmas Parliament by the king and his council elected by the community of England.'[5]

Henry himself was no less aware than were the reformers of the significance of a meeting of parliament. Writing from France, in January and in February 1260, to forbid the great officers of state and the councillors in England to summon any parliament in his absence, he said ' We wish no parliament to be held in England before we return there: we order you that you should in no wise cause any writ to be sealed in our name for the holding of parliament there before our return to England ',[6] and ' we order you to postpone and completely to set aside any parliament, . . . permitting no parliament to be held, and giving orders for none before our return to England, since, once we have returned there, by your counsel . . . we shall provide for holding parliament, as may be most suitable for us and for our realm.'[7] Or again, ' Concerning what you have told us about holding a *colloquium*, we inform you that it does not accord with our will that any parliament should be held in our realm in our absence, since this is not fitting, and we think it would not redound to our honour '.[8] Henry would not

[1] *Supra*, p. 79, n. 1.   [2] *Supra*, p. 79, n. 2.   [3] *Supra*, p. 79, n. 3   [4] *Supra*, p. 79, n. 4.
[5] *Supra*, p. 79, n. 5.   [6] *C.R. 1259-1261*, p. 235.   [7] *Ibid.* p. 268.   [8] *Ibid.* p. 273.

have written so peremptorily and so insistently had nothing more
than a routine session of the exchequer or of the law courts been the
business of the parliament which he was so concerned to prohibit;
nor would he, after his return to England in the spring of 1260, have
tried to convict Simon de Montfort of treason on a charge of having
defied the royal prohibition by attempting to hold a parliament in
Henry's absence,[1] if all that Simon had done in those crucial weeks
had been to insist that the courts of justice and the exchequer
should continue to meet as usual. It was politics, not law and
fiscal administration, that had stirred these men so deeply that they
had been brought face to face on the brink of civil war.

The men who framed the Provisions of Oxford were perfectly
explicit upon the function and purpose of parliament as they understood the word and as they intended to operate the institution which
it designated. For in their hands what had hitherto been merely an
occasion was converted into a political institution, and a vague,
untechnical colloquialism became a clearly defined and precise
constitutional term. They decreed [2] that parliaments should meet
three times a year at specified dates almost mathematically equal
intervals apart from each other: they laid it down that to all of
these parliaments the members of the council of fifteen and the twelve
elected to represent the *communitas* were to come without waiting
for a summons, though they might also be summoned specially
for emergency meetings should need arise. And the declared
purpose of these parliaments is ' to review the state of the realm and
to deal with the common business of both the kingdom and the
king ': the twelve are elected ' to treat at the three parliaments
each year with the king's council, on behalf of the *communitas*, upon
the common business, the business of the king and of the realm ',
and the *communitas* ratifies in advance whatever the fifteen and the
twelve shall do together. Parliament, in short, was to be the
systematized and organic form of the consultation between the
king and the *communitas* always implied in feudal custom, but now
made explicit. Its purpose was to ensure that this consultation
should be regular and frequent, that it should no longer be left to
the king's whim to decide when and whom he should consult, and
that the consultation should be completely effective in controlling
royal policy in all matters of the public interest. In particular,
the aim of these consultations in parliament was to reform the state
of the realm by means of edicts and ordinances discussed, adopted
and promulgated in the parliaments themselves, as was stated
explicitly in the commissions issued for the enquiry into individual
grievances in August 1258,[3] and in the proclamation of the

[1] C. Bémont, *Simon de Montfort, Comte de Leicester* (Paris, 1884), pp. 350–2.
[2] *Supra*, p. 79, nn. 1, 2.
[3] *Supra*, p. 79, n. 6.

Provisions and Establishments of Westminster in November 1259.[1] The making of appointments [2] and the control of foreign policy [3] through meetings of the parliament were further aspects of this insistence upon consultation in parliament.

When, after their victory at Lewes on 14 May 1264, the reformers once more controlled the government of England, the writs of summons to the two parliaments which they called, stated more explicitly their conception of parliament as a forum for consultation, approval and proclamation. The four knights summoned from each shire to the June parliament of 1264 were to come ' to treat with us (and with our prelates, magnates and other faithful men) concerning our business and that of the realm '.[4] The main purpose of that parliament was to adopt the *Forma Pacis*, including the *Forma Regiminis*, which was to be the provisional constitution of the government of England until a more lasting constitution and settlement could be provided by means of arbitration.[5] The formal proclamation of this *Forma Pacis* describes it as ' an ordinance made in the parliament held at London about the feast of the Nativity of St. John the Baptist last ', and as having been ' enacted in parliament at London '; and again, as ' the ordinance made at London with the consent, approval and command of the lord king and of the prelates, barons and the *communitas* there present at that time '.[6] The recalcitrant royalist Marchers, though they prudently disobeyed the summons, had, like the rest, been summoned ' to treat of the state of the king and of the realm '.[7] The writs of summons issued for the famous parliament of January 1265 declared that ' the prelates, magnates and nobles of our realm have been summoned to our forthcoming parliament at London . . . for the matter of the release of Edward our eldest son and for other matters affecting the *communitas* of our realm '; [8] that the barons and bailiffs of each of the Cinque Ports were to send four representatives to the parliament ' to treat with us and with the aforesaid magnates of our realm and to lend counsel on the aforesaid matters, since the king urgently needs their presence and that of our other faithful subjects ';[9] other cities and boroughs were required, in similar terms, to send their representatives to the parliament,[10] and from each county two knights were summoned ' to be present with us in our parliament at London . . . and to treat with us and with our counsel upon the release of Edward our dearest son, and to arrange security therefor, and also for other difficult business concerning our realm '.[11] As the practice developed of widening the basis of parliament by extending its membership by means of representation, the writs of

[1] *Supra*, p. 79, n. 5.   [2] *Supra*, p. 76, n. 9.   [3] *Supra*, p. 76, nn. 6, 7, 8.
[4] *Supra*, p. 80, n. 1.   [5] *Supra*, p. 80, n. 2.   [6] *Ibid.*
[7] *Supra*, p. 80, n. 3.   [8] *Supra*, p. 80, n. 4.   [9] *Supra*, p. 80, n. 5.
[10] *Ibid.*   [11] *Supra*, p. 80, n. 6.

summons more than ever before emphasized its purpose as a consultative assembly for discussing, determining and proclaiming
joint decisions upon the highest and the most general matters of
public importance for the kingdom as a whole. Justice will still
be done in parliament—witness the writs of summons to Peter of
Savoy at Pevensey, John de Warenne at Lewes, Hugh Bigod at
Bosham and William de Valence at Brehendon ' to come before us
and our council in our next parliament at London on 1 June (1265)
to do and receive justice ';[1] or the implication in the grant to
Isabella de Fors, ' until our next parliament at London on 1 June ',
of the custody of her late brother's lands;[2] or the command to the
over-hasty bishop of Bangor to revoke the interdict which he has
placed on the chaped of Llywelyn ap Gruffydd, ' or at least to
respite it until our forthcoming parliament which we are to hold
at Westminster, where you and the other prelates of our realm
will be present at our command, so that then, having discussed
these matters, we may do to both sides whatever in justice should be
done '.[3] But these judicial matters, however important or interesting in themselves, were merely items which it was convenient to
settle at the forthcoming parliament: the purpose of the parliament
itself remained essentially political.

The use of the word ' parliament ' in this political sense grew
up with the institution which it came to describe, though the germ-
inating seeds of the institution may be discerned perhaps as much
as thirty years before the term, in this special political sense, began
to be applied to it. By 1240 the word, especially in its French form
' parlement ', was in the air, in fairly common and unspecialized
use among the men who together constituted political circles in
England. Evidently these men were beginning to use the word to
describe large and important political assemblies in which the king
consulted with the great men of the land, both spiritual and secular,
upon matters of state of all kinds. As yet this political usage was
neither systematic nor exclusive, for some of the most important
assemblies of the years between 1242 and 1258 were at no point in
the chancery rolls described as ' parliaments '. But, though the
term was at first slow to establish itself in the chancery records, it
is highly significant that, while its first occurrence there, in 1242,
was casual,[4] the second was portentous, for it shows that by 1244
the king's clerks had come to think of the famous meeting between
King John and his barons in 1215 as ' the parliament of Runnymede '.[5]
Of the ten occurrences, on eight separate occasions, of the use of the
word ' parliament ' in the printed chancery rolls before 1258, only
three were judicial in their context, the other seven being general or
political and including such high matters as the refusal of the

[1] *Supra*, p. 80, n. 8. [2] *Supra*, p. 74, n. 9. [3] *Supra*, p. 75, n. 1.
[4] *Supra*, p. 74, n. 1. [5] *Supra*, p. 76, n. 1.

magnates to allow the papal grant to the archbishop of Canterbury of the first fruits of vacant benefices in lay gift,[1] the consideration of the king's request for an aid from his magnates,[2] and the withdrawal of the severe reassessment of the Crusading tenth made by the papal envoy Rostand.[3] In face of this evidence, it is impossible to doubt the mainly political significance of the word ' parliament ' used by the king's clerks in the chancery records before 1258: justice was indeed done at the parliaments, or at least during their time of session, but the parliament itself was essentially a political occasion for discussions between the king and his great men. So essential was the attendance of the magnates in great force when a ' parliament ' was summoned that Henry thought it necessary to give formal written permission to a newly elected bishop who could not conveniently attend the parliament, and at the same time to insist that the bishop-elect should be represented by proctors with full powers.[4]

We can only guess what brought the word ' parliament ' into official use in the chancery records in this somewhat haphazard way in the years 1242–58. It is tempting, and not unreasonable, to link its appearance in the rolls with the recurrent political crises of 1242–44 over finance, military service, and the misconduct of the war in France, crises which led to repeated demands for political reforms foreshadowing so closely those which were eventually adopted at the Parliament of Oxford in 1258. Perhaps the word ' parliament ' was used sufficiently often by those who urged reform for it to have become familiar and fairly common usage in political and governmental circles during these years, and so to have found its way without conscious premeditation into the official documents of the chancery. It is significant that in 1246, so soon after the ferment of the years 1242–4, Matthew Paris first used the word in his great chronicle, and that he should have felt it necessary to provide an explanation of the new word in high-sounding descriptive terms emphasizing the completeness of the assembly, the importance of the occasion, and the general character of the business to be treated, touching the whole state of the disordered realm.[5]

This slow and haphazard beginning was suddenly and greatly accelerated, and was also given much sharper definition, by the revolutionary developments of the years 1258–65. Even if we omit the vitally important references in the texts of the Provisions and Establishments of Westminster, as well as those in the official records of Henry's complaints against Simon de Montfort, and of Simon's replies in 1260, we still find the word employed forty-three times in thirty-three different letters patent and letters close in the seven years between 1258 and 1265. Characteristically enough,

---

[1] *Supra*, p. 77, n. 1.   [2] *Supra*, p. 77 n. 3.   [3] *Supra*, p. 77 n. 2.   [4] *Supra*, p. 77, n. 3.
[5] *Supra*, p. 72 nn. 1, 2.

after Evesham the word again became somewhat rare, occurring in the chancery rolls only five times in the remaining seven years of Henry's reign. While it would be absurd to attempt to draw precise statistical conclusions from evidence of this kind, we cannot escape the deductions which this overwhelming disproportion in frequency of usage forces upon us. Nor is it only a matter of frequency of usage: it is, even more, one of definition. The men of 1258 changed parliament from an occasion into an institution, an institution which they used as the fundamental source of authority for the government of England and for the adoption and execution of their plan of reform. To them parliament was no mere occasion for holding judicial pleas or settling fiscal transactions in the exchequer: it was the means whereby the king, in full consultation with the great men of the land and with such others as might be required, considered all the needs of himself and of his realm and people, and decided what action was required to satisfy those needs in every field—political, administrative, financial, military, diplomatic, or whatever else they might be, even were it ecclesiastical. Parliament was the seat of discussion and decision, and the source of all reform. It is not too much to say that they acted as if they saw in parliament the sovereign authority of the land, for the king was not to act without it, and he was bound to obey its advice. So frequently does the word appear in the chancery records during these seven years, and in so clearly-defined and fundamental a context, that it seems to have had for them something of the hypnotic appeal of a political slogan, the name of a magical panacea to cure all the ills of the age, like the ' constitution ' of the continental liberals of the nineteenth century.

Because they could not trust Henry to decide the occasions and the frequency of the meetings of parliament, the magnates set themselves to regulate these matters by formal constitutional documents, written constitutions converting an irregular occasion into a formal institution with a defined and nominated membership meeting at exactly prescribed times and charged with highly important functions. We see in these selected texts how under the pressure of political exigency, they even extended the basis of the membership of parliament by calling in the representative element, speaking for the shires and the boroughs, to take part in the process of discussion and decision which was the essence of parliament. These same texts show us how these men sought to define the relations of parliament to the king, to the privy council, to the whole body of the *communitas,* and to the officials, clerks and servants who governed England in the king's name. In the record of the great debate between Henry and Simon de Montfort in the summer of 1260,[1] as in Henry's insistent letters from France in January

---
[1] Bémont, *loc. cit.*

and February of that year,[1] we can even see, sharply contrasted
with each other, the royal and the Montfortian views of the essential
nature of parliament.   To the king it was a body existing only in
virtue of his pleasure and his summons, having no authority save
what it derived from him, so that it was indecorous and shameful
to contemplate its meeting without him or against his orders, and
treason to attempt to hold it in his absence or against his prohibition—a view which he still asserted in 1269,[2] long after the
troubles were over.   To Simon, on the other hand, parliament
was an institution created by the Provisions of Oxford, which
had given to it separate existence and independent authority,
had prescribed the dates of its meetings and laid heavy responsibilities upon it.

   This view of parliament could not prevail in the political climate
of thirteenth-century England.   Forced into premature development
by Henry III's utter incompetence to cope with the problems of
governing his kingdom, the reformers' conception of parliament
was put to the test before the political education of the English
baronage had advanced sufficiently to enable them to stand the
strain imposed upon it.   Kenilworth and Evesham were no more
inevitable than Lewes had been: but it is hard to see how much
longer Simon de Montfort could have kept England to his chosen
path even had he escaped from the trap which the Lord Edward's
military genius had so successfully improvised for him in the summer
of 1265.   In fact, Evesham put an end, for the time being, to the
Montfortian view of parliament, and in the remaining seven years
of Henry III's reign the Chancery records show the king's conception of parliament re-established.   It is once more an occasion,
rather than an institution; but, though it is now seldom mentioned,
it is still an occasion of great moment, when the king will consult
with his great men upon important matters of general public
concern—the formal submission of rebels,[3] the fate of the city of
London after the rebellion,[4] the projected crusade against the
infidel,[5] and the affairs of the realm at large.[6]   And the king's
presence in person is essential to its meeting, for when illness
prevents the enfeebled old king from attending parliament on the
appointed day at Midsummer, 1269, he asks the magnates, ' out
of reverence and honour for him ', to await his coming to begin
his colloquy with them.[7]   Parliament was, it seemed, back where it
had been before 1258.

   The appearance, however, was deceptive.   After the tremendous
events which had convulsed England so many times between 1258
and 1267, Henry's conception of kingship, already challenged as

---

[1] *Supra*, p. 83, nn. 6, 7, 8; p. 84, n. 1.   [2] *Supra*, p. 78, n. 5.   [3] *Supra*, p. 78, nn. 2, 3.
[4] *Supra*, p. 78, n. 1.   [5] *Supra*, p. 78, n. 4.   [6] *Supra*, p. 78 n. 5.
[7] *Ibid.*

long ago as 1215, could not for long endure.   The idea of parliament as the organized and regular means of consultation between the king and his magnates had in reality been impressed indelibly upon the political consciousness of all classes of Englishmen who played any part in public affairs, and the same Lord Edward who had done so much to bring to nought the parliaments of Simon de Montfort was, as king in his turn, to make parliament into one of the most important institutions in English political machinery.   And despite the immensely important growth of the judicial and fiscal aspects of parliament in his reign, it remained what it had been from the first, an essentially political assembly.   In France and in Scotland, as in most other medieval states, the corresponding national assembly became known as the Estates General or by some such term: in England the word 'parliament' prevailed.   That the English parliament never dwindled to a mere court of law like the French 'parlements', and that our national assembly did not become known as another 'States General', was largely due, in the first place, to the fact which these instances from the chancery records of Henry's reign abundantly show, that, from the first uses of the word in matters of government, Englishmen thought of 'parliament' as a primarily political assembly; and in the second place, to the achievement of the reformers of 1258–65 in stamping that conception of parliament upon English political consciousness for ever.

University College, Aberystwyth   R. F. TREHARNE

ADDENDUM

After the final proofs of this article had been corrected and returned, and too late for alterations to be made in its text, Dr. E. B. Fryde, who was using the proof copy for some work of his own, pointed out to me that my article omits reference to two further entries, on the Close Rolls for 54 and 56 Henry III, in which the word 'parliament' occurs. On 24 August 1270, in an apologetic letter (*C. R. 1268–1272*, pp. 290-1) which thrice uses the word 'parliament', Henry asks Llywelyn ap Gruffydd to send envoys to Westminster for 'the forthcoming parliament in the quinzaine of Michaelmas', instead of to a previously arranged conference in the Marches, in order to discuss Llywelyn's charges that Henry's men of Montgomery have broken the peace : Henry explains that the impending departure of the Lord Edward and many of the magnates of England for the Crusade has made it necessary for him to summon all of his great men (including the English delegates to the proposed border conference) to attend the parliament to which Llywelyn's envoys are now invited.   A letter of 17 September 1272 (*ibid.* p. 524), addressed to Ralph of Hengham and his fellow-justices on eyre in Shropshire, asks them to postpone 'from month to month until they can finally do justice in them', all pleas brought by or against Roger de Mortimer and his sons, and certain named associates, since the king has required their attendance at 'the forthcoming parliament at Westminster in the quinzaine of Michaelmas', and therefore they cannot be present at the opening of the eyre in Shropshire.   These two entries, one adding to the numbers of those which show that foreign affairs and the planning of a Crusade could both be dealt with in parliament and both showing plainly that the king, even after the end of the civil war, urgently required his magnates to attend at parliament, strengthen slightly the main contentions of this article.   I regret the omission of these two references all the more because both were cited in the appendix to Mr. H. G. Richardson's valuable article (cited *supra*, p. 71, n. 1).

                                                                R. F. T.

3

INTRODUCTION TO
MEMORANDA DE PARLIAMENTO, 1305[1]*

by F. W. Mautland

THE LENTEN PARLIAMENT OF 1305

On 12 November 1304, King Edward issued from Burstwick writs for a parliament to be holden at Westminster on 16 February 1305.[2] He was on his way back from Scotland. He kept Christmas at Lincoln and was there as late as 12 January. On the 22nd he was at Spalding and thence he issued a second set of writs. Events, he said, had happened which made it impossible for him to be at Westminster on the appointed day, so the parliament was postponed to the 28th of February.[3] Slowly and by a circuitous route he travelled southward, for we hear of him at Walsingham, Swaffham, Thetford, Bury St Edmunds, Exning, Wilbraham, Royston, Braughing, Standon, Wades Hill, Ware, Waltham. On 26 January he addressed a letter under his privy seal to the chancellor, which may perhaps explain the postponement. He expected that in the ensuing parliament the clergy would call him in question and he directed that a search should be made in the chancery for any documents which might bear upon the matters in dispute.[4] By other letters under the privy seal dated on 5 February, of which we must speak at greater length hereafter, he directed the appointment of receivers and auditors of petitions; he desired that the petitions should, so far as was possible, be disposed of before his arrival at Westminster. Meanwhile the

---

[1] *Records of the Parliament holden at Westminster...in the thirty-third year of the reign of King Edward the First*, edited by F. W. Maitland, Rolls Series, 1893. [Reprinted in Maitland, *Selected Essays* (Cambridge, 1936), pp. 1–72. Alternative title, *Memoranda de Parliamento*. References so indicated below are to the Rolls Series volume. Section I of the introduction, dealing with the make-up of the roll, and with the two classes of Ancient Petitions, numbering 16,000 in all, preserved in the Public Record Office, is omitted, as are the Calendar and Lists that make up the last section.]

[2] *Parliamentary Writs*, vol. I, p. 136.   [3] *Parl. Writs*, vol. I, p. 138.

[4] Chancery Warrants, Series I, no. 5263 [*Cal. Chanc. Warrants*, vol. I, p. 246]: 'por ce que nous entendons qe le dit Ercevesqe e autres du clergez nous voudront paraventure aresoner a nostre prochein pallement [*sic*] sur aucunes choses touchantz lour estat.'**

sheriffs of Kent, Surrey and Sussex had been bidden to send up
great quantities of corn and ale to Westminster for the maintenance of the king's household.[1] On the 27th he entered London
and stayed at the Hospital of St Katharine near the Tower. On
the 28th the parliament was opened at Westminster.[2]

It was a full parliament in our sense of that term.[3] The three
estates of the realm met the king and his council. The great
precedent of 1295 had been followed and, if the writs of summons
were punctually obeyed, the assembly was a large one. By rights
there should have been present some ninety-five prelates, about
145 representatives of the inferior clergy, nine earls (if we include
the Prince of Wales and the Earl of Angus), ninety-four barons,
seventy-four knights of the shires, and about 200 citizens and
burgesses; altogether some 600 men. Besides these we must take
account of thirty-three members of the king's council to whom
writs were sent, and, as we shall see hereafter, there were yet other
men present and performing important duties, men who had a
special knowledge of Scotland and Gascony.

This assembly was kept together for just three weeks. On
21 March a proclamation was made telling the archbishops, bishops
and other prelates, earls, barons, knights, citizens and burgesses
in general that they might go home, but must be ready to appear
again if the king summoned them.* Those bishops, earls, barons,
justices and others who were members of the council were to
remain behind and so were all those who had still any business to
transact. But the 'parliament' was not at an end. Many of its
doings that are recorded on our roll were done after the estates
had been sent home.[4] The king remained at Westminster, surrounded by his councillors, and his parliament was still in session
as a 'full' and 'general' parliament as late as the 5 and 6 April.[5]

---

[1] *Parl. Writs*, vol. I, p. 407.   [2] *Annales Londonienses*, p. 134.

[3] [The medieval term for describing a parliament containing elected representatives would seem to be *general*. See Powicke, *The Thirteenth Century*,
p. 343. The phrase *in full parliament* appears to mean 'in open and formal
session'. See below, pp. 58, 80, 94.]

[4] [It must be remembered that the roll does not set out to give a full
account of the proceedings. See Richardson and Sayles in *The Bulletin of the
Institute of Historical Research* (cited henceforth as *B.I.H.R.*), 1928–9, pp. 132,
149–50, for detailed analysis of the rolls edited by Maitland.]

[5] *Memoranda de Parliamento*, pp. 4, 293, 297. See also *Parl. Writs*, vol. I,
p. 158. On 6 April the king releases one of his councillors, Master Robert
Pickering, from further attendance.**

Easter day fell on the 18th of that month, and its approach seems to have put an end to the prolonged session. Early in May the king began a tour through the home counties. He proposed to hold another 'parliament', which however, so far as we know, was not to be an assembly of the estates, on 15 July, but this he postponed first to 15 August and then to 15 September.[1]

THE KING'S COUNCIL: ITS COMPOSITION

Now if we are to frame any exact conception of the body or various bodies of men by whom the business that is recorded on our roll was transacted, and of the mode in which they dealt with that business, it seems necessary that we should understand the composition of the king's council. Unfortunately, as is well known, the council of Edward I is still for us an ill-defined group of men.[2] Writs of summons and writs for wages will often teach us the names of all the barons who were called to a parliament and enable us to know who it was that represented the pettiest boroughs, and yet we cannot enumerate with any certainty the members of the council. We can indeed make a list of those of its members who, not being prelates or barons, were summoned by name to be present at a given parliament. On the present occasion no less than thirty-three men were thus summoned. The list included Philip Willoughby the chancellor of the exchequer, the justices of the two benches and the barons of the exchequer, several men who were being employed as justices in eyre and thirteen masters of the chancery or clerks of the council. The title 'masters in chancery' is one which may lead us astray by suggesting that those who bear it are, like their successors in later days, principally engaged in performing certain subordinate functions in a great court of law and equity. But this is not so. If, with Dr Stubbs, we say that at this time the chancellor is 'the principal secretary of state for all departments', we may call these masters the 'under-secretaries of state'. Though already a keeper of the privy seal is beginning to intervene between the king and his chancellor, though already the king, at least at times, seems to have one yet more intimate clerk who is known as his secretary, the chancery is still the great secretarial department; it does nearly all the king's writing for him, whether such writing concerns foreign affairs or the govern-

[1] *Parl. Writs*, vol. i, pp. 158–60.   [2] Stubbs, *Const. Hist.* §230.

ment of England.[1] If for a moment we may use such modern terms, we may say that the chancery is Home Office, Foreign Office, Board of Trade, Local Government Board all in one; in short it is a general secretarial bureau, which exercises a certain control even over the only other great official 'department' that there is, namely the exchequer. Thus when the king is surrounded by the masters or principal clerks of the chancery, he has at his side the men who know most about the way in which England is governed and foreign affairs are managed, 'permanent', or fairly permanent, 'under-secretaries of state', and yet men who are on their promotion, for some of them may well look to being chancellors or treasurers before they die. It is among them also that the king finds his diplomatists. The thirty-three names therefore upon our list represent almost all that England has to show in the way of legal learning, official experience and administrative ability.[2]

But then of course it is certain that there are members of the council who are not upon this list. They have been otherwise summoned. In the first place there are the two great ministers. The treasurer, Walter Langton, has been summoned as bishop of Lichfield; he is King Edward's right-hand man. The chancellor, William Hamilton, who, when compared with Langton, seems an insignificant person, can appear as dean of York.[3] But there must be other prelates and there must be lay nobles who are members of the council. On the other hand it is difficult, if not impossible, to believe that every prelate or baron is a member of the council. We see this from that proclamation of 21 March which has already been mentioned. On that day the mass of prelates and nobles is

[1] In 1299 John Banstead is described as 'secretarius regis'; *Foedera*, vol. I, p. 916. In 1306 the same title is given to Philip Martel, doctor of civil law; *Prynne Records*, vol. III, p. 1095. In each case, however, this occurs in a document relating to foreign affairs, and we cannot be sure that in addressing foreign powers the king did not sometimes give to his clerks titles that had no very definite significance in England. As to the title 'clericus Regis', this may be borne at one and the same time by a large number of persons. [According to Tout 'Secretary at that date meant little more than confidant and keepers both of the Great and the Privy seal might be so described'. In 1305 Benstead was Controller of the Wardrobe and keeper of the Privy Seal, and 'in the front rank among Edward's confidential agents'. *Mediaeval Administrative History*, vol. II, pp. 18–19. See also *Essays in History presented to R. L. Poole* (Oxford, 1927), pp. 332–59.]*

[2] [On secretaries and king's clerks, see, besides Tout, Powicke, *Henry III and the Lord Edward*, pp. 293–7, 696–7; G. P. Cuttino, *English Diplomatic Administration* (1940); 'King's clerks and the Community of the Realm', *Speculum* (1954), pp. 396–409 and F. Pegues in *E.H.R.* (1956), pp. 529–59.]

[3] The chancellor seems to have had no summons, except as dean of York.

sent home; but the members of the council are to remain behind. Now it would be a hard task were we to seek to recover the names of all those who in any given year were King Edward's sworn councillors. Still certain materials exist, by a circumspect use of which we might arrive at some tentative but serviceable conclusions. We will fix our attention on the months of March and April in the year 1305 and see by whom it is that the king is surrounded. Our parliament roll will give us some help, while some help may be derived from the contemporary charter roll.[1] It is well known that a royal charter—and herein lies the chief formal difference between a charter and a mere patent—purports to have been delivered by the king in the presence of several witnesses whose names are given. We must not for one instant suggest that by merely collecting the names of such witnesses we could frame a list of those men of high station who were sworn members of the council. In the first place a man may be a member of the council and yet for many months together may never be in the king's presence. Sickness, old age, a mission to foreign parts, may keep him away; or again he may be in opposition or disgrace. No law obliges the king to consult all his councillors. For example, during the year in question we hardly ever see the Archbishop of Canterbury in the king's presence. In all likelihood he is still a member of the council; but he is in opposition and disgrace. And then on the other hand we may not infer that a man is a member of the council merely because he witnesses the grant of a charter. Not only may he be a casual visitor to the royal court, but even if his name appears habitually, this may be because he holds some not very important office about the king's person, and we can not be certain that the occupants of all such offices were usually sworn of the council. Still we may reasonably ask what great men were constantly in the king's presence during these two months, and the answer that we get to this question may be of some value.

The parliament, we have said, met on 28 February. Between that date and 21 March, when the assembly of the estates was dissolved, the king's charters were thus witnessed:

5 *March.* Earls of Lincoln, Gloucester, Hereford, and Warwick, Aymer de Valence, Hugh le Despenser, Robert Fitz Roger, Robert de la Warde (steward of the household).

[1] [For an application of this technique to the year 1252–3, see 'History from the Charter Roll', *E.H.R.* (1893), p. 23: *Collected Papers*, vol. II, pp. 298–312.]

7 *March.* Earls of Lincoln, Gloucester, Hereford, and Warwick, Aymer de Valence, Hugh le Despenser, Robert de la Warde.

8 *March.* Archbishop of Canterbury, Bishop of Lichfield (Treasurer), Bishops of Lincoln, Salisbury, and Carlisle, Earls of Lincoln, Lancaster, Gloucester, Hereford, and Warwick, John of Brittany, Hugh le Despenser, John de Segrave, Roger le Brabazon (C.J.B.R.), Robert de la Warde.

10 *March.* Earls of Lincoln, Gloucester, Hereford, and Warwick, Aymer de Valence, Hugh le Despenser, Robert Fitz Roger, Robert de la Warde.

10 *March.* The same with John of Hastings.

14 *March.* The Treasurer, the Bishop of Durham, the Earls of Lincoln, Lancaster, and Hereford, John of Brittany, Aymer de Valence, Robert Fitz Roger, Robert de la Warde.

20 *March.* The Treasurer, the Bishops of Durham, Carlisle, and Glasgow, the Earls of Lincoln, Gloucester, Hereford, Warwick, and Carrick, John of Brittany, Aymer de Valence, Robert Fitz Roger, Robert de la Warde. [A Scottish charter.]

20 *March.* The Treasurer, the Bishops of Durham and Carlisle, the Earls of Lincoln, Lancaster, Hereford, and Warwick, Aymer de Valence, Hugh le Despenser, Robert Fitz Roger, Robert de la Warde.

On the next day the assembly of the estates was dissolved. We shall see, however, that the king retains all or most of those who have been witnessing his acts.

28 *March.* The Treasurer, the Bishops of Durham, Carlisle, and Glasgow, the Earls of Lincoln, Gloucester, Hereford, Warwick, and Carrick, John of Brittany, Aymer de Valence, Robert de la Warde.

29 *March.* The Treasurer, the Bishops of Durham, Salisbury and Carlisle, Earls of Lincoln, Hereford and Warwick, Henry de Percy, Hugh le Despenser, Robert de Clifford, John de Segrave.

30 *March.* The Treasurer, the Bishops of Durham and Carlisle, the Earls of Lincoln, Hereford, and Warwick, John of Brittany, Aymer de Valence, Hugh le Despenser, John de Segrave, Robert de la Warde.

5 *April.* The Treasurer, the Bishops of Durham and Carlisle, the Earls of Lincoln, Gloucester, and Warwick, Henry de Percy, Robert de Clifford, Robert de la Warde.

5 *April.* The Treasurer, the Bishops of Durham and Carlisle, the Earls of Lincoln, Gloucester, and Hereford, Aymer de Valence, Henry de Percy, John de Hastings, Robert de Clifford, Robert de la Warde.

5 *April.* The Treasurer, the Bishops of Durham and Carlisle, the Earls of Lincoln, Gloucester, Hereford, and Warwick, John of Brittany, Henry de Percy, Hugh le Despenser, Robert de la Warde.

8 *April.* The Treasurer, the Earls of Lincoln and Hereford, John of Brittany, Aymer de Valence, Hugh le Despenser, Robert de la Warde.

10 *April.* The Treasurer, the Bishops of Salisbury and Carlisle, the Earls of Lincoln, Gloucester, and Hereford, Aymer de Valence, Hugh le Despenser and John de Hastings.

15 *April.* The Treasurer, the Bishop of Durham, the Earls of Lincoln and Hereford, John of Brittany, Aymer de Valence, Henry de Percy, Hugh le Despenser, Robert de la Warde.

The Easter holiday now intervenes. In May and June, as in January and February, we may see the king travelling about the country, and when this is the case his charters have fewer witnesses—perhaps the treasurer, perhaps the Bishop of Durham, with an earl or two earls and three or four barons, or some men, it may be officers of his household, who are not of baronial rank. The most regular of all the witnesses to a royal charter is the steward of the household; at this moment he is Robert de la Warde.

We may now turn to the parliament roll and make further pursuit for the names of councillors. Nicholas Segrave has to answer for his offences 'in full parliament, in the presence of the king himself, the Archbishop of Canterbury, and many bishops, earls, barons, and others of the king's council'.[1] Then on Monday, 29 March, certain persons presented themselves 'before the king himself and his council' as willing to go bail for Segrave, and on the following Wednesday their bond was witnessed by the treasurer, the Bishops of Durham and Carlisle, the Earls of Lincoln and Warwick, and the two chief justices.[2] On 13 March Almaric de St Amand is bailed before the treasurer, the chief justice of the king's bench, 'and others of the king's council', by six great men, all of whom may themselves be members of the council, the Earl of Lincoln, John of Brittany, Hugh le Despenser, Hugh de Vere, Thomas of Berkeley, and Adam of Welles.[3] Another case was heard by the treasurer, the chief justice of the king's bench, John of Berwick, 'and others of the king's council'.[4] But by far the longest list of councillors that we get is contained in an elaborate notarial instrument which describes how on 5 April the titular bishop of Byblos appeared 'before the bishops and other prelates, earls, barons, justices, and divers other noble clerks and laymen, councillors of the magnificent prince, the lord Edward, the illustrious king of England', proffered a papal bull, and received a short answer to the effect that this bull was of no avail in England. Then the notary tells us how these things were done in the presence of the treasurer, the Bishops of Durham and Carlisle, the Earls of Lincoln, Hereford, and Warwick, twenty-four persons

---

[1] *Memoranda de Parliamento,* no. 449, pp. 255f.
[2] *Ibid.* no. 449, pp. 258–60.   [3] *Ibid.* no. 452.   [4] *Ibid.* no. 420.

who are described as knights, three who are 'discreet men', and three who are clerks. The list is worthy of some further analysis. Of the twenty-four 'knights', ten have received the baronial summons to this parliament (Valence, Percy, Clifford, Vere, Teye, Welles, William de Grandison, Rither, Deyncourt, Burghersh), eight have received the councillor's summons and are justices or barons of the exchequer (Brabazon, de L'Isle, Bereford, Howard, Hengham, Spigurnel, Malorie and Inge). The others are John of Brittany, who apparently was not summoned, but who is the king's nephew and one of his trustiest captains and advisers;[1] John de Botetourte, who is warden of the western parts of the Scottish march;[2] John Wogan, who is justiciar of Ireland; John of Havering, who may be of baronial rank and who at any rate is just being appointed to be seneschal of Gascony;[3] Ralph of Sandwich, who is constable of the Tower; and Nicholas Fermbaud, who is constable of Bristol. The three 'clerks' (Reginald Brandon, Robert Pickering, and William of Kilkenny) have all had the councillor's summons. As to the three 'discreet men', they have none of them been summoned. They are, we may guess, too 'discreet', that is, too intimately connected with the king's person, to need any writ. They are John of Drokenesford, the keeper of the wardrobe, the head, that is, of a department which has a great deal to do with military and other expenditure; John of Banstead, who is or has been the king's secretary, and who before the year is out will be chancellor of the exchequer,[4] and John of Berwick, another clerk, who has long been in the service of the king and queen; possibly he holds the privy seal.[5] Then three notaries of the apostolic see, two of whom, John Bush and John of Caen, are also clerks of the English chancery,* perfect the instrument with all due solemnity.

Then we may see a committee of the council appointed. It consists of the treasurer, the Bishop of Durham, the Earl of

[1] His father, John Duke of Brittany, is living, but dies in this year. He is subsequently summoned as Earl of Richmond.

[2] Bain, *Calendar*, vol. II, no. 1659.**

[3] *Memoranda de Parliamento*, App. II.

[4] *Foedera*, vol. II, pp. 916, 974.

[5] Already in 1292 he is 'discretus vir', 'clericus Regis'; *Foedera*, vol. II, p. 766. He has lately been negotiating the peace with France. He was dean of Wimborne and a canon of York. He was one of Queen Eleanor's executors; Foss, *Judges*, vol. III, p. 237. [Berwick never kept the privy seal. For further details on the three discreet men, all wardrobe clerks, see Tout, *Administrative History*, vol. II, pp. 42, 83, and the Index in vol. VI.]

Lincoln, Aymer de Valence, John Drokenesford, and John Banstead. They are to discuss the affairs concerning which a certain 'Dominus de Cuk' has come to the king from foreign parts.[1] He, we take it, is Jehan lord of Cuijk in Brabant. He was over here in 1297 as an envoy of the Count of Flanders,[2] and on the present occasion he has apparently come to negotiate about certain debts that are due from the king to the Duke of Brabant.[3]

In the autumn of this year the king held another 'parliament'. So far as we know he did not call in the prelates or barons in mass, nor did he summon any representatives of the shires or the towns. The names of those whom he ordered to appear are for the more part names with which we are by this time growing familiar. The treasurer was summoned and the Bishop of Worcester, the Earls of Lincoln and Hereford, Hugh le Despenser, Henry Percy, John of Hastings, John Botetourte, and William Martin; three justices, two barons of the exchequer; Philip Martel and another master of the chancery;[4] John of Banstead, and John of Sandale, the chamberlain of Scotland; and besides these the Abbots of Westminster and Waverl[e]y and Friar Hugh of Manchester.[5] It was by these twenty men (for John of Hastings was too ill to come), in conjunction with ten representatives of the various estates of Scotland, that the great Ordinance for the affairs of Scotland was drawn up.[6] Almost immediately after this, six out of these twenty men were commissioned as ambassadors to the pope, namely, the treasurer, the Bishop of Worcester, the Earl of Lincoln, Despenser, Banstead and Martel.[7]

Now the constitution of the body which was to treat with the Scottish commissioners may give us a valuable warning; for it is somewhat artificial; the representatives of Scotland are to be

---

[1] *Memoranda de Parliamento*, no. 454.

[2] *Foedera*, vol. I, pp. 853, 856; *Annales de Wigornia*, p. 529.

[3] *Memoranda de Parliamento*, App. III.

[4] [For Philip Martel see Cuttino, *English Diplomatic Administration*, Index. There is no evidence that he was a chancery clerk and no proof that he was a sworn councillor. He was keeper of diplomatic records and attended the king's council in a professional capacity in 1305.]

[5] The 'parliament' was postponed from time to time, and some men who were summoned in the first instance were not (so far as we know) summoned after the postponement, namely, the Bishops of Durham, Salisbury, and Carlisle, the Prince of Wales, the Earls of Lancaster, Gloucester, and Warwick, Aymer of Valence, John of Brittany, Clifford, Burghersh, Thomas of Berkeley, Roger la Warre, and certain justices and clerks; *Parl. Writs*, vol. I, pp. 159–61.

[6] *Parl. Writs*, vol. I, p. 161.   [7] *Foedera*, vol. II, p. 974.

outnumbered by just two to one; there are to be just two English bishops, two English abbots, two English earls. The two abbots are probably not sworn members of the council, but every great interest is to be represented and there are two Scottish abbots to be balanced. We may well believe that according to the notions of this age the king has a clear right to call upon any one of his subjects to give him counsel; and bold would have been the man who either refused to come, or who refused to sit beside any one whom he found at the council board. This makes it exceedingly hard for us to say that one man is while another man is not a permanent councillor.

The difficulty may be illustrated by the case of the most famous of the English nobles. Seven earls were summoned to the parliament, besides the Prince of Wales and Gilbert of Umfraville, who was Earl of Angus in Scotland. Five of these we have seen about the king's court, the Earls of Lincoln, Gloucester, Hereford, Lancaster, and Warwick; and, by the way, it must not escape us that the king is surrounded by his kinsfolk: Thomas of Lancaster and John of Brittany are his nephews, Hereford and Gloucester are his sons-in-law, Aymer de Valence is his cousin. Then the Warenne earldoms of Surrey and Sussex we may perhaps describe as being in suspense. The heir to them, the young John of Warenne, has not been summoned to the parliament; probably he is under age and not yet belted; but we happen to know that he is present, for on 15 March the king 'in his own chamber at Westminster in his Parliament' offers the hand of his granddaughter, Joan of Bar, to the young earl, who gratefully accepts the offer.[1] Edmund, the heir of Arundel, is another infant. The two earls whom we have not mentioned are those of Oxford and Norfolk. We can hardly doubt that the marshal of England is at least a titular councillor; but he is not being consulted; we do not know that he came to this parliament. He has been in disgrace. Three years ago he had to surrender his estate and office to the king, and take them back on terms which will make him the last of his great race.[2] There is no quarrel now. On 14 March the king 'because of his great affection'—so runs the chancery formula—forgives him the debts that he owes.[3]

---

[1] Rot. Cl. 33 Edw. I, m. 18d.*

[2] The surrender was made in April, the regrant in July 1302; *Foedera*, vol. I, pp. 940–1.

[3] Rot. Pat. 33 Edw. I, pt. 1, m. 16: 'ob grandem affectionem'.**

He may well be an old, disappointed, broken man; death is at hand and the days of the Bigods are over; but for all this he is probably entitled to call himself one of the king's councillors.

When, however, all due allowance has been made for all our doubts and mistakes, we have to picture to ourselves the council as being in the main a body of officers, of ministers, of men who in one capacity or another are doing the king's work and receiving the king's pay. Even those prelates and barons who remain at Westminster, when their fellows have gone home, are hardly mere prelates and barons. The Bishops of Durham and Carlisle are not just two bishops; the magnificent Anthony Beck, the strenuous John Halton, we might almost call provincial governors, the military governors of districts which are exposed to invasion. Clifford and Despenser are not just two powerful barons; they are the two forest justices, and as such they are at this moment two very important ministers. Valence and Brittany are the king's best generals. The Earl of Lincoln, the faithful Henry Lacy, is as near to being a prime minister as a layman can be. And then the council embraces all the great courts and all the great boards. A full meeting of the council is a full meeting of the king's bench, of the common bench, of the chancery, of the exchequer: it is this and more than this.[1]

So much as to men; one word as to places. The parliament was held at Westminster, and the proclamation that invited petitions was made in 'the great hall'. Nevertheless, it is not in the royal palace that we can lay the one scene of which we have a full account; it was not there that the Bishop of Byblos came before the council. The king, we are told, was dwelling and the council was assembled in the house of the Archbishop of York.[2] Another document tells us that on 22 February a sum of £6. 12s. was paid from the wardrobe to Walter, the chaplain of the palace, in order that the archbishop's house might be prepared for the reception of the king and queen.[3] The temporalities of the archiepiscopal see were in the king's hands; William of Greenfield, the elect archbishop—he had lately resigned the chancellorship—had gone to the pope for

---

[1] I have not come upon any contemporary and official authority which shows that the king has more than one council, or which qualifies the term *consilium* with any such adjectives as *ordinarium, privatum,* or the like. [See below, p. 133, n.3.]   [2] *Memoranda de Parliamento,* no. 464.
[3] Exchequer: Q.R. Various Accounts: Wardrobe and Household. [E 101/366/24.]

E

confirmation. Already in 1293 the king had held a parliament at the same place,[1] and thus early had York House, standing where the White Hall was to stand in later days, become the scene of royal councils.

THE BUSINESS OF A PARLIAMENT

And now we may ask the question, what does our record tell us of the part played in this parliament by the king's council, and by those who constituted or represented the three estates of the realm? We may bring the business of a medieval parliament under five heads, namely—(1) the discussion of affairs of state, more especially foreign affairs; (2) legislation; (3) taxation or supply; (4) the audience of petitions; (5) judicial business, the determination of causes criminal and civil.

(1) *General discussion*

The king had summoned the estates in order that he might treat 'of certain matters specially touching our realm of England and the establishment of our land of Scotland', and no doubt the state of Scotland was one of the main matters which required his attention and the advice of his councillors. Let us remember that just at this moment Edward was at the full height of his power. All looked well; it seemed as if the evening of his reign was to be peaceful and glorious. He had lately traversed Scotland from end to end hardly finding an enemy, save in the garrison of Stirling Castle, and now even Stirling was his. Wallace, it is true, was in all probability still at large when our parliament was sitting at Westminster; but he was a hunted outlaw and his capture, when it took place soon afterwards, cannot have been an unlooked-for event. As for the young Earl of Carrick, Edward had no reason for suspecting him of a grand ambition; we see him taking part in the parliament as one whom the king trusts. The task in hand was to provide for Scotland a settled form of government, a task that might demand prolonged debates, but not, it would seem, a hopeless task. What Edward did at this parliament was to call upon the Bishop of Glasgow, the Earl of Carrick, and John Mowbray to say how Scotland should be represented at another parliament to be holden later in the year. They reported that two bishops, two abbots, two earls, two barons, and two men elected

---

[1] *Rolls of Parliament*, vol. I, p. 91.

by the community of Scotland would be representatives enough. As to the place at which the parliament should meet, they left that to the king; as to the time, the Scots could hardly be ready before Midsummer. Thereupon the king fixed London and 15 July as the place and date for the assembly.[1] Afterwards he postponed that date until 15 September, and then at Westminster the ten Scottish representatives and twenty members of the English council drew up the important 'Ordinatio super stabilitate terræ Scotiæ'. However, at the moment what should interest us most is this, that in our lenten parliament the three Scottish spokesmen did not answer the question that had been put to them until after the assembly of the English estates had been dissolved. Those who were not members of the council had been sent home on 21 March; not until the 26th did the Bishop of Glasgow, Robert Bruce, and John Mowbray bring in their report.

Whether Edward had sought advice in this matter from the mass of the clergy, baronage, and commoners, we cannot say; nor do we know that the affairs of Gascony afforded material for a general debate, though there was an enormous mass of Gascon business to be transacted. Edward had lately recovered his French provinces, and was just sending out a new set of representatives. John of Havering, who had been justiciar of Wales, was to be in supreme command as seneschal of the duchy; Richard of Havering, lately the escheator north of Trent, was to be constable of Bordeaux; William Dene, seneschal of the Agenais; Frisot de Montclar, treasurer of Agen. Vast quantities of writs had to be issued for the payment of arrears of many kinds.[2]

To come nearer home, we have seen how the king expected that the clergy would make an attack upon him. He was now quite strong enough to meet, to forestall, such an attack. He had not forgotten the humiliation that he had suffered at the hands of Archbishop Winchelsea. With his very good will, as we may well suppose, a petition was presented by the barons and commons complaining that the monks, more especially the Cistercians, sent large sums of money out of the country to alien mother houses.[3] Of this matter we must speak under another head, but it may have been discussed in many meetings by the assembled laity. The

[1] *Memoranda de Parliamento*, nôs. 13, 458.

[2] This information is derived from the Gascon Roll. *Memoranda de Parliamento*, App. II.   [3] *Ibid.* no. 486.

treatment of the offending archbishop, who had lately been giving a fresh cause of complaint by 'visiting' the king's free chapel in Hastings Castle,[1] was a subject to be debated rather at the council board than before the estates of the realm.

(2) *Legislation*

In the way of legislation this parliament did little. No statute was passed which at once found a place upon the statute roll; but there are several acts of a more or less legislative character which should be briefly mentioned.

In answer to the petition of the laity touching the revenues of the religious houses the following reply was given: 'The king in his full parliament, by the consent of the prelates, earls, barons, and others of the realm, has ordained and established a certain statute about this matter.'[2] Our roll, as will now be seen for the first time, goes on to add—'in the form that follows'. But nothing follows; a blank space is left; the statute, if drawn up, was kept in abeyance. Two years afterwards it was formally enacted or re-enacted at another parliament and became the well-known Statute of Carlisle, 'De asportatis religiosorum'.[3] The reasons for this delay are not obvious; but we have to remember that at the date of our parliament the papacy was vacant, and that Edward may have had several reasons for keeping in suspense over the future pope a statute which might prevent the flow of money from England to Rome or Avignon.[4]

There has passed into our collections of statutes out of the Vetus Codex an 'Ordinance for Inquests' made at this parliament.[5] It is an answer to a petition presented by Simon Parker, and provides in general terms that an inquest to which the king is

---

[1] *Ibid.* no. 204.   [2] *Ibid.* no. 486.

[3] *Statutes of the Realm*, vol. I, p. 150.

[4] Dr Stubbs, *Const. Hist.* §181, writes thus: 'In the February parliament of 1305 the consent of the barons had been given to a statute forbidding the payment of tallages on monastic property and other imposts by which money was raised to be sent out of the country. Not being fortified by the assent of the clergy or commons this Act was not published until 1307, when in the parliament of Carlisle held in January it was formally passed.' This may be so, and certainly the recitals in the Statute of Carlisle seem to point this way. But our roll very distinctly claims for the statute made in our parliament the consent of the prelates, earls, barons, and others of the realm. Benedict XI died on 7 July 1304; Clement V was not elected until 5 June 1305.

[5] *Statutes of the Realm*, vol. I, p. 143.

party is not to be stayed merely because the king's pleaders assert that some of the jurors are not favourable to the king. This was agreed and ordained 'by the king and his whole council'.[1] Such an ordinance was beneath the dignity of the statute roll, and we should have great difficulty in proving that it had the assent of the estates. But it was a concession by the king, and the king's ordaining power would easily cover the making of such a concession.

An Ordinatio Forestae which is on our roll was placed also upon the close roll; it has been received into our printed statute books.[2] It is the king's answer to certain petitions and does not purport upon its face to bear the authority of the assembled estates or even the authority of the council.[3] The king has been compelled to consent to a perambulation (*puralee*) of his forests, and now some of those who have been 'put out of the forest by the perambulation' want both to be quit of their old burdens and yet to enjoy their accustomed advantages; they do not want to provide 'poture', meat and drink, or money instead of meat and drink, for the foresters as of old, and yet they want to keep their old easements and rights of common within the forest. The king tells them that they must make their choice; they cannot be both inside and outside the forest and the forest law. It was not he who called for the perambulation; the demand for it should not have been made; but he has granted that demand and will keep his word. The justices of the forest are to see that effect is given to this answer. We can hardly treat this as an act of legislation; certainly we cannot treat it as an act in which the estates of the realm took part. But no doubt at their meetings there was much talk about the forests, and discussion of those grievances which in the next year were met by an ordinance of sufficient importance to be placed upon the statute roll.[4]

Lastly, there is, or rather once was, on our roll what was called in the margin thereof 'Ordinatio de trailbastons'.[5] The king has

---

[1] *Memoranda de Parliamento*, no. 10.   [2] *Statutes*, vol. i, p. 144.
[3] *Memoranda de Parliamento*, no. 461.
[4] The Ordinatio Forestae of 1306; *Statutes*, vol. i, p. 145. This is dated on 28 May, that is to say, two days before the day fixed for the parliament. The enacting words are 'concordatum est et statutum', and it calls itself 'istud statutum'.
[5] This seems to be the first appearance in an official document of the curious word 'trailbaston'. There can be little doubt that it signified a 'club-man', a vagabond with a big stick. [For a fourteenth-century miniature showing a trailbaston in action, see H. M. Cam, *The Hundred and the Hundred Rolls* (1930), p. 180.]

appointed justices to inquire of, hear and determine divers felonies and trespasses. Their commissions are upon the patent roll; the earliest is dated on 6 April.[1] The king now gives them certain instructions as to their proceedings. These will be of some importance in later history, for 'a commission of trailbaston' becomes one of the known forms of commission with which justices can be equipped. But this again we can hardly regard as a legislative act. The king has always enjoyed and still enjoys a very large discretionary power of sending justices when and whither he pleases, and of defining the matters about which they are to inquire. Even were we to examine the new commission minutely, we might find in it little that was very new or to us very striking, nevertheless the issue of it was the one thing done in this parliament that all the chroniclers have thought worthy of note; indeed, a certain annalist speaks of this year as the year of trailbaston.[3] This vigorous attempt to free the land of vagabonds takes its place along with the execution of Wallace, the disgrace of the archbishop, and the coronation of a new pope; they are the memorable events of the year, at least so it strikes a contemporary.

(3) *Taxation*

As to taxation, we have every reason to believe that on the present occasion no tax of any kind was imposed, and we have no evidence to show that the king asked for money. He seems to have been very poor. The salaries of his justices and his clerks were in arrear, and they had to be told that they must wait for better times.[4] It is of course possible that some statement of his necessities was laid before the assembled magnates, clergy and commons, but we read nothing of any 'supply' or of any demand.

There are, however, three matters which deserve a brief notice in this context. 'The bishops, abbots, earls, barons, and others of the realm' petitioned that, whereas they had done their military service in Scotland in the campaigns of 1300 and 1303, they might take scutages from their tenants.[5] The request was granted. 'The

---

[1] *Parl. Writs*, vol. I, p. 408.

[2] See Pike, *Introduction to Year Book*, 14–15 Edw. III, pp. xxx–xxxvi.

[3] *Liber de Antiquis Legibus*, App., p. 250: 'L'an de Treyle baton'. See also *Flores Historiarum*, vol. III, p. 122; *Annales de Wigornia*, p. 557; Rishanger, *Chronica*, p. 224; *Annales Londonienses*, p. 134; *Trivet*, p. 404.*

[4] *Memoranda de Parliamento*, nos. 80, 175.

[5] *Ibid*. no. 198.

earls, barons, and others who owe the king military service' also complained that though they had done their service, the officers of the exchequer were charging them with scutages for all their fees. The answer was that the king in the presence of the whole council had ordained that relief should be given to them by a writ directed from the chancery to the exchequer, and that the form of the writ was to be settled by the council.[1] Thirdly, 'the archbishops, bishops, prelates, earls, barons, and other good men of the land' asked that, as the king had lately tallaged his demesnes, they also might be allowed to tallage those parts of the ancient demesnes of the crown which were in their hands.[2] To this the response was a simple *Fiat ut petitur*.[3] In all these cases the petitioners seem to have been asking for no more than they were entitled to, though the only procedure by which they could obtain it was a petition.

(4) *Audience of petitions*

But by far the greater part of our parliament roll is occupied by entries which concern the audience of petitions. Before we discuss any of the many questions which such entries suggest we must remember that many of the original petitions exist, and the external form of a petition should be briefly described.

It will in general be a strip of parchment about five inches long, while its breadth will vary from three inches to a bare inch. On the front of this strip and along its length the petitioner's grievance and prayer will be written, usually in French, rarely in Latin, and will be addressed 'to our lord the king' or 'to our lord the king and his council'. On the back of this strip and across its breadth

---

[1] *Memoranda de Parliamento*, no. 203. [For Edward's ultimately unsuccessful attempt to turn the scutage into a general tax, see H. M. Chew in *E.H.R.* (1922), pp. 321 ff.]   [2] *Ibid.* no. 87.

[3] In 1304 Edward had taken a tallage of a sixth from his demesnes; Stubbs, *Const. Hist.* §181. It would not be true to say that on the present occasion the king allowed the magnates 'to tallage their demesnes'. A landlord may always tallage his villains, and it is by his villains that the greater part of his demesnes are occupied. At all events, though he may thereby be breaking manorial custom, no court of law will prevent him doing this. But when one of the manors which are the ancient demesne of the crown has been granted to a mesne lord, he may only tallage the *homines de antiquo dominico coronae* when their compeers on the manors which have not left the king's hand are being tallaged by the king. And even this, so it would seem, he can only do by the king's permission. See Vinogradoff, *Villainage*, pp. 92–3. [See also R. S. Hoyt, *The Royal Demesne in English Constitutional History* (Ithaca, 1950), pp. 204–6.]

there will almost always be written some words, usually in Latin, rarely at this time in French, which either prescribe the relief which the petitioner is to have or send him away empty. Then below this endorsement there will very often occur the syllable *Irr̄*, while just now and again we find the full *Irrotulatur*.[1] Then, if we are lucky enough to connect this document with an entry on the parliament roll, the relation between the two will be of this kind: By means of the formula, *Ad petitionem A. de B. petentis quod, etc., Ita responsum est quod, etc.*,* the roll will first state the substance of the petition, having turned its plaintive French into businesslike Latin and pruned away its immaterial details, and then it will give with absolute accuracy the words of that response which is endorsed on the petition.[2]

And now we may glance at the grave question, How and by whom and when and where was this business, this long and laborious business, transacted? We know that for some time past the multitude of petitions presented at the king's parliaments had been giving trouble and had been met by various expedients. In the eighth year of the reign we hear that 'the folk who come to the king's parliament are often delayed and disturbed to the great grievance of them and of the court by the numerous petitions which are presented to the king, many of which might be " exploited " before the chancellor and the justices'. It is, therefore, provided that these petitions are to be sorted. Those which concern the seal are to come before the chancellor, others are to be sent according to their nature to the exchequer or to the justices, or to the justices of the Jewry. Only those 'which are so great or so much of grace' that they cannot otherwise be dealt with are to come before the king in order that his pleasure may be taken, and they are to be brought before him and his council by the chancellor and the other chief ministers, so that he and his council may have leisure to attend to the great affairs of his realm and of other lands.[3] Then in the twenty-first year it was ordained that all petitions which thenceforth should be proffered at the parliaments should be handed in to receivers appointed by the king in order that they might be examined. Five bundles were to be made, one for the chancery, another for the exchequer, a third for the justices, a

---

[1] On several occasions I have seen *Irrotulatur* at full length, and have never noticed an *Irrotuletur*.   [2] [See below, p. 135, for an example.]
[3] Ryley, *Placita*, p. 442; Stubbs, *Const. Hist.* §231.**

fourth for the king and his council, while the fifth was to contain those which had already been answered.[1]

(a) *Procedure in 1305.* On the present occasion we obtain yet fuller information. Already on 5 February, three weeks before the day fixed for the parliament, Edward, who was then at Swaffham in Cambridgeshire, wrote to his chancellor about this matter.

We bid you [he said] along with the treasurer, to whom we have issued a similar command, proclaim that all those who have petitions to deliver to us and our council at our forthcoming parliament shall deliver them day by day to those who are assigned to receive them between now and the first Sunday of Lent [7 March] at the latest. And do you and the others of our Council in London 'deliver' as many of these petitions as you can before we come, so that no petitions shall come before us in person, save only those which cannot in anywise be 'delivered' without us, and these last you are to have well tried and examined and set in good order. This proclamation should be made in the great hall at Westminster, in the chancery, before the justices of the bench, in the Gildhall, and in Westcheap, and the names of those who are to receive petitions must be declared. You are to let me know without delay in what manner you have fulfilled this command and whom you have appointed to receive the petitions.[2]

From this it would seem that the work of examining and even of answering the petitions—for to 'deliver' a petition is to answer it—was to be taken in hand by those members of the council who were in London some days before the date appointed for the parliament.

Whether this order was obeyed or revoked we cannot say for certain. Our roll opens with just such a proclamation as the king had prescribed, and but for his letter we should naturally have supposed that it was not made until 28 February, the first day of the parliament. Be this as it may, the persons appointed to receive the petitions were Gilbert Roubury,[3] a justice of the king's bench, John Kirkby, the remembrancer of the exchequer, and two clerks of the chancery, who were also notaries of the apostolic see, John Bush and John Arthur of Caen. Their duty was, we take it, to receive and to sort the petitions.

[1] Ryley, *Placita*, p. 459; Stubbs, *Const. Hist.* §231.*

[2] Chancery Warrants, Series I, no. 5274. [*Cal. Chanc. Warrants*, vol. I, p. 246.]

[3] [Gilbert of Rothbury, justice of king's bench 1295–1316, was the clerk of the parliament 1290–1307. He was also clerk of the king's council 1290–5. See Richardson and Sayles, 'The King's Ministers in Parliament', *E.H.R.* (1931); Sayles, *Select Cases in King's Bench* (Selden Society, 1936), vol. I, p. lxi.]

Then we read that the king has appointed certain men to receive
and to answer all those petitions presented by the folk of Gascony
that can be answered without the king. These men, we may say,
constitute a very strong committee for Gascon affairs. They are
the treasurer, the Earl of Lincoln, Aymer de Valence, John of
Brittany, John of Havering, Arnaud de Caupenne,[1] the Prior of
le Mas, Master Piers Arnaud de Vic, Master Piers Aimery, and John
of Sandale. John of Havering is at this parliament appointed
seneschal of Gascony; he has some title to be called an English
baron, though apparently he has not received the baronial summons on the present occasion. John of Sandale has received no
summons; but he is a trusty clerk; he is now chamberlain of
Scotland, and will be Bishop of Winchester and Chancellor of
England; he has had experience in Gascony.[2] Sir Arnaud de
Caupenne, the Prior of le Mas, Piers Arnaud, and Piers Aimery
have not received any summons of the ordinary kind and we can
in no sense call them Englishmen. Piers Arnaud is provost of
Bayonne, he has recently been one of the two royal lieutenants in
Gascony and Arnaud de Caupenne has been with him.[3] Piers
Aimery has at times been about the king's person[4] and in 1302 he
was summoned to a parliament among the king's clerks;[5] but he
is or was a canon of the church of St Severin,[6] and is at this
moment retiring from the office of constable of Bordeaux. Sir
Arnaud de Caupenne is seneschal of the Limousin, Périgord, and
Quercy. As to the Prior of le Mas, his name is Bernard Pellet or
Pelleti, he is a doctor of both laws, and has lately been engaged
for our king's service by the Earl of Lincoln at a yearly salary of
£250 tournois. We cannot yet treat the auditors of petitions as a
committee of the English house of lords.[7]

[1] On p. 3 of the *Memoranda de Parliamento* this name by a deeply regretted
error has been given as Campenne. There is more than one Caupenne (Calva
Penna) in the south of France.

[2] *Foedera*, vol. II, p. 934.

[3] In 1294 Master Peter Arnaldi 'de Bik' is a king's clerk in Gascony;
Foedera, vol. II, p. 807. In 1300 and 1301 he was one of the king's 'locum
tenentes' in his 'duchy of Aquitaine', *ibid.* pp. 902, 934. On the Gascon Roll
for our year (m. 24) he appears as provost of Bayonne on 30 March 1305.
I assume that 'de Bik' and 'de Vico' have the same meaning. There are several
places called Vic in the south of France.

[4] *Foedera*, vol. II, p. 876.   [5] *Parl. Writs*, vol. I, p. 113.

[6] *Foedera*, vol. II, p. 920.

[7] As to these Gascon auditors, see *Memoranda de Parliamento*, App. II.

To answer those petitions from Ireland and the Channel Islands which can be answered without the king, a less dignified group of men is constituted. It consists of John of Berwick, one of those very 'discreet' clerks who have not received writs of summons, Hervey of Stanton, who has not been summoned, but has been employed as an itinerant justice and will soon be a justice of the common bench, William Mortimer, an itinerant justice who has received the councillor's writ, Roger de Beaufou, who has not been summoned but is going to be employed as a justice of trailbaston, and lastly, William de Dene, who is on the eve of being appointed seneschal of the Agenais; if he was in any sense an Irishman, he was the one Irish member of this Irish committee.[1]

For Scottish petitions a third set of men is appointed. It includes William Inge and Henry of Guildford, English justices, who have been summoned as councillors (Inge is soon to be a justice north of Forth),[2] Richard of Havering who has not been summoned (he is one of the king's clerks, has served him in Scotland,[3] and is now to go out as constable of Bordeaux),[4] and two men neither of whom has been summoned but who probably know more than any other men about the king's proprietary interests in Scotland, namely, James of Dalilegh, escheator south of Forth, and John Weston, the king's receiver; they have lately been taking account of all the king's demesnes as far north as Orkney.[5] We are told that these people are to receive, not that they are to answer, the Scottish petitions, but as it seems plain that in the first instance all petitions are to pass through the hands of Roubury, Caen, Kirkby, and Bush, we may perhaps believe that the committee for Scotland had the same power that was given to the committees for Gascony and for Ireland, that it consisted not merely of receivers and sorters of petitions, but of triers and auditors.

For the English petitions no auditors were, so far as we know, expressly appointed. And here it may be remarked that this roll gives us the first evidence that we have of the appointment of auditors, nor do we get any other evidence for another ten years.[6]

---

[1] There had been a William de Dene who held land in Ireland; but he was dead; Sweetman, *Calendar*, 1302–7, p. 157.

[2] Bain, *Calendar*, vol. II, p. 457.   [3] *Ibid.* p. 294.

[4] *Memoranda de Parliamento*, App. II.   [5] Bain, *Calendar*, vol. II, p. 438.

[6] At the autumn 'parliament' of this year 1305 Roubury, Kirkby, Caen, and Bush were again appointed to receive the petitions, but of auditors we read nothing; *Parl. Writs*, vol. I, p. 160.

In 1316 there were three parties of auditors; one for England, a second for Gascony and the Isles, a third for Wales, Ireland, and Scotland. On that occasion the English committee consisted of three bishops, two barons, a justice, a baron of the exchequer, and a clerk of the chancery.[1] Perhaps in 1305, without any formal appointment, a small group of councillors was busy over the English petitions, but the constitution of that group may have varied from day to day, as now this man and now that could be spared from other employments. Some of the most important councillors had been told off for the Gascon petitions, the treasurer, the Earl of Lincoln, Aymer de Valence, and John of Brittany. The chancellor may have presided over the English committee and have had with him the Bishops of Durham and Carlisle, the Earls of Hereford, Gloucester and Warwick, some barons, some justices, perhaps the two chief justices, and some clerks. About this matter we cannot be certain; and it is possible that there was more than one committee for England; the endorsements on the various English petitions were not all written by one and the same hand.

Then we can see that some of the petitions were reserved for the king's eye or ear, while others were reserved for plenary meetings of the council. We come across a petition which has an endorsement of the usual character, a response defining the relief that the suppliant is to have, but that response is preceded by the words 'Coram Rege' or 'Coram Consilio', and often we can be sure that those words were not written by the hand that wrote what follows them. Here we seem to have in the first place a statement by the receivers or the auditors that this petition is one which must come before the king himself, or, as the case may be, before a full meeting of the council, followed by the order that was made when the king or when the council had considered the supplication. In one instance the endorsement of a petition which has thus been reserved for the king's audience is followed by an interesting note—'These thirty-two petitions were expedited before the king on the first Sunday of Lent.'[2] It is an interesting note, for it shows us that already on 7 March, just a week after the opening of parliament and on the very day that had been fixed as the last for the receipt of petitions, considerable progress had been made in the work of 'delivering' or 'expediting' them;

[1] *Rotuli Parliamentorum*, vol. I, p. 350.
[2] *Memoranda de Parliamento*, no. 77.

already thirty-two of the reserved petitions had come before the king and they, having been duly 'tried' by the auditors, had been answered by him in the course of a single Sunday. Then we find another petition which in effect asks for an original writ of a kind as yet unknown in the chancery.[1] It bears two endorsements made by two different hands. The first says that at the end of the parliament this petition must come before all the justices; the second says that it is agreed by the council that a writ shall be framed to suit the petitioner's case.[2] From this it would seem that towards the end of the parliament, the various committees having done their work, full meetings of the council were held for the discussion of novel and arduous cases. We have seen above how on 5 April the Bishop of Byblos found at least thirty-three men assembled in one place to hear his petition.

(b) *The parliament rolls and the petitions.* However, we must not hope that any study of our roll, however careful, will enable us to set in their true chronological order all the acts done in this parliament. We have but too good reason to believe that a parliament roll is not in the very strictest sense of the term a contemporary record, and that it does not always say first what happened first. In one instance this is clear enough. Our roll begins with the proclamation concerning the delivery of petitions. This is immediately followed by the proclamation of 21 March, which sends all but the king's councillors back to their homes. From this we must not infer that all the subsequent entries on the roll represent events which occurred after that day. On the contrary we have seen that already on 7 March the king had answered a considerable number of petitions. What is more, a glance at the patent or the close roll will show us that long before the 21st the chancery was busily engaged in issuing the writs which carried into execution the responses given to the petitions. Thus, to take one example, we find on the third membrane of our roll an entry telling us how a favourable reply was given to a request by Robert Fitz Walter concerning a chapel in London which had formerly been a synagogue of the Jews; and then on the patent roll we find that Robert had got his writ as early as

---

[1] *Memoranda de Parliamento*, no. 251.

[2] This is just such a case as is contemplated by that famous clause, Stat. West. II, c. 24. The clerks of the chancery will not make a new writ, so the matter is brought before 'the next parliament', and the writ is provided by the 'jurisperiti'.

8 March. We may perhaps suppose that the first membrane with its account of the dissolution of the assembly was prefixed by way of frontispiece to a roll that had been already made up; but we have other reasons for suspecting that the larger part of our parliament roll is in a certain sense a secondhand record. We shall probably come to the conclusion that the entries on the roll stand to the endorsed petitions in the relation of copies to original documents.

Already we have said that on the back of the petition we may generally find the word *Irrotulatur* in some abbreviated form. This, we take it, has been put there by the clerk who wrote the parliament roll. It means, 'I have enrolled this petition and answer'. He did not sit writing his roll in the room in which the petitions were being heard. They were brought to him as they were 'expedited', perhaps at the close of each day's session, and his *Irrotulatur* serves as a 'tick' to show which of them he has already entered on his roll. Then he sends the originals to the chancery. In the margin of the roll, whenever that margin is still undecayed, we may read opposite almost every entry that concerns a petition, *Lib' in Canc'*, which we may expand into *Liberatur in Cancellariam*. The clerk having done with the petitions sends them off to the chancery, and we may say puts a 'tick' on his roll to show that this has been done. Then in the chancery the original endorsed petition will be the warrant for further proceedings. The chancellor will seal some patent writ or some close writ, or, it may be, some charter and vouch his warrant for so doing by the words *per petitionem de consilio*, or *per petitionem retornatam de consilio*. He finds his authority not in the entry on the parliament roll, which perhaps is not in his custody, but in the original endorsed petition. The endorsement itself is the order that has been made, the entry on the roll is a copy of that order. We are putting no slight upon the parliament roll by saying this and must hasten to add that the roll now before us shows every sign of having been drawn up while the work of hearing petitions was still in progress. To take one example, on the sixth membrane of the roll we read how an addition was made to the response given to a petition of the prior of Bridlington. That petition has been reported on the third membrane, and looking back to the report of it we find that the additional words stated on the sixth membrane have also been introduced by way of postscript into the entry on the third membrane.[1] The third

---

[1] *Memoranda de Parliamento*, nos. 49, 170.

membrane of our roll, therefore, had been written before the addition was made to the response that had been given to the prior. Still it seems that the endorsement itself and not the entry on the roll should be considered as the first hand and the authoritative document.

This may serve to explain a remarkable fact in the history of the parliament rolls. To all seeming the practice of enrolling such petitions as those which are entered on the roll that is now before us was abandoned early in the course of the fourteenth century. Such rolls as we have of Edward II's day are very like this roll, that is to say, they are largely occupied by the petitions of private persons who are seeking redress or favours at the hands of the king or at the hands of the king and his council. On later rolls we may find petitions enough; we shall find many petitions presented by one or more of the estates, and also a few petitions which the estates have in effect made their own; but we shall not find, at least not in any number, petitions addressed by private persons to the king or the king and council. We have every reason to believe that such petitions were still presented, for large quantities of them still exist, and some of them have been printed, also that they were presented in parliament, for we find auditors still appointed to hear them; but they are not entered on the parliament roll. If the printed book be a safe guide, there is no parliament roll even of Edward III's day that in this most important respect resembles our roll.[1] The explanation of this we take to be that the enrolment of the petition and its response is all along somewhat of a luxury, for it is not the entry on the roll but the writing on the back of the original petition that serves as a warrant for all subsequent proceedings.[2]

[1] If the printed *Rotuli Parliamentorum* give a different impression, this is because their editors have hardly distinguished with sufficient emphasis the matter that they took, at first or second hand, from parliament rolls, from the matter which they took, at first or second hand, from the original petitions. I do not think that they used, at first or second hand, as many as 1600 petitions, while the two classes of 'Ancient Petitions' and 'Ancient Petitions —Exchequer' contain together about 16,000 documents.

[2] See Hale, *Jurisdiction of the House of Lords*, p. 64: 'Some [petitions] were delivered over by the receivers of petitions either to the *consilium regis* or the *auditores petitionum* and by them indorsed. And these petitions are not entered on the parliament roll, but were entered [that is, were preserved] *in bundellis petitionum parliamenti* with their answers.' This seems to describe correctly the practice which obtained from Edward III's day onwards; but in earlier days the petitions disposed of by the auditors or by the council were not only endorsed but also enrolled; at least so it seems to me.

We may venture on one other speculation. May it not be that the many sad gaps which occur in the series of parliament rolls are due partly to the fact that at many parliaments, even of the later years of Edward I, no roll was made, and that if a roll was made, it was not treated as being of very high value?[1] The suggestion has been offered that many early rolls were deliberately destroyed by kings who wished to be quit of uncomfortable precedents. But this hardly accords with the nature of those rolls which have come down to us. By far the greater part of them is filled by what we may call private petitions, and no great store may have been set by them because what they recorded was sufficiently recorded elsewhere. If any dispute arose about a petition, the original could be found upon the chancery file, and possibly the reason why our oldest parliament rolls come from the exchequer and not from the chancery is that they were intended to serve as a check on a chancellor who had got the original documents and was bound to execute the orders endorsed upon them. Then a statute would go on to the statute roll, an ordinance would go on to the patent or the close roll, while as to the *placita*, those heard by the king in parliament were sometimes put upon the 'coram rege' roll, the roll of the king's bench.[2] May it not be then that the first parliament roll was a somewhat superfluous document? At any rate it is a most remarkable fact that we have at this day got most of the membranes that were used by the maker of the Vetus Codex and very few membranes that he did not use. Miserably defective though our series may seem, it may be nearly as perfect as it was in the middle of the fourteenth century; it may perhaps be nearly as perfect as it ever was.

(c) *Petitions are to king and council.* The petitions of which our roll speaks are neither petitions by parliament nor yet are they petitions addressed to parliament. We see at once that they are very different from those petitions of the commons (*petitions de la commune, petitions des communes*) which will occupy the greater part of almost any

---

[1] [For a close examination of the early records of the parliaments see Richardson and Sayles in *B.I.H.R.* vols. v and vi (1927–9), and their introduction to *Rotuli Parliamentorum Anglie hactenus inediti* (Camden Series, 1935).]

[2] Hale, *Jurisdiction*, p. 53: 'And it is observable that most of the great cases, which are recorded *inter placita parliamenti E. i.*, which were in their nature cognizable by the king's bench, are likewise entered *inter placita coram rege*, as if transacted and judged in that court.'

parliament roll of Edward III's day. But again they are not addressed to 'parliament', or to 'the lords of parliament', or to either house of parliament. They are addressed either 'to the king' or 'to the king and his council'. In a certain sense they are parliamentary petitions, they are presented in or at a parliament. But at present 'parliament' or 'a parliament' is not conceived as a body that can be petitioned. A parliament is rather an act than a body of persons. One cannot present a petition to a colloquy, to a debate. It is but slowly that this word is appropriated to colloquies of a particular kind,[1] namely, those which the king has with the estates of his realm, and still more slowly that it is transferred from the colloquy to the body of men whom the king has summoned. As yet any meeting of the king's council that has been solemnly summoned for general business seems to be a parliament.[2] These petitions are not addressed to parliament, nor are they addressed to the assembled estates, nor are they addressed to the earls, barons, and prelates. They are addressed either simply to the king or to the king and his council. The formal title for them which is in use in the chancery is 'petitiones de consilio', 'council petitions'.

When we examine the character of these petitions we soon see that for the more part they were not fit subjects for discussion in a large assembly. They do not ask for anything that could be called legislation; the responses that are given to them are in no sort 'private acts of parliament'. Generally the boon that is asked for

[1] [The thesis of Richardson and Sayles that *parliamentum* had acquired a technical meaning before the accession of Edward I has been forcibly contested by Powicke, *Henry III and the Lord Edward*, p. 341, and by Plucknett, who considers the term still equivocal in 1336. See *The English Government at Work, 1327–1336* (Cambridge, Mass., 1940), vol. I, pp. 82–90.]*

[2] Stubbs, *Const. Hist.* §230: 'The name of parliament, the king's parliament, belonged to the sessions of each of the three bodies thus distinguished, the terminal session of the select council, the session of the great council, the session of the commune consilium of the three estates.' Langlois, *Revue Historique*, vol. XLII, p. 90: 'Parlement, ce mot vague, synonyme barbare, à l'origine, d'assemblée et de *colloquium*, s'est précisé vers la même époque en Angleterre et en France.' The personification of 'parliament', which enables us to say that laws are made by, and not merely in, parliament, is a slow and subtle process. The same process is now at work upon other words; we begin to personify the Church Congress and so forth; even our 'meetings' pass resolutions. As to the word 'council', it is important to remember that in the Middle Ages no distinction was or could be drawn between 'council' and 'counsel'; both were *consilium*. [On the word 'parliament', see Langlois, reviewing the *Memoranda* in *E.H.R.* (1894), pp. 755 ff., and H. G. Richardson on 'The Origins of Parliament', *Trans. R. Hist. Soc.* (1928).]**

is one which the king without transcending his legal powers might either grant or deny. Sometimes we may say that, if the facts are truly stated by the petitioner, the king is more or less strictly bound by the rules of common honesty to give him some relief: The king owes him wages, or his lands have been wrongfully seized by the king's officers. At other times what is asked for is pure grace and favour: The petitioner owes the king money and asks that he may be allowed to pay it by instalments, or that in consideration of his poverty part of his debt may be forgiven, or perhaps the University of Cambridge asks that the king will found a college.[1] As yet no hard line is drawn between the true petition of right which shall be answered by a *Fiat justitia* and all other petitions. 'Right' and 'grace' shade off into each other by insensible degrees, and there is a wide field for governmental discretion. Probably there would be an outcry if the religious houses could not pretty easily obtain licences for the acquisition of a reasonable quantity of land; if the nobleman who is going abroad were not suffered to appoint a general attorney; if the burghers of this or that town could not without much difficulty get leave to tax themselves and their neighbours by way of murage, pontage, or pavage; still, in any particular case the request may be refused and no reason given for the refusal.

(*d*) *The responses to the petitions.* Further, we see that the response to the petition seldom gave to the suppliant all that he wanted. He had only, we may say, 'made a *prima facie* case' for relief, and he obtained only a preliminary order. He did not get what he wanted, he was merely put in the way of getting it. Hale has stated this matter very well:

But although the council received the petitions from the hands of the receivers, yet they rarely (if at all) exercised any decision or decisive jurisdiction upon them, but only a kind of deliberative power, or rather direction, transmitting them to the proper courts, places, or persons where they were proper to be decided.... Hence it is, that most of the answers that the council gave were in the nature of remissions of the petitions to those persons or courts that had properly the cognizance of the causes.[2]

That is so; but it does not imply that, had there been no petitions, those persons or courts would have been competent to entertain

---

[1] [The enrolment, answer, petition and endorsement are given below (p. 135).]
[2] *Jurisdiction*, pp. 67–8.

those causes or to have given relief to the aggrieved. These petitions and responses are not nugatory. Nothing in the age that we are studying is more remarkable than the narrowly limited powers of the courts of law, of the exchequer, of the chancery, more especially in all such matters as concern the king. The courts of law can in general only entertain such causes as are laid before them by a writ issued from the chancery. For ordinary cases the chancery has a store of 'writs of course', and no doubt they are issued as a mere matter of routine upon receipt of the proper fees; but if anything that is in the least unusual is required, the chancellor will do nothing without a warrant from the king or council, and this warrant will be carefully noted at the foot of the writ. Some day, when the excellent work of calendaring the patent and close rolls has been completed, we shall know how much and how little a chancellor dared to do without an express warrant; apparently he dared do but little. This roll of ours contains a memorandum telling how on 6 April 'in full parliament' (it was a full parliament though the assembly of the estates had been dissolved a fortnight ago) the king prohibited his chancellor, William Hamilton, from issuing letters of protection for men who were in Ireland.[1] At present the warrant upon which the chancellor proceeds may well be oral instructions given to him immediately by the king, or brought to him by a member of the council, by John of Banstead, Henry Percy, the Bishop of Durham, Aymer de Valence, the Earl of Lincoln, or it may be a writ under the privy seal, or again it may be an endorsed petition.[2] Hence the need for so many petitions. As to the exchequer, the man who wants any relief there which is not to be had as a mere matter of routine must petition the king, and if his petition receives a favourable reply, even this will not send him directly to the exchequer; on the

---

[1] *Memoranda de Parliamento*, no. 459.

[2] I understand the note *per ipsum Regem* to mean at this time, 'My warrant is the king's word of mouth heard by me'; *per ipsum Regem nunciante J. de Benstede*, 'I act upon an oral message brought to me from the king by John of Banstead'; *per breve de privato sigillo*, 'For this I have a writ under the privy seal'; *per consilium*, 'I heard the council authorise me to do this'; *per petitionem de consilio* or *per petitionem retornatam de consilio*, 'I rely upon the endorsement of a petition presented to the council'. The 'sign manual' does not belong to this age. [For the beginning of the sign manual, under Edward III, see Tout, *Administrative History*, vol. v, p. 61; for various forms of chancery warrant, see Maxwell-Lyte, *Historical Notes on the use of the Great Seal of England* (1926), pp. 141 ff., 179 ff.]

contrary it will send him first to the chancery for a writ directed to the treasurer and barons.[1] The king has a very tight and immediate control not only over all purely governmental affairs, but also over all 'administrative justice'. This control is exercised for him in his 'parliaments' by his council or by committees of his council, the greater cases and those which have most of 'grace' in them being reserved for his own hearing. The exchequer, the financial department, is controlled by the chancery, the secretarial department, and the chancery is controlled by king and council. Often enough the man who wishes for relief in the exchequer must go first to the council for an endorsement and then to the chancery for a writ. There is already a great deal of what an impatient reader may call circumlocution and red tape. The petition will perhaps in the first instance be endorsed with a *Coram Rege*; it will then be taken before the king and another endorsement will be made upon it; a note of it will then be made upon the parliament roll; then it will be delivered into the chancery; from the chancery a writ will be sent to the exchequer but not until it has been copied on the close roll; when it gets to the exchequer, copies of it will be made by the remembrancers upon their memoranda rolls; and after all this the treasurer and barons will only begin to consider whether justice requires that the suppliant should have any relief. All this formalism is worthy of study; it is the necessary groundwork for ministerial responsibility and government by discussion.

The petitioner, we have said, had only 'to make a *prima facie* case'. Occasionally we find him sending in some evidence along with his petition, for example, a copy of a charter, or of an inquisition. This, however, is rare, and a petition hardly ever ends with a formal offer of proof such as that which every plaintiff makes in the courts of law. Still it seems plain that those who heard the petitions must have had before them more than the suppliant's bare and unsworn word about the facts of his case. True that they were seldom going to give him any final relief; usually they would do no more than set some inquiry going in the courts of law, the chancery or the exchequer. But then the institution of such inquiries cannot possibly have been a mere matter of course; had it been such, a clerk of the chancery might have been set to endorse the petitions with cut and dried formulas.

---

[1] See the learned and triumphant argument of Lord Somers in The Bankers' Case, *State Trials*, vol. xiv, p. 1.

The truth probably is that as regards the king's interests—and it is just because the king has some interest in the matter that most of these petitions are presented—the council is exceedingly well informed; potentially it is almost omniscient. In these parliaments the whole governmental force of England is brought into a focus. Not only are all the great officers there, but most of their principal subordinates are there or within call. A petitioner can hardly make a statement about the king's finances, the king's estates, or even the course of justice, that cannot at once be checked, if not by one of the auditors, then by some judge, clerk, remembrancer or escheator who is close at hand, or by a few recent rolls which are within easy reach. This, we take it, is what is meant by that 'trying' of petitions of which we hear. The petitions reserved for the king himself are not to be placed before him until they have been sufficiently 'tried', that is to say, he expects that when a petition is brought before him there will be some minister at hand to say whether there is any truth in the petitioner's allegations. We know that the work of hearing petitions was long and laborious; it had threatened to deprive the king and his chief advisers of any leisure for the great affairs of state; and we may well believe that the four hundred and fifty endorsements recorded by our roll represent the work of many hours.

When a petition was to be heard, did the petitioner appear either in person or by attorney prepared to supplement or support by oral argument the written statement of his grievance? Probably this was unusual, but still we seem to have evidence that the petitioner's presence might be required and that his petition might be 'dismissed for want of prosecution'. An entry on our roll tells us how one William of Whitewell presented a petition complaining of the misconduct of John Bacon, a clerk of the court, who was seemingly lying in gaol for his offences, and by way of response we have this: 'William of Whitewell being solemnly called has not prosecuted this petition, therefore let the said John go quit thereof for the present.'[1] Then the next entry is concerned with another charge against this same John Bacon. Ralph of Cokethorpe accuses him of making fraudulent erasures on the plea rolls and asks for relief. 'Roger de Fresnes', we are told, 'has presented this petition before the council on Ralph's behalf, but on being asked whether he is Ralph's attorney, he says that he is not;

[1] *Memoranda de Parliamento*, no. 266.

therefore he is told to cause the said Ralph to appear and prosecute the petition should Ralph wish to do so.' 'Afterwards', says our record, 'it was testified by [the chief and another justice of the king's bench] that Ralph came before them and confessed that it was not by his authority that Roger prosecuted the said petition, nor had he any complaint to make. Therefore let the said John go quit thereof for the present.'[1] These two cases stand a little outside the general run of petitions, in that a very definite complaint is brought against a royal officer, but still it is evident that at least in some instances a petitioner was expected to be at Westminster by himself or his attorney, and that his petition might be rejected if he was not there to explain and support it.

(e) *Petitions by communities.* Sometimes the petition comes from an individual, sometimes from a community. Of petitions presented by communities we have a considerable number. To say nothing of the religious houses and the two universities, we have petitions by the communities of boroughs and by the communities of counties. And here we may perhaps see one of the duties of the knight who appears on behalf of a shire and of the representative burgess: he brings in and, it may be, urges by oral argument the petitions of that community which has sent him to the parliament. Then, again, we seem to have petitions which must have been drawn up during the parliament. Some instances we have already mentioned. 'The bishops, abbots, earls, barons, and others of the realm' ask the king's aid in collecting their scutages. 'The archbishops, bishops, prelates, earls, barons, and other good men of the land' ask that they may tallage such of the ancient demesnes of the crown as are in their hands. Such petitions seem to imply meetings at Westminster of those who were interested in them: they may imply regular sessions of the lords and the commons. By some resolution or another someone must have been authorised to write down these demands on strips of parchment. But so far as we can see these petitions are treated like the other petitions; on the parliament roll they are indiscriminately mixed up with the other petitions. We pass from a petition of the rector of Winchelsea, asking that the king will not take quite all the tithes of his church, to a petition presented by the magnates, and thence to a petition by the Abbot of Osney concerning certain financial operations in which he has taken part on the king's behalf. Then again wedged

[1] *Memoranda de Parliamento*, no. 267.

between a petition of Roland of Okestead and a petition of the citizens of Lincoln we find two petitions which seem to come from the assembled commons and to be the outcome of their deliberations. 'The poor men of England' complain that juries are corrupted by the rich, and that ecclesiastical judges meddle with temporal suits.[1] In each case the king civilly refuses to do anything. If juries are corrupt, those who are injured can have a writ of attaint; a writ of prohibition will confine the courts christian within their proper bounds. By no sharp line can the petitions of the assembled lords and commoners be marked off from the general mass of those petitions which are to be 'expedited' in the parliament by the king and his council. At a somewhat later date the line will be drawn; the petitions of the assembled commons, the petitions of 'the community of the land', will be enrolled along with the king's answers to them; petitions addressed to either of the two houses will be enrolled, if they have received the assent of both houses and of the king; but the ordinary petitions presented to the king and council by those who have grievances will not be enrolled, though as of old many of them will be answered in parliament by committees of auditors. *

(*f*) *Action of the commoners.* As to what was done by the assembled commoners during the three weeks that they spent at Westminster, we shall hardly get beyond guess-work. All that we learn from our roll is, first, that they joined in a petition with the magnates about the exportation of the wealth of the monasteries, to which petition the king gave his assent, though he did not at once convert it into a statute; and secondly, that they presented two petitions of their own, which were refused. The king, so far as we know, did not ask them for money, nor did he desire their consent to any new law. The doctrine that in these days the representatives of the shires and towns were called to parliament not in order that they might act in concert on behalf of the commons of England, but in order that each might represent before the king in council the grievances and the interests of the particular community, county or borough, that sent him thither,[2] may easily be pressed too far, but we shall

---

[1] *Memoranda de Parliamento*, no. 472. The 'pauperes homines terrae Angliæ' seem to be the assembled commons. The original French petition may have run somewhat as follows: 'A nostre seigneur le Rei prient les povres gentz de sa terre.'

[2] [For a sound criticism of this doctrine see G. L. Haskins, 'Petitions of representatives in the parliaments of Edward I', *E.H.R.* (1938).]

probably think that there is no little truth in it, if we ask what the knights and burgesses were doing while the king and his councillors were slowly disposing of this great mass of petitions, many of which were presented by shires and boroughs. Official testimony the council can easily obtain; but it wants unofficial testimony also; it desires to know what men are saying in remote parts of England about the doings of sheriffs, escheators, and their like, and the possibilities of future taxation have to be considered. Then, again, there are many appointments to be made; for example, it is the fashion at this time to entrust a share in the work of delivering the county gaol to some knight of the county, very often to one of the knights who is representing or has represented that county at a parliament. Without denying that the germ of a 'house' of commons already exists, without denying that its members hold meetings, discuss their common affairs and common grievances, without denying that Edward has encouraged them to do this—at the present moment he has a quarrel with the clergy, at least with the archbishop, and no doubt is glad when the assembled commons protest that there are abuses in the church—without denying all this, we may still believe that the council often gives audience, advice, instructions to particular knights and burgesses. After all we have to fall back upon the words of the writ of summons: the commoners have been told to come in order that they may do what shall be ordained.

(5) *Judicial business*

We pass to judicial business, noticing that the line between this and the hearing of petitions is not very sharp.

(a) *The Placita.* The *Placita* which came before this parliament were few but miscellaneous.

In the first place we have the very famous case of Nicholas Segrave.[1] Segrave and Cromwell had been serving with the king in his Scottish campaign; Segrave had brought an accusation against Cromwell and a judicial combat had been waged between them in the king's court.[2] Then, however, Segrave, perhaps because he knew that the king would stop the duel, challenged his adversary

---

[1] *Memoranda de Parliamento*, no. 449.

[2] ['Waged' is used here in the technical sense of giving an undertaking to prove your charge by your body or otherwise as the court may determine, at an appointed time.]

to fight him in the court of the king of France; he withdrew himself from the English host and was endeavouring to make his way to France when he was captured. He confessed this grave offence—it was nothing less than treason. Edward then asked his council what was the punishment meet for such a crime. Their answer was—Death. The king, however, of his special grace was content that Segrave should find seven manucaptors who would undertake that he would render himself to prison if ever the king should call upon him to do so.[1]

As regards the tribunal before which Segrave stood we can say this much: The sheriff of Northampton was told to bring him before the king in the forthcoming parliament at Westminster, so soon as the king should arrive there: He made his appearance 'in full parliament in the presence of the king, the archbishop of Canterbury, and divers earls, barons and others of the king's council': When sentence was to be pronounced the king asked the advice of 'the earls, barons' (not, it will be observed, the prelates, for there was like to be a judgment of blood), 'and others of his council': it is said by a chronicler that they discussed the matter for three days:[2] Segrave's manucaptors appeared 'before the king and his council' on 29 March and executed their bond on the 31st in the presence of the treasurer, three other bishops, the two chief justices, and others. The assembly of the estates had been dissolved on the 21st. It is very possible, however, that the trial took place while all the magnates were still at Westminster; Segrave was a baron and had been summoned as such to the parliament.[3]

The citizens of Salisbury had refused to submit to a tallage set upon them by the bishop under the authority of a charter granted to one of his predecessors by Henry III. On 5 March a writ went to the sheriff of Wiltshire bidding him summon the mayor, citizens, and the whole community of the city to be 'before us and our council' at Westminster on Mid Lent Sunday (28 March). On that day four men appeared bearing full powers from the civic com-

---

[1] [See Pollock and Maitland, vol. II, p. 508; and, for the setting and sequel of the case, Powicke, *The Thirteenth Century*, pp. 331–2.]

[2] *Flores Historiarum*, vol. III, p. 122.

[3] Nicholas Kingston, accused of complicity in Segrave's crime, waged his law (*Memoranda de Parliamento*, no. 450). It is said that he made his law on Friday, 2 March. The 2 April was a Friday; the 2 March was a Tuesday and the third day of the parliament. As Segrave had been convicted before Kingston was accused, it seems probable that 2 April is the true date.

munity; two of them were, if we may already use such a phrase, the sitting members for Salisbury, a third had represented the town at a former parliament.[1] They and the bishop plead, and then the matter having been discussed 'before the king and his council', a judgment is pronounced. 'The king wills and commands' that the citizens do pay the tallage on this occasion, while as to the future they must choose between submitting to tallage and abandoning their franchises. They take the latter course, and on 6 April 'before the whole council' the mayor surrendered the mayoralty into the king's hand. It is clear that in this case the trial did not take place until the assembly of the estates had been dissolved.[2]

Next we read how on 13 March certain great folk, all of whom may themselves have been members of the council, undertook in the presence of the treasurer, the chief justice of the king's bench, 'and others of the king's council', to produce Almaric of St Amand and William of Montacute before the king whenever they should be called upon to do so; and then how on the 19th Almaric undertook to produce John of St Amand.[3] Almaric was the governor of Oxford castle, and in and about Oxford castle there had been a serious riot, in which some clerks of the university had taken their full and accustomed share. The subsequent proceedings assumed the form of an information—and, be it noted, an information of felony—lodged by the king's serjeant in the court of king's bench, and one offender of humble rank went to the gallows. As we read the record which tells this picturesque tale, we shall notice that between the king's council and the king's bench there was still in Edward I's day a very close connection.

A citizen of Bayonne, a hostage in the king's hand, had been committed to the care of the citizens of Winchester, but had escaped. For his escape the citizens were to answer by their mayor, bailiffs and six other representatives 'before us and our council in our forthcoming parliament at Westminster' on the last day of February. At that day nine of the Winchester folk appeared 'before the king and his council in the said parliament'. Further proceedings took place on 4 March, and on a yet later day the citizens made fine with the king 'before the king himself and his council'.[4]

(b) *The council and the courts.* Such records as these—and many

---

[1] *Parl. Writs*, vol. I, p. lxxxi.   [2] *Memoranda de Parliamento*, no. 451.
[3] *Ibid.* nos. 452–3.   [4] *Memoranda de Parliamento*, no. 456.

others of a like kind might be cited from other rolls—bring us within sight of an often debated and still debatable question. What in Edward I's day was the jurisdictional competence of the king's council, and in particular what was the relation in matters of judicature between the council and the nascent house of lords?[1]

Perhaps some new light might fall upon this old question were we to view it from what might be called the archivist's standpoint, were we to say for the moment that every one of the high courts in England must have a separate set of rolls. If we take up this not indefensible position, and leave out of sight the chancery and the exchequer and also the courts of the itinerant justices, we shall then hold that Henry III during the last half of his reign has two, and only two, high courts of law. The one of these is 'the bench'; it has a separate set of records, 'the *de banco* rolls'. The other is professedly held before the king himself; it follows him in his movements; it has a separate set of records, 'the *coram rege* rolls'. For ordinary purposes this latter court consists of a few professional justices; later in the reign a chief justice is definitely appointed to hold the pleas *coram rege*; but at any moment this court can be afforced by the presence of the king, of his councillors, of numerous barons and prelates. Now and again its roll will bear as a title 'Pleas before the King and his Council'.[2] It is superior to 'the bench', for it can correct the errors of 'the bench'.[3] Then early in Edward I's reign a further differentiation takes place. The court held *coram rege* when it assumes its everyday shape—that of a tribunal consisting of a few professional justices—becomes 'the king's bench'; what has formerly been 'the bench', though it always preserves this title, becomes, in common parlance, 'the common bench'; at a later day it will be the court of common pleas. But there is a greater change than this. A new set, unfortunately a meagre, disjointed set, of plea rolls (which, however, are not pure plea rolls, for they deal also with petitions and other

[1] [See *Select Cases before the King's Council*, 1243–1482, ed. J. F. Baldwin and I. S. Leadam, Selden Society, 1918; G. O. Sayles, Introduction to *Select Pleas in King's Bench* (Selden Society, 1936), vol. I.]   [2] Hale, *Jurisdiction*, p. 51.
[3] I may perhaps be allowed to refer to what I have elsewhere written about this matter; Bracton's *Note Book*, vol. I, p. 56; *Select Pleas of the Crown*, Selden Society, p. xii. Two points seem to be too easily forgotten. (1) *The Bench* is the formal title, not of the King's Bench, but of the Court of Common Pleas. (2) The two benches were not in all respects courts of co-ordinate jurisdiction; error lay from the Common Pleas to the King's Bench. See Blackstone's *Commentaries*, vol. III, pp. 410–11; Hale, *Jurisdiction*, p. 126.

matters) begins to appear. A court which is to stand above the king's bench is being evolved out of the old court held *coram rege*; its rolls are the 'parliament rolls'. But the process is slow. For a while this highest tribunal is hardly distinct from the king's bench. Every plea in the king's bench is in theory a plea *coram ipso domino rege*, and the rolls of the king's bench never cease to be the *coram rege* rolls. The superior tribunal is rather, if we may so speak, an afforced, an intensified form of the inferior tribunal than a separate court; a plea that is put upon the parliament roll may be put upon the king's bench roll also; the justices of the king's bench are members of the council, and a case heard at a full meeting, a parliament, of the council, is heard by, among others, the justices of the king's bench. A plea may be adjourned from a parliament to the king's bench or from the king's bench to a parliament without breach of continuity.

A new tribunal is evolved, or rather, two tribunals become three. We can see this development taking place in the pages of Bracton and Fleta. Bracton knows but two of those courts of which we are speaking: there are justices resident at the bench; there are yet more exalted justices attending the king's person.[1] Fleta knows three: there are justices resident at the bench; there are other justices who fill the king's own place, but above even them there is another tribunal, 'for the king has his court in his council in his parliaments, in the presence of prelates, earls, barons, nobles, and other learned men, where judicial doubts are determined, and new remedies are established for new wrongs, and justice is done to every one according to his deserts'.[2] Bracton has to account for two sets of rolls; Fleta for three. Whether we ought to say that the highest of the three tribunals is the new one, whether we ought to describe the process as the deposit of a middle tribunal between the lowest and the highest, whether both of these phrases are not too definite and too modern to describe the real facts—these are grave problems which must be left to others. Our imaginary archivist would perhaps say that he could not decide them until

---

[1] Bracton, f. 108.

[2] Fleta, lib. II, c. 2: 'Habet enim Rex curiam suam in consilio suo in parliamentis suis, præsentibus prælatis, comitibus, baronibus, proceribus, et aliis viris peritis, ubi terminatæ sunt dubitationes judiciorum et novis injuriis emersis nova constituuntur remedia, et unicuique justitia, prout meruit, retribuetur ibidem.' In many handwritings *viris peritis* and *iurisperitis* would be indistinguishable.

he had made up his mind on the humbler question whether many parliament rolls have been lost. Our present point must be that before the end of Edward's reign there are three courts each with its roll.

(c) *The highest tribunal.* What is the nature of the highest of these three? Is it council, is it house of lords? Fleta will warn us that we are asking an almost unanswerable question. 'Habet enim Rex curiam suam in consilio suo in parliamentis suis, præsentibus prælatis, comitibus, baronibus, proceribus et aliis viris peritis', that is all that we can safely say. The highest tribunal of the realm is the king in council; it is the king in his council in his parliaments, in the presence of prelates, barons, and other learned men. To deny that it is the king in council is impossible; to deny that it is the king in parliament, or rather that its sessions are parliaments, is impossible.

Events which were still in the future when the great Edward died, decided that the highest ordinary tribunal of the realm should be 'the king in parliament', and that this term should mean the house of lords; they decided that this tribunal should become for the more part but a court of error, and during the rest of the Middle Ages and far into modern times should have exceedingly little to do;[1] they decided also that the king in council should dispense an extraordinary justice and this on a very large scale. If asked to mark the difference between ordinary and extraordinary justice, we can hardly do better at the present moment than place ourselves once more in the archivist's room, and say that the court of ordinary jurisdiction keeps a proper Latin plea roll and that the council keeps none. This is no insignificant detail. When the time has come for abolishing that court of star chamber which is one of the forms that the council has assumed, this will be charged against it as one of its many irregularities—it has no proper Latin plea roll.[2] In the eyes of the lawyers of the seventeenth century this want of a roll goes far to prove that the council board is an upstart tribunal. What has been its strength in time gone by when, having no stiff Latin record to draw up, it could modify its procedure to suit every new want, has become its weakness in the age of Coke and Prynne, an age which demands a parchment title for every unpopular institution.

---

[1] Hale, *Jurisdiction*, chap. xxx; see also Hargrave's Introduction, p. vi.

[2] Stat. 16 Car. I, c. 10: 'And by another statute...it is...enacted...that all pleas...shall be entered and enrolled in Latin.'

Long ago the parliament roll has passed from the custody of the council. Long ago it has become the record of those meetings of the estates of the realm which have acquired an exclusive right to the name of parliaments, and more particularly it has become the record of the house of lords. Long ago the rule has been that those members of the council who are not peers of the realm, but yet are summoned to parliament, are to sit in the house of lords as 'mere assistants', are not to vote, are not to speak unless their opinions are demanded. This being so, we are apt to approach the parliament rolls of Edward I's reign with a certain prejudice in our minds. They ought, so we think, to be the records of the estates of the realm; in so far as they are judicial records, they ought to be the records of the house of lords. It is hard to think away out of our heads a history which has long lain in a remote past but which once lay in the future; it is hard to be ever remembering that such ancient terms as *house of lords* and *peers of the realm* were once new terms; it is hard to look at the thirteenth century save by looking at it through the distorting medium of the fourteenth. And so we are apt to approach our earliest parliament rolls with a belief that they ought to be rolls of the house of lords and not rolls of the king's council, that the supreme tribunal of England ought to be the house of lords and not the king's council, that whatever upon our record makes against this belief should be explained away as irregular or anomalous.

Even if he had settled opinions about debatable questions of constitutional history, it would be wrong for the editor of such a book as this is to thrust them forward. The most that he can legitimately do is to provide materials for the formation of opinions. In so doing, however, it may perhaps be lawful and desirable that he should remind his readers of some facts that are like to be forgotten. And in the present case he may be allowed to say once more that we have very few parliament rolls of Edward I's reign, to remark that his son's reign was filled with momentous events, and to plead that those events may not be suffered to cast their shadow over the past. We must judge the rolls of Edward I's reign on their own merits, without reference to the parliament rolls of his grandson's, or of any later, reign. As regards the matter that is now before us, the jurisdictional competence of the parliaments, there seem to be some special reasons why this warning should not be neglected.

We are dealing with something that is new. However ancient may be the roots whence the jurisdiction of 'the king in his council in his parliaments' draws its nourishment, it is a new thing that men should see three different tribunals rising one above the other; it is a new thing that they should see a yet higher court above that court which is held in theory *coram ipso domino rege*. The competence of this highest court is as yet indefinite. Fleta uses vague words about it. He has a fairly clear view of the competence of the king's bench; it hears criminal causes; it corrects the errors and false judgments of all justices, except when such matters are brought before the king himself and his council or before auditors specially assigned for the purpose. But of the justice that is done by the king 'in his council in his parliaments' we must speak loosely: Judicial doubts are there decided, new remedies are provided for new wrongs, and justice is done to every one according to his merits. We can see, however, that this tribunal is not solely a court of error; it has a far wider power than the house of lords will have in later days. This doctrine is fully borne out by the parliament rolls. The causes which come before the parliaments do not usually come there by writ of error. The jurisdiction that is exercised is more commonly than not a jurisdiction of first instance. If we ask why a case comes before a parliament rather than before the king's bench or the common bench, often we can give no certain answer. We may say perhaps—to take examples from our own roll—that Nicholas Segrave is tried in a parliament because he is a baron charged with treason; but why should the citizens of Winchester be haled before a parliament for suffering a prisoner to escape, and why should not the Bishop of Salisbury urge his claim to tallage the men of Salisbury before one of the two benches, or even before the exchequer? Seemingly all that we dare say is that the causes heard in parliament are important causes, important because they concern the king, or because they concern very great men, or because they involve grave questions of public law, or because they are unprecedented. We must not miss the 'equitableness' of this tribunal. When Fleta says that it provides new remedies for new wrongs, and that justice is done to every man according to his deserts, he means that this supreme court can look at 'the merits of the case' with some disregard for technicalities. We are dealing with a court that has large, indefinite powers.

And then we are dealing with Edward I, the wise and vigorous king. Under his hand institutions which to our eyes seem to have in them many flaws, flaws which may easily become yawning clefts, are doing their appointed work without much friction. We can hardly look back to his time through the fourteenth century without imagining that there must be some jealous dislike of the council, an aristocratic jealousy on the part of the nobles, a professional jealousy on the part of the judges and common lawyers. But do we really see this? If not, then our problem as to the constitution of the supreme tribunal becomes simpler. It may be further simplified if we try to make it a concrete problem. Indubitably this supreme tribunal is the council. The question whether it is also the house of lords may be divided into two. First, we ought to ask whether every prelate and baron had a right to sit in the council though he had not been invited to do so. Secondly, we ought to ask whether those members of the council who were neither prelates nor barons were fully competent members of the tribunal.

To neither of these questions must we here give a dogmatic answer, but in connection with the first it may be right that we should ask a yet further question, namely, whether we are not introducing an inappropriate idea and burdening ourselves with an unnecessary anachronism when we talk of any man having a right to sit in this or any other court of law? We must put duty in the first line, right in the second. We have learnt to do this when discussing the constitution of those county courts which send knights to the house of commons; must we not also do it when we are discussing the constitution of the house of lords and of the council? In 1305 the baron, who had come from Yorkshire or Devonshire, had been compelled to spend three weeks in London at his own cost, for he was paid no wages. Did he very much want to spend another three weeks there hearing dreary petitions concerning the woes of Scots and Gascons? At a later time a desire for political power and for social pre-eminence will make the English baron eager to insist on his right to a writ of summons, eager to take a part, however subordinate, in all that is done by the house of lords. But in Edward I's day the baronage is hardly as yet a well-defined body, and it may be that there are many men who, unable to foresee that their 'blood' is being 'ennobled' for ever and ever, are not pleased when they receive a writ which tells them that, leaving their homes and affairs, they must journey and labour in the king's service, and all this at their own cost. Thus for many years one great constitutional question can remain in suspense. It is not raised, no one wishes to raise it. So long as the king does not impose taxes or issue statutes without the consent of the baronage, the baron hopes that the king will mind his own business (and it is his business to govern the realm) and allow other folk to mind theirs.[1]

Of the second of our two questions but one word can here be said. If we fix our gaze on the council which remains in constant session and 'in full parliament' at Westminster for several weeks after the generality of prelates and barons have departed, we shall have some difficulty in believing that those councillors who are neither prelates nor barons are taking but a subordinate part in the work that is done; for example, that when the council is sitting as a judicial tribunal, the opinions of the two chief justices, Brabazon and Hengham, are of less importance than the opinions of two barons who are no lawyers. Once more let us remember that until very lately the jurisdiction of the king's council has been regarded as being substantially the same thing as the jurisdiction of that court over which Brabazon presides.[2]

CONCLUSION

Perhaps more than enough has already been said about these controverted matters; but it seemed necessary to remind readers, who are conversant with the 'parliaments' of later days, that about the parliaments of Edward I's time there is still much to be discovered, and that should they come to the opinion that a session of the king's council is the core and essence of every *parliamentum*, that the documents usually called 'parliamentary petitions' are petitions to the king and his council, that the auditors of petitions are committees of the council, that the rolls of parliament are the records of the business done by the council—sometimes with, but much more often without, the concurrence of the estates of the realm—that the highest tribunal in England is not a general assembly of barons and prelates, but the king's council, they will not be departing very far from the path marked out by books that are already classical.[3]

---

[1] [For evidence, however, as to the active co-operation of the baronage in Edwardian parliaments, see Powicke, *The Thirteenth Century*, pp. 343-8.]

[2] Hale, *Jurisdiction*, pp. 59, 156, holds that the judges were in Edward I's day the most important members of the tribunal which heard pleas in parliament.

[3] The one point about which I venture to differ from what seems to be the general opinion of modern historians (and I am uncertain as to whether this

F

Those who have done most for the constitutional history of the middle ages would probably be the first to admit that much more remains to be done. And much more can and will be done in due course. Only a very small portion of the records that bear on the history of the council of the thirteenth and fourteenth centuries has yet been published.[1] It is true that the parliament rolls are in print, but we have no such rolls for Henry III's reign, very few from the days of the first two Edwards, and even when we have a parliament roll it does not tell us by any means all that we ought to know if we are to know the council. On the other hand there is an inexhaustible supply of rolls of other kinds. The contents of this book, for example, represent but a little part of the writing that was done at Westminster in consequence of one particular session of the council, that which was held in the spring of the year 1305. It would have been easy to have filled another volume with documents occasioned by that session, writs of all sorts and kinds issued *per consilium* or *per petitionem de consilio*, including the very numerous letters that were sent to Gascony, inquisitions of all sorts and kinds that were made under the authority of those writs, proceedings before the king's bench and proceedings in the exchequer which took place because the council had ordered them. I am persuaded that if the charter, patent and close rolls, the privy

difference is real) is that I cannot find in the official language of Edward I's time any warrant for holding that the king has more than one *concilium*, or rather *consilium*; any warrant, that is, for holding that this term is applied to two or three different bodies of persons, which are conceived as permanently existing bodies, or any warrant for holding that the term should be qualified by some adjective, such as *commune*, or *magnum*, or *ordinarium*. We might like to ask the question whether every prelate and every baron is a member of *the* magnum consilium, whether every representative of a shire or a borough is a member of *the* commune consilium regni. The Latin language knows no article definite or indefinite; the language of the time knows no difference between counsel and council. One thing is clear: an order sending to their homes the prelates, earls, barons, knights, burgesses, and other commoners, 'sauve les Evesques, Contes et Barouns, Justices et autres, qui sount du Counseil nostre seigneur le Roy' is an intelligible order.* [Maitland's statement here differs hardly at all from that of Stubbs in §§ 230–1 of the *Constitutional History*. On the question of council or councils, his view is now generally accepted.]

[1] [Since Maitland wrote, the series of calendars of the medieval close, patent and charter rolls have been completed. The curia regis rolls down to 1220 have been printed in full, and a selection of pleas from the *coram rege* rolls is being published by the Selden Society. No comprehensive collection of early council proceedings has been published, nor any memoranda roll of the exchequer later than 1200.]**

seals, the memoranda of the exchequer, and the *coram rege* rolls were used skilfully and in combination, our historians would be able to give us an account of many a session or parliament of the council of which we have not yet heard, to tell us who were present and what business was transacted. The task that has to be performed is indeed a gigantic task, that of calendaring mile after mile of closely written parchment, and fitting thousands of undated documents into their proper places; but it can be accomplished by prolonged, sustained, and well-directed efforts, and it ought to be accomplished. He would be a bold man who said that there is any question about the government of England by Edward I which cannot be answered.

APPENDIX 1*

Ad petitionem Universitatis de Cantebrigia petentis auxilium domini Regis quod ipse velit esse fundator unius domus quam eadem Universitas ordinavit pro pauperibus scolaribus in eadem Universitate commorantibus sustentandis et quod domus illa dotari possit de terris et redditibus usque ad summam xl. lib. vel plus vel minus pro voluntate Regis:—

Ita responsum est: Rex vult certiorari per vicecomitem si sit ad commodum vel ad dampnum Regis.

Ancient Petitions, 13758.

A nostre seignur le Roy qe Deu gard moustrent le Chaunceler, Mestres, e Clers de sa Universite de Cauntebrige par la ou il ount...e purveu pur lestat de Seynt Eglise e profit de la terre al eyde de Deu, une collegion de povres escolers a estre trovez sustenance en la dite Universite, parmy vostre eyde chere Syre si vous plest, e autries almoignes des clers e des lays qe lur voylent pur Deu eyder et [avaun]cer, vous prions pur lamour de Dieu, e les almes vostre piere, miere, cumpaigne e vos auncestres voyllet de cele mesun estre fundur e qe ele seit en vostre proteccion e qe ele puisse estre dowe par purchas en almoignee de ceaux qe les voillent avauncer des terres ou des rentes a la value de quaraunte livrees, ou plus, ou meyns, a vostre vollente, nient countreesteaunt vostre estatuz des teres e tenemens alyenez en morte mein, dount les escolers la demeraunz puissent estre sustenuz, issint qe ceaux escolers soient esluz, receus, demoraunz e governez par le Chaunceler e la fraunchise de la dite Universite, cum autres escolers iloqes estudiaunz.

(*Endorsement*.) Rex vult certiorari per vicecomitem si sit ad commodum vel ad dampnum Regis.

Domino Cancellario.[2]

---

[1] *Memoranda de Parliamento*, no. 50.
[2] At the foot of the back of the petition, by way of address.

4

THE *PLENA POTESTAS* OF ENGLISH PARLIAMENTARY REPRESENTATIVES*

by J. G. Edwards

UNTIL the year 1872, and for nearly six centuries before, the writs ordering the election of knights and burgesses for Parliament directed that the persons chosen should come having 'full and sufficient power to do and consent to those things which then and there by the Common Council of Our said . . . Kingdom . . . shall happen to be ordained upon the aforesaid affairs, so that for want of such power . . . the aforesaid affairs may in no wise remain unfinished'.[1] The purpose of this essay is to consider the significance of the formula and of its long persistence.

It is in 1294 that the formula emerges in its substantially final shape, but it is not in the writs of 1294 that the demand for full power first appears. The history of the demand before 1294 is therefore the first point to be examined. The most convenient starting-place is the well-known assembly of 1254. For that, each shire had to choose two knights from the shire, to come *vice omnium et singulorum*** in the shire, to provide, along with the knights from the other shires, what aid they would give to the king.[2] These words, while implying that the knights were to come as representing their shire, make no specific demand that they should come with full power. The terms used in connexion with Simon de Montfort's two assemblies of 1264 and 1265 are of the same general kind: the knights in 1264 are spoken of as coming *pro toto comitatu*,[3]† and in 1265 as coming *pro communitate comitatus* and *ex parte communitatum comitatuum*.[4]†† So far, the terms used are the same as, or similar to, those used in the plea rolls to describe the capacity in which knights came from the shires to 'bear record' before the king's justices of proceedings in the shire court.[5]

---

1 Anson, *Law and Custom of the Constitution*, i (5th ed.), p. 62.
2 *Peerage Report*, App. i. 13; Stubbs, *S.C.* (9th ed.), p. 366.
3 *Foedera* (ed. 1816), i. 442; Stubbs, *S.C.*, p. 400.
4 *Peerage Report*, App. i. 35.
5 Adams, *Origin of the English Constitution* (enlarged ed.), p. 321.

In 1268, however, a rather different course was being contemplated by the government. The king decided in that year to summon representatives of twenty-seven boroughs to meet the council at Westminster, and ordered the representatives to bring with them letters patent drawn up in accordance with a form enclosed with the writ of summons, and these letters patent were to be sealed with the borough seal. The letters patent whose form was thus prescribed by the government were in fact formal powers of attorney, authorizing the borough representatives to act 'in the name of' the 'whole community' of their respective boroughs. In effect, therefore, the government required that the representatives of the boroughs in 1268 should come with full powers.[1*]

The writs for the two parliaments of 1275 keep to the less explicit formulas of 1264 and 1265. The summons to the spring parliament of 1275 says nothing of the capacity in which the representatives were to come: they were merely summoned *ad tractandum*.[2] The summons for the autumn parliament of that year states that the two knights were to come *pro communitate dicti comitatus*.[3**]

The next available writs, those for the assemblies of 1283, show some interesting variations. Early in the year there were two simultaneous meetings, one at York for the five northern shires, the other at Northampton for the other shires of England. The representatives of the shires and of the boroughs on this occasion were ordered to come *habentes plenariam potestatem pro communitatibus eorundem*.[4†] Here was a specific demand for full powers. Later in the year, however, representatives of shires and boroughs were called to an assembly at Shrewsbury to witness the trial and punishment of Prince David. On this occasion nothing was said about full powers: the representatives were merely summoned *nobiscum . . . locuturi*.[5]

The next surviving writs are those summoning representatives of the shires to an assembly in the summer of 1290.

---

[1] 'Et nos quicquid ipsi in premissis nomine nostro fecerint ratum habebimus et acceptum' is the closing sentence of the prescribed form of letters patent. The documents are printed, with comments, by Mr. G. O. Sayles in *E.H.R.* xl. 580–5.††

[2] *E.H.R.* xxv. 236; Stubbs, *S.C.*, pp. 441–2.

[3] Stubbs, *Const. Hist.* ii. (4th ed.), pp. 234–5, n. 5.

[4] Ibid., i. 10; Stubbs, *S.C.*, p. 458.   [5] *Parl. Writs*, i. 16; Stubbs, *S.C.*, p. 461.

These demanded that the persons chosen should come *cum plena potestate pro se et tota communitate comitatus.*[1]*

Next come the writs of 1294, to which reference has already been made. These called for knights to come from the shires *cum plena potestate pro se et tota communitate comitatus ... ita quod pro defectu potestatis huiusmodi idem negotium infectum non remaneat.*[2] The additional sentence, *ita quod pro defectu potestatis huiusmodi*, &c., was obviously intended to draw attention to the preceding demand for full power. From 1294 onwards, both the demand for full power and also the sentence emphasizing the necessity of such power were equally part of the normal and traditional form in which representatives were summoned to the English Parliament.**

That the emergence and definition of this demand for full power were the outcome of a gradual process is evident. Has the fact any significance, or is it merely a negligible accident? The answer to this question depends partly upon our answer to a further question. Is there any reason to suppose that contemporaries attached any importance to the demand for full power—did those who made the demand think it of any importance, and did those to whom the demand was addressed think it important?

Let us consider first those who made the demand. The framers of the writs were the chancery clerks: they were skilled lawyers and busy practical administrators, and *a priori* there is no reason to suppose that they would introduce the demand for so specific and legal a thing as *plena potestas* for no purpose; or that having introduced it, they would over a period make it in varying terms for no reason whatever— they who were ordinarily so respectful of precedent. But there are more than *a priori* indications that the demand for full power was made quite consciously and with some definite purpose, and that the framers of the writs regarded this full power as being a matter of some moment. One indication is the sentence *ita quod pro defectu potestatis huiusmodi idem negotium infectum non remaneat*, which was introduced into the writs from 1294 onwards. Another indication is given by an incident in that same year. The writ of 1294 to the

---

1 *Parl. Writs*, i. 21; Stubbs, *S.C.*, pp. 472-3.
2 *Parl. Writs*, i. 26; Stubbs, *S.C.*, pp. 476-7.

sheriffs summoning from each shire two knights with full power is dated 8 October. There was also directed to the sheriffs a second writ, dated 9 October, ordering them to cause to be chosen from each shire, in addition to the two knights with full power, two other knights, who should come to Westminster at the same time as the two knights with full power. But nothing is said about full power in the case of the second pair of knights: they are simply ordered to come *ad audiendum et faciendum quod eis tunc ibidem plenius iniungemus*.[1]* It is therefore evident that the chancery clerks did not demand full power indiscriminately.

We may now consider the views of those to whom this demand for the full power was addressed. For a considerable time after 1294 the borough representatives commonly appeared in Parliament bringing with them a formal document, sealed with the borough seal, stating that the mayor and the whole community of the borough concerned had given them full power to act. A number of these formal 'powers' of the borough representatives still survive in the Public Record Office: they are fairly numerous in the fourteenth century, and some boroughs went on sending them even in the fifteenth century.[2] We also find that at first the sheriffs, too, in returning the names of the persons chosen to be knights of the shire, not infrequently add the formal statement that the knights chosen have received full power from the community of the shire concerned.[3] The officials in the constituencies, therefore, recognized that the demand for full power was not an empty or negligible formality.

The demand also attracted the attention of some contemporary writers. The *Modus tenendi parliamentum*, as is well known, makes emphatic reference to the full powers of the

[1] Mr. Sayles shows that the two knights summoned by the writ of 9 October were probably intended to act as collectors of the tenth granted by the assembly. *Bull. of Inst. of Hist. Research*, iii. 110.

[2] Examples are printed in Prynne, *Brevia Parliamentaria Rediviva*, pp. 274, 284–5, 287, 355–6, 359–60 (this last is dated 1435). The Oxford Chamberlains' accounts for 1370–1 record a payment 'in vino potato per maiorem, Johannem de Stodle et alios *tempore sigillacionis commissionis dictorum maioris et Johannis burgensium parliamenti*:** *Munimenta Civitatis Oxonie*, ed. Salter, p. 273. Stodle and the mayor were returned by Oxford for the Parliament of Feb. 1371.

[3] *Parl. Writs*, i. 21 (9), 23 (18), 38 (18), 39 (19), 41 (27), 58 (21), 58 (26), 59 (27), 60 (35), 61 (39) are examples.

knights and burgesses.[1] More interesting, however, is another reference, this time from a writer of Edward I's time. It is a familiar point, which has been strongly stressed by some recent writers on the early history of Parliament, that the chroniclers of the thirteenth century say very little, except incidentally, about the growth of representation in Parliament under Henry III and Edward I: thus Dr. Pasquet writes that 'the entry of the knights of the shires and the representatives of the towns into the great council of the kingdom passed quite unnoticed by contemporaries: under Edward I, as under Henry III, the chroniclers continue to mention only the presence of the magnates in Parliaments at which, as we know from official documents, there were also representatives of the "community of the land".'[2] In actual fact it is not accurate to say that the appearance of representatives in Parliament went 'quite unnoticed' by contemporary chroniclers. Their appearance was noticed by one of the best chroniclers of Edward I's reign, the careful, well-informed monk of Norwich named Bartholomew Cotton. In the course of his account of Edward I's reign, he records the assembly of 1294 which has been mentioned above as one of the gatherings to which knights were summoned to come from the shires, bringing full powers. Cotton duly notes the summoning of these knights, and it is interesting to observe what he says about them.

'Eodem anno vocati sunt quatuor milites de quolibet comitatu Angliae, qui haberent potestatem obligandi comitatum et faciendi quod per consilium domini regis ordinaretur, et quod comparerent coram consilio predicto in crastino Sancti Martini in Novembri ubi ordinatum fuerit quod decima daretur domino regi in forma quae sequitur.'[3*]

The sentence *qui haberent potestatem obligandi comitatum* is a clear reference to the knights' full power which the writs of summons required them to bring. Here, then, is a contemporary chronicler who does specifically notice the summoning

---

[1] Ed. Hardy, pp. 9, 11.

[2] Pasquet, *The Origins of the House of Commons*, trans. Laffan, p. 14. 'Complètement inaperçue des contemporains' is the phrase in the original French version.

[3] Cotton, *Hist. Anglicana* (Rolls Ser.), p. 254. The chronicler is mistaken in supposing that the four knights had power to bind the shire. As already noticed above (p. 144), only two of the four knights had full power.

of knights from the shires to the great council of the kingdom, and the point which he remarks upon in connexion with them is that they had *potestatem obligandi comitatum*, or, in other words, that they had full power.

These various facts seem to indicate that the full power of the representatives was recognized as being of material importance not only by persons in legal and official circles— chancery clerks, sheriffs, and borough officers—but also by intelligent contemporary observers outside. This being so, one may proceed to a further question. Why did the king and his lawyers, in summoning representatives, demand that those representatives should come with full power?

The extract already quoted from Bartholomew Cotton suggests a useful clue to an answer: after recording the summoning of the knights he goes straight on to say that when the assembly met it was ordained that a tenth be given to the king. Cotton obviously realized, and meant to suggest, that on this occasion in 1294 there was a definite connexion between the *potestatem obligandi comitatum* and the grant of a tenth. Bearing this clue in mind, it is instructive to look again at the earliest assemblies to which representatives with full power were called, in order to see what business they transacted. The first occasion, that of 1268, is unfortunately obscure: the precise nature of the business contemplated is not known, nor is it certain that the summons was effective.[1] For Edward I's reign, however, more information is available. By the closing years of the reign—say by 1297—the demand for full power had become a regular feature of the writs. If we examine the writs of the fourteen years between January 1283, when the demand for full power first appears in Edward I's reign, and (say) October 1297, we find that full power was required on every recorded occasion except one—the assembly of September 1283. We also find that on those same occasions taxation was granted by every recorded assembly except one—the assembly of September 1283. It is hard to avoid the conclusion, already suggested by the contemporary chronicler, that there was a direct connexion between the demand for full power and the granting of taxation. It follows that during the central years of

[1] See Mr. Sayles's remarks, *E.H.R.* xl. 583.

Edward I's reign, during the years 1283–97 when the demand for full power was defined and grew into common form, the king and his lawyers required that the representatives should possess the full power in order thereby to secure grants of taxation which should, through the consent of fully empowered representatives, be legally binding upon the communities of shire and borough which they represented.

To suggest such a conclusion is to tread disputed ground, and to tread it, perhaps, in a rather old-fashioned way.[1] Dr. Pasquet has maintained that 'the desire to obtain the preliminary consent of the counties and towns to the levying of aids . . . was not the sole or even the principal purpose for which Edward I assembled them';[2] and both Dr. Pasquet and Dr. Riess appear to hold that the king was under no legal necessity of obtaining the consent of shires and boroughs to taxation.[3] As to the first point, one can agree that the obtaining of consent to aids was not the sole purpose for which Edward I assembled representatives of shires and boroughs, for if one takes his reign as a whole there are several occasions, as Dr. Pasquet points out, when representatives were summoned though no demand for an aid seems, on the evidence available, to have been made. All that is being asserted here is that during the period of Edward I's reign between 1283 and about 1297—the period during which the demand for fully empowered representatives grew into common form—the question of consent to taxation seems to have been uppermost in the mind of the king and his lawyers. As to the opinion that the king was

---

[1] Two very recent essays by distinguished American scholars, however, show a similar tendency. Professor Carl Stephenson, in an essay on 'Taxation and Representation in the Middle Ages', writes that the object of his essay 'has not been to prove that taxation was the only important factor in the evolution of the representative system, but to insist that it should not be so hastily passed over as it has been in some recent books'; *Haskins Anniversary Essays*, pp. 311–12.* Professor C. H. McIlwain, in his chapter on 'Medieval Estates' in the *Cambridge Mediaeval History*, vol. vii, goes so far as to concede that 'if we confine ourselves to the beginnings of these innovations [*sc.* of representation in Parliament], while Henry III was still alive, the contemporary evidence is strongly in favour of Bishop Stubbs's view that the original motive behind the beginning of these changes was almost entirely fiscal'; op. cit. vii. 678. I had not the advantage of reading these two essays until after the present paper was written.

[2] Op. cit., pp. 196–7.

[3] Pasquet, op. cit., pp. 178–83; Riess, *Geschichte des Wahlrechts*, pp. 8–14.**

under no legal necessity of obtaining the consent of shires and boroughs to taxation, one can only say that no convincing evidence has yet been adduced in support of it, and that a good deal of evidence tells directly against it. There is no doubt, of course, that the king had legal rights to tax *sections* of his subjects without their consent. But what the king required, in the interests both of productivity and administrative convenience, were taxes which were uniform and general. It has yet to be proved that the king possessed, or even claimed, legal rights to impose general and uniform taxes upon the movables of *all* his subjects without their consent. But waiving these questions, it may at any rate be suggested that the full powers demanded of the representatives of shire and boroughs did provide a practical legal solution of a problem that evidently caused some difficulty during the thirteenth century. The problem concerns consent to taxation.

The general setting of the problem in the thirteenth century is sufficiently familiar. By that time the king's extraordinary revenue derived from feudal sources—the aids of the tenants-in-chief and the tallages levied on the royal domain—had proved unsatisfactory for two reasons: they lacked uniformity and they were not sufficiently productive. The solution of these two difficulties was gradually sought by having recourse to the systematic taxation of movables. It was already a well-established rule of feudal law that the king could not legally take an extraordinary aid from his free tenants without their consent.[1] Any general and uniform taxes which included the free tenants in their scope would therefore legally need consent. Moreover—and this added a further complication—it seems clear that men in the thirteenth century inclined to the belief that consent to taxation should be a personal, individual consent: there are several interesting indications, to which Professor S. K. Mitchell has already drawn attention in his valuable *Studies in Taxation under John and Henry III*, that men were not yet clear in their own minds that the consent of a majority, in matters of taxation, bound

---

[1] Even the civil lawyers, who were not inclined to belittle the prerogatives of the Prince, did not agree that the Prince had the power to take a man's property against his will. Carlyle, *Hist. of Mediaeval Political Theory*, v. 102–3.

a dissentient minority, or that the consent of those present necessarily, on matters of taxation, bound those who were absent. That was the position which the king and his ministers had to face: as practical administrators they had to find some practical and legal means of overcoming these difficulties. It is not perhaps entirely fanciful to suggest that one may trace something of the gradual development of the means by which the king and his ministers ultimately solved the problem.

During the first half of the thirteenth century they seem to have tried to surmount their difficulties by the expedient of asserting that the corporate consent of the great council of leading tenants-in-chief was binding upon everybody.[1] But this attempt failed. The tax-payers—including the greater magnates themselves—showed that they were not prepared to acquiesce.[2]

It is in the writs summoning representatives of the shire in 1254 that the chancery clerks show the first sign of finding a legal solution of the difficulties about consent. The knights in 1254 were to come, the writs specified, *vice omnium et singulorum* in the shire, so that what they did would be done *vice omnium et singulorum*. And 'all and sundry' is a comprehensive term—it includes everybody. But although comprehensive it was evidently not satisfactory, for it does not appear again: 'all and sundry' rather suggests a mass of individuals. In the next writ, that of 1264, the phrase is different: the knights were to come *pro toto comitatu*. 'The whole shire' gets away from the mass of individuals, and suggests a single whole. In 1265 there is still another change: the representatives were to come *pro communitate comitatus*. *Communitas*—here evidently was the *mot juste*, for once this word *communitas* has appeared in 1265, it steadily persists in the later writs: it appears in 1268, in 1283, in 1290, in 1294, and subsequently. It was the *mot juste* because the inhabitants of the shire had long been regarded in English law as a *communitas*, as an organic body with common knowledge, common responsibilities, and (above all) a common will. Now

---

[1] Mitchell, op. cit., ch. x.

[2] The well-known episodes of 1220 and 1254 are the clearest evidence. *Letters of the reign of Henry III* (Rolls Ser.), i. 151-2, ii. 101-2.

in law the common will of a community transcends the individual wills of those who make up the community, without, however, being something alien or entirely external to those individual wills. It was precisely upon this common will of shires and of boroughs—for boroughs were *communitates* even more obviously than shires—that the lawyers of Henry III and Edward I laid hold as providing the key to the problem of consent. By basing consent on a common will they found a means, sound in law and justifiable in reason, of eliminating the troublesome necessity of reckoning with individual wills as such.

They next moved on to demand that each community should give full powers to its representatives to act on its behalf: each community would thereby be legally bound by the acts of its representatives. It was therefore necessary to define the nature of these full powers in adequate terms. An examination of the writs between 1268 and 1294—the period in which the specific demand for full power emerged —suggests that they show a progressive clarifying and refining of the idea of full power. The king in 1268 required that each borough should bind itself to hold as *ratum et acceptum* whatever its representatives should do in its name. The writ of 1283, when full power was next asked for, required that the representatives should bring *plenariam potestatem . . . ad audiendum et faciendum ea quae sibi ex parte nostra faciemus ostendi.** Both these formulae are very general: they bind the communities in advance to do they know not what. Neither formula appeared again, so they were evidently not satisfactory. The next demand, in the writs of 1290, was phrased quite differently: the representatives were to come *cum plena potestate pro se et tota communitate comitatus praedicti, ad consulendum et consentiendum pro se et communitate illa hiis quae comites, barones et proceres praedicti tunc duxerint concordanda.*** The phrasing on the next occasion, in 1294, is very similar in form and identical in substance. As compared with that of 1268 and 1283, this phrasing is an improvement: it is more specific—the communities are to bind themselves to consent to what is agreed upon by the earls, barons, and magnates, men who are the natural leaders of the country, and who are not likely to agree upon anything unreasonable.

Nevertheless, the things to which the representatives are to have full power to consent are things agreed upon by earls, barons, and magnates, persons who are distinct from and in a sense external to the representatives themselves. At any rate the formula was not satisfactory, for it was not repeated after 1294. In 1295 still another formula appears. The representatives were to come with full power *ad faciendum quod tunc de communi consilio ordinabitur.** This formula, with the addition of the words *et consentiendum* during Edward II's reign, became the traditional formula which continued till 1872. One may suggest that it became substantially fixed in 1295, and remained substantially unaltered through six centuries, after the various permutations prior to 1295, because it satisfactorily expressed what the king's lawyers wished to attain. Its exact implications are worth noticing. It does not demand that the representatives should come with full power to bind their respective communities to do 'what shall be shown to them on the king's behalf'—to do they know not what. Nor does it demand that they should come with full power to bind their communities to do things agreed upon by earls and barons and magnates—by persons distinct, in a sense, from themselves. What the communities are required to bind themselves, through their fully empowered representatives, to do is 'to do what shall be ordained by common counsel'. In other words, the king's lawyers have taken the idea of the common will one step farther, and have taken it to its logical conclusion. Already they had, as it were, merged individual wills in the common will of the community of shire or borough. But shires and boroughs are not the only communities in England: around them and above them there towers another community—the community of the realm, the community of England, which blends, transcends them all. 'What is ordained by common counsel' is the common will of this community of the realm of England. It is precisely this common will of the community of the realm of England that the lesser communities of shire and borough bind themselves through their representatives to do. The common will of the community of the realm of England is not something alien to the common wills of the lesser communities of shire and borough. Nor is the common will of the community of shire or borough something alien to the individual wills of those who make up that community. Thus the practical problem of consent is solved. And by this solution, incidentally, the venerable maxim, *quod omnes tangit ab omnibus approbetur,** is literally and legally fulfilled.[1]

The importance of the *plena potestas* was not exhausted in the period of origins, and its survival through nearly six centuries of later parliamentary history was not the mere continuance of inert common form. A good illustration of its continued importance as one of the underlying ideas in the theory of Parliament is provided by the growth of the doctrine of the legal sovereignty of Parliament. The historical origin of that doctrine is obviously a matter of very great interest in constitutional history. One obvious root is to be found in the fact that the English representative parliament grew out of the older *parliamentum* of the king's council, which was the king's council acting in the supreme plenitude of its power and thereby acting as the highest court of the realm. There has been a strong tendency, confirmed perhaps more especially by Professor McIlwain's illuminating work on *The High Court of Parliament*, to regard the high-court character of Parliament as being historically not merely one root, but the root of the modern legal sovereignty of Parliament. There is room for legitimate doubt, however, whether this high-court theory really accounts for all that has to be accounted for under the heading of the legal sovereignty of Parliament. The high-court theory explains the origin of Parliament's judicial attributes, and of its power over administration, and it explains the origin of much of its legislative power. But it hardly explains the origin of all the legislative power of Parliament, for it does not seem to account satisfactorily for Parliament's legislative power in taxation.[2] To

---

[1] The solution is also a very good illustration of Gierke's remark that 'Political Thought when it is genuinely medieval starts from the Whole, but ascribes an intrinsic value to every Partial Whole down to and including the Individual'. *Pol. Theories of the Middle Age*, trans. Maitland, p. 7.

[2] It is true that a Chief Baron of the Exchequer did argue in 1441 that tenths and fifteenths were revenues of the court of Parliament like attainders and forfeitures. But the comment of the Chief Justice of Common Pleas on the same occasion put the matter in the right light: 'The fifteenth granted to the King by his people cannot be called a perquisite or profit of his Court of Parliament, for the perquisites or profits of his courts are things which accrue to him through a forfeiture to his law.'

explain this it seems necessary to bring in a second factor. What this second factor was is indicated very clearly by Sir Thomas Smith in his classical work, *De Republica Anglorum*, published in 1583. As is well known, Smith emphasizes the fact that Parliament is a high court, but he was aware that Parliament was something more than a high court in a merely judicial sense, for among his examples of the diverse powers of Parliament he includes the fact that it 'appointeth subsidies, tailes, taxes, and impositions'.[1] Parliament, according to Smith, possesses its wide and various powers because it

'representeth and hath the power of the whole realme both the head and the bodie. For everie Englishman is entended to bee there present, either in person or by procuration and attornies, of what preheminence, state, dignitie, or qualitie soever he be, from the Prince (be he King or Queene) to the lowest person of Englande. And the consent of the Parliament is taken to be everie mans consent.'[2]

The 'attornies' here obviously include the knights of the shire and burgesses, for they were, in virtue of their *plena potestas*, the attorneys of their respective communities, to do and consent to whatever should be ordained by common counsel.[3] In Smith's view, therefore, what made Parliament 'the most high and absolute power of the realme of Englande' was not merely the fact that it was a high court, but the fact that it was a high court in which there were present the fully empowered attorneys of shires and boroughs; for by their presence every Englishman could legally be understood to be present, and by their presence the consent of Parliament could legally be taken to be every man's consent. Nor was this doctrine a mere ingenious invention of Smith's. In a case argued in the court of Exchequer Chamber in 1480

The case is discussed by Mr. T. F. T. Plucknett in *Tudor Studies*, ed. Seton-Watson, pp. 162–8.

[1] Ed. Alston, p. 49.   [2] Ibid.

[3] The two burgesses for Scarborough in 1384 are referred to as 'attornati' in the formal document giving them full power; Prynne, *Brevia parliamentaria rediviva*, p. 285. The two burgesses for Southampton in 1332 are called *attornatos nostros* in the formal powers; P.R.O. Parlty. writs and returns, 5/11. The two citizens for Norwich in 1335 are called *attornatos seu procuratores nostros* in the formal powers; ibid., 5/18. The *Modus tenendi parliamentum* speaks of the representatives of the Cinque Ports as *attornati*; ed. Hardy, p. 9. The effective phrase of the full powers, *ratum et gratum habituri*, &c., was the normal formula in powers of attorney: see the specimen power of attorney in Madox, *Formulare Anglicanum*, p. 346.

counsel for the Crown remarks that an Act of Parliament binds every one to whom it extends, 'because,' he explains, 'every man is privy and party to the parliament, *for the Commons have one or two for each community to bind or unbind the whole community.*'[1] The doctrine of Sir Thomas Smith was thus in accord with the established tradition of the English common lawyers. It suggests that historically the legal sovereignty of Parliament sprang, not from a single but from a double root. One root was the character of Parliament as a high court. The second root was the *plena potestas* of the representatives of the Commons.

---

[1] 'Par chescun act de parlement chescun a qi act extend serra lie, pur ce qe chescun homme est prive et partie al parlement, car les communes ont un ou ii pur chescun com. pur lier ou deslier tout le com.' *Les reports des cases en ley* (ed. 1680), xxi Ed. IV, no. 6, p. 45. Mr. Plucknett discusses the case in another connexion in *Tudor Studies*, pp. 172–7. He translates 'com.' as 'county', but it seems probable that 'com.' really stands for 'commune', i.e. community. On the adjacent pages 40, 51, and 52 of the *Reports*, the word for county is 'coûty' or 'county'.

5

THE PERSONNEL OF THE COMMONS IN PARLIAMENT UNDER EDWARD I. AND EDWARD II.*

by J. G. Edwards

RECENT teaching on the history of the mediæval English parliament has shown a distinct tendency to question many of the accepted opinions as to the place and importance of the Commons in the parliaments of the 14th century. The conclusions which are now becoming fashionable have been reached by various lines of study. Only one of these lines—the investigation of the personnel of the Commons in parliament—concerns us here. It has of late attracted several scholars, and has led some of them to propound a number of rather iconoclastic conclusions.[1] We are now taught that when the constituencies—particularly the borough constituencies—were ordered to elect representatives, they quite commonly omitted to do so. Even when an election was made we are told that the representatives elected often failed to appear in parliament. It is asserted, moreover, that "members were rarely re-elected".[2] From all this it is inferred that representation in parliament during the 13th and 14th centuries was regarded as a burden and was avoided as far as possible both by the representatives and by the constituencies. It is inferred, too, that the borough members, comparatively numerous on paper, were in actual fact a minority of the Commons and were outnumbered by the knights of the shire.[3] The object of the present paper is to attempt a synopsis of a few of the primary facts and to test the validity of some of the canons of interpretation that have hitherto been observed in dealing with the evidence. Consideration will be given mainly to the reigns of Edward I. and Edward II., except when lack of material from those two reigns makes it necessary to take account of the 14th century as a whole.

A word must first be said about the evidence. The main sources are the sheriffs' returns and the enrolments of writs *de expensis.*[4]

---

[1] Pasquet, *Essai sur les Origines de la Chambre des Communes* (1914) ; Lapsley, *Knights of the Shire in the Parliaments of Edward II.* (*Eng. Hist. Rev.* 1919) ; Pollard, *Evolution of Parliament* (1920).**

[2] Pollard, p. 8.   [3] *Ibid.*, p. 319.

[4] Printed *in extenso* for the reigns of Edward I. and Edward II. in Palgrave's *Parliamentary Writs.* The enrolled writs *de expensis* are also printed in Prynne's *Fourth*

A certain amount of additional information, scattered but not insignificant, may also be obtained from the rolls of parliament and from
borough accounts. There are two difficulties about this evidence.
In the first place, it is incomplete. For gatherings earlier than the
colloquium of July 1290 the surviving returns are too few and fragmentary to be of much value for the present purpose. After 1290
the evidence is more satisfactory : there are only two assemblies,
those of November 1294 and November 1296, for which the names of
the elected representatives are entirely lacking ; [1] for the remainder,
except for that of May 1300, reasonably full particulars are forthcoming.[2]
Still it must be remembered that these particulars are only reasonably
full : they are not complete. Thus it is only for six assemblies between
1290 and 1327 that the lists even of knights of the shire are absolutely
complete [3] : during the same period there is only one constituency,
York county, for which it is possible to make a list of members
which (save for the meetings of November 1294 and November 1296)
is quite full. Every statement made about the personnel of the
Commons in parliament is therefore made subject to these numerous
gaps in the evidence. The second difficulty is not so persistent, but is
apt nevertheless to cause occasional embarrassment. This is the
difficulty of mediæval names. Owing to the constant recurrence of
the same christian names in the same family and to the careless fashion
in which " senior " or " junior " or local descriptions are inserted or
omitted in the returns, it is not always possible to be sure about
identifications. Fortunately this difficulty does not arise as often as
might be expected, and the resultant error is not likely to be serious :
but the possibility of error on this score is there, and allowance must
be made for it. With these reservations in mind, we may now attempt
a synopsis of the primary facts in tabular form, and in doing this, it
is convenient to keep the shire constituencies distinct from the cities
and boroughs.

Between July 1290 and January 1327 (excluding the meetings of
November 1294 and November 1296 for which, as has been said, no
returns are available) there were 34 assemblies, variously styled
parliaments or *colloquia*, to which the shires were ordered to send
representatives. Tables A and B give a statistical summary of the
shire representation.

Part of a Brief Register of Parliamentary Writs. The returns are analysed in the *Return
of Members of Parliament (Parl. Papers*, 1878, vol. lxii. pts. i.-iii.).
    [1] Except for London for 1296 ; Sharpe, *Cal. of Letter Books : Letter Book C*, p. 24.
    [2] Returns discovered since 1878 have been entered in manuscript in the copy of the
Return of Members of Parliament kept in the Round Room at the Public Record Office.
These additions, which are not very numerous for the reigns of Edward I. and Edward II.,
have been noted in preparing the statistics given below.
    [3] The meetings of October 1302, February 1305, September 1313, January 1315,
February 1324 and October 1324. Northumberland made no election for the parliaments
of January 1315 and October 1324 owing to Scottish raids.

TABLE A (Shires)

PARLIAMENTS.	Col. 1.	Col. 2.	Col. 3.	Col. 4.	Col. 5.	Column 6.									
						2.	3.	4.	5.	6.	7.	8.	9.	10.	11.
July 1290	28	64	64	..	..	..	..	..	..	..	..	..	..	..	..
November 1295	35	73	65	..	8	8	..	..	..	..	..	..	..	..	..
October 1297	32	64	55	..	9	7	2	..	..	..	..	..	..	..	..
May 1298	35	70	47	13	23	21	2	..	..	..	..	..	..	..	..
March 1300	33	66	43	15	23	14	8	1	..	..	..	..	..	..	..
May 1300	14	39	22	8	17	12	4	1	..	..	..	..	..	..	..
January 1301	35	70	16	*41	54	31	15	6	2	..	..	..	..	..	..
October 1302	37	74	39	10	35	24	8	2	1	..	..	..	..	..	..
February 1305	37	74	37	19	37	18	12	5	1	1	..	..	..	..	..
May 1306	34	68	31	19	37	15	9	7	6	..	..	..	..	..	..
January 1307	36	72	49	10	23	12	7	3	1	..	..	..	..	..	..
October 1307	34	68	34	14	34	16	10	4	3	1	..	..	..	..	..
April 1309	36	71	26	10	45	19	6	10	4	6	..	..	..	..	..
August 1311	36	72	25	16	47	23	11	7	3	3	..	..	..	..	..
November 1311	36	72	11	53	61	18	19	9	7	5	3	..	..	..	..
August 1312	28	56	30	9	26	7	7	4	5	1	1	1	..	..	..
March 1313	33	65	30	8	35	14	9	4	2	3	2	1	..	..	..
July 1313	25	50	16	18	34	16	8	3	2	4	..	1	..	..	..
September 1313	37	75	16	26	59	18	21	8	3	2	5	1	1	..	..
September 1314	33	66	45	8	21	7	4	6	1	2	..	1	..	..	..
January 1315	36	72	38	12	34	16	7	5	1	1	3	1	..	..	..
January 1316	33	57	31	9	26	12	4	3	4	..	..	3	..	..	..
May 1316	19	38	19	8	19	8	5	3	3	..	..	..	..	..	..
July 1316	36	68	23	19	45	21	9	8	2	4	..	..	1	..	..
October 1318	34	68	34	10	34	13	8	2	7	2	..	1	1	..	..
May 1319	35	70	40	14	30	13	9	2	1	4	1	..	..	..	..
October 1320	37	73	40	9	33	14	6	5	2	3	3	..	..	..	..
July 1321	36	71	28	9	43	17	7	7	4	3	4	1	..	..	..
May 1322	36	71	31	12	40	20	10	4	2	1	1	2	..	..	..
November 1322	32	64	33	11	31	11	8	6	2	3	..	..	1	..	..
February 1324	37	74	35	13	39	16	6	6	4	3	3	..	..	1	..
October 1324	36	72	42	6	30	13	6	5	2	1	..	3	..	..	..
November 1325	36	72	36	11	36	15	7	4	3	1	2	..	3	..	1
January 1327	35	70	33	7	37	18	11	4	1	1	..	..	1	1	..

* Re-elected from the parliament of March 1300.

Table A is arranged by parliaments, and gives the following information for each of the 34 assemblies to which shire representatives were called :

Column 1—number of shires known to have returned or sent members;[1]
Column 2—number of members known to have been returned or to have attended ;
Column 3—number of members returned or present for the first time known;

---

[1] " Returned or sent " because the names are derived partly from the sheriffs' returns, partly from the enrolled writs *de expensis*, and occasionally the persons who were actually sent were not the persons who had been returned by the sheriff : when this occurs, the names given by the enrolled writs *de expensis* have been taken in preference.

Column 4—number of members known to have been returned to or present in the parliament immediately preceding;

Column 5—number of members known to have been returned or to have attended *for the particular shire* on any previous occasions;

Column 6—an analysis of the figures in column 5, showing the numbers returned or present for the second time, the third time, etc., respectively.

TABLE B

Shires.	Col. 1.	Col. 2.	Column 3. 1.	2.	3.	4.	5.	6.	7.	8.	9.	10.	11.
Bedford	65	30	14	7	4	2	1	2	..	..	..	..	..
Berkshire	66	36	25	4	2	2	1	..	2	..	..	..	..
Buckingham	66	31	14	11	2	2	1	..	..	..	..	..	1
Cambridge	68	35	23	2	4	5	..	..	..	..	1	..	..
Cornwall	57	33	22	6	1	2	..	2	..	..	..	..	..
Cumberland	55	32	18	8	4	1	1	..	..	..	.˙.	..	..
Derby	58	25	11	4	7	1	..	1	..	1	..	..	..
Devon	64	34	19	10	2	1	..	1	..	..	1	..	..
Dorset	65	38	24	6	5	2	..	1	..	..	..	..	..
Essex	66	30	12	8	5	2	3	..	..	..	..	..	..
Gloucester	59	35	22	7	4	..	1	1	..	..	..	..	..
Hereford	64	40	23	13	3	..	..	1	..	..	..	..	..
Hertford	60	18	3	6	2	4	..	1	..	1	1	..	..
Huntingdon	68	33	20	5	3	1	1	1	2	..	..	..	..
Kent	61	31	18	5	3	2	2	1	..	..	..	..	..
Lancashire	56	33	19	8	3	3	..	..	..	..	..	..	..
Leicester	58	31	18	6	3	3	..	..	1	..	..	..	..
Lincoln	61	35	23	5	3	2	1	1	..	..	..	..	..
Middlesex	54	24	13	5	2	1	1	..	1	..	1	..	..
Norfolk	63	27	15	6	1	1	..	2	1	..	..	1	..
Northampton	61	37	26	5	3	2	..	..	..	1	..	..	..
Northumberland	50	31	23	3	2	1	1	1	..	..	..	..	..
Nottingham	56	31	19	4	6	..	1	1	..	..	..	..	..
Oxford	61	28	15	8	1	1	..	1	..	1	1	..	..
Rutland	61	37	23	8	4	..	2	..	..	..	..	..	..
Shropshire	63	27	15	5	1	2	..	2	1	1	..	..	..
Somerset	67	43	30	5	6	1	1	..	..	..	..	..	..
Southampton	64	34	19	8	3	1	2	1	..	..	..	..	..
Stafford	65	27	8	12	3	1	1	1	..	..	1	..	..
Suffolk	62	25	10	5	5	3	..	..	1	1	..	..	..
Surrey	59	23	12	2	3	3	..	1	..	2	..	..	..
Sussex	56	23	11	4	2	3	..	2	1	..	..	..	..
Warwick	67	36	21	5	7	2	..	..	1	..	..	..	..
Westmorland	56	27	14	7	1	2	2	..	1	..	..	..	..
Wiltshire	59	33	19	8	4	..	..	2	..	..	..	..	..
Worcester	59	29	12	9	3	5	..	..	..	..	..	..	..
Yorkshire	69	42	24	12	4	1	1	..	..	..	..	..	..
Total	2269	1164	657	242	121	65	24	27	12	8	6	1	1

Table B is arranged by constituencies, and gives the following information for each of the 37 shires which returned members to the assemblies of 1290–1327:

Column 1—total number of returns or attendances during the period;

Column 2—total number of persons returned or attending during the
period ;

Column 3—an analysis of the figures in column 2, showing the number
of persons returned respectively once, twice, three times, etc.,
during the period 1290–1327.

When we turn to the boroughs it is necessary to make a selection.
During the years 1290–1327 some 175 cities and boroughs were ordered,
at one time or another, to elect representatives for parliament, and
from almost all these there are returns still extant. But owing to a
variety of causes, the number of surviving returns is much greater
from some boroughs than from others. Between 1290 and 1327 there
were 28 assemblies (excluding that of November 1296, the returns for
which are not available) to which borough representatives were called.
From a good many boroughs returns survive for only one or two of these
gatherings. From others, the series is almost complete : thus there
are returns from the borough of Bedford for 27 out of the 28 meetings.
The majority of the boroughs fall somewhere between these two
extremes. A selection must therefore be made of those boroughs for

TABLE C (39 Boroughs)

PARLIAMENTS.	Col. 1.	Col. 2.	Col. 3.	Col. 4.	Col. 5.	Column 6.											
						2.	3.	4.	5.	6.	7.	8.	9.	10.	11.	12.	13.
November 1295	33	65	65	..	..	..	..	..	..	..	..	..	..	..	..	..	..
May 1298	34	68	57	11	11	11	..	..	..	..	..	..	..	..	..	..	..
March 1300	11	22	16	4	6	4	2	..	..	..	..	..	..	..	..	..	..
January 1301	29	57	37	10	20	14	4	2	..	..	..	..	..	..	..	..	..
October 1302	33	66	46	13	20	10	7	1	2	..	..	..	..	..	..	..	..
February 1305	39	77	48	16	29	20	6	2	1	..	..	..	..	..	..	..	..
May 1306	35	64	37	18	27	17	5	4	..	1	..	..	..	..	..	..	..
January 1307	36	72	52	5	20	12	6	1	..	..	1	..	..	..	..	..	..
October 1307	35	70	30	6	40	16	11	7	3	2	..	1	..	..	..	..	..
April 1309	35	68	42	12	26	11	7	3	2	2	..	..	1	..	..	..	..
August 1311	38	76	43	9	33	16	6	8	..	2	..	..	..	1	..	..	..
November 1311	34	68	21	34	47	25	10	5	4	..	2	..	..	..	1	..	..
August 1312	17	34	20	6	14	6	5	2	..	1	..	..	..	..	..	..	..
March 1313	35	70	30	6	40	16	14	2	3	2	..	2	..	..	..	1	..
July 1313	17	34	15	10	19	8	6	2	2	1	..	..	..	..	..	..	..
September 1313	39	78	28	16	50	20	10	9	2	3	4	..	1	..	..	..	1
September 1314	29	58	29	9	29	14	5	3	3	..	3	..	1	..	..	..	..
January 1315	37	74	30	16	44	14	8	9	4	4	1	3	..	1	..	..	..
January 1316	9	18	12	4	6	2	3	..	..	..	1	..	..	..	..	..	..
October 1318	34	67	33	3	34	17	7	3	4	1	1	..	1	..	..	..	..
May 1319	36	71	41	14	30	10	9	5	1	2	2	1	..	..	..	..	..
October 1320	34	68	35	11	33	12	7	5	3	1	..	2	2	1	..	..	..
July 1321	31	61	31	11	30	10	4	4	4	1	1	3	1	2	..	..	..
May 1322	35	70	42	9	28	10	4	3	5	1	1	2	1	1	..	..	..
November 1322	28	56	27	8	29	11	5	3	4	1	1	1	2	..	1	..	..
February 1324	39	78	42	10	36	16	9	2	2	2	2	1	1	..	..	1	..
November 1325	36	72	37	18	35	13	8	6	1	2	3	..	1	1	..	..	..
January 1327	30	60	34	7	26	11	5	2	1	1	1	3	..	..	1	..	1

which the data are reasonably complete. Accordingly, attention is here limited almost entirely to cities and boroughs which can show returns for 20 or more of the 28 parliaments of the period under consideration : 39 of these borough constituencies have been taken, spread over most of the shires of England. Tables C and D give, for the 39 boroughs named, information similar to that given for the shires in Tables A and B.[1]

TABLE D

Boroughs	Col. 1.	Col. 2.	Column 3.												
			1.	2.	3.	4.	5.	6.	7.	8.	9.	10.	11.	12.	13.
Bedford . . .	53	28	16	6	3	2	..	..	..	1	..	..	..	..	..
Reading . .	46	27	18	4	2	1	2	..	..	..	..	..	..	..	..
Wallingford .	42	19	9	7	..	1	..	..	1	1	..	..	..	..	..
Cambridge . .	46	26	16	4	2	4	..	..	..	..	..	..	..	..	..
Bodmin . .	37	31	28	1	1	1	..	..	..	..	..	..	..	..	..
Launceston .	38	24	15	6	2	..	1	..	..	..	..	..	..	..	..
Carlisle . .	37	20	12	4	2	1	..	..	..	1	..	..	..	..	..
Derby . .	48	30	18	6	6	..	..	..	..	..	..	..	..	..	..
Exeter . .	47	29	19	6	1	2	1	..	..	..	..	..	..	..	..
Totness . .	41	21	13	5	1	..	1	..	..	..	..	1	..	..	..
Shaftesbury .	42	31	25	4	1	..	..	1	..	..	..	..	..	..	..
Colchester .	39	14	9	1	1	1	..	..	..	1	..	..	..	..	1
Bristol . .	40	29	23	3	1	2	..	..	..	..	..	..	..	..	..
Gloucester .	42	24	17	3	2	..	1	..	..	1	..	..	..	..	..
Hereford . .	50	23	10	6	4	1	..	2	..	..	..	..	..	..	..
Huntingdon .	52	28	17	6	2	2	..	..	..	..	1	..	..	..	..
Canterbury .	44	26	16	5	3	1	1	..	..	..	..	..	..	..	..
Rochester .	44	18	11	3	1	..	..	1	..	1	..	1	..	..	..
Leicester .	46	30	19	8	1	2	..	..	..	..	..	..	..	..	..
Lincoln . .	44	24	15	4	2	..	3	..	..	..	..	..	..	..	..
Norwich . .	50	27	19	2	2	2	..	1	1	..	..	..	..	..	..
Yarmouth .	49	25	15	6	1	1	1	..	..	..	..	1	..	..	..
Northampton .	48	25	14	6	2	1	1	..	..	1	..	..	..	..	..
Newcastle-on-Tyne	32	16	8	3	2	3	..	..	..	..	..	..	..	..	..
Nottingham .	46	25	14	5	3	2	1	..	..	..	..	..	..	..	..
Oxford . .	48	15	10	..	1	1	..	..	..	..	2	..	..	..	1
Shrewsbury .	52	24	14	3	5	..	..	..	..	1	1	..	..	..	..
Bridgwater .	50	40	32	6	2	..	..	..	..	..	..	..	..	..	..
Ilchester .	40	22	17	2	..	1	1	..	..	..	..	1	..	..	..
Winchester .	46	31	22	5	2	2	..	..	..	..	..	..	..	..	..
Stafford .	41	19	7	6	3	2	1	..	..	..	..	..	..	..	..
Dunwich .	45	20	12	2	1	3	..	1	..	1	..	..	..	..	..
Ipswich . .	46	21	11	6	1	1	1	1	..	..	..	..	1	..	..
Guildford .	40	17	9	2	3	1	1	..	..	..	1	..	..	..	..
Appleby .	42	29	21	5	2	..	1	..	..	..	..	..	..	..	..
Salisbury .	52	36	26	6	3	..	1	..	..	..	..	..	..	..	..
Wilton . .	45	28	17	7	3	..	1	..	..	..	..	..	..	..	..
Worcester .	46	30	22	3	3	1	1	..	..	..	..	..	..	..	..
York . .	46	28	18	6	3	..	..	..	1	..	..	..	..	..	..
Total . . .	1742	980	634	173	80	42	21	6	5	7	5	4	1	..	2

[1] London has been omitted because the city during the latter half of Edward II.'s reign frequently elected three, four and (on one occasion) six representatives, giving power to any two or three of them to answer for the city. This practice distorts the figures for London, and makes them misleading as statistics. On the number of London's representatives see Prynne, *Brevia Parliamentaria Rediviva*, pp. 374-80.

Now these arid statistics, whatever their limitations, are at any rate quite sufficient to dispose of the theory that members were rarely re-elected. That theory may of course be understood in more than one sense. If it is taken in its most natural meaning, it does not in the least square with the facts. A comparison of the figures in columns (3) and (5) in Tables A and C will show that in almost any parliamentary assembly of the period 1290–1327 a considerable proportion of the representatives were persons who had been elected on one or more previous occasions. Taking the shire constituencies in Table A, it will be seen that in several parliaments persons who had been elected on one or more previous occasions form a distinct majority of the shire representatives : this is true of about ten parliaments, *e.g.* August 1311 (47 : 25), September 1313 (59 : 16), May 1322 (40 : 31). Slightly more numerous are the parliaments in which the knights of the shire who had been elected on previous occasions are exactly or approximately equal in number to those then elected (so far as is known) for the first time : this is true of about a dozen parliaments, *e.g.* October 1302 (35 : 39), October 1318 (34 : 34), November 1325 (36 : 36). In about eleven parliaments the knights of the shire who had been elected on one or more previous occasions are outnumbered by those elected for the first time, *e.g.* March 1300 (23 : 43), September 1314 (21 : 45), October 1324 (30 : 42) : even here, however, their numbers are by no means negligible. Taking now the 39 borough constituencies in Table C, it will be seen that there are some half-dozen parliaments in which a distinct majority of the burgesses are persons who had been elected on one or more previous occasions, *e.g.* October 1307 (40 : 30), September 1313 (50 : 28), January 1315 (44 : 30). There are some half-dozen other parliaments in which the burgesses who had been elected on one or more previous occasions are exactly or approximately equal in number to those elected for the first time : examples are the parliaments of September 1314 (29 : 29), October 1318 (34 : 33), November 1325 (35 : 37). In some fifteen parliaments, however, the re-elected are distinctly outnumbered by those elected for the first time, *e.g.* October 1302 (20 : 46), January 1307 (20 : 52), May 1319 (30 : 41). It would seem, therefore, if one may generalize from the 39 boroughs taken in Table C, that re-election was rather less common in the boroughs than in the shires. Nevertheless, it was so common both in shires and boroughs that it cannot be regarded as in the least exceptional.

The point may be demonstrated in another way if we now consider the evidence by constituencies instead of by parliaments, and make use of the facts summarized in Tables B and D. These tables show for each constituency (so far as the materials allow) the total number of elections made, the total number of persons elected, and the extent to which these persons were re-elected, during the period

1290–1327. Thus for Bedford borough the total number of elections is 53 : the total number of persons elected is 28 ; of these 28, 16 are elected once, 6 twice, 3 three times, 2 four times and 1 eight times, making the total of 53 elections. Taken together, Tables B and D are conclusive against any theory that members were rarely re-elected. They show that practically all the constituencies have examples of persons elected four times ; that a good proportion of the constituencies had members who were elected five and six times ; and that some of them were represented by persons who were elected as often as ten, eleven and thirteen times.[1] These statements may be illustrated by a few examples. Cambridgeshire has one member elected 9 times ; Salop has one member elected 7 times and another elected 8 times ; Oxfordshire has one member elected 8 times and another elected 9 times ; Westmorland has one elected 7 times ; Buckinghamshire has one elected 11 times. Even more surprising is the evidence from some of the boroughs. Bedford, Gloucester, Wallingford and Dunwich each have one member elected 8 times ; Rochester has one elected 8 times and another elected 10 times ; Yarmouth, Totness and Ilchester each have one elected 10 times ; Colchester has one elected 8 times and one elected 13 times ; Oxford has two members elected 9 times and one elected 13 times. It is not, however, upon these examples that the main emphasis must be laid, otherwise one might easily be deceived into thinking that Our Old and Respected Member was already a familiar flower of the constitution. The evidence of the two Tables must be taken as a whole if its full force is to be fairly shown. And its full force is greater than appears at first sight. What one sees at first sight is that in the shires there are 657 persons elected once as against 507 persons elected more than once, while in 39 boroughs there are 634 persons elected once as against 346 persons elected more than once. This, it may be urged, proves indeed that re-election was common, but proves also that the majority of members were not re-elected. That is certainly a very important truth : undoubtedly the majority of members during the period 1290–1327 were not re-elected. But that truth must not be allowed to hide another truth equally important. It is this : that in the shires, 657 persons elected once account for 657 elections, whereas 507 persons elected more than once account for 1612 elections ; that in 39 boroughs, 634 persons elected once account for 634 elections, whereas 346 persons elected more than once account for 1108 elections. To get the whole truth we must not only count heads ; we must also count elections. Even then, it must be remembered, we shall not have reached quite the whole truth about re-election. For the figures given above have been obtained by taking each constituency by itself and ignoring the fact that the same person might be elected at various

---

[1] This fact was duly noted by Prynne ; *Brev. Parl. Red.*, p. 137.

times by more than one constituency, so that his first election for one constituency might not necessarily be his first election to parliament. Thus a Gerard of Braybrook was elected for Buckinghamshire to the parliaments of January 1301 and April 1309 ; for Hertfordshire to the parliaments of January 1307 and October 1307 ; for Bedfordshire to the parliaments of August 1311, November 1311 and (probably) August 1312. If, as seems likely, this Gerard is one and the same person, it will be seen that his first election for Hertfordshire was really his second election to parliament, while his first election for Bedfordshire was his fifth election to parliament. Other examples of this kind occur from time to time, at any rate in the shires. It is impossible, however, to take account of them without first establishing identifications, and this unfortunately is too lengthy a task for the present paper.[1] Accordingly these elections have had to be left out of account in compiling the accompanying Tables. If they had been included, the case against the theory that members were rarely re-elected could have been made rather stronger than it is already. But it scarcely need be pressed further. If any one is still unconvinced he might perhaps care to continue the discussion with Chaucer's Franklin. The opinions of that worthy vavasour should be interesting. For he was knight of the shire " ful ofte tyme ".

So far we have taken the theory that members were rarely re-elected in its natural meaning. It might, however, be understood in another sense. It might be taken to mean that members were rarely re-elected to two or more immediately successive parliaments. Stated in this way the theory, without being wholly true, would be much more true than it is in the sense previously discussed. Column 4 in Tables A and C shows for each parliament the number of its members known to have been also elected to the parliament immediately preceding. It proves that a certain proportion of the members of any parliament were persons who had been also elected to the parliament next preceding. The proportion varies, among knights of the shire from one in twelve (October 1324) to one in three (September 1313), and among the burgesses from one in fourteen (January 1307) to one in four (November 1325).[2] These, however, are probably minimum figures. At any rate it is clear that election to two consecutive parliaments was by no means unusual, though it was not the common rule. The further question —how far members were re-elected to a series of consecutive parliaments —cannot be satisfactorily answered owing to the gaps in the evidence, but a few facts are worth noting. It would seem that election to three immediately successive parliaments, though not common, was by no

---

[1] See Palgrave's introduction to the alphabetical digest of persons ; *Parl. Writs*, vol. i.
[2] Re-election was enjoined upon the constituencies by the writs summoning the assemblies of January 1301 and November 1311, and then the proportions are rather higher. But normally the constituencies were left to do as they pleased.

means unknown : during the period 1290–1327 there are about 60 examples to be found in the shires and about 30 in the boroughs mentioned in Tables C and D.   Election to more than three consecutive parliaments was obviously unusual, but the examples available ought not therefore to be ignored.   In the shires one can find 14 examples of election to four consecutive parliaments, 5 examples of election to five consecutive parliaments, 1 of election to six consecutive parliaments,[1] and 1 of election to seven consecutive parliaments.[2]   In the boroughs there are 9 examples of election to four consecutive parliaments, 4 of election to five consecutive parliaments, 1 of election to seven consecutive parliaments,[3] and 1 of election to ten consecutive parliaments.[4]   These examples might be slightly multiplied if complete returns were available.   The fact remains, however, that re-election to a series of immediately successive parliaments was unusual under Edward I. and Edward II.   Interpreted in this sense, the statement that members were rarely re-elected might be accepted : but even in this special sense it would still be subject to exceptions which, though relatively small in number, are yet sufficiently numerous to be worth bearing in mind.

Two other matters now demand consideration.   Granted that constituencies which obeyed the writ of summons often re-elected the same persons, how far did constituencies ignore the summons and omit to elect at all ?   And supposing that an election was made, to what extent did the representatives elected actually attend in parliament ?

It seems to have been unusual for shire constituencies to refuse or omit to elect : there appear to be no more than four examples between 1290 and 1327, and in each case the shire's failure to elect is explained in the return as being due to some special cause.[5]   In borough constituencies, on the other hand, omissions of election are thought to have been very common.   This point was first emphasized by Riess, and it has been stressed again more recently by M. Pasquet.[6]   They call attention to the fact that the sheriffs in their returns frequently report that boroughs " nihil responderunt " or " nullum dederunt responsum"[*] to the precept of election : the sheriffs say this, as Riess rightly remarks, of boroughs great and small in all the shires of England.   But there is evidence that a *nullum dederunt responsum* did not neces-

---

[1] Richard of Chessbech for Devonshire to the parliaments of July 1321–November 1325.

[2] William of Scalebrok for Oxfordshire to the parliaments of May 1306–August 1312.

[3] William Amerose for Yarmouth to the parliaments of April 1309–September 1313.

[4] Andrew Pirie for Oxford borough to the parliaments of March 1300–November 1311.

[5] *Parl. Writs*, I. p. 60 (36) ; p. 176 (44) ; II. ii. p. 145 (66) ; p. 322 (27).

[6] Riess, *Die Geschichte des Wahlrechts zum englischen Parlament im Mittelalter*, pp. 17-24 ; Pasquet, pp. 183-92.   Riess's essay is an acute and valuable study, but it is not always accurate in details, and its use of evidence is sometimes unsatisfactory.[**]

sarily mean that a borough failed to elect. Thus Colchester made no answer to the sheriff of Essex for the parliament of February 1305, yet at least one burgess for Colchester actually attended that meeting, since a writ *de expensis* is enrolled for him.[1] Again Grimsby " nullum dedit responsum " to the sheriff of Lincoln for the parliament of September 1313, yet two burgesses of Grimsby received writs *de expensis* for that parliament.[2] Again Ipswich is returned by the sheriff of Suffolk as having made no answer for the parliament of April 1328 ; but two burgesses were as a matter of fact elected and they received writs *de expensis* for attending. An interesting letter from the bailiffs of Ipswich to the Chancery rather suggests that the sheriff did not receive their answer in time to include the names in his return.[3] That this sort of thing might easily occur is proved by one of Riess's own examples. He cites Scarborough as giving no answer for the parliament of August 1311.[4] Now the sheriff of Yorkshire certainly did enter in his return that the bailiff of Scarborough had made no answer, but Riess does not seem to have observed that this entry was afterwards cancelled,[5] and that the names of the Scarborough burgesses are actually inserted underneath. In this case the sheriff presumably received the names at the last moment and amended his return accordingly. All that a *nihil responderunt* need mean, therefore, is that the sheriff had received no answer up to the time of sending his own return to the Chancery. It may sometimes also mean that no election was made. The difficulty is to know which meaning is to be understood in any given case. *Nullum dederunt responsum* must therefore be handled with care : Riess's interpretation of it involves a dangerous argument *ex silentio*, and may easily dispose one to exaggerate the omissions of election in the boroughs.[6]

We now come to what is perhaps the most important question of all. To what extent did the representatives elected actually attend in parliament ? Recent teaching has been leaning towards the view that elected representatives very frequently failed to attend. The evidence vouched in support of this doctrine is contained chiefly in the enrolments of writs *de expensis*. The number of members for whom these

---

[1] *Parl. Writs*, I. p. 143 (18) ; p. 157 (47).

[2] *Ibid*. II. ii. p. 108 (39) ; p. 116 (57).

[3] P.R.O. Parl. Writs and Returns, Bundle 5, Board 4. The bailiffs' letter is printed (a little carelessly) by Prynne, *Brev. Parl. Red.*, p. 271 : they say that they have informed the sheriff of the names of those who had been elected, " et coment qe le dit viescounte eit certefiee la court de meme respounse ou noun, nous, qe prests susmes en taunt qe nous poems suffire a obeyr as maundementz de nostre seignour lige ensi qe de droit susmes tenutz, vous certifioms, sires, qe de nostre commun assent avoms eleuz nos comburgeis Geffrei Stace et Cristophre del Boys ", etc.*

[4] Riess, pp. 21-2, n. 2.

[5] Palgrave indicates this by his usual sign ; *Parl. Writs*, II. ii. 46 (6).

[6] Thus Pasquet (pp. 184-5) gives Yarmouth as one of two examples of towns which " refusent presque systématiquement de répondre ". Yet returns are extant for Yarmouth for 24 out of 28 parliaments between 1290 and 1327.

writs are enrolled is nearly always considerably less than the number of persons returned by the sheriffs as having been elected : this is especially true of the borough representatives, but it also applies, though in a much lesser degree, to shire members as well, at any rate under Edward I. and Edward II.   From this it has been inferred that while the number of members returned was over three hundred, the number who actually attended was commonly no more than about a hundred, the great majority of whom were knights of the shire. These inferences are sound provided that the enrolments of writs *de expensis* are exhaustive.   It is thought that for the shire members, at any rate, these enrolments are exhaustive, since they usually account for all or most of the full complement of 74 knights of the shire.   It is admitted, however, that they are not quite exhaustive for the burgesses : some fifteen cities and boroughs, it has been suggested, may have paid their members independently of writs *de expensis*, and were therefore actually represented in parliament though their burgesses do not usually figure in the enrolments of writs *de expensis*.[1] But apart from these few exceptions, it is thought that the number of burgesses for whom writs *de expensis* are enrolled may be taken as a fairly accurate indication of the number of borough representatives actually present in parliament.   This assumption has recently been challenged by Miss May McKisack in a paper on *Borough Representation in Richard II.'s Reign*.[2]   There is other evidence from previous reigns which indicates that her challenge is well founded.   In the parliament of March 1340 a committee of Lords and Commons was appointed to consider certain petitions.   The names of the persons chosen—who were presumably actually present in parliament—are recorded in the parliament roll.   Among them are six citizens and burgesses.   Yet no writ *de expenses* is enrolled for a single one of the six.[3]   It is not often, however, that the rolls of parliament help in this way.   But there are other sources which furnish additional tests.   Specially valuable for this purpose are the borough accounts, which often record payments made for the expenses of the borough's representatives in parliament. Unfortunately these accounts have usually survived only in an imperfect condition, and very few even of those that do survive have been systematically printed or calendared.   They nevertheless supply some useful instances.   Thus the excerpts from the borough accounts of Reading printed by the Historical Manuscripts Commission show that representatives of the borough were actually present in at least 8

---

[1] Professor Pollard suggests (pp. 317-18) London, York, Bristol, Winchester, Salisbury, Southampton, Norwich, Yarmouth and the Cinque Ports.   It may be worth mentioning in passing that all these boroughs (except the Cinque Ports) do occasionally appear in the enrolments of writs *de expensis*.

[2] *Eng. Hist. Rev.* xxxix. pp. 511-25.

[3] *Rot. Parl.* ii. p. 113.   The names are : Thomas of Wycombe (constituency unknown), Robert of Morwode (Nottingham), Philip of Cayly (Cambridge), John of Rattlesden (Colchester), John of Preston (? Wycombe), Thomas But (? Norwich).

parliaments between April 1354 and September 1388 ;[1] yet no Reading burgesses are mentioned in the enrolments of writs *de expensis* for a single one of those same parliaments.   Again in the excerpts from the borough accounts of Lynn printed by the same Commission, there are entries which show that burgesses received payments for attending 8 parliaments between February 1328 and February 1338 ; but writs *de expensis* for Lynn members are enrolled for only 2 of those parliaments.[2]   Similarly, a few extracts printed from the borough accounts of Shrewsbury record expenses paid to members of 4 parliaments between August 1311 and September 1336 ; but the enrolled writs *de expensis* do not mention Shrewsbury burgesses in 3 of the four parliaments in question.[3]   These are facts gleaned from mere scattered abstracts and unsystematic summaries of very incomplete borough accounts.   It is interesting to turn to a set of borough accounts which have survived in a fairly continuous series (though there are several gaps of one or more years even here) and which have been published in a form which makes their contents pretty accurately known—the accounts of the borough of Leicester.   Between 1301 and 1324 these accounts record payments to the borough representatives (sometimes one but generally two) for attending 13 parliaments : for 10 of these parliaments no writs *de expensis* are enrolled for Leicester members.[4] During the reign of Edward III., the accounts show payments to Leicester members for attending at least 23 parliaments ; yet no writs *de expensis* are enrolled for Leicester for 18 of these 23 meetings.[5] It will be observed that none of the boroughs that have been adduced are among those which are supposed to have paid their members

[1] *Hist. MSS. Comm. Report XI.*, Appendix, Pt. vii. pp. 171-2.   The parliaments are: April 1354, May 1368, January 1380, November 1380, April 1384 (?), November 1384, October 1385, September 1388.

[2] *Hist. MSS. Comm. Report XI.*, Appendix, Pt. iii. pp. 213-16.   The parliaments are: February 1328, March 1332 (?), September 1332, September 1334, March 1336, September 1336, and two of the three parliaments of March 1337, September 1337 and February 1338.   Writs *de expensis* are enrolled for the parliaments of February 1334 and September 1336.

[3] *Hist. MSS. Comm. Report XV.*, Appendix, Pt. x. p. 27 ; Owen and Blakeway, *History of Shrewsbury*, i. p. 546.   The parliaments are: August 1311, March 1330 (or November 1330), September 1331 (?), March 1336 (or September 1336).   A writ *de expensis* is enrolled for the parliament of March 1330.

Bateson, *Records of the Borough of Leicester*, i. pp. 235, 246, 248, 267, 278, 296, 300, 320, 324, 328, 333-4, 339, 344, 347.   The parliaments are: January 1301, May 1306, April 1309, November 1311 (or August 1312), September 1314, January 1315, January 1316, October 1318, May 1319, October 1320, July 1321, May 1322, February 1324. Writs *de expensis* are enrolled for September 1314, January 1315 and January 1316.

[5] *Ibid.* ii. pp. 11, 14, 17, 26, 41-2, 45, 46, 47, 48, 60, 75, 77, 80, 91, 108, 110, 144, 147, 148, 158.   The parliaments are : September 1332 (?), December 1332, February 1334, September 1334, May 1335, March 1336, February 1338, February 1339, October 1339, January 1340 (?), April 1341, June 1344, February 1351, January 1352, September 1353, April 1354, February 1358, May 1360, June 1369, February 1371 (?), November 1372 (?), November 1373, January 1377.   (Payments for other parliaments which cannot be definitely assigned will be found *ibid.* pp. 28, 141.)   Writs are enrolled for the parliaments of December 1332, February 1334, February 1351, April 1354, February 1371.

without recourse to writs *de expensis*. Their example proves that we cannot rely upon the enrolled writs *de expensis* as being in any sense an exhaustive record of the borough members who actually attended mediæval parliaments. And there are other pieces of evidence which, though less definite than the facts just cited, appear to point to the same conclusion. One of these pieces of evidence may be referred to here. A parliament which met in February 1371 made a certain grant of money to the King. After the members had dispersed, the King found that it would be necessary to revise the terms of the grant. In order to save the trouble and expense of reassembling all the members, he issued a writ in April 1371 ordering the sheriffs to send from each shire one of the Knights and from cities and boroughs one of the citizens and burgesses who had come to the parliament in February, to meet at Winchester in June to revise the grant.[1] The names and respective constituencies of the members whom the sheriffs were thus ordered to send are enrolled in the Close Roll. Here then we have what purports to be a list of some of the members who " came " (*venerunt*) to the parliament of February 1371, and we may compare it with the enrolled writs *de expensis* for that parliament. Of course we must move cautiously : *venerunt* may be common form, and in the deserts of common form the unwary traveller may easily be duped by a verbal mirage. In this case " who came " may possibly mean no more than " who were elected to come ". The wording of the writ, however, appears to keep a clear distinction between the two expressions : it says that if any of the persons named " qui . . . ad dictum parliamentum . . . venerunt " are no longer alive, then " socios suos qui cum eis de veniendo ad parliamentum predictum electi fuerunt " are to be ordered to come instead of them. Again if " venerunt " meant merely " who were elected to come ", one would expect to find representatives summoned from more than two boroughs of a county like Wiltshire, where the boroughs electing representatives were at that time normally more numerous : yet two only of the Wiltshire boroughs are mentioned in these writs of April 1371. On the whole there is some justification for inclining to the view that " venerunt " here may very well mean " came ". If that is indeed its meaning, then these writs would imply that in the parliament of February 1371 no less than 83 boroughs were actually represented, though not necessarily by two members apiece in every case.[2] Yet it is for 18 boroughs only that writs *de expensis* are enrolled for the parliament of February 1371. The discrepancy is so serious that if it stood alone it might be passed

---

[1] *Report on the Dignity of a Peer*, i. Appendix, pp. 650-52. The persons summoned are described in the writ as persons " qui . . . ad dictum parliamentum [in February] de mandato nostro venerunt ".

[2] That is possibly the implication of the juxtaposition of " venerunt " and " electi fuerunt ". The enrolled writs *de expensis* prove that some boroughs were represented by two members each.

over. But taken with the proved discrepancies between the enrolled writs *de expensis* and the borough accounts of Shrewsbury, Reading, Lynn and above all Leicester, it cannot be lightly dismissed as incredible, and it is a warning against too hastily assuming that the citizens and burgesses were very remiss in attending and that they were a numerical minority of the Commons.

We may now turn to the shires. As is well known, the enrolments of writs *de expensis* are sometimes quite complete for all 37 shires, and in any case they always account for a greater proportion of the county than of the borough constituencies. It has therefore been supposed that for the shires, at any rate, these enrolments may be taken as exhaustive. It is very rarely that they can be tested, as the shires unfortunately had no records corresponding to the borough accounts. But occasionally a test is possible. For the parliament of March 1340, writs *de expensis* are enrolled for 61 county members drawn from 33 shires. Two of the shires for which no writs are enrolled are Oxford and Surrey. Yet at least one member was present from each of those shires, for they are mentioned in the parliament roll as appointed to serve on a committee to deal with petitions.[1] Again, it is known that Henry of Keighley, one of the knights for Lancashire, was present in the parliament of January 1301, since it was he who bore to the king the " bill " of grievances drawn up on that occasion.[2] Yet no writ *de expensis* is enrolled for him. These two examples are definite proof that the enrolments of writs *de expensis* are not necessarily exhaustive even for the shire members. The example from 1340 is especially noteworthy. An enrolment of writs *de expensis* for so many as 33 out of 37 shires might naturally be thought exhaustive. Yet it is clear that two shires which had members actually present on that occasion are omitted from the enrolment. Now the enrolments of writs *de expensis* for the shires during the reigns of Edward I. and Edward II. are often nothing like so full as that of March 1340. Thus for the parliament of January 1301 only 25 shires are enrolled, for that of May 1306 only 20, for that of October 1318 only 28, for the two York parliaments of 1322 only 19 apiece. It being certain that 33 out of 37 is not an exhaustive enrolment in 1340, one can scarcely feel confident that 28 out of 37 is exhaustive in 1318, and still less that 19 out of 37 is exhaustive in 1322. On the whole, one is forced to the conclusion that the enrolments of writs *de expensis* cannot safely be taken as exhaustive, either for the shires or for the boroughs.[3]

The foregoing considerations suggest that the evidence of sheriffs'

[1] *Rot. Parl.* ii. p. 113. Thomas de la More (Oxford) and John of Hayton (Surrey) are the two members of the committee for whom writs *de expensis* are not enrolled.

[2] Stubbs, *Const. Hist.* ii. (4th ed.) pp. 157-8. In the following June he was imprisoned for the part he had played.

[3] This conclusion was long ago reached by Prynne ; *Fourth Part*, pp. 11-12, 76, 177.

returns and enrolled writs *de expensis* may easily prove misleading unless interpreted with great caution. This is especially true when that evidence is used as an index to the contemporary attitude of constituencies and representatives towards the mediæval English parliament. There seems to be a growing opinion that mediæval constituencies were reluctant to elect, that their representatives were still more reluctant to attend, and that down to the 15th century, at any rate, this general reluctance so far prevailed that a considerable proportion of the constituencies were commonly represented in parliament only on paper, so to speak. Various facts seem to indicate, however, that these opinions need some qualification before they can be accepted with any confidence. Thus it is possible to prove, even from the enrolments of writs *de expensis* as they stand, that a good many of the members who were frequently elected actually attended a large proportion of the parliaments for which they were returned. Between 1290 and 1327, Bedfordshire returned Peter le Loring and John Morteyn 6 times; Loring was present 6 times and Morteyn 5 times: Buckinghamshire returned Robert Malet 11 times and he attended 9 times: Baldwin of Stowe was returned 9 times by Cambridgeshire, and attended 6 times: Richard of Chessbech was returned 9 times by Devonshire and was present 8 times: John Peverel was elected 6 times by Dorsetshire, and was present 6 times: Hertfordshire elected Geoffrey de la Lee 9 times and Richard Perers 8 times; Lee attended 8 times and Perers 5 times: John Waldeshef was elected 7 times by Huntingdonshire and attended every time: Lancashire returned Gilbert of Singleton, William of Slene and Edmund Nevill each 4 times, and each was present 4 times: Richard of Walsingham was elected 7 times by Norfolk and attended 7 times: Richard of Horseleye was elected 6 times by Northumberland and attended 5 times: John of Croxford was returned 9 times by Oxfordshire and was present in parliament every time: Shropshire elected Richard of Harley 8 times and he attended 8 times: Yorkshire returned Gregory of Thornton 5 times and he attended 5 times: even in the incomplete enrolments for the boroughs there are Exeter, Lincoln and Worcester each with a burgess elected 5 times and present 4 times,[1] and Bedford with William Costyn elected 8 times and present at least 5 times. But the most interesting examples from a borough come from Oxford d ring the period 1368–1404. Writs *de expensis* are enrolled for Oxford burgesses for every parliament except three between May 1368 and January 1404.[2] An analysis shows that Edmund Kenyon was elected 9 times and attended 9 times; that William Dagevill was elected 7 times and attended 6 times; that William of Codeshale was elected 5 times and attended 5 times; that

---

[1] Matthew of Crouthorne (Exeter), Henry Stoil (Lincoln), Richard Coliz (Worcester).
[2] The enrolled writs are printed by Prynne; *Fourth Part*, ss. iii.-v.

G

Adam River and John Hicks were each elected 5 times and were present in parliament 4 times.   It may be urged that all these may have been exceptional cases which do not necessarily invalidate the inference that reluctance to attend was the general rule.   It may therefore be interesting to test the members who were elected only once : among these, if anywhere, one might expect to find the persons who were reluctant.   The lists for the period 1290–1327 show some 650 shire members elected (so far as is known) only once : the enrolled writs *de expensis*, incomplete as they probably are, show that at least 380 of these actually attended.   For the boroughs no comprehensive test is possible : but it may be noted that in Bedford during the same period 16 burgesses were elected once, and that at least 8 of them actually attended ; and that in Oxford during the period 1368–1404 19 burgesses were elected only once and 18 are known to have attended. Taken together, these figures suggest that reluctance to attend was quite possibly not a general and almost certainly not a successful attitude.   The well-known case of Chipping Torrington is worth recalling in this connection.[1]   It is usually quoted as proof that the men of Torrington were anxious to avoid sending representatives to parliament.   But it also proves that they had not been allowed to act in the matter as they pleased—in short, that their reluctance to attend had not been a successful attitude.   There are some other facts which convey a similar impression.   In 1383 the burgesses of Colchester obtained a charter exempting them for five years from sending burgesses to parliament, on account of the expenses of fortifying the town ; in 1394 they obtained a similar exemption for three years on the same ground ;   in 1404 they obtained a similar exemption for six years " provided that they keep and support all statutes and ordinances and charges made and granted in the said parliaments ".[2]   In 1388 Maldon obtained an exemption from sending representatives for three years in order to assist in rebuilding its bridge ;   in 1392 it obtained a second exemption for the same reason, this time for seven years.[3] Most interesting of all is an example from Hull : in October 1384 the burgesses were excused from sending representatives *to the next parliament* of November 1384, because of the great expense of fortifying the town.[4]   These facts, while they certainly show that the three boroughs concerned were quite prepared to forgo parliamentary representation in order to further their local enterprises, also seem to show that they did not regard themselves as entirely free to neglect their parliamentary duties at pleasure ;[5] they apparently thought that their

---

[1] *Rot. Parl.* ii. pp. 459–60 ;   Prynne, *Fourth Part*, pp. 319–20.
[2] *Cal. Pat. Rolls*, 1381–85, p. 214 ;   1391–6, p. 379 ;   1401–5, p. 355.   The proviso in 1404 suggests that the king regarded the presence of representatives as of some importance from the point of view of legal forms.
[3] *Ibid.* 1385–88, p. 508 ;   1391–6, p. 187.   [4] *Ibid.* 1381–85, p. 475.
[5] See also the letter of the bailiffs of Ipswich, *supra*, p. 207, note 3.

reluctance to attend had better be a chartered reluctance if it was to be a really successful attitude.   Their example suggests that the reluctance of constituencies and representatives, even if it were proved, may not be the only factor to consider.   The mediæval English parliament was the handiwork of kings.   We must not too readily assume that those kings were always half oblivious of their handiwork ; for they were strong kings and they ruled in " a small, well conquered, much governed kingdom ". [1]

[1] Maitland, *Law Quart. Rev.* xiv. p. 33.

6

THE LEGISTLATORS OF
MEDIEVAL ENGLAND[1]*

by H. M. Cam

THERE HAS been so much discussion, and that so learned, of the nature of law in the Middle Ages, that it will be well for me to begin with a disclaimer. What I am concerned with is not so much law as laws, not so much theory as practice, not so much forms as forces. The great American school of legal historians may be right in saying that none save God could *make* law in the Middle Ages, but the student of medieval English government is confronted with assizes, establishments, provisions, ordinances, proclamations, and statutes that men observed or infringed and that judges enforced. They existed, and they mattered; they are both a monument to human activity and an indication of human intentions and opinions. In asking how and why they came to be there I am seeking the originating impulse for legislation rather than investigating its technical validity or the authority and status of the legislator.

In Dr. Ivor Jennings's book on parliament in the twentieth century[2] there is a chapter headed "Who makes the laws?" For one who seeks the substance rather than the form, he says, the answer to this question "The King in Parliament" will not do. Even if you admit that the responsibility for all legislation today rests with the government, you have still to find the government's source of inspiration. He appends to his discussion an analysis of the legislation of one year. Seventy acts were placed on the Statute Book in 1936-7, and he traces each of them to its originating agency—King Edward VIII, the Dominions, the Cabinet, the various Government Departments, Government Commissions, the Bench, Local Authorities, "public demand" in the Press, and

[1] The Raleigh lecture on history, read to the British Academy 13 June 1945. Reprinted from the *Proceedings of the British Academy*, vol. xxxi.
[2] Cambridge, 1939.

what he calls associated interests, such as the Society for the Prevention of Cruelty to Animals, the National Union of Teachers, the Central Council for Rivers Pollution, the National Farmers' Union, the Trade Marks, Patents and Designs Federation, and the Salvation Army. Finally, there is Mr. A. P. Herbert.

Who made the laws in medieval England? That is the question that I want to put, limiting myself to the last three centuries of the Middle Ages, to which the bulk of the enacted laws belong. There can be little hope of obtaining results comparable with Dr. Jennings' from such remote records, but the question is worth asking. Though, as he says, the law knows nothing of the legislative process,[1] the historian of civilization must be concerned with it. By and large, we are a law-abiding people, approximating to Burke's ideal of a disposition to conserve with an ability to improve. Our legislative machinery is the oldest in Europe, and if it has stood up to a good deal of criticism from outside in the last twelve years and survived more serious menaces from within, it has been mainly by virtue of its contacts with the opinion of the country at large. At the moment when it is about formally to renew that contact by our customary rough and clumsy methods it is not irrelevant to consider the earlier, experimental period in the evolution of the legislative process, and the nature of the contacts of law and opinion in the thirteenth, fourteenth and, fifteenth centuries.

There are three main sources of legislative activity in medieval England: the directive or planning urge in the ruler, the need for clarifying and defining experienced by the judicature, and the demand from the ruled for redress of grievances.

To the first source, the desire of the executive for order, we can attribute a large part of the legislation of the thirteenth century —such measures, for instance, as the police code built up by Henry III and Edward I from the Assize of Arms to the Statute of Winchester, the order for the holding of hundred courts in 1234, the succession of decrees on the coinage, the series of exchequer ordinances down to Stapleton's of 1323, and Edward I's great Statute of Wales, the first colonial constitution. We have a glimpse

[1] *Parliament*, p. 232.

of one of the departmental discussions, which produced such regulations in the preamble to the *Provisio super vicecomites et clericos suos* of 1298, which shows how three bishops, the king's treasurer, the barons of the exchequer, the justices of the Bench, and others of the king's council, being assembled in the exchequer on the feast of St. Valentine, had before them the problem of the literate but dishonest clerk who made out writs for levying excessive dues, and thus involved his illiterate but innocent chief, the sheriff, in penalties for extortion. They took counsel for a remedy and provided that henceforth the clerk should share his master's responsibility to the exchequer.[1] Official decrees of this sort might or might not need wide publicity, and a large proportion of them were not promulgated in parliaments. I do not propose to discuss them at length; administrative legislation is with us today and we know all about it and its sources. But the directive impulse of the administration, and above all of the council, is a continuing influence throughout the Middle Ages, originating, selecting, and amending the measures that become laws, not least in the period when the forms of legislation would seem to suggest a receptive rather than constructive attitude on the part of the government.

The second source, the judicature, is most important in the first of our three centuries. The judgement in a particular case, formally recorded as a precedent for the direction of future judges and litigants, belongs to the period when parliaments are still preeminently judicial occasions, and there are several instances of such *ad hoc* legislation on the rolls of Edward I's parliaments. The Statute of Waste of 1292, as is well known, is the judgement in the case of *Butler* v. *Hopton* after long discussion among the king's justices in full parliament.[2] The two "explanations" attached to the Statute of Gloucester, in effect revisions of a clumsily drafted enactment, have been traced by Mr. Sayles to two lawsuits, of 1278 and 1281, in which Eleanor Percy and the mayor and bailiffs of London, respectively, were involved.[3] The Ordinance *de Proteccionibus* in 1305 arose out of the particular

[1] *Stat. R.,* i. 213.   [2] *Stat. R.* i. 109 f.; *Rot. Parl.* i. 79.
[3] *Eng. Hist. Rev.,* 1937, pp. 468 ff.

grievance of the prior of St. Oswald's, who could not get redress from a defendant who was wrongfully pleading the king's protection.[1] In 1315 the *specialis petitio* of Katharine Jordan as to some sharp practice in a plea of Novel Disseisin produced a *generalis responsio* imposing penalties to be enforced by the justices in all such cases.[2] The transition from judicial to legislative remedy is perhaps indicated in a petition of 1318, when, in response to Robert of Mouhaut's complaint as to the penalizing of an attainted jury, the council reply that to change the laws of the realm requires the greatest deliberation, and that in full parliament.[3] Aside from judgements, it was, of course, in the great statutes of Edward I from 1275 onwards, modifying and defining the operation of the Common Law, that the judges made their greatest contribution to the statute book.

But the most abundant source of law-making is the third: public demand, direct or indirect, implicit or explicit; and parliaments were at once the field in which such impulses could work and, as time went on, the institution by means of which men could assert and enlarge their claims to law and justice. It is mainly, though not solely, with legislation in parliaments that we shall be concerned.

It is only possible to attempt such a survey by standing on the shoulders of others. The field opened up by Maitland in 1893 and McIlwain in 1910 has since then been explored by so many scholars on both sides of the Atlantic that the history of parliamentary legislation has been completely transformed. G. B. Adams, W. S. Holdsworth, M. V. Clarke, Eileen Power, Professors Plucknett, Morris, and Gray, Mr. Edwards, and Mr. H. G. Richardson are only a few of those on whose work I have relied in attempting to examine the processes of legislation from Magna Carta to the Reformation.

We all know that Magna Carta is the first statute on the statute roll, but we should not find it a perfectly simple matter to answer the question who made the charter enrolled there, for it took

---

[1] *Memoranda de Parliamento* (R.S.), p. 59; cf. p. 17, petition no. 15.
[2] *Rot. Parl.* i. 289.   [3] Cole, *Documents of English History*, p. 26.

twelve years to make, and there were many hands employed. We begin with its only begetter, Stephen Langton, holding up the Coronation Charter of Henry I to the assembled barons at St. Paul's, if the St. Albans' Chroniclers tell the truth, in August 1213;[1] we go on to the unknown framers of the "Unknown Charter of Liberties", to the equally unknown "men of the school of Glanvill and Hubert Walter" who, as Professor Powicke tells us,[2] must have helped to draft the carefully worded clauses of the articles submitted to John in May 1215,[3] to the barons who took part in the "Parliament of Runnymede", to the faithful supporters of John's young son who cut out the revolutionary clauses in 1216 and incorporated the amendments and additions of 1217. By now we have run through the whole gamut of baronial and official opinion, from the extreme Left-wing views of the five-and-twenty overkings (though even these have been recently rehabilitated by Mr. Richardson)[4] to those Right-wing moderates who stand out as the first English statesmen to catch the Whigs bathing and steal their clothes. The final version of the Charter, issued "freely and spontaneously" by the young King Henry in 1225, the statute cited in the courts and enforced by the judges from 1226 to 1920, owes perhaps less to him than to any of the other legislators, known and unknown, whose ideas and endeavours it incorporates.

Of the fifty or sixty other legislative acts of Henry III's reign only two have achieved anything like fame, and the first of these, though studiously noted in their handbooks by generations of medieval lawyers, is chiefly notorious today for the clause that is not there. In the Council of Merton in January 1236 all the learning and all the arguments from natural and divine law, from canon and civil law, and even, as he asserted, from the ancient custom of the land were on the side of Robert Grosseteste in urging

---

[1] The reliability of Roger of Wendover, the sole authority for this incident, is very doubtful, and there is good reason to credit the barons with independent initiative in demanding a charter. See V. H. Galbraith, *Roger of Wendover and Matthew Paris* (1944) and J. C. Holt "The Barons and the Great Charter" *Eng. Hist. Rev.*, 1955.

[2] *Stephen Langton*, p. 122.

[3] Accepting Mr. Holt's dating in *Eng. Hist. Rev.*, 1957, pp. 407–8.

[4] *John Rylands Bulletin*, 1944, "The Morrow of the Great Charter".

the simple and humane proposal to bring the common law of England into line with canon and civil Law by providing that children born out of wedlock should be held legitimate after the marriage of their parents. The bishop of Lincoln and the reform party were just about 700 years ahead of their times; but the diehards who declared "We will not change the laws of England" clearly implied that they could have changed them if they liked, in this agreeing with Grosseteste when he wrote to Justice Raleigh: "I am not so inexperienced—*nec tam idiota sum*—as to imagine that you or anyone else can make or change laws without the king and the magnates being consulted."[1] Then, as now, the reformer had to have the public opinion that counted on his side if he was to get anything done.

The other statute that is in all the law-books, the Statute of Marlborough, is also the product of discussion and compromise. It began with the Petition of the Barons, presented at the Parliament of Oxford in June 1258, containing the grievances both of great men like the earls of Gloucester and Hereford, of their tenants, and of the communities of the shires. The agenda of the *ad hoc* council of reform noted that the justices and other learned men were to consider the amendment of the laws before the next parliament.[2] Dr. E. F. Jacob[3] has traced the evidence of their labours in the various drafts of the document, which, after being held up by the obstructionist tactics of the greater men and forwarded by the publicity given by the heir to the throne to the protests of the middling men, was solemnly promulgated as the Provisions of Westminster by Henry III in October 1259. Of its twenty-four clauses, ten are based on the petition presented at Oxford fifteen months earlier. Though, as Mr. Jolliffe has said,[4] it was a document of the opposition, and a revolutionary opposition at that, it was enforced in the courts, reissued by Henry III ir 1263 as a conciliatory gesture,[5] and reissued again by Simon de Montfort's government after Lewes, though it may have been

---

[1] Grosseteste, *Epistolae* (R.S.), Ep. 24, p. 96.
[2] *John Rylands Bulletin*, 1933, Richardson & Sayles, "The Provisions of Oxford".
[3] *Baronial Reform and Rebellion*, Oxford, 1925.
[4] *Constitutional History of Medieval England* (London, 1937), p. 335 n.
[5] Jacob, *Baronial Reform*, pp. 76 ff.

suspended by his defeat and death. Finally, two years after Simon de Montfort had fallen at Evesham and his followers had been disinherited at Winchester, "The lord king wishing to provide for the betterment of his realm and for such administration of justice as the royal office entails, having called together the more discreet men of the realm, both greater and lesser, provided, established and ordained" at Marlborough a set of enactments which incorporated the whole of the "revolutionary" legislation of 1259, with eleven additional clauses.[1] The concerns of the great men for their feudal dues, the complaints of the countryside against the oppressions of sheriffs, of magnates, and of royal justices, the grievances of tenants against their lords, the skilful devices of the legal experts, who may even have included Bracton himself and, at the latest stage, the pacific influence of the papal legate—all these interests and agencies went to the making of the Statute of Marlborough.

A hundred years later we shall find out best examples of the interplay of interests and agencies in the processes of law-making in the field of economic affairs. All England, from the king to the agricultural worker, is out to make money, and the tussle between high politics and local jealousies, associated interests and class antagonisms is informing the experimental and occasionally amateurish legislation of council and parliament. Eileen Power has depicted the interplay of motives among the different parties concerned in the establishment of parliamentary control of the wool taxes. I should like to glance at two other examples of economic legislative experiment involving various interests, and consider the Statute of the Staple of 1354 and the Ordinances and Statute of Labourers of 1349-52.

The staple for English merchants set up by Edward I had been at Bruges, Antwerp, and St. Omer by turns when, in the Parliament of York in 1318, the question of the establishment of home staples was mooted, and a conference was arranged in the following year between the merchants and the exchequer officials with others of the council, which reported in favour of the establish-

---

[1] *Stat. R.* i. 19-25. Professor Powicke considers that the hand of Ottobuono is traceable in the drafting of this preamble.*

ment of home staples.[1] Political factions in the council, it seems, held up action till 1326 when, under the influence of the younger Dispenser,[2] ordinances made "by us and our council for the common profit and relief of the people of all our realm and power" set up the fourteen home staples and laid down regulations for native and alien merchants, purchasers, and manufacturers.[3] In 1328, however, the matter was reopened and the different towns were asked to send delegates to an assembly of merchants at York. The London delegates, writing back to the city for further instructions, indicate the difficulties of the assembly; the towns cannot agree, the merchants of the staple want a foreign staple, and they are all afraid of incurring the enmity of the king and council if they fail to make a recommendation.[4] The compromise suggested by the city fathers in their reply was in fact accepted, the ordinances of 1326 were repealed in the Parliament of Northampton, and free trade "after the tenor of the Great Charter" was established for the time being. A petition from the good folk of the community in the Parliament of York of 1334 for the restoration of the home staples was rejected and in 1340, the war with France having begun, Edward III established an overseas staple at Bruges in the lands of his continental ally. In the April parliament of 1343, in response to an inquiry from the council, the merchants put forward a long and reasoned statement in favour of home staples,[5] but foreign policy still outweighed their arguments and it was not till 1353 that they had their way. In September of that year a Great Council was held, expressly to deal with the maintenance and good government of the staple. A set of carefully drafted ordinances, drawn up by the king's council at least three months earlier, according to Mr. Richardson,[6] was read aloud to the prelates, magnates, and commons assembled in the White Chamber of Westminster Palace; any amendments proposed to be given in writing. The commons demanded a copy of the ordinances; one was given to the knights and another to the burgesses,

[1] Eng. Hist. Rev., 1914, Bland, "Establishment of Home Staples".
[2] Cal. Pat. Rolls, 1324-7, p. 274.
[3] Bland, Brown, and Tawney, Documents, pp. 181-4.
[4] A. H. Thomas, Cal. of Plea and Memoranda Rolls, 1323-64 (Cambridge, 1926), p. 52.
[5] Rot. Parl. ii. 143.   [6] Bulletin Inst. Hist. Research, No. 25 (1931), p. 13, n. 4.

and after great deliberation had amongst themselves they gave
their opinion in writing. The magnates having read and discussed
this written statement, the ordinances were issued in their final
form. Only one amendment of the commons is recorded; they
proposed to add eight more towns to the list of staples, bringing
the number up to seventeen. The king accepted the suggestion
only as far as regarded Canterbury "in honour of St. Thomas".
The commons further petitioned that the articles of the ordinances
should be recited at the next parliament, and entered on the roll of
parliament, so that ordinances and agreements made in council
should not be on record as if they had been made in common
parliament, and to this the king assented.[1] Thus in the following
April the chief justice expounded to the lords and commons in
parliament how the king had established the staple in England,
and how no staple could be maintained without fixed laws and
customs, and therefore he had deputed the wise men of his council
and the prelates, dukes, earls, barons, justices, serjeants, and others
of the commonalty to ordain and make such laws and ordinances;
and because he wished them to endure for ever he now caused
them to be recited in parliament to endure for ever as a statute.
Once again the knights of the shire were invited to get written
copies and study them and, if they wished, propose amendments
in writing. And after good deliberation the commons found the
ordinances good and profitable for king and people and prayed
that they might be confirmed, putting forward a number of
supplementary proposals, most of which were accepted, and the
ordinances, being confirmed, with these additions, by the king
and the magnates, were finally placed on the statute roll.[2]

So much for the genesis of the Statute of the Staple of 1354,
the fruit of thirty-five years of bargaining, diplomacy, and compromise between king, merchants, burgesses, knights of the shire,
magnates, and council. The history of the Statute of Labourers,
as traced for us by that great American scholar Bertha Putnam,[3]

---

[1] *Rot. Parl.* ii. 246–53; *Stat. R.* i. 332–43. *

[2] *Rot. Parl.* ii. 254, 257, 261 f.; *Stat. R.* 348 f.

[3] *Toronto Law Journal*, 1944, pp. 251–81. See also *Enforcement of Statutes of Labourers*,
New York, 1908; and *The Place in Legal History of Sir William Shareshull* (1950), pp. 51,
53, 68–72.

opens up another window on the processes of law-making. She appears to have caught the architect of the law in his workshop. It begins with the first ordinance "against the malice of labourers" issued by the council in June 1349 while the Black Death was still raging, a hastily drafted emergency measure designed to check the rise of wages and prices and to prevent labourers from breaking their contracts. Its ineffectiveness was soon evident; grievous complaints reached the council of the black market in labour which made it impossible for the employers of labour to pay any taxes. In November a second ordinance was issued, providing that all excess wages might be levied from the recipients and applied to the reduction of the taxpayers' burden, and a new commission to the justices of the peace charged them with the enforcement of both ordinances. By 1351 the government felt it was safe to summon a parliament again, and in this petitions were put forward by the commonalty for the better enforcing of both ordinances. The statute purporting to be a reply to these petitions betrays the hand of the expert lawyer as well as the experienced administrator; and the subsequent petition of the commonalty[1] laid down the terms of the grant of the next triennial subsidy with such skill, closing all the gaps through which the over-paid labourer might escape, the tax collector cheat, or the locality be unduly penalized or favoured in the matter of tax-relief, that Miss Putnam again detects the expert adviser. The parliament roll speaks of long treaty and deliberation by the commons, and of magnates sent to advise with them, so there is evidence to bear out her contention that the inspiration of the measure comes from the council.[2] Miss Putnam goes farther and names the specific councillor who she believes devised the ingenious financial and legal details of the whole scheme, if not the original plan of a nation-wide regulation of wages. Her legislator is William Shareshull, justice of the peace, justice itinerant, junior judge in Common Pleas, Exchequer, and King's Bench, and chief justice of King's Bench from 1350 to 1361, in which capacity he opened

[1] *Stat. R.* i. 327.

[2] *Rot. Parl.* ii. 237. Elsewhere it is referred to as "an ordinance made by the king's council". Putnam, *Enforcement of Statutes of Labourers*, p. 268.

five successive parliaments during his term of office. He attended the councils which drafted the first and second ordinance; he was himself an employer of labour in Oxfordshire; he was holding sessions in the summer of 1349 which could have brought him in close touch with the *popularis conquaestio* of the taxpayers; he enforced the ordinances as justice of the peace, and in opening the parliament of 1351 he told the lords and commons that the matters chiefly needing amendment were the failure to keep the peace and the refusal of labourers and servants to work as they used to do. Whether his share in the legislation of 1349-52 was great or small, we cannot mistake the combined action of the views of the employing and taxpaying class, the policy of the government, the experience of the administrator, and the skill of the legal expert in producing the first labour legislation of this country. It is noteworthy also that there were channels by which public opinion could speedily reach the government when parliaments were temporarily suspended.

What were these channels? Stubbs, seeking the origins of the importance of the commons in parliament, found it in the local juries, whose knowledge of their countryside was ascertained for the use of the central government, and in the ancient communal responsibilities of township, hundred, and shire blending naturally with the newer chartered responsibilities of the urban communities to produce the representative element in parliament. Along this line, reinforced as Dr. Post is teaching us,[1] by canonist doctrines of corporate responsibility imposed from above, we might arrive at the commons' share in taxation, but hardly at their share in legislation. It is true that the grievances of the countryside presented by a jury or elicited by inquest might, and did, issue in legislation—witness the relation of the first Statute of Westminster of 1275 to the Hundred Rolls inquest of the previous year*—but a more spontaneous means of expressing the subjects' plaints and prayers was needed for parliament to become the national tribunal for righting nation-wide wrongs. That means was the petition or bill, and it is above all in the study of the process of petitioning

[1] *Speculum*, 1943, pp. 211-32; *Traditio*, 1943, pp. 355-408.**

that the most valuable additions to our knowledge of parliamentary evolution have been made in recent years. The trail was
blazed by Maitland in 1893, but only in the last twenty years has
exploration been seriously undertaken, notably by Mr. Richardson[1] and Professor H. L. Gray,[2] but also most usefully by Mr.
G. L. Haskins, Miss D. Rayner, and Mr. A. R. Myers.* The
petition, by its freedom from set forms and by its deferential
method of approach, offered opportunities for the spontaneous
expression of opinion; down to 1914 it was·recognized as the
natural vehicle for requests from the unenfranchised.[3] We have
already noted its close verbal relation to legislation in the history
of Magna Carta and the Statute of Marlborough: the same point
has recently been made by Mr. Edwards in connexion with the
Confirmation of the Charters in 1297.[4] A less close but highly
significant relationship is traceable in the preambles to a whole
number of statutes, beginning with those of that great autocrat
Edward I. A king cannot be coerced, says Bracton, but you can
always supplicate him. *Locus erit supplicationi.*

In the Tudor *Discourse upon the Understanding of Statutes* recently
edited by Dr. Thorne,[5] and ascribed by Professor Plucknett to
Sir Thomas Egerton, later Lord Ellesmere,[6] the reader is warned
against taking the preamble to a statute too seriously.[7] This is a
very sound warning for Tudor times, but as regards the medieval
statute there is a good deal to be said for Dyer's description of the
preamble to a statute as "a key to open the minds of the makers
of the act and of the mischiefs they intend to remedy". I will
quote some of Edward I's alleged reasons for legislation in chronological order. "Because our lord the King greatly desires to redress the state of the realm where it needs amendment, and that
for the common profit of Holy Church and of the realm" (1275);
"the king providing for the fuller administration of right as the

---

[1] *Bulletin Inst. Hist. Research*, 1927–34 (Nos. 15, 17, 18, 23, 25, 33); *Eng. Hist. Rev.*, 1931,
1932; *Rotuli Parliamentorum Anglie hactenus inediti* (Camden Series), London, 1935; *Select
Cases of Procedure without Writ* (Selden Society), London, 1941.

[2] *The Influence of the Commons on Early Legislation*, Cambridge, Mass., 1932.

[3] See P. Fraser, "Public Petitioning and Parliament before 1832". *History*, 1961, pp. 195–
211.

[4] *Eng. Hist. Rev.*, 1943.   [5] San Marino, California, 1942.

[6] *Law Qaurterly Review*, 1944, pp. 246–7.   [7] *Discourse*, ed. Thorne, p. 114.

royal office demands" (1278); "because merchants have fallen into poverty through failure to recover their debts" (1283); "to make good the oppressions and defects of former statutes" (1285); "of his special grace, and for the affection that he bears towards prelates, earls, barons and others of his kingdom" (1290); "since the Abbots of Fécamp and St. Edmunds and divers others supplicated in parliament" (1290); "at the instance of the magnates of his realm" (1290); "on the grievous complaint both of religious and of others of the kingdom" (1292); "understanding by the public and frequent complaint of the middling folk . . . we have decreed in parliament for the common welfare" (1293); "having diligently meditated on the defects in the law and the many grievances and oppressions inflicted on the people in time past we wish to provide a remedy and establish the certainty of the law" (1299); "in favour of the poor workmen of this city who live by the work of their hands, lest they should lack meat and be impoverished" (1302); "since those who have been put out of the forest by the perambulation have made request at this parliament"[1]—that is, the parliament of 1305, on whose rolls four such petitions are recorded.[2]

If these preambles give the key to Edward's mind, we seem to see a benevolent and order-loving legislator, passing from concern for a complete and coherent system of law to a growing consciousness of personal and class grievances calling for redress. Without any intention of calling the nation into partnership with him, it is clear that Edward was to some extent permitting his subjects to suggest, if not dictate, matter for legislation. He was making his parliaments, held twice or thrice a year "for the providing of new remedies for new wrongs, and for the doing of justice to all according to their need", the occasions for receiving petitions from all and sundry.

It used to be assumed that one of the functions of elected representatives was to hand in such petitions on behalf of their constituents. It may have become their function at a later date, but

---

[1] *Stat. R.* i. 26, 47, 53, 71, 107; *Rot. Parl.* i. 35, 41, 79, 117; *Stat. R.* i. 128; *Rot. Parl.* i. 147, 177.

[2] *Memoranda de Parliamento* (R.S.), pp. 18, 67, 89, 155 ff.

Mr. George Haskins[1] has proved conclusively that it was not so in Edward I's reign, for petitions were presented in large numbers in parliaments to which no representatives came, and it can be shown occasionally that special delegates were appointed by a community to present a petition when other men had been chosen as its representatives. In its origins, petitioning was a direct approach by the subject or group of subjects to the king. If the grievance alleged was a personal or local one, concerning the petitioner alone, it was most likely to demand executive or judicial action on the part of the crown, though judicial action might in a test case, as we have seen, produce legislation. Not until the fifteenth century, it seems, were the answers to requests for special or for localized favours for individuals, groups, or localities cast into legislative form. The main source of legislation was not the special but the general or common petition, which, as defined in 1346, was a petition "that might turn to the common profit",[2] as distinct from one that concerned special or private interests. Such a petition might be presented by one or by many; it would be worded in such a way as to suggest that it had widespread support. From a letter of Edward's printed by Stubbs we know that the petition of twelve articles that purported to express the demands of the whole community of the realm,[3] was presented in the parliament of Lincoln in 1301 by Henry of Keighley, one of the knights of the shire for Lincolnshire; Edward himself later described Keighley as acting for the Archbishop of Canterbury and other magnates of the realm who had pressed the king outrageously at that parliament.[4] In 1301 the "community of the realm"—the medieval equivalent for "public opinion", that is, the body of those politically conscious and politically active—was still predominantly aristocratic. But from 1297 onwards the lesser folk, both knights and burgesses, were being drawn more and more into the vortex of politics, and the reign of Edward II established both the political value to the magnates of co-operation with the "knights and the folk of the boroughs who came to the king's

---

[1] *Eng. Hist. Rev.*, 1938, "Petitions under Edward I".

[2] *Rot. Parl.* ii. 160.   [3] Palgrave, *Parliamentary Writs*, i. 104 f.*

[4] Stubbs, *Const. Hist.* ii, at § 181 (p. 151, 2nd ed.). See also Powicke, *The Thirteenth Century*, 1953, p. 704.

parliament at the king's command for themselves and for the people", as they described themselves in 1309,[1] and also the practical uses to which the petitioning technique could be put. As the fourteenth century advanced, the lords were claiming a share in the hearing and answering of petitions, and it suited them well to inspire and promote petitions which purported to be in the common interest and which were presented by those who were not of their order.

Thus, early in the reign of Edward III, though parliament was still the tribunal where remedies were sought for private wrongs, the tide of petitions of national scope calling for political or legislative action had mounted so high that deliberate classification became necessary. Miss Doris Rayner, in a close' and careful study of the technique of petitioning,[2] has shown how between 1324 and 1334 the chancery clerks who kept the records of parliaments were working out a solution of the problem. By 1339 the two categories are officially recognized; the singular or private petition is that which concerns the individual or private interest, and it must be delivered to the auditors and triers, who will pass it on to the appropriate authority for judicial or executive action. The common petition is that which concerns the common interest, and it must be delivered to the clerk of the parliament for reference sooner or later to the king and the lords of the council, with or without the endorsement of the commons as a body. Their endorsement or avowal certainly gives it a better chance of being accepted and becoming the basis of a statute or ordinance.

As Stubbs said long ago, nearly all the legislation of the fourteenth century is based upon parliamentary petitions. According to Professor Gray, this is equally true of the first half of the fifteenth century: then the tide turns, and a growing number of statutes omit all reference to the popular request. With the accession of Edward IV the bulk of legislation shrinks markedly, and under Richard III and Henry VII only a small proportion of the acts of parliament originate formally with the commons.

---

[1] *Rot. Parl.* i. 444.
[2] *Eng. Hist. Rev.*, 1941, "The Machinery of the Commune Petition".

Whereas under Henry V sixty-nine of his seventy statutes were based on petitions, of the 114 public acts of Henry VII, only seventeen purport to be passed at the request of the commons.

Professor Gray, following Stubbs, interprets this whole movement as the rise and decline of popular power as contrasted with that of the king, the council, and the lords. There is admittedly still much to be done in clearing up the relations of lords and commons in the fourteenth and fifteenth centuries, on which it may be hoped that the *History of Parliament* launched by Lord Wedgwood will throw further light, but I think we are already in a position to say that a petition purporting to come from the commons in the fifteenth century, like a petition presented on behalf of the community of the realm in the fourteenth century, might in fact have originated in a variety of sources. The petition of the magnates and community which produced the Statute of Carlisle in 1307 almost certainly was inspired by Edward I.* We saw that the act prescribing the technique for applying labour fines to the relief of taxation was based on a petition that was probably dictated by a member of the council. Indeed the roll of parliament refers specifically to the advice given on this occasion by certain great men "both with regard to the aid and for the making of petitions touching the common people of the land".[1] In the parliament of 1401 a petition touching the Cistercian order was referred to the commons by Henry IV for their consideration, and they approved it. From another entry on the roll it appears that the petition was originally handed in by Archbishop Arundel, but the statute formed on it is described as being granted at the instance and request of the commons.[2] Anyone who could make out a good case for his particular demand being in the common interest might claim or allege the backing of the commons. As far back as 1327 the commons were protesting against having bills put forward in their name without their endorsement or "avowal",[3] and this practice of backing or avowing a bill put forward by an individual, or originated by the lords, or put into their mouths by king or council, is traceable

[1] *Rot. Parl.* ii. 237.
[2] *Rot. Parl.* iii. 457, 464; *Stat. R.* ii. 121.   [3] *Rot. Parl.* ii. 10-11.

throughout the period when Professor Gray is crediting them
with something like the monopoly of initiative. Much of the
autocratic legislation of Richard II's last parliament was formally
petitioned for by the commons. To name a few instances from
1382 to 1423, petitions from the Lombard Merchants in England,
from the mayor and aldermen of London, from the dean and
chapter of Lincoln, from the poor commons of Northumberland,
Cumberland, and Westmorland, from the captains who had
served in the French wars under Henry V, from the master of the
mint and from magnates like Henry Prince of Wales or John
Duke of Bedford are put forward on their behalf by the commons
and bear fruit in legislation.[1] In 1423 the lords referred to the
commons a petition which they had received from the merchants
of the Staple, "to have their opinion", and the commons sent it
back to the lords "as one of their common petitions.[2]"

One result of this practice is that in the fifteenth century it
becomes usual for outside bodies to address their petitions to the
commons, in the hope that they will present them to the king and
the lords. The development of this technique has been fully
described by Mr. A. R. Myers.[3] A pictorial representation of
the process is to be found in the muniments of King's College,
Cambridge. On the Parliament Roll of 1444[4] is a petition from
the Provost and Scholars of the College Royal of our Lady and
St. Nicholas addressed to the "right wise and discrete Commons
of this present Parliament" requesting them to pray the king to
establish, by the advice of the Lords Spiritual and Temporal and
by authority of parliament all the articles annexed, and grant
to the college his letters patent to that effect. The charter based
on the resulting act of parliament is preserved at King's College,
and on its first sheet are a series of miniatures arranged like a
flight of steps: in the left-hand margin kneel the commons with
the speaker, bearing a roll, at their head. He says: "Priount les
Communes." Above are the lords headed by the chancellor who

---

[1] *Rot. Parl.* iii. 138, 429, 581; iv. 74, 143, 177 f.

[2] *Ibid.*, iv. 250; cited by Stubbs, *Const. Hist.* iii, at § 440 (footnote).

[3] *Eng. Hist. Rev.*, 1937, "Parliamentary Petitions in the Fifteenth Century"; *Toronto Law Journal*, 1939, "The Commons in the Fifteenth Century".

[4] *Rot. Parl.* v. 87.

says: "Nous le prioms aussi." In the centre kneels Henry VI
himself, saying "Fiat" and adoring the Virgin and St. Nicholas
depicted above him to the right.[1]

Legislation originating in a petition may give the petitioners
something different from what they requested. Henry V's promise
in 1414* not to enact statutes whereby the commons might be
bound contrary to their asking was, as has been pointed out by
several scholars,[2] no security that a statute would conform to
the terms of the request, nor did it assure to the petitioners the
chance of discussing and rejecting amendments. Nine years later
a council minute instructed the clerk of parliament to show the
acts that had been passed in the last parliament to the justices of
both benches, so that they might be rendered into clear language;[3]
the final wording of the statutes was not controlled by parliament.
Thus the device of "the bill containing the form of the act desired
to be enacted" which is coming into use from the middle of the
fifteenth century is an important development in legislative
procedure. It probably originated in private demands for royal
grants like the King's College bill; it was used for measures
promoted by the Crown before it was employed for the common
petition originating *bona fide* with the commons. It not only
led, if Professor Plucknett is right,[4] to more exact drafting and to
stricter interpretation of statutes, but it also involved parliament
itself more actively and intimately in the legislative process.
Legislation was no longer "the government's vague reply to
vaguely worded complaints, but rather the deliberate adoption
of specific proposals embodied in specific texts emanating from the
crown and its officers". More than that: though the formal
initiative might be temporarily lost to the commons in the Tudor
period, their discussions and criticisms of measures would have a
more practical effect on the form and content of the statutes to
which, having ceased to be petitioners, they were more truly
assenters than when they had claimed that function in 1414. If

[1] *Proceedings of Cambridge Antiquarian Society*, 1931-2, p. 87.
[2] S. B. Chrimes, *English Constitutional Ideas in the Fifteenth Century* (Cambridge, 1936),
pp. 161 ff., citing Dr. Pickthorn.
[3] Nicolas, *Proceedings and Ordinances of the Council*, iii. 22.
[4] *Law Quarterly Review*, 1944, pp. 248 ff.

Professor Plucknett is also right in his suggestion that the change in attitude towards the statutes evinced in Egerton's *Discourse* is the product of procedural change rather than political theory, we should have an admirable illustration of Dicey's thesis that laws create opinion almost as much as opinion produces laws.

In scrutinizing the channels by which public opinion was conveyed to the legislative agencies we have lost sight of the sources of that opinion. "The connexion between legislation and the supposed interests of the legislators is obvious", says Dicey.[1] Almost every interest in medieval society, almost every element in its make-up, has left its trace on the legislation of council and parliament.

Take first the legal profession. "We made the statute and we know what it means", said Hengham, speaking for the Edwardian bench. Judges, according to Dicey, aim rather at securing the certainty than at amending the deficiencies of the law,[2] and Magna Carta and the Petition of Right exemplify that attitude. The *Quo warranto* legislation of Edward I, embodying the Bractonian theory that all governmental functions exercised by a subject must expressly be delegated by royal act or sanction illustrates well the policy of definition applied in the royal interest. The Treason Law of 1352, assigned by Miss Putnam, like the labour legislation, to Chief Justice Shareshull,[3] also extends by defining. The judges who were instructed to put the good points of the Ordinances of 1311 into the statute of 1322[4] were the forerunners of those who were charged a hundred years later to clarify the wording of the acts that had just passed through parliament.

As for the common lawyers, they were undoubtedly pursuing their own interests in seeking to limit the scope of equitable jurisdiction, both in council and in chancery, by those fourteenth-century statutes to which seventeenth-century enemies of the Star Chamber were to appeal. The attack on the lawyers' membership of parliament in 1372, from whatever quarter it came, was

---

[1] *Law and Public Opinion in England during the Nineteenth Century* (London, 1905), p. 13.
[2] *Ibid.*, p. 362.   [3] See above, p. 176, n. 3.
[4] J. Conway Davies, *Baronial Opposition to Edward II* (Cambridge, 1918), p. 583; cf. p. 492.

unsuccessful.[1] Possibly their help in formulating and presenting petitions was making it as useful to others as it was profitable to themselves to be elected to the common house.

The interest of the clergy is easily detected. Their hand is traceable in a series of measures, from *de Bigamis*, recorded before clerics and lawyers and accepted and published by the king's council in 1276, down to the statute for the clergy based on their *querimonia* in 1316.[2] In 1401, besides the statute about the Cistercians promoted by archbishop Arundel, there is the famous *de heretico comburendo*, which corresponds closely clause by clause to the long Latin petition of the clergy, drafted presumably in Convocation, up to the point when the statute replaces the petition that the lay authorities shall deal with the convicted heretic "as is incumbent on them" by the direction "that they shall cause him to be burned before the people in some public place".[3]

The share of the lay magnates in legislation is constant and obvious. To take one field where their interests conflicted with that of the Church, Edward I's statement that he passed the Statute of Mortmain at their instance is borne out by the fact that the first attempt to limit the acquisition of land by an ecclesiatical corporation was made by the barons at Oxford in 1258. In all the anti-papal protests and enactments from 1307 onwards, as in the anti-clerical proposals of the fifteenth century, the voice of the lay landlord and patron is clearly heard. How far the magnates pulled wires in the fifteenth-century House of Commons is a matter of debate, but, as we have seen, there is no question that many of the petitions addressed to the king and the lords of the council in the fifteenth as in the fourteenth century had been inspired by some of those who had the considering of them. "They procure petitions in the name of the commons which touch the commons not at all." The law against poachers of 1293 and the ordinance on maximum prices of 1315 were instigated by the magnates and can fairly be ranked as class legislation.[4] So, in a different sense, was the *Provisio per milites* of 1292—a code of rules for tournaments drafted by knights who

---

[1] *Eng. Hist. Rev.*, 1931, pp. 377-81. [2] *Stat. R.* i. 42-3, 175 f.
[3] *Rot. Parl.* iii. 466-7; *Stat. R.* ii. 125-8.* [4] *Rot. Parl.* i. 101, 295.

took a part in such exercises, which was approved by the earls and other magnates who then requested the king to ratify them. Edward, himself an ardent jouster in his younger days, approved them as being for the common good, confirmed them by letters sealed, and ordered the sheriffs to co-operate in enforcing them.[1] It is as if the cup-tie regulations were issued by order in council.

There was, of course, no hard-and-fast line in England between the greater and the lesser baronage, the nobility and the gentry. Magnates and knights of the shire were at one, for instance, in supporting the Statute of Labourers. But in one legislative episode to which Miss Putnam has introduced us[2] there is a tug of war between magnates and county gentlemen. For some sixty years of the fourteenth century various experiments were being tried to solve the problems of keeping the peace in the counties.* The magnates advocated the appointment of one or two great men to "keep the counties" and act as local justices, and got their way three times (in 1328, 1330, 1332); in the commons petition after petition reiterated the demand that those smaller men who since 1307 had been entrusted with the police duties of inquiry and arrest of suspects should be given judicial powers also, so that they could try and sentence peace-breakers. Such powers were given and taken away time after time; but in the end the commons had their way; the justices of the peace were to be local knights and squires, and plenty of them; not one or two great lords with estates in half a dozen counties.

A longer and less conclusive tug of war concerned another office held by country gentlemen—the sheriffdom. The tussle of the sheriffs and the exchequer reveals something like a vested interest working in the House of Commons. The sheriffs, who were responsible to the exchequer for the profits of local government, made up these profits in large part from the sums paid to them by their subordinates, the hundred bailiffs to whom they sublet the hundreds. Under the Statute of Lincoln of 1316, which purported to remedy the grievances of the magnates against oppressive and extortionate sheriffs, they were forbidden

[1] *Ibid.*, 85.   [2] *Trans. R. Hist. Soc.*, 1929.

to charge too high a rate.[1] But the kings found the office of hundred bailiff a useful piece of royal patronage,[2] and in the early fourteenth century they were constantly separating hundreds from their shires by giving them to protégés who kept all the profits of office for themselves and paid nothing to the sheriff, who was nevertheless expected to pay in the same sum to the exchequer as before. Naturally he tried to recoup himself from those parts of the shire which were still in his control, so that the practice was justly described as being "to the great damage of the people and the disherison of the sheriffs". The Statute of Northampton for 1328 provided that all hundreds thus granted away should be rejoined to their shires, and that no such grants should be made in future.[3] A few grants were rescinded "according to the form of the agreement of the common council of the realm made in parliament at Northampton",[4] but the number of petitions from sheriffs and ex-sheriffs in the next few parliaments shows how little had been effected.[5] The terms of these petitions, incidentally, indicate a growing reliance on parliamentary legislation. In the parliament at York in 1333 a petition from all the sheriffs of England evoked an order to the exchequer to enforce the statute of 1328,[6] and steps were taken in ten counties;[7] but in the following year counter petitions from the ousted bailiffs produced a reversal of policy.[8] In 1336 the sheriffs had further backing from the knights of the shire and the commons, and the prelates and magnates agreed that the statute should be enforced.[9] During the years 1328-36, according to Miss Wood Legh,[10] some seven to ten sheriffs had been elected to every parliament. In 1339 a common petition demanded that they should

---

[1] *Stat. R.* i. 174-5.

[2] See *Fine Roll Calendars, passim.*

[3] *Stat. R.* i. 259, cap. 12.

[4] *Fine Roll Calendar,* 8 July 1328 (p. 97); *Close Roll Calendar,* 28 October 1328 (p. 346).

[5] *Rot. Parl.* ii. 33 (No. 11); Ancient Petitions, No. 548; C. 202/C. 28, No. 229.

[6] *Fine Roll Calendar,* p. 348.

[7] *Close Roll Calendar, 1333-7,* pp. 63, 65, 72, 106, 114, 116, 117, 121, 125, 127, 174, 175, 176.

[8] *Rot. Parl.* ii. 73-84; cf. Richardson, *Rotuli Parliamentorum,* pp. 232-9; *Close Roll Calendar,* pp. 210, 215, 216, 221-2; *Fine Roll Calendar,* pp. 364, 395, 443.

[9] *Stat. R.* i. 277.

[10] *Eng. Hist. Rev.,* 1931, p. 373.

be excluded from parliament. Their numbers dropped markedly, and the agitation in their interest ceased.

With the accession of Richard II the subject was raised again in a slightly different form. The sheriffs asked for an allowance at the exchequer in respect of franchises or hundreds granted out, and, though the minority government demurred at first, in 1381 the concession was made by a statute that sanctioned the rendering of accounts at the exchequer on the accountant's oath.[1] But the exchequer, it would seem, refused to be bound by the act of parliament. Repeated petitions, both from the commons as a whole and from the communities of the shires affected, demanded the enforcement of the statutes of 1316, 1328, and 1381, but the answer was always the same:[2] "Apply to the council, which will consider your case." Henry IV and Henry V in their first parliaments showed signs of yielding, but it was always the same story; the treasurer and barons refused to surrender an inch.[3] By the first parliament of Edward IV the commons had a scheme completely worked out—a bill containing the form of an act[4]—and a committee of lords, according to the Fane fragment, was appointed to "oversee the bill made for the ease of sheriffs" and "thereupon to make report to the king".[5] But, as before, the answer was *le roi s'avisera*,* and 150 years after the tussle began the sheriffs were still accounting for their ancient farms, depending upon the good will of the exchequer and not on their own oaths. It is a clear instance of the limitation in practice, rather than in theory, of the effectiveness of parliamentary legislation.

After the country gentry came the merchants, who had been called into consultation by Edward I from 1275 onwards for the fixing of the old and the new customs and for the drafting of the two statutes which regulated the acknowledgement and collection of debts. We have seen their collaboration in the framing of the Statute of the Staple of 1354. Eileen Power has described their

---

[1] *Rot. Parl.* iii. 45, 116; *Stat. R.* ii. 21.

[2] *Rot. Parl.* iii. 211 f., 247, 266, 280, 290, 305, 330.

[3] *Bulletin Inst. Hist. Research*, xi. 158; *Rot. Parl.* iii. 446, 469, 478, 495; iv. 11 f.

[4] *Rot. Parl.* v. 494 f.

[5] W. H. Dunham, *The Fane Fragment of the 1461 Lords' Journal* (London, 1935), p. 19.

consultative assemblies in the fourteenth century, and their constant influence on fifteenth-century legislation, not only with regard to the changes in the location of the staple, but also in relation to the export of bullion and the minting of coin.[1]

If the burgesses had played their part under Edward III by combining with the woolgrowers against the great financial interests of the merchants, under Richard II we begin to be aware of them as craftsmen. The internecine war between the victualling guilds of London and their opponents is reflected in the legislation of 1383-4—the passing and the rapid repeal of the statutes against victuallers and fishmongers.[2] The regulation of crafts by statute begins with the prohibition of shoemakers from being tanners in 1389 and the statute for girdlers in 1391.[3] The apprenticeship regulations of the City of London are given statutory force in 1430,[4] and with the accession of Edward IV the anti-alien sentiment of the London handicraftsmen is given free vent in legislation prohibiting the importation of a long list of manufactured goods. The first of these must, I think, be the bill "containing the hurts and remedies of merchandises" described in the Fane Fragment as having been put in by the king's own hand;[5] if so it was not carried in that parliament, but in the following one of 1463.[6] It is in connexion with this protectionist movement that a women's interest makes itself felt in parliament, in the petitions of the silkwomen and throwsters of London in 1455 and 1463 against the importation of various small manufactured silk goods.[7] They were a body of domestic workers, less well organized than the crafts of cordwainers, horners, pattenmakers, bowyers, shearmen, and fullers, who also secured protective legislation in their own interests between the years 1464 and 1486.[8]

Lastly there are the special needs of the localities, in which perhaps we get nearest to the voice of the man in the street: the

[1] *The Wool Trade in Medieval English History*, Oxford, 1941; Power and Postan, *Studies in English Trade in the Fifteenth Century* (London, 1933), pp. 293-320.

[2] Unwin, *The Gilds and Companies of London* (London, 1908), pp. 146-52; *Rot. Par.* iii. 142-3.

[3] *Stat. R.* ii. 66, 81; *Rot. Parl.* iii. 271, 296.   [4] *Stat. R.* ii. 248.

[5] *The Fane Fragment*, pp. 18-19.   [6] *Stat. R.* ii. 396 ff.

[7] *Rot. Parl.* v. 325, 506; *Stat. R.* ii. 374, 395 f., 493.

[8] *Rot. Parl.* v. 566 f.; *Stat. R.* ii. 414-16, 494, 520.

grievous clamour and complaint of the men of Shropshire seeking protection from the lawless men of Cheshire; those of Tewkesbury asking that the Severn crossing may be better guarded from the Welshmen and those of the Forest of Dean; the prayer for bridges on the road between Abingdon and Dorchester; the petition of the clothworkers of three Devonshire hundreds; the boroughs of Northampton and Leicester demanding a restriction of their municipal franchise; the mayor and community of Dover praying that their town may be the only exit port for travellers to the Continent; the parishioners of St. Faith's and St. Gregory's by St. Paul's asking for regulations to restrict the slaughtering of beasts in their vicinity "since they have oftentimes been greatly annoyed and distempered by corrupt airs engendered in the said parishes by blood and other fouler things, complaint whereof by the space of sixteen years hath been made as well by the canons of the said Cathedral Church as by many others of the king's subjects of right honest behaviour".[1] Such petitions, promoted by the commons, leave their mark on the statute book alongside the regulations by which the Yorkist and Tudor kings are restoring order to a polity broken by the civil war.

Where, in all this, we may ask, is the ordinary citizen? Is there any legislation which reflects anything more general than a class or a sectional interest? Mr. McFarlane has called the politics of the fourteenth and fifteenth centuries a joint-stock enterprise,[2] and the same description might well be applied to their legislation. The king and council undoubtedly were the guiding spirits throughout the Middle Ages, and towards the end of them the initiative was almost entirely in their hands; but that did not mean that the king's will alone was involved, nor did men think so. Egerton, writing in the early years of Elizabeth's reign, points out that it is difficult to be sure of the intent of a statute because of the number who have had a hand in it: "So manie hedes as there were, so manie wittes; so manie statute makers, so manie mindes."[3] "The public opinion which finds expression in legisla-

[1] *Rot. Parl.* iii. 440; iv. 156, 345; vi. 431 f.; *Stat. R.* ii. 417, 421, 527.
[2] *Trans. R. Hist. Soc.,* 1944, p. 73.
[3] *Discourse on the Understanding of Statutes,* p. 151.

tion is", as Dicey says, "a very complex phenomenon; often a compromise resulting from a conflict between the ideas of the government and the feelings and habits of the governed."[1]

I suggested that the medieval equivalent for "public opinion" is "the community of the realm" and at the Oxford Parliament of 1258 "le commun de la terre" is precisely equated with the baronage.[2] By 1509 it takes two words to say it in English; the *commonalty* is an estate of the realm of long standing, taking its share, but having its place beside the lords spiritual and temporal; but there is a larger whole, a *commonwealth* of England which includes all the orders of the realm, and which is defined by Sir Thomas Smith as "a society or common doing of a multitude of free men collected together and united by common accord among themselves".[3] Not the least important of the common doings that had brought the commonwealth into being had been common action in legislation.

This common action was forced on them partly by the Crown, partly by their own interests. It is perhaps unfortunate that it takes a common danger or a common enemy to evoke a common consciousness and common action. The dislike of the king's foreign servants in the thirteenth century, the anti-papal and anti-clerical feeling of the fourteenth, the jealousy of the alien merchant and craftsman in the fifteenth were probably truer expressions of community feeling than any constructive zeal. But the common action they they provoked was itself an education; the habit of anti-clerical legislation was preparing the ground for an ecclesiastical revolution. And the common action was creating the new entity—the parliament by whose authority laws were made, to whose authority as legislator the individual would appeal.

Moreover the legislative process was familiarizing men with the notion of a common weal. The conception paternalistically expounded in the preambles of Edward I's statutes had been taken over by the fourteenth-century members of parliament

[1] *Law and Public Opion*, p. 10.
[2] Stubbs, *Charters* (9th edition), cf. pp. 381 and 383 on the election of the twelve to treat at parliaments.
[3] *De republica Anglorum* (Cambridge, 1906), p. 20.

who accepted the distinction between the singular needs of the individual and proposals that might turn to the common profit. All those who, in forwarding their own interests, were alleging the common welfare as their motive, were helping to build up the tradition—the magnates conferring with the commons, the councillors and civil servants who drafted the petitions for them, the over-mighty subjects, the merchants, and the poor folk of the shires alike.

Again, through the practice of making the commons the channel by which the ordinary citizens' petitions are transmuted into laws, the doctrine of the electors' responsibility for their representative's financial undertakings has been extended to legislative activities also. "Every man is bound by every act of parliament," says Catesby in 1481, "for every man is privy and party to parliament, for the commons have one or two representatives for each community who can bind the whole."[1] They not only accept the authority of parliament; they see themselves as constituting that authority. "Every Englishman is intended to be there present."[2] By whatever road it had travelled, parliament had come to be the embodiment of national unity.

By common action, in pursuit of a dimly realized common good, and by acceptance of a common responsibility, parliament had come to be at once the school and the expression of common consciousness. The machine and the power to drive it had developed together; the ship had found herself and was ready for the Tudor captain. If the public opinion of the sixteenth century was more truly national than that of the thirteenth, one at least of the causes had been the combined endeavour of so many sorts and conditions of men over 250 years to make and mend the laws of the land.

[1] Year Book, Mich. Term, 21 Ed. IV, cited by Thorne, *Discourse on the Understanding of Statutes*, p. 20, n. 37.
[2] Smith, *De republica Anglorum*, p. 49.

7

PARLIAMENT*

by Theodore F. T. Plucknett

1. DEFINITION OF PARLIAMENT

NO English institution has been studied with such ardor, and with so little definite result, as parliament. For a century and a half the larger part of its records have been accessible in print, and yet the more they are scrutinized, the more obscure and varied are the interpretations put upon them.[1] This is not the place for a general review of parliamentary problems, yet they cannot be altogether avoided. The aim of this series of monographs is to present, in as objective a fashion as possible, a picture of the English government at work during the first ten years of Edward III. The obvious first step is to establish a list of the parliaments which met during that period — and immediately we are faced with the much disputed problem: what is a parliament?

Writing with especial reference to the period now under review, Mr Richardson and Dr Sayles have put forward a theory that only those assemblies are to be accounted parliaments which have been summoned by writs in which the word 'parliament' appears. Their remarks deserve quoting:

It may be asked how a great council is to be distinguished from a parliament: can we rely on the form of the writ of summons, seeing that in previous reigns the formulas were not settled and undoubted parliaments were summoned by

[1] An elaborate bibliography of recent work on parliament would overburden this essay. Access to the modern literature of the subject is easily obtained through the notable articles by H. G. Richardson and George Sayles in the *Bull. Inst. Hist. Research*, v (1927), 129–154; vi (1928), 71–88; I (1928), 129–135; VIII (1930), 65–82; IX (1931), 1–18, and in *E. H. R.*, XLVII (1932), 194–203, and in Richardson's articles in the *Trans. R. H. S.*, 4th Series, XI (1928), 137–183, and in the *Law Quarterly Review*, L (1934), 201–223, 540–570; much valuable chronological and bibliographical material appears in the *Interim Report of the Committee on House of Commons Personnel and Politics* (1932, Cmd. 4130). Much interesting new material will be found in *Rotuli Parliamentorum Anglie hactenus Inediti*, edited by Richardson and Sayles (Camden Society, 3rd Series, vol. LI). We shall cite it as *Rot. Parl. Inediti*. Further material and comment is to be found in M. V. Clarke, *Medieval Representation and Consent* (London, 1936), Bertie Wilkinson, *Studies in the Constitutional History of the Thirteenth and Fourteenth Centuries* (Manchester, 1937), and J.E.A. Jolliffe, *Constitutional History of Medieval England* (London, 1938).

writs which omitted the word *parliamentum?* There seems no doubt, however, that although the practice had hitherto varied, the tendency from about the year 1300 had been to insert the word *parliamentum* in writs summoning to parliament: this is the invariable rule under Edward III.[1]

The last phrase of this quotation looks very much like begging the question; if we reject all summonses which omit the word *parliamentum* then indeed we can establish a rule that all true parliaments were summoned under that style. But how can such an 'invariable rule' be deduced until we have proof that the word *parliamentum* from 1327 onwards was a technical term for an institution with a technically precise identity?

There are really two problems here. First, did there exist during our period a technical distinction between parliaments and those other assemblies of lords spiritual and temporal and commons which these two writers describe as 'great councils'?* Second, is the word *parliamentum* the infallible touchstone which will distinguish the one from the other?

From time to time a variety of functions have been suggested as distinctive of parliament, but it is now well established that great councils also performed identical duties. During the first half of the fourteenth century we find great councils legislating, adjudicating, taxing, and answering petitions.[2] It is safe to say that, in the present state of knowledge, there is no function which was the exclusive right of parliament during our period. An examination of what a particular assembly did will therefore provide no answer to the question whether that assembly was a parliament or not.

Furthermore, the distinction between parliaments and great councils based upon their composition, which was currently drawn down to the days of Stubbs, has likewise proved to be illusory. An assembly of king, lords spiritual and temporal, and elected commons may be a parliament, but it may equally well be (according to the distinction drawn by Mr Richardson and Dr Sayles), a great council.[3] Conversely, it is generally recognized that many early assemblies were described by contemporaries as parliaments although the commons were not summoned to them. The examination of the composition of a particular assembly is thus of no service whatever in determining its constitutional character, if the Richardson-Sayles theory is adopted.

The first of our two problems, then, leads us to the conclusion that

[1] Richardson and Sayles, 'The Parliaments of Edward III,' *Bull. Inst. Hist. Research*, VIII (1930) 67.**

[2] Detailed citations in support of this are collected by Richardson and Sayles in the *Bull. Inst. Hist. Research*, VIII (1930), 75–76.

[3] A striking example is the assembly at Lincoln on 10 Sept. 1327 (*Dignity of a Peer*, IV, 376; *Bull. Inst. Hist. Research*, VIII, 1930, 66, 71), which will be discussed later.

neither the functions nor the composition of large assemblies will serve
to determine whether they are parliaments or great councils. Is it still
possible that the word *parliamentum* should possess some significance?
Mr Richardson has provided rich material for attacking this, the second
of the two problems involved in the passage quoted on an earlier page.

This historic word began its public life as a colloquial expression which
careful writers seemed to avoid. Official documents, in particular, hardly
ever employed it, and only very gradually did its popularity and undoubted convenience win it a place in the political vocabulary of Englishmen. Its original sense might vary considerably; any sort of conference
or discussion might be a *parliamentum*.[1] The expression 'great council'
was equally loose in its significance, and had to wait even longer before
it obtained the sanction of official recognition. The chancery contented
itself with the expression *colloquium et tractatus*, which was its usual
formula for summonses to all sorts of large deliberative conferences —
and this term persisted in summonses to parliaments even when, in the
fulness of time, parliament had become a true institution. It is likewise
true that these later parliaments were summoned by writs which usually
contained the word *parliamentum* as well as *colloquium et tractatus*. But
it is impossible to maintain that *parliamentum* was a technical term until
there was an idea to which it could be attached with precision. Mr
Richardson and Dr Sayles have shown that the word *parliamentum* was
sometimes misused — from the standpoint of their theory — in various
documents, official and unofficial. As explanation they cite the inevitable slips and even ignorances of contemporaries.[2] The explanation is
surely too simple. If *parliamentum* were a technical term with a precise
meaning, it would have been used, like other legal expressions during this
period, with technical accuracy. It would, moreover, correspond to an
institution with precise distinguishing characteristics. In short, it would
be a distinction corresponding to a constitutional difference. The principal objection to the Richardson-Sayles theory is that it asserts that
there was a verbal distinction, but no actual difference; and this objection
seems fatal.[3]

Soon after our period the powers and composition of parliament became settled and distinct from those of other assemblies and it therefore
became possible, and indeed, necessary, to have a technical word for a

---

[1] This is well discussed and illustrated by Richardson (*Trans. R. H. S.*, 4th Series, xi, 1928, 137 ff).

[2] *Bull. Inst. of Hist. Research*, viii (1930), 71. As we shall have occasion to observe later, there
is a similar lack of definition in the use of the terms *parliamentum* and *convocatio* in connection with
the meetings held under the *premunientes* clause: see Felix Makower, *Constitutional History and
Constitution of the Church of England* (London, 1895), p. 356, n. 14.

[3] For the suggestion that a 'right to petition' may have constituted the difference between parliaments and other similar bodies, see below, p. 88.

H

technical thing: that word was *parliamentum*. It is, however, an anachronism to apply such a distinction to our period, and especially to the earlier years of it.   In 1327 the clear-cut technical distinction which separated parliaments from other great assemblies was still unformed, and to understand the position of these *colloquia et tractatus*[1] in the national economy we must forget the future and think solely of those who lived during the first ten years of Edward III's reign.   If we confine ourselves to that period we shall find that the king frequently summoned assemblies of notable persons to give him advice generally, or on some specific matter; sometimes, too, for other purposes (especially financial and military) as well.   One feature is common to them all, and that is the individual summons by writ under the great seal of the more distinguished of these persons, if not of all of them.   The writ of summons will describe the meetings in various terms — *colloquium, tractatus, parliamentum, consilium, deliberacio*, or some combination of these expressions — but the writ of summons is the product of a simple and significant fact: these persons are not, for the most part, ordinarily attendant upon the king and so must be summoned away from their ordinary activities.   As soon as they have discharged the duties for which they were called, they will disperse.   By the year 1327, moreover, about half these assemblies will be further enlarged by the addition of the commons — knights of the shires, citizens, and burgesses — whose election is ordered by writs in regular forms.

In the course of history it was these larger assemblies attended by the commons which became the most important.   A prescient statesman with some political imagination might have guessed this even in 1336; but there still remained several fundamental questions.   Was this particular type of assembly to acquire peculiar constitutional powers differentiating it from other types of assembly?   Was it to receive a name which should be technically its own?   Was its composition to be more settled, or less settled, than that of the other types of large assembly then in common use?   The fact that we can now answer these questions must not tempt us to ascribe this knowledge to the councillors of Edward III; on the contrary, it will be a warning that when we single out for special emphasis those meetings which consisted of lords spiritual and temporal and commons, we are placing an emphasis on these assemblies which contemporaries would have regarded as exaggerated, and are slighting those great councils which then occupied so prominent a place in public life.

---

[1] The ancient formula *colloquium et tractatus* might even be used of very small casual consultations without implying the existence of any institution, e.g., the summonses dated 5 Nov. 1331, in *Dignity of a Peer*, IV, 405.

Bearing these considerations in mind, we can now make a tentative list, such as the following:

CHRONOLOGICAL LIST

of all assemblies summoned by writ under the great seal which comprised all the bishops, abbots, and peers usually summoned; in the second column an asterisk indicates that the sheriffs of all the usual English counties were ordered to return two knights of the shire and two citizens and two burgesses from every city and borough; a dagger indicates that the *premunientes* clause was used, and a double dagger that it was repeated in a second letter. The third column shows the styles used in the writs, and the fourth, gives the reference to the text of the writs in *Dignity of a Peer*.

Date and Place of Meeting	Composition	Style in Writs of Summons	Page
1 Edw. III			
3 Feb. 1327, Westminster	* † †	Parliamentum: colloquium: tractatus	III, 369
15 Sept. 1327, Lincoln	* † †	Colloquium: tractatus (parliamentum in the margin of the roll)	IV, 376
2 Edw. III			
7 Feb. 1328, York	* † †	Parliamentum: colloquium: deliberacio	378
24 Apr. 1328, Northampton	* †	Parliamentum: colloquium: tractatus	381
31 July 1328, York	* † †	Consilium: deliberacio: tractatus	384
16 Oct. 1328, Salisbury	* † †	Parliamentum: colloquium: tractatus	386
3 Edw. III			
9 Feb. 1329, Westminster	*	Parliamentum (adjourned from 16 Oct. 1328)	389
23 July 1329, Windsor		Colloquium: tractatus	390
4 Edw. III			
11 Mar. 1330, Winchester	* † †	Parliamentum: colloquium: tractatus	391
9 July 1330, Osney		Colloquium: tractatus	394
15 Oct. 1330, Nottingham		Colloquium: tractatus	395
26 Nov. 1330, Westminster	* †	Parliamentum: consilium: tractatus	397
5 Edw. III			
5 Apr. 1331, Westminster	*	Parliamentum: colloquium: tractatus (cancelled)	400
30 Sept. 1331, Westminster	* †	Parliamentum: colloquium: tractatus	403
20 Jan. 1332, Westminster		Colloquium: tractatus[1]	406
6 Edw. III			
16 Mar. 1332, Westminster	* † †	Parliamentum: colloquium: tractatus	408
Sept. 1332, Westminster	*	Parliamentum: colloquium: tractatus	411
Dec. 1332, York	*	Parliamentum: colloquium: tractatus (prorogued to 20 Jan.)	416
20 Jan. 1333, York	*	Parliamentum (prorogued from 4 Dec.)	418

No great assemblies were summoned for the 7th regnal year

[1] A writ of military summons dated 28 Jan. 1332 seems to refer to this assembly as a parliament *Dignity of a Peer*, IV, 407).

Date and Place of Meeting	Compo-sition	Style in Writs of Summons	Page
8 Edw. III			
21 Feb. 1334, York	* † †	Parliamentum: colloquium: tractatus	422
19 Sept. 1334, Westminster	* † †	Parliamentum: colloquium: tractatus	427
9 Edw. III			
26 May 1335, York	* † †	Parliamentum: colloquium: tractatus	443
10 Edw. III			
11 Mar. 1336, Westminster	* † †	Parliamentum: colloquium: tractatus	454
23 Sept. 1336, Nottingham	* † †	Colloquium: tractatus: consilium (in margin; also contained 4 elected and 37 nominated merchants)	460
13 Jan. 1337, York	* † †	Parliamentum: colloquium: tractatus (prorogued until the 11th year)	464

The exclusion of several assemblies of merchants, some nominated and some elected, of all provincial convocations of clergy, and of a few assemblies of selected peers, still leaves us therefore with the above list of twenty-five assemblies to which the whole body of lords spiritual and temporal was summoned. If we omit the seventh year of our period when the crisis of the Scottish war prevented normal political activities, we get an average of very nearly three summonses a year, and, considering the expense and difficulty of travelling, these summonses must have been burdensome to the prelates and peers, whose reluctance to obey was not without foundation.

Of these twenty-five assemblies, four may immediately be set aside, for no commons were summoned to them. We shall follow the convenient modern convention of calling them 'great councils,' although recognizing, as Mr Richardson and Dr Sayles have remarked, that this is not a contemporary technical term.[1]

We are left with twenty-one assemblies whose composition is identical: all the bishops, an ascertainable list of abbots and peers, certain councillors, two knights from every county, and two citizens and two burgesses from a more fluctuating list of cities and boroughs. This, in fact, is the classical constitution of parliament, and we suggest that no study of parliament is complete which neglects any of them. In writing the history of parliament as an institution, all the assemblies which contained the later parliamentary elements must evidently be considered.

Furthermore, serious consideration must be given to the question whether we are justified in describing them, not merely as prototypes of parliament, but as true parliaments. In our period the writs vary slightly

[1] *Bull. Inst. Hist. Research*, VIII (1930), 69. The four great councils were all styled *colloquium e tractatus*, the last having the word *consilium* in the margin. They were on 23 July 1329 (Windsor) 9 July 1330 (Osney), 15 Oct. 1330 (Nottingham), 20 Jan. 1332 (Westminster).

in the style they employ. In fourteen of these twenty-one cases the words used are *parliamentum, colloquium et tractatus;*[1] once we find *parliamentum, colloquium et deliberacio,*[2] and once *parliamentum, consilium et tractatus;*[3] the two writs of prorogation use *parliamentum* simply.[4] As for the remainder, one is called *colloquium et tractatus* (with *parliamentum* in the margin),[5] another is a *consilium, deliberacio et tractatus,*[6] and the third is *colloquium et tractatus* with *consilium* in the margin.[7]

What significance have these variations in terminology when the assembly, in any case, was the same, and the functions were the same? In any study of the history of parliament all these meetings should surely be considered as forming part of an unbroken series of parliamentary assemblies, with the sole peculiarity that the word 'parliament' had not yet become the exclusive technical designation for them.

If we follow the insistence of Mr Richardson and Dr Sayles upon the need for the word 'parliament' in the writ to constitute a valid parliament, then we have to find some other category in which to place the three assemblies of 15 September 1327 (Lincoln), 31 July 1328 (York), and 23 September 1336 (Nottingham), and we shall have to find some rational distinction to accompany the verbal difference. It is quite incredible that there should be two distinct institutions consisting of the same people unless there was a substantial difference in powers or functions to justify the technicality. These two authors have in fact felt the difficulty, and they suggest (with obvious hesitation) that assemblies of lords spiritual and temporal and commons under the style of *parliamentum* conferred a general right to petition, and that such assemblies without the word *parliamentum* gave no such right:

> In one respect, at least, parliament seems to be distinguished from a great council — in the one there is or ought to be a general opportunity to petition and a right to be answered, in the other this opportunity is not given, and the right is not recognised.[8]

In support of this novel theory[9] no evidence whatever is produced.

---

[1] 3 Feb. 1327 (Westminster), 24 Apr. 1328 (Northampton), 16 Oct. 1328 (Salisbury), 11 Mar. 1330 (Winchester), 15 Apr. 1331 (Westminster), 30 Sept. 1331 (Westminster), 16 Mar. 1332 (Westminster), 9 Sept. 1332 (Westminster), 4 Dec. 1332 (York), 21 Feb. 1334 (York), 19 Sept. 1334 (Westminster), 26 May 1335 (York), 11 Mar. 1336 (Westminster), 13 Jan. 1337 (York).

[2] 7 Feb. 1328 (York).

[3] 26 Nov. 1330 (Westminster).

[4] 9 Feb. 1329 (Westminster), 20 Jan. 1333 (York).

[5] 15 Sept. 1327 (Lincoln).   [6] 31 July 1328 (York).

[7] 23 Sept. 1336 (Nottingham). This assembly, besides the normal prelates, peers, and commons, also contained 37 nominated and 4 elected citizens and merchants who were called 'to advise.'

[8] *Bull. Inst. Hist. Research,* VIII (1930), 76.

[9] In the introduction to *Rot. Parl. Inediti,* p. x, this position is stated with less emphasis than in the *Bulletin;* it does not seem to have been expressly withdrawn, however.

We are given no contemporary statements that this right existed in parliament or was absent in great councils. Indeed there is direct evidence to the contrary. These two authors have themselves shown that on occasion petitions were answered in great council, sometimes even petitions which had not been answered in a previous parliament.[1] A tentative suggestion that Edward II once tried to deny the right to petition in parliament rests on very slender inferences from a complaint that there was no one assigned for the purpose of receiving them, to which the king replied by promising to make suitable administrative provision.[2] Further, was this right a right of the lords, the commons, the whole parliament, or the public generally? And was the right to be answered satisfied by the usual response, 'le roy s'avisera'? If petitioning is indeed to be the test, then it will have to be pointed out that an important prayer that actions of trespass should not be discontinued by the demise of the crown was presented at the meeting of 15 September 1327 (Lincoln),[3] and that magnates and commons joined in asking for the enforcement of a certain ordinance at the meeting of 23 September 1336 (Nottingham).[4]

We believe that this right has not so far been established and that the distinction based upon it is non-existent. Nothing seems more sure than that petitions from all sorts of people, on every imaginable subject, and in a great variety of forms, oral and written, were constantly being presented to the crown on all sorts of occasions — in parliaments, great councils, or at any other time. The fact that certain petitions remained unanswered for three successive parliaments during our period with no more protest than a 'prayer' from the commons (who make no appeal to rights and assert no principles) seems strong evidence that the answering of petitions in parliament, as elsewhere, was a matter of absolute discretion in the crown.[5]

Here we are concerned with Edward III's government in action rather than in theory, and from this point of view the inclusion of the three assemblies of 1327 (Lincoln), 1328 (York), and 1336 (Nottingham) seems to us inevitable;[6] the slight discrepancies in their titles merely show that

---

[1] *Bull. Inst. Hist. Research*, VIII (1930), 76.

[2] *Bull. Inst. Hist. Research*, VI (1928), 75; VIII (1930), 73; *Rot. Parl.*, I, 444.

[3] P.R.O., Ancient Petitions, Nos. 13017–13018; *Bull. Inst. Hist. Research*, VIII (1930), 76, n. 5.

[4] *C. P. R. 1334–1338*, 367–368.

[5] 'Item prie la commune qe touz les billes nient responduz donez par la commune as divers parlementz en temps nostre seigneur le roi qore est soient duement responduz et execut a ceo parlement' (*Rot. Parl. Inediti*, p. 225 [6]). The curious words of the *Modus Tenendi Parliamentum* in the chapter 'De Particione Parliamenti' are not helpful in this discussion; the assertion that the king is 'perjured' if he dismissed parliament before all the petitions have been dealt with, is obviously a strong expression of the writer's political views and not a statement of existing constitutional law: he may be alluding to the Ordinances (1311), c. 29.

[6] Their omission from the list in the *Interim Report* is unfortunate.

we have not quite reached the age when the word 'parliament' became a technical term.

2. PARLIAMENTARY RECORDS

Such then were the great assemblies summoned during our period; and those to which we must give special attention are the ones we have ventured to call parliaments — not because this was already their technical name in the opening years of Edward III, but because they are in the direct historical line of development which gave us that institution.

The next enquiry must be directed to the archives which parliaments created, both as the machinery of their current work, and as the permanent memorials of their acts. Attention has several times been drawn to the defects of the old *Rotuli Parliamentorum*, and it is a matter of congratulation that much new material has now been admirably edited by Mr Richardson and Dr Sayles for the Royal Historical Society under the title *Rotuli Parliamentorum hactenus Inediti*.[1]

In editing one of the many parliament rolls which escaped the notice of the eighteenth-century compilers of the *Rotuli Parliamentorum*, Maitland propounded a theory which has ever since deeply influenced writers on the subject.[2] Taking some words of *Fleta*[3] (which have since become widely known) and contrasting them with the statements of Bracton, he emphasized the significance of parliament as a recent addition to the system of common law courts. Where Bracton, in the middle of the thirteenth century, knew only two such courts (common pleas and king's bench), *Fleta* was able to describe a third, 'the council in parliament.' Moreover, Maitland was able to point to a particularly cogent piece of evidence in support of *Fleta's* statement. This was the appearance of a third sort of plea roll corresponding to the new institution, which we can only describe as parliament rolls.

This conclusion has been accepted by most modern scholars (though not by all) and widely applied. Maitland's reservations, however, should be observed: only 'now and again' are these rolls entitled plea rolls, and at best we have but 'a meagre, disjointed set of plea rolls (which, however, are not pure plea rolls, for they deal also with petitions and other matters).' These warning words are confirmed by the more detailed researches of Mr Richardson and Dr Sayles who amply show how miscellaneous and unorganized these rolls are. It is even overstating the facts

---

[1] Bibliography for records (parliamentary rolls and petitions): *Rot. Parl. Inediti*, pp. viii–xxii; R. L. Atkinson's introduction, prefixed to P.R.O. copy of index to the Ancent Petitions.

[2] Maitland, *Memoranda de Parliamento* (Rolls Series, London, 1893), pp. lxxix–lxxxi.*

[3] *Fleta*, ed. John Selden (London, 1685), Bk. II, cap. 2.**

to call them a set of rolls, for the collection is to some extent the work
of later archive keepers and not a contemporary *fonds*.

In our own ten-year period this disjointed collection is particularly
defective. First, it is necessary to observe that we cannot properly call
every document which at some time has been rolled up a parliament roll,
simply because it has some relation to the work done at a parliament;
there are, however, a few rolls during our period which were expressly
drawn up to serve as a record of parliamentary work, and of these a few
words must be said. There is a roll of 'Records and Memorials' *memoranda* of things which took place in parliament summoned to Westminster on 26 November 1330, handed in to the chancery by Henry
de Edenestowe, clerk of the parliament; an endorsement asserts that
Edenestowe handed in the roll on 8 November 1331. A second roll with
a title in French instead of Latin, but to the same effect, comes from the
next parliament (30 September 1331) and the endorsement shows that
Edenestowe handed it in on 25 February 1332; the following parliament
of 16 March 1332 has likewise left a roll which Edenestowe handed in on
an unstated day. A single membrane deals with the next parliament
(9 September 1332), and a last membrane deals with the next two parliaments (4 December 1332 and 20 January 1333). At some later date
all these separate rolls were sewn together to form Chancery, Parliament
Roll, No. 2 which was finally printed in *Rot. Parl.*, II, 52–69. There is
no trace of any other rolls of this description during this period,[1] and
none of them can be described as plea rolls in any way comparable to
the orderly sets which the common law courts have left us.

The first three rolls are expressly associated with Edenestowe as clerk
of the parliament;[2] and, in fact, if he compiled them (as seems very
probable), there can be little doubt from the similarity of style that the
last two membranes are from the same source. It will be noticed that
the rolls cover six consecutive parliaments, that the first parliament takes
up three membranes, the second, third and fourth take one membrane
each, while the fifth and sixth take a membrane together. We can therefore see Edenestowe's ardor steadily decline, but all the same we must
give him credit for making an interesting experiment, and for continuing
his effort for over two years.

The significant fact in all this is that down to the end of our period
there is nothing like a consistent set of rolls forming part of the ordinary
administrative machinery used by successive parliaments. We have the

---

[1] Fuller descriptions, and the text of the endorsements (which were not printed in *Rot. Parl.*)
will be found in the articles by Richardson and Sayles in *Bull. Inst. Hist. Research*, IX (1931), 17.

[2] This is the contemporary form of his name: Richardson calls him 'Edwinstowe.'

experiment of Edenestowe, like the earlier experiment of Ayrmin under Edward II, but they both seem the product of individual initiative rather than of administrative necessity.[1] The difference between these memorials and true parliamentary archives is analagous to the difference between a person's diary, consciously written up, and his letter files and business papers. Most of the parliaments managed to do their work without even a memorial roll. If such is the general characteristic of the rolls there is little to be learned, beyond the facts which they narrate, from an analysis of their form and content. The first and longest of these rolls plunges without any preamble into a long state paper, the attainder (for such it virtually was) of Mortimer and his partisans. Then comes a petition presented by the city authorities of London, which is followed by a plea of the crown in Latin (as pleas should be). Finally the roll concludes with a number of petitions and their answers, arranged in descending order of importance, but intermingled with a few general orders of an administrative and legislative character.

The second and third rolls contain more narrative, giving notes of the opening orations and proclamations, and fairly full accounts of political decisions, while the succeeding rolls maintain the same style although they are much briefer.

We are therefore not dealing with a series of records which formed an integral part of the administration of a great institution. Broad conclusions on issues of national importance are interesting enough to the political historian, but we miss in these rolls the detail inseparable from administrative machinery. It is difficult to believe that there was any real need for Edenestowe's memorial rolls, and indeed other parliaments during this period dispensed with rolls; hence the light which they throw on parliamentary working is necessarily colored by the compiler's own outlook and interests. There may be one other element common to Ayrmin's roll and Edenestowe's: both seem to try to record the political happenings in parliament at moments of extreme tension and even of constitutional crisis. But once again, this is an abnormal factor which distinguishes them from the ordinary run of current records.

Apart altogether from any question of memorial rolls, it must be remembered that the work of several hundred persons cannot well be organized without some recourse to writing; a certain amount of quill-driving there must have been, and material of this sort is especially significant, for it formed part of the administrative procedure of parliament. Thus

---

[1] It is worth recalling that Ayrmin in 1316 claimed to be specially named and deputed to the task of compiling this roll; Edenestowe makes no such claim, and so it would seem that the government felt no pressing necessity for resuming the plan.

we have original rolls[1] (and some late copies[2] of lost originals) which contained transcripts of petitions evidently made in the normal course of parliamentary procedure: we also have an informal breviate of certain petitions headed *coram rege*, seemingly memoranda for submission to the king or his closest advisers;[3] official copies of petitions may be placed on the dorse of the close rolls,[4] and much more rarely we find a lengthy record of litigation.[5]

Besides copies made in the course of administrative procedure, we have original petitions. Some of these are, in fact, made up in the form of rolls — thus from the Candlemas parliament of 1327 we have a roll of forty-one petitions from *la comune de la terre* and the answers annexed;[6] the Londoners put in a formidable screed more than once,[7] while the smaller slips of parchment from all sorts of petitioners survive in considerable numbers, although unhappily dispersed in several groups. Many are among the Ancient Petitions, some of which have been printed (either from the originals or from later transcripts) in the *Rotuli Parliamentorum*. The majority, however, have never been printed anywhere. The classes of council and parliamentary proceedings, both exchequer and chancery, contain others. When these documents bear precise indications in the text by a definite connection with a dated enrolment or by a dated endorsement to show that they were indeed discussed in parliament, there is little difficulty; but the absence of such indications is not conclusive, and many of the undated and unendorsed petitions in these classes may have come before parliament without leaving any trace of the fact. It will be noticed that the printed *Rotuli Parliamentorum* contain numerous examples of such petitions whose connection with parliament is attested (if at all) only by the statements of the Stuart antiquaries who copied them.

A few casual rolls, and a fair mass of usually uncommunicative petitions, therefore, form the sum of our parliamentary records. When we think of the imposing array of Edward III's peers, prelates, commons, and clergy in parliament, of the size of the assembly, the frequence of its meetings, the momentous decisions it reached, and the wide jurisdiction

---

[1] Such as those printed in *Rot. Parl. Inediti*, pp. 186–215 (1330), and 216–223 (1332).

[2] An imposing roll of eleven membranes is represented by the late transcripts now printed in *Rot. Parl. Inediti.*, pp. 141–179 (which supersedes the much more fragmentary abstracts in *Rot. Parl.*, II, 430–440 (1327).

[3] *Rot. Parl. Inediti.*, pp. 181–185 (1328).

[4] *Rot. Parl.*, II, 5–6 (1327); cf. *C.C.R. 1330–1333*, 286, 291, *et passim*.

[5] *Rot. Parl. Inediti*, pp. 240–266 (1336).

[6] *Rot. Parl.*, II, 7–11 (1327); for other versions see *Rot. Parl. Inediti*, pp. 101–103, 116–126. Two other petitions of the commons are printed, *ibid.*, pp. 224–230 (1333), and pp. 232–239 (1334).

[7] *Rot. Parl. Inediti*, pp. 126–141 (1327); cf. *Rot. Parl.*, II, 54 (1330)

it exercised, this handful of records seems painfully meagre and altogether unworthy. And yet from another point of view, there may come
an explanation. Administrative records in the middle ages are likely to
fail us at the one critical moment when decisions are being taken. The
subsequent stages of a transaction are easily traced through the long
series of rolls and files, but the initial exercise of discretion and the
choice of a course of action have often left little or no trace. Regarded
from this point of view, the very poverty of our parliamentary records
is a measure of the vital importance of the institution, and an indication
that it was not merely a cog in the administrative machine, but an institution at the very heart of things, where the most intimate process of
government — the exercise of discretion — took place.[1]

3. THE COMPOSITION OF PARLIAMENT

It is very difficult to speak briefly of the composition of parliament,
so many and so obscure are the problems involved. The writs of summons are enrolled on the dorse of the close rolls during our period, and
have been printed in full in the appendices to the *Report of the Lords'
Committees on the Dignity of a Peer of a Realm* (1826). One great distinction is immediately apparent between the persons summoned by individual writ (now represented by the house of lords) and those who
were summoned indirectly through the sheriffs and bishops (whose modern representatives are the house of commons and convocation).

Taking the individual summonses first, we find four groups. First
come the diocesan bishops, twenty-one in all, who are regularly summoned to all parliaments[2]— and we may note in passing that the four

---

[1] An instructive parallel will be found in the later attempt by John Prophete to establish a roll
of council proceedings (printed in Baldwin, *King's Council*, pp. 489–504); here, too, an executive
body soon found it irksome to maintain a formal record, although the office of the privy seal, which
was closest to the council, kept files which must once have been voluminous.

[2] There is one exception which is significant enough to be mentioned in some detail. Adam of
Orlton had been regularly summoned as bishop of Worcester until the autumn of 1333 when he
was translated to Winchester by the pope at the request of Philip VI of France; a bull dated 7 Dec.
1333 appointed Simon of Montague as his successor at Worcester. Edward III was greatly in-
censed at this arrangement and refused to recognize it. Hence we find that Adam was still summoned as bishop of Worcester to the parliament of Feb. 1334 and John of Stratford was still summoned as bishop of Winchester, although he had been translated to Canterbury. As for Canterbury, Edward chose to regard it as still vacant, and so summoned the guardian of the spiritualities.
The quarrel lasted almost two years. In the parliament of Sept. 1334 the see of Winchester was
completely unrepresented, neither Adam nor a guardian of its spiritualities being summoned; Simon,
however, was now summoned as bishop of Worcester and John of Stratford as archbishop of Canterbury. Adam got his temporalities in Sept. 1334 but was still not summoned — and his see was still
unrepresented — in the parliament of May 1335. At last he received his parliamentary writ for
the parliament of March 1336. While disputes of this sort were almost normal at this date, it is
remarkable that the king should have withheld the parliamentary summons for so long.

Welsh bishops were summoned, although the Welsh commons do not regularly enter parliament until two hundred years after our period closes.[1] The question, much agitated in later centuries, whether the bishops attended by reason of their dignity or of their tenure had hardly arisen as yet, but it is significant that an absent bishop is represented by his vicar-general, and a vacant see by the guardian of the spiritualities,[2] both of whom are ecclesiastical officers. These arrangements seem to imply that the episcopate attended parliament by reason of its spiritual, rather than its supposed tenurial, position.

The second group of individual summonses concerns the abbots, many of whom were evidently of equal consequence with the bishops, though they were summoned with rather less regularity. A few occasional failures to summon may be due to special causes but the omission of the abbot of Battle from the parliament of July 1328, and thenceforward is noticeable.[3] In the first two or three parliaments of our period there were about eighteen abbots, but the rest show a fairly steady list of about thirty; the single exception was in March 1332, when in addition there were called twenty-eight abbots 'who are not usually summoned to parliaments' (says the close roll), making an exceptionally large total of fifty-eight.[4] At various times during the fourteenth century certain abbots procured exemption from parliamentary attendance, often alleging tenurial considerations.[5] It seems that during a vacancy, no one was summoned.

The third group, the baronage (to use a modern term), has aroused even more controversy. The fundamental questions of the relation of peerage to tenure and the significance of the writ of summons must be left to the constitutional historians and their natural adversaries, the peerage lawyers. The house of lords in a long series of decisions on peerage claims has laid down a great deal of 'history' which only lawyers would accept, a purely conventional history which historians are unanimous in rejecting at many points.*

We are not yet in the period when baronies were conferred by patent, and consequently there is nothing in a man's style to show that he was

---

[1] See below, p. 102, n. 1.

[2] *Dignity of a Peer*, iv, 376, 379, etc. In the lenten parliament of 1336 the archbishop of York was allowed to send a proxy (*ibid.*, p. 457; cf. p. 461).

[3] There was no vacancy at this date, and apparently no charter of exemption. Battle re-appears in the lists in 1348 and again in 1370, and is often summoned from the reign of Richard II onwards.

[4] *Dignity of a Peer*, iv, 409.

[5] Examples will be found in Stubbs, *C.H.E.*, iii, 459; cf. H. M. Chew, *The English Ecclesiastical Tenants-in-Chief and Knight Service, especially in the 13th and 14th Centuries* (London, 1932), pp. 172–179.

a baron;[1] on the rolls he is simply John Pecche, Simon Warde, or Henry
de Percy.   The only territorial titles during our period are the earldoms,
of which there were six at the beginning and ten at the end.   Three of
them are notable since the titles were derived from Scotland, the English
holders of them claiming by inheritance from Scottish ancestors.[2]   An
Irish title, Ormond, was conferred on James Butler, who had married
Edward III's aunt.

There is a good deal of consistency in the summonses of magnates,
although anomalies occasionally occur.   Once summoned, a magnate is
almost always resummoned,[3] and it is already general for his heir, if of
full age, to succeed him.   Once we find the son of an aged magnate summoned in his stead during his father's lifetime;[4] it is also a general practice not to summon minors, although there are exceptions here too.[5]

In numbers, the lay peers below the degree of earl naturally varied,
and even within the short period of the present ten years they were as
few as forty-seven on one occasion, and as many as sixty-seven on another.   Hence the lay lords together could hardly have out-numbered
the bishops and abbots by more than a very small figure; generally both
classes seem to be about evenly balanced.

We now pass to the fourth class of persons who received individual
summonses, and with them we are conscious of approaching the true
centre and heart of Edward III's parliaments.   A curious circumstance
that must first be noted is that when writs are enrolled on the dorse of
the close roll, those to the spiritual lords come first, then come the writs
to the lay lords, and then the writs to the sheriffs for the elections to
commons; last come the fourth group, whom we shall call the councillors.
It seems, therefore, to have been felt that there was a distinct difference

[1] It has been suggested that some of the lords of parliament were not barons but bannerets; on
this obscure point see Tout, *Chapters*, III, 296, n. 1; Tout, *Collected Papers* (Manchester, 1934),
II, 180.

[2] They were Henry of Beaumont, earl of Buchan (by his marriage with a Comyn), Gilbert of
Umfravill, earl of Angus (through his mother), and David Strabolgi, earl of Atholl (through his
father who was regarded in Scotland as having forfeited the title).   The facts were simple: Edward
III summoned three pretenders to Scottish earldoms to his parliaments, on the assumption, no
doubt, that their presence there would be politically useful; Edward I had adopted the same device,
but modern theory has found it necessary to confer on them imaginary English baronies.

[3] The suggestion that some of the irregularities may be due to military service in Scotland did
not commend itself to the late J. H. Round, *Family Origins* (London, 1930), p. 191.

[4] Thus John Cobham was apparently summoned instead of his father, Henry, in Jan. 1333
(*Dignity of a Peer*, IV, 418).   Both before and after this exceptional summons among the lords, John
was an elected knight of the shire for Kent.   His father, Henry, died in 1339 but John's summonses
to the lords do not become a regular series for some years after (1350); his summons in 1333 seems
to have escaped G.E. Cokayne, *The Complete Peerage of England, Scotland, Ireland, Great Britain
and the United Kingdom* (London, 1887–1898; 2d ed., 1910— , 9 vols. published).

[5] John of Eltham (the king's brother) was summoned as earl of Cornwall eleven times during
our period, although he was only twenty when he died in 1336 (Cokayne, *Peerage*).

between the councillors and the lords spiritual and temporal. Moreover, the prelates and peers are called to be 'present with us and with
the other prelates, lords and magnates'; the fourth group, however, are
to be 'present with us and with the others of our council.' Again it
seems implied that the councillors will be rather a group apart from the
prelates and peers. Marked as it is, too much emphasis must not be
placed upon this distinction; it seems the rule indeed with parliaments,
but in the summonses to great councils where no commons were called,
it is usual to find that the councillors and peers are named together in
one list as receiving identical summonses.[1] Clearly, then, there was no
great social gulf between the councillors and the peers (several of them
in fact rose to be prelates and chancellors), but the grouping was an
administrative one which was felt to be requisite in parliaments, although
not in the great councils.

In numbers the councillors were never very considerable in comparison
with the lords spiritual and temporal. During our period they reached
a maximum of twenty-three in September 1334, although they had been
but eight in February 1328. A list of all such councillors who had been
summoned at any time to parliaments within our period would contain
forty-two names, from which it will be apparent that fluctuations were
frequent. Indeed, only two of them — Geoffrey Scrope, chief justice of
the king's bench, and William Herle, chief justice of the common pleas —
were summoned to every one of the parliaments during this period. The
group is sometimes referred to by modern historians as 'the judges,' but
not all the judges were summoned, nor was a puisne judge who had once
been summoned necessarily re-summoned.[2] A seat on either of the
benches did not carry with it a summons to parliament, therefore; nevertheless, the judicial element, as we have seen, was constant, if not strong.
No doubt the legal business before parliament required the best expert
attention, but it must also be remembered that these judges did not
confine themselves to legal problems. They were men of affairs and
administrators who had sometimes reached the bench after careers in
the civil service as well as at the bar. Bourchier was a soldier, who like
Baynard, Willoughby, Cambridge, and Parning, had been knight of the

[1] *Dignity of a Peer*, IV, 390, 395, 396–397, 406. In all three of the disputed parliaments of our
period—1327 (Lincoln), 1328 (York), and 1336 (Nottingham)—the summonses of the councillors
were enrolled separately, as for normal parliaments.

[2] It must be remembered that during this period judges were removed from court to court and
promoted or demoted in grade with bewildering rapidity. Many, but probably not all, of these
changes appear in the patent rolls. When they can be traced they do not always coincide with
summonses to parliament. Several English lawyers and judges were commissioned to the Irish
bench, but the late Dr F. E. Ball, *The Judges in Ireland* (London, 1926), doubted whether some of
them ever acted.

shire before becoming judge, while Travers' tenure of a seat in the common pleas merely interrupted a long career at the head of the finance of
Gascony.[1]   Many of them were, or had been, barons of the exchequer,
while Travers and Norwich had been lord treasurer's remembrancers and
were therefore experts in the inner working of the accounting machinery.
Useful as their legal learning was, it is clear that the king did not want
merely judges, as such, but a few judges whose experience in many fields
of activity made them especially valuable as advisors and in selecting
them he was unfettered by tradition or prescriptive rights.

Beside judges we sometimes find that there were summoned prominent serjeants-at-law, especially from those who were retained as king's
serjeants; unfortunately, the absence of reliable lists* makes it difficult to
say whether all of the latter class were summoned; Toudeby and Parning
were the best-known members of this group.   On the border between
law and finance were the barons of the exchequer who were occasionally
summoned, although many of the judges held (or had previously held)
these offices; two chancellors of the exchequer were summoned during
our period (but not regularly), while the treasurer was also occasionally
called.

Finally, there was among the councillors an interesting little group of
clergy.   Indeed, those chancellors and treasurers of the exchequer who
were summoned were, in fact, clergy, well provided with archdeaconries
and prebends; other councillors, however, were doctors of law, civilians,
and diplomatists, like Shoreditch and Sampson, or canonists managing
the king's litigation at Avignon, like Adam of Murimuth and Weston.

These, then, were the *curiales*, lay and clerical, men of undoubted ability, who in offices, in courts, on the bench, and on foreign missions bore
the hard, steady toil which alone would keep the machinery of state in
motion.   In experience and in ability they could hardly have had any
equals among the lords, save those prelates who had already obtained
the rewards for similar careers of devotion and untiring work for the
crown.   It is hardly possible to imagine a mediaeval parliament working unless such men as these were at the centre.   The very fact that they
were to be initiators and actors, rather than mere onlookers in the work
of parliament, must be taken as the explanation of the shifting character
of the group; officials they were, but they were not present *ex officio*.

As we approach the centre of parliament, it becomes more difficult to
speak with assurance on several matters.   One in particular must be
mentioned: did this group of separately summoned councillors coincide
with the king's council?   If it did, it would be sufficient to search the

---

[1] For the nature of his office of constable of Bordeaux see Tout, *Edward II*, p. 392, and E. C. Lodge,
Gascony under English Rule (London, 1926), p. 140.

parliamentary writs in order to establish a list of the king's council at any particular date. It has generally been recognized that this is quite an inconclusive method, and so it would seem that, although these persons were summoned as councillors, yet the council *en bloc* was not summoned by means of individual writs to its members. It is highly probable, however, that some of them attended, if not openly, at least behind the scenes, while it would obviously be superfluous to issue an elaborate summons under the great seal to persons who held no high dignity, and who were always at hand. We ought probably to assume, then, that the enrolled lists of councillors were not exhaustive of this group.[1]

We now come to the large group of persons who were summoned to parliament indirectly. Within this class are two main groups, clergy and laity.

The position of the lower clergy in the early parliaments of Edward III is of particular interest, for the king was trying an experiment which, if successful, would have given us a very different sort of parliament from that which in the event grew up. The story is complicated and only the main outlines have as yet been established. Unfortunately, the subject has been studied, except in recent years, entirely from political motives at moments when history was being used in connection with a succession of crises in ecclesiastical affairs.

In the thirteenth century it was admitted that the clergy were an order apart, and that their spiritual property was not subject to taxation unless they, as an organized body, gave their consent.[2] This assent was

---

[1] The recent suggestion made by J. E. A. Jolliffe (*The Constitutional History of Medieval England*, London, 1937, p. 340), that the council was of the essence of parliament needs mention here in spite of its exaggeration. He writes: 'An assembly embodying prelates, magnates, knights and burgesses without the council, and summoned *ad colloquium habendum*, would be no parliament — in the reign of Edward III it would be called a *Magnum Consilium*. A meeting only of the king, the council, and the justices to try *placita* and hear petitions was, on the other hand, perfectly a parliament.' It is true that there was no separate list of summonses of councillors to many great councils, but their names will generally be found mingled with those of the magnates; even if they were not summoned by writ, it is hardly conceivable that a large assembly could do its work without such a nucleus of experts to organize it. The second of the sentences quoted is an extension of Maitland's view, which was already dangerously near to paradox; cf. p. 90 above.

[2] The further proposition that papal permission for such a grant was necessary need not detain us, although it was politically of some consequence. The landed estates of bishops and abbots were regarded as temporalities, and were taxable in parliament. The lower clergy subsisted for the most part on tithes, offerings, and the profits of ecclesiastical jurisdiction; these were spiritualities, and, in the thirteenth century, pope and king competed for the right to tax them. The consent of the lower clergy to taxes on their spiritualities was regularly sought in either case, although the popes made some claim to tax by prerogative. See W. E. Lunt, 'The Consent of the English Lower Clergy,' in *Persecution and Liberty, Essays in Honor of George Lincoln Burr* (New York, 1931), pp. 117-170. Much material concerning the clergy in parliament and in convocation, and clerical taxation, is collected in D. B. Weske, *Convocation of the Clergy* (London, 1937), and in M. V. Clarke, *Medieval Representation and Consent* (London, 1936).*

usually given in assemblies summoned by the primate of each province, either expressly for the purpose or for general ecclesiastical business, at the request of the crown.

Under Edward II and Edward III the inconveniences of this arrangement became obvious. If the crown wanted supplies, it generally wanted them quickly, and, impatient at the delays of ecclesiastical assemblies, sometimes spoke sharply to the prelates. The primates stubbornly refused to accept royal commands to hold assemblies, and insisted that they would only act in response to a request couched in terms which made it clear that the crown was asking favors and not asserting rights. Attempts to circumvent the primates by inducing the bishops to hold diocesan assemblies for clerical grants of taxes aroused determined opposition from the inferior clergy. A third scheme, which was being tried during our period, was to combine the assemblies for clerical grants with parliament. This had the obvious advantage that all the financial resources of the country would thus be brought into a single negotiation. A clause (called the *premunientes* clause), added as early as 1290 to the summonses of the bishops, required them to 'warn' the dean (or prior) of their cathedral and all the archdeacons of their diocese to appear in person at parliament, while the cathedral chapter was to elect one proctor, and the rest of the clergy of the diocese two proctors for the parliament. The summonses to all the parliaments in our period, as listed above, contain the *premunientes* clause with the exception of those called for April 1331, September 1332, and December 1332. The clause is substantially the same in all cases, with the sole exception that the heads of the cathedral chapters (prior or dean as the case may be) were not called to the parliament of February 1334.[1]

The *premunientes* clause aroused opposition from the clergy whose reluctance to obey it is possibly reflected in the fact that its provisions were generally[2] repeated in a second letter to each of the two primates, who were expected to issue mandates giving it effect concurrently with the orders of the diocesan bishops, whose failure to act seems indeed to have been taken as certain. This second letter afforded the means of a compromise. The clergy took less and less notice of the *premunientes* clause in the writs to the diocesan bishops, and so maintained their principle that the king should not compel them to merge with the laity in parliament. The primates, however, compromised with the crown by disobeying both the first *premunientes* clause (as did the diocesan bishops) and the second mandate; instead, the primates summoned the provincial

---

[1] The proclamation calling together on 9 Feb. 1329 the parliament of the preceding autumn which had been adjourned makes no mention of the inferior clergy.

[2] The three exceptions were the parliaments summoned for April 1328, Nov. 1330, and Sept. 1331.

convocations. The working out of this arrangement took place in our period, and the gradual establishment of the procedure can be traced in the variations of the mandates to the primates. Occasional traces of the attendance of clerical proctors are to be found at various dates,[1] but soon it became customary for convocations to be summoned instead, although the composition of convocation was rather different from that which the *premunientes* clause would have produced. The very next year after our period the crown recognized the new device by sending a request to summon convocations instead of the second letter of *premunientes* to the primates; the clause (now meaningless, however) continues to appear in the summonses to the diocesan bishops down to the present day.[2]

The second group of persons indirectly summoned is the one which eventually became the dominant partner in parliament — the commons. To every sheriff in England[3] (except to those of Durham and Chester) went a writ ordering him to cause to be chosen two knights of his county, two citizens from every city, and two burgesses from every borough from the most discreet and hard-working, and to cause them to come to the parliament provided with full and sufficient power to do and consent to whatever may be, with God's favor and common counsel, ordained; the king's business is not to be delayed by any defect in these powers, and the writ is to be returned with the names of the knights, citizens and burgesses.[4]

To comment adequately on these writs would mean writing the longest chapter in English constitutional history. Here only a few remarks are possible, directed in particular to describing the nature of parliament as the apex of the administrative machinery, as it existed during the ten years of our period. We have seen that the magnates were summoned to treat and to give counsel; the commons, however, were not called to give advice, nor to treat and to reach decisions. Probably all that was

---

[1] E. C. Lowry and A. E. Levett, 'Clerical Proctors in Parliament and Knights of the Shire,' *E.H.R.*, XLVIII (1933), 443–455; in March 1336 the Canterbury clergy granted a tenth in parliament (Stubbs, *C.H.E.*, II, 398), which seems to be an exception to the rule (*C.H.E.*, III, 340). The latest discussion of these obscure changes is by Clarke, *Medieval Representation and Consent*, especially Chs. I and VII. For traces of indirect elections, see *ibid.*, pp. 326 ff.

[2] The above is a summary of a complicated process which in fact was not so simple nor so regular. It is further confused by the loose use of the words parliament and convocation in the sources. Fuller details and access to original materials can be found in Makower, *Constitutional History of the Church of England*, pp. 200–207, 359–365. In the P.R.O. (Special Collections 10) there are a few original procurations of inferior clergy.

[3] The warden of the Cinque Ports was likewise ordered to return two 'barons' from each port, the writ being, *mutatis mutandis*, the same as to the sheriffs.

[4] The importance of these powers has recently been emphasized by J. G. Edwards, '*Plena Potestas* of English Parliamentary Representatives,' in *Oxford Essays in Medieval History Presented to H. E. Salter* (Oxford, 1932), pp. 141–154.*

required of them was authority to do and to consent to whatever might be ordained. In this respect their position is the same as that of the lower clergy under the *premunientes* clause.

The commons naturally fall into two sub-groups, the knights of the shire, and the citizens and burgesses. On the rare occasions during this period when we hear of the commons apart from the whole parliament, it is generally the knights of the shire who are mentioned; clearly, it was they who mattered most. Thirty-seven shires[1] returned seventy-four county members, and several studies of their personality have been made on a county basis, with interesting results. Taking the most recent of these, we find that Bedfordshire was represented by men whose careers can be summarized thus:

JOHN DE BEAUCHAMP. Of good family but unimportant; arrested for breach of the peace, but acquitted as it appears that he was in fact maintaining it; J.P.; twice M.P.

JOHN MORTEYN. Nine times M.P., 1307–1330; large landowner, several times summoned for military service; friend of Edward II and the Despensers; a strong partisan in politics with so many enemies that the king gave him permission to ride always armed; frequently on commissions of taxes and array.

ROGER DE NOWERS. Seven times M.P. for Beds. or Oxon. Active partisan of Mortimer; 'extremely turbulent'; imprisoned for killing a coroner.

WALTER DE HOLEWELL. Fought for Edward II at Boroughbridge and later in Scotland; four times M.P.; commissioner of array and of taxes; accused of theft and of maintaining false charges in the king's bench.

RICHARD DE LA BERE. Constantly on commissions of taxes and array; much land in several counties; sometime sheriff; five times M.P.

THOMAS DE STODLEGH. Thrice accused of house-breaking; often on judicial commissions (and once accused of misconduct therein); served on financial commissions (accused and once convicted of irregularities); seven times M.P.

ROGER LE MARESCHAL. Frequently on judicial and fiscal commissions; once M.P.; his son was M.P. later.

GERARD DE BRAYBROK. Great landowner; sixteen times M.P. in twenty-six years; apparently liked this service, for when sheriff he returned himself; his father had been seven times M.P. and his son became bishop of London and chancellor; frequently on judicial commissions.

JOHN DE MEPERTESHALE. Ten times M.P.; many years coroner; charged with corruption while commissioner of array, but 'rather more law-abiding than his fellows.'

HUGH CROFT. Five times M.P.; in 1335 sat for Hunts., as well as Beds., constantly on all kinds of commissions.

[1] The last parliament of Edward II, which became the first of Edward III, contained representatives from Wales. The only other occasion before the statute 34–35 Hen. VIII, c. 26, was in 1322.

THOMAS FREMBAUD. Constantly in debt; fined £2000 for various acts of violence; six times M.P.; fought at Crecy; sheriff; escheator (imprisoned for arrears of accounts).

WALTER POUL. Deputy-sheriff and apparently concerned mainly with the clerical duties of that office; twice a knight of the shire and three times burgess for Bedford.

These are most of the members who sat for Bedfordshire in our period;[1] the study of other counties produces similar results. It is not necessary to stress the number of seeming crooks and bandits who were elected, for it must be remembered that their generation was one of fierce faction and sometimes of civil war, which will explain most of the assaults, homicides, and house-breakings of which we hear. As for financial probity, it must likewise be remembered that handling or collecting public funds was a difficult task which often placed the official between the upper and nether millstone. The system was complicated and ineffective, and the crown bore hard upon its agents who in turn had to get the money where they could find it. These men were not necessarily criminals, though there is no need to assume that even the best of them were ever very scrupulous. Some of them had taken part in the *chevauchées* of which contemporary sources speak with equanimity, and so had well-marked party affiliations, while all of them had filled offices which were a rough school of administration and politics. The work they did on the countless commissions of oyer and terminer, gaol delivery, the peace, array, assessment and collection of taxes, as keepers of castles and sequestered estates, as sheriffs, escheators, and coroners, was hard, responsible, and exacting; the assembly of some seventy such men must have brought together a vast amount of local knowledge and experience in local administration. Besides all this, it is already apparent that several of them were acquiring parliamentary experience through their attendance at numerous parliaments. The importance of this is hardly seen during our period, but its results are obvious shortly afterwards when the frequent association of men of this calibre produced truly independent action by the knights of the shire in parliament.[2]

---

[1] These details are drawn from the illuminating thesis on the knights of the shire for Bedfordshire by Margery Fletcher (1933) in the library of London University.* Other county monographs on similar lines are listed in the *Interim Report*, pp. 12–13. The initials M.P. are here used for convenience; it is of course well known that the expression 'member of parliament' is post-mediaeval, and that the commons during the middle ages regarded themselves as present *at* parliaments rather than members *of* parliament.

[2] The election to parliament of sheriffs during their term of office is not unusual during our period, for we find as many as 10 acting sheriffs sitting at one time; they were excluded by statute in 1372 (*Rot. Parl.*, II, 310), together with practising lawyers, from being knights of the shire. At least 12 of the commons during our period rose to judicial office, and so presumably were already lawyers.

Of the citizens and burgesses it is less easy to speak.[1]   That they were an important element we can infer from those occasions on which the crown summoned special assemblies of nominated or elected townsmen in times of serious crisis.[2]   The names of some hundreds have come down to us, but it is difficult to form a just impression of their careers until municipal archives have been more fully explored; London and York, for example, generally sent to parliament merchants who were business men of national importance, while lesser towns naturally sent their best — that is to say, members of their own office-bearing class. There is little likelihood, however, of finding in our period the richness of detail which is available in the fifteenth century — the age when the town members begin to play a distinctive part in parliament.

That they were numerous seems beyond doubt; something like one hundred and forty boroughs and cities returned members at one time or another between 1294 and 1337.   At any one parliament, however, the number of town constituencies would have fallen short of this number rather considerably; between eighty and ninety seems a reasonable estimate.[3]

There is a great deal of obscurity about election procedure.   The county members were certainly chosen in the county court, which indeed would be the only convenient opportunity, and it is clear that the normal county made the choice.[4]   There is no evidence of reluctance to elect,[5] nor on the other hand is there any indication during our period (as there is fifty years later) of any competition for election; as yet, it was still considered satisfactory for the election to take place in the ordinary meeting of stewards and bailiffs which seems to have constituted the normal county court.

The election of the citizens and burgesses raises special problems.   The most recent investigations suggest that, although the returns were made by the sheriff, the elections took place in the towns to which the sheriff sent his precept.   It is likewise becoming apparent that the towns took

---

See L. Wood-Legh, *Sheriffs, Lawyers and Belted Knights in the Parliaments of Edward III, E.H.R.*, XLVI (1931), 272, and *Knights' Attendance in the Parliaments of Edward III, E.H.R.*, XLVII (1932), 398–413.

[1] Much material has been collected by M. McKisack, *The Parliamentary Representation of the English Boroughs during the Middle Ages* (London, 1932), Ch. VI.

[2] For example, the assemblies at Oxford, 27 May 1336 (88 elected merchants), Northampton, 28 June 1336 (105 nominated merchants), and at London and Norwich (mayors and 3 or 4 men from 70 towns); all the writs are in *Dignity of a Peer*.

[3] Cf. *Interim Report*, p. 114.

[4] Cf. *Rolls from the Office of Sheriff of Beds. and Bucks.*, ed. G. H. Fowler (Apsley Guise, 1929), ·p. 38, No. 88, and *Official Return*, I, 79, note ¶.

[5] Northumberland, however, refused to elect once on the ground that it was too poor to pay the knight's wages, and again because of the danger of war with Scotland (*Official Returns*, I, 79, note †, 99, note †).

the matter seriously and that their members attended with considerable regularity.[1]

How did the sheriff decide which boroughs ought to return members to parliament? A place might be regarded as a borough merely because it was always reputed to be one, or because it had a charter, or because it was taxed at a higher rate than the county, or because it had a gild merchant. More particularly, were places taxed as boroughs because they returned members to parliament, or did sheriffs only call on those places which already paid the higher rate of tax? These problems have been carefully investigated,[2] with the result that priority between taxability and representation appears to be unascertainable. Anomalies also seem fairly frequent. Some boroughs paid the higher rate and were not represented; others were represented but paid the lower rate. It would seem that sheriffs and taxers both exercised discretion in selecting boroughs, but there is a growing tendency for their lists to be similar. During our period the list of parliamentary boroughs was certainly not fixed, nor was it consistent from the standpoint of wealth or population as revealed in the tax rolls. It is curious that the south-western counties should have had such a disproportionately high number of boroughs, both parliamentary and fiscal.

The grand total seems therefore something like this:[3]

Spiritual lords (21 bishops, 31 abbots)	52
Temporal lords (11 earls, 66 barons)	77
Councillors	10
Knights of shires	74
Citizens and burgesses	160
Inferior clergy (20 deans, 58 archdeacons, 63 proctors)[4]	141
Total	514.

4. PARLIAMENT AT WORK

It is now time to follow the normal course of a typical parliament during our period, as far as it is ascertainable. The writs normally

---

[1] McKisack, op. cit., pp. 66–81.

[2] J. F. Willard, 'Taxation Boroughs and Parliamentary Boroughs,' Historical Essays in Honour of James Tait, pp. 417–435. It is not unnatural that some boroughs disagreed with the sheriff on the matter; thus Richmond and Ripon refused to obey the sheriff's precept, alleging that they were not liable to parliamentary representation (William Prynne, The First Part of a Brief Register. Kalendar of the Several Kinds, Forms of All Parliamentary Writs, London, 1659–64, iv, 318 (1328).

[3] These figures (so far as concerns the lords) refer specifically to the parliament of September 1332.

[4] These figures are the attendance which would have resulted from the premunientes clause if it had been literally obeyed; if instead the primates had summoned the convocations a rather different composition would have resulted. If the northern province, moreover, elected its parliamentary proctors by archdeaconries instead of by dioceses (as it did its convocation proctors) then the total of proctors would become 73 instead of 63.

gave about forty days' notice of the date of meeting, although sometimes
a crisis compelled more haste.[1]   The prelates and peers caused considerable difficulty through their reluctance to appear punctually, if at all.*
Thus the poor attendance at York in February 1328, is given as the
reason for another parliament at Northampton in April, while the lack
of magnates at the parliament (*tractatus*) of July in the same year made
a fourth assembly necessary in October.   At the October meeting the
earls of Lancaster and Kent were conspicuous absentees, and John
Stratford, bishop of Winchester, was summoned into the king's bench
to answer for his leaving parliament without permission.[2]   Once the
peers were warned that they would not be allowed to send proxies,[3] and
at least one parliament, that of December 1332, was a complete fiasco;
the handful of lords who came declared that they could do nothing until
the absentees were present; so fresh writs were sent out to those who
had not appeared.[4]   These re-summonses are enrolled;[5] we learn that
only three out of twenty-one bishops turned up, only three out of thirty-
one abbots, and only thirty-four out of seventy-six peers.   The disparity
between the defaults of the clergy and those of the peers is striking; so,
too, is the fact that the absentees included not only those who took little
interest in politics, but such outstanding figures as John Stratford, bishop
of Winchester, and Adam Orlton, bishop of Worcester, and the Mow-
brays, Zouches, Beauchamps, and Courtenays among the baronage.

It is now generally agreed that the commons attended in fairly large
numbers.   The writs de expensis which they sued in order to get their
wages show conclusively that many of them attended, and it is now
known that those who did not sue the writ (or whose writ was not enrolled) cannot be assumed to have been absentees.   We now know that

[1] The parliament for Nov. 1330 was called at 31 days' notice; the 40 days' rule goes back to
Magna Carta (1215), c. 14.

[2] The summons is in *Dignity of a Peer*, IV, 389, and part of the record is in 4 *Inst.*, 15–16; the
report is in Year Books 3 Edw. III, foll. 18–19; for further references see H. G. Richardson, 'Year
Books and Plea Rolls as Sources of Historical Information,' *Trans. R.H.S.*, v (1922), 59.

[3] *Dignity of a Peer*, IV, 408: *procuratores seu excusatores*, the latter probably being the 'essoins in
parliament' mentioned in *Year Books Edward II* (Selden Society, London, 1934), XX, 38–40.   By
means of a proxy an absent prelate or peer could appoint deputies to serve in his place, undertaking
to abide by whatever they had consented to in his name.   Alternatively, a letter might be sent praying to be excused from attendance.   In the P.R.O. Special Collections 10 are some 450 'parliamentary
proxies' within our period.   Many of them are appointments of deputies to replace absent bishops,
abbots, priors, and archdeacons, and a very few such proxies created by temporal lords.   There are
also a number of procurations by capitular bodies appointing their parliamentary representatives.
When the crown knew that attendance was impossible the writs might omit the clause de comparendo
personaliter (*Dignity of a Peer*, IV, 461).

[4] *Rot. Parl.*, II, 67b.   Even the lawyers failed to attend.

[5] *Dignity of a Peer*, IV, 418–419.

not all writs were enrolled, and that wages were obtainable without suing the writ.[1]

Writs to the sheriff were sometimes accompanied by covering letters. Thus in 1330 the sheriffs were required to return non-partisan knights or sergeants, for in the past there had been returned unscrupulous persons who made it their business to prevent the discussion and redress of grievances;[2] similarly, the writs for the Easter parliament of 1328 recall the losses caused to localities where parliament meets, owing to the tumult of armed followers, and so magnates and commons alike are told to bring only reasonable and orderly retinues.[3]

The political and military situation is clearly responsible for the fact that more than half the parliaments during our period met outside Westminster — in the north (York, Lincoln, Nottingham) with variations in Oxford, Salisbury, Windsor and Winchester. When they arrived at the appointed place, the lords and commons generally heard a proclamation, partly based on the statute of Northampton, (c. 3, 1328), forbidding the bearing of offensive weapons by all degrees, while children are not to play 'bar' nor snatch at people's hoods, under pain of imprisonment.[4] Then came a formal oration on the causes for summoning a parliament, delivered by some distinguished prelate or officer. On one occasion there were three such speeches, one by the archbishop of Canterbury, one by the bishop of Winchester (as chancellor), and finally one by Sir Geoffrey Scrope, the chief justice.[5] It was Scrope, in fact, who seems to have made the really important speeches which placed details of policy before the parliament with definite proposals upon which debate was to follow.

After petitions were presented, a deliberative stage was reached, when it seems to have been most usual for the magnates to consult apart from the prelates, but permanent grouping can hardly be discerned in this period. In due course each group returned and announced its decision by the mouth of a spokesman,[6] and sometimes even the individual mem-

---

[1] The problem is discussed with references to recent controversial literature in Miss McKisack's excellent study, *Parliamentary Representation of English Boroughs*, Ch. iv; also J. G. Edwards, 'The Personnel of the Commons in Parliament under Edward I and Edward II,' *Essays in Medieval History Presented to Thomas Frederick Tout* (Manchester, 1925), pp. 197–214.*

[2] *Foedera*, ii, Pt. ii, 800; *Rot. Parl.*, ii, 443. Generally it was immaterial whether the person elected was a knight, as long as he was of knightly rank; for sergeants see Tout, *Collected Papers*, ii, 282, n. 1.

[3] *Dignity of a Peer*, iv, 383 ff.

[4] 2 Edw. III, c. 3; *Rot. Parl.*, ii, 64; for 'hot words' between two lords in the presence of the king and council, see *Rot. Parl.*, ii, 65a.

[5] During our period it would seem that the commons were not always present at these opening proceedings.

[6] *Rot. Parl.*, ii, 64b.

bers gave their opinion separately as well as in a group.[1] Once we find the bishops and the proctors of the inferior clergy consulting together,[2] and once we find the curious grouping of six named prelates, two earls and four barons into one group, the rest of the earls, barons and the clerical proctors into a second, and the knights of the shire and the commons into a third group.[3] The admission of the commons into the work of deliberation seems directly due to the failure of many of the prelates and magnates to attend. In any case, the joint deliberation of the lay barons and the clerical proctors shows how very flexible the internal organization of parliament still was. Groups such as these sometimes drew up valuable reports upon the problems referred to them,[4] which provided reasonable bases for action. One further point needs mention: the habit of separate deliberation in temporary groups has every appearance of being normal, and so a united public session of prelates and peers might be reserved for the preliminary orations, the statement of problems, the delivering of opinions, and the announcement of decisions. These occasions seem to be what is meant by *plein parlement* — or, to borrow the language of Geneva, plenary sessions. It is clear that *plein parlement* does not necessarily imply the presence of the commons.[5]

Our period has a somewhat archaic air. Very shortly after its close parliament underwent profound changes. The knights of the shire became more prominent, and even the citizens and burgesses played a more important part, with the result that the prelates and peers drew closer together as the commons grew more powerful.

As we have observed, this machinery could hardly work without clerical assistance. Hence we find the approval of set forms of words drafted beforehand: 'un accord se fist en mesme le parlement en cest forme,' the text whereof follows.[6] Occasional scraps of parchment which

---

[1] *Ibid.*, p. 60b.

[2] *Ibid.*, p. 64b.   [3] *Ibid.*, p. 69.

[4] See the long reports by lords and bishops separately, *ibid.*, pp. 64–65.

[5] Occasionally it is explicitly stated that the commons were present in *plein parlement* (*Rot. Parl.*, ii, 61, No. 6; 65, No. 5). More generally it is apparent that *plenum parliamentum* included the prelates, earls, and barons only (*Rot. Parl.*, ii, 56–57; 64, No. 4). The suggestion made above that *plenum parliamentum* implies a united session of lords in contrast to sectional meetings is offered with some hesitation as an alternative to the two conflicting views at present held. According to one of these, the word 'full' does not refer to the numbers present but to the openness of their proceedings (A. F. Pollard, *The Evolution of Parliament*, 2nd ed., London, 1926, pp. 33–34, 57–58); hence even the councillors alone without magnates could describe themselves as *plenum parliamentum*. This view has been criticized by Wilkinson (*Studies in the Constitutional History of the Thirteenth and Fourteenth Centuries*, Manchester, 1937, Ch. i), who holds that the phrase implies the presence of the general body of lords. The sense of the phrase may well have varied at different dates and in different contexts, and the suggestion above is confined to the period of the early years of Edward III.*

[6] *Rot. Parl.*, ii, 62, No. 9.

appear to be drafts of resolutions or speeches are yet to be found in the Record Office.[1]

Judicature in parliament is a many-sided subject which is obscured rather than clarified by studying parliament as an institution. A body of such varied origins cannot be treated as if it were the court of common pleas. The best approach to the jurisdictions of parliament, the council, chancery, and like bodies, is an administrative one; for the ultimate form is the result of developing procedures, rather than of developing institutions.

Examining the procedures in use during our period, we find that parliament might employ several different forms. Taking first the criminal cases, we see two well-defined courses. The first is that which brought Lancaster to the block in 1322 and Mortimer in 1330. The fact that the former case was out of parliament, and the latter in parliament, is of little moment; the really important element is the procedure rather than the institution. In the former, the king assembled some magnates and 'recorded' his personal knowledge that Lancaster had committed various treasons which were notorious to all the world.[2] Judgment immediately followed.[3] Mortimer's case ran the same course.[4] The *recordatio* was here represented by a schedule of charges, followed by a demand for judgment from the assembled earls and barons. In like manner Simon de Bereford was condemned, although the lords made the notable protest that Simon was not their peer and so they were not bound to judge him, whereupon the king promised that this case should not be taken as a precedent.[5] Clearly, the lords deemed it a duty based upon their feudal position to render judgment in such cases, and a feudal-romanesque origin for the procedure may be suspected.[6] It is natural that there should have been dissatisfaction with this old procedure; in 1327 Lancas-

---

[1] Chancery, Parl. Proc., 6/13, may be an example. E 175/2/18 seems to be notes of the king's speech to a parliament.

[2] The record of Lancaster's trial is printed in *Foedera*, II, Pt. i, 478, from the patent roll, and is recited verbatim in the reversal of the judgment in 1327 printed in *Rot. Parl.*, II, 3, from the close roll. For a fuller discussion of this and similar cases, see T.F.T. Plucknett, 'Rise of the English State Trial,' *Politica*, II (1937), 542–559.*

[3] This denial to the accused of any opportunity of defending himself is the result of the principle that the prosecution could only succeed if it made out an overwhelming case; defence was therefore superfluous; see J. F. Stephen, *History of the Criminal Law of England* (London, 1882), III, 351–354. For the incontrovertibility of the king's word, see Frederick Pollock and F. W. Maitland, *The History of English Law before the Time of Edward I* (Cambridge, 1895), II, 669, and the additional material in S. E. Thorne, 'Courts of Record in England,' *West Virginia Law Quarterly*, XL (1934), 350, n. 11.

[4] *Rot. Parl.*, II, 52.

[5] *Rot. Parl.*, II, 53.

[6] Slightly modernized by the association with it of the commons, this procedure seems to have grown into the act of attainder.

ter's case had been reversed and condemned, but this did not prevent Mortimer's trial by substantially the same method.

The second course available in criminal trials was clearly based upon the common law. The prisoner, Sir Thomas de Berkeley, was arraigned, allowed to defend himself, and tried by a jury of twelve knights, for he, too, was not a lord of parliament.[1]

A third procedure, available both in criminal and civil cases, was the correction of error on the records of inferior courts, and even of errors in pleas held 'by the council in the new exchequer.'[2] It is obvious from the year books that these proceedings in parliament closely resembled those in the common law courts, and were argued by counsel. They began by petition to the king in council; the approval of the petition was authority for issuing the writ of error which brought up the record complained of, and served as the commission by which parliament was empowered to examine and redress the errors.[3] Parliament was therefore exercising a jurisdiction delegated from the council, just as the chancellor did at the end of the century. Throughout the middle ages error was but rarely brought in parliament, as far as we can ascertain, and such trace as it may have left would normally be on the roll of the lower court,[4] for as we have seen, parliament soon abandoned the attempt to keep a plea roll.[5]

Rather more frequently we find parliament acting as a court of discussion to which courts of first instance would adjourn difficult points.[6] Examples of this are fairly frequent in the reign of Edward II, for which we have available modern editions of the year books and the accompanying records.[7] The best-known example is Staunton v. Staunton, just after our period,[8] which shows how a case could move from court to court, including parliament, without discontinuing the record — such removals could be made by the court itself when faced with a difficulty, or procured by a party if he successfully petitioned the king in council or in parliament.[9] Although some magnates may have attended pro-

---

[1] *Rot. Parl.*, II, 57. The peers made a general protest saving the principle that they were not bound to judge commoners (*ibid.*, p. 54).

[2] Year Books 2 Edw. III, foll. 24–25.

[3] Lancaster's case is typical (*Rot. Parl.*, II, 3).

[4] This is explained in Y. B. 33 Hen. VI, fol. 17.

[5] By 1366 the common pleas declined to recognize such activity of the council in the name of parliament, saying that the council 'is not the place where judgments can be reversed,' Y. B. 39 Edw. III, fol. 14.

[6] In the fifteenth century the exchequer chamber often took its place for this purpose.

[7] *Year Books Edward II* (Selden Society), II, 52; XII, 83; XVIII, 179; cf. XXI, 58–60.

[8] *Year Books 13–14 Edward III* (Rolls Series), pp. xxxvii–xliv, 18; *Year Books 14–15 Edward III* (Rolls Series), pp. 288–300. The judges showed some resentment at the proceedings and in fact frustrated them.

[9] *Year Books Edward II* (Selden Society), XI, 130.

ceedings such as these, it is not necessary to assume that the whole peer-age took part unless the case was closely associated with party politics;[1] on such occasions we may even find the commons mentioned as partici-pating in the judgment. In more normal cases it is clear that the council, the judges, and the officials were those most concerned.

Although these are all well-defined procedures, the bulk of parliament's judicial business falls into a fifth category. The matters involved are immensely varied in type and importance, but we suggest that they have one element in common, that is to say, their connection with adminis-trative law. One of the results of the system of feudal law was that matters of public concern often arose in litigation between private parties, and a further result was that the crown had claims of a feudal nature arising out of countless private estates. The office which managed most of this huge mass of business was the chancery, and it was recognized that proceedings in common law courts might often be interrupted while the chancery ascertained how the crown's rights were affected. Every mediaevalist is familiar with some of the great heads of chancery's com-mon law jurisdiction — inquests of office, *ad quod damnum*, and the like. To these must be added matters arising out of the king's grants (and hence the interpretation of grants of, and the title to, franchises of all sorts), all kinds of litigation which had been suspended *rege inconsulto*, and all matters relating to lands in the king's hand, whether by escheat, wardship, forfeiture, or otherwise. Much of this work was purely ad-ministrative and was transacted by the chancery clerks, but some of it was quasi-judicial and came before the council. It is not surprising therefore to find that the close and patent rolls contain abundant traces of this sort of adjudication credited to parliaments. As Mr Richardson and Dr Sayles have observed:

There come before parliament questions of property in which the king is, or is supposed to be, interested: if complaints are made as to the action of the escheators, or if there is a question of a man's accountability for the issues of a manor, the case is likely to be settled in parliament. Questions of franchises, disputes between town and gown and other university affairs, disputes between a bishop and his chapter, disputes between native and alien merchants, grants by the king, a countess's dower, a whole miscellany of petty administrative questions are parliamentary business.[2]

[1] Examples are Lancaster's case (1327): *Rot. Parl.*, II, 5a; the record and judgment of Mortimer's case was shown to the 'knights of the shires and other commons' as well as to the lords when it was reversed for error in 1354: *Rot. Parl.*, II, 255 (cf. *ibid.*, p. 257, No. 15).

[2] *Bull. Inst. Hist. Research*, IX (1931), 5. Matters of this sort generally reached parliament after having been raised in earlier private litigation. If the crown wished to initiate litigation on these subjects, the chancery, exchequer, or king's bench would be the more usual place. The reason given for this in 1342 is that 'the king will not sue by petition in parliament for matters which concern him'

In a sense it is true, for the documents expressly associate parliament with these affairs; but it is unnecessary to assume that parliament, as we understand the institution, was troubled with any but the most important of them. There is every cause for believing that, while parliament was sitting, the council regarded itself as part of parliament, and its acts might therefore be described as the acts of parliament. It is likewise important to remember that parliament was a convenient occasion, since several officials and judges were taken momentarily away from their posts and assembled in conference. In short, whether we examine parliament as a court or as an administrative body, it is for the most part only a reflection of the council, which exercised its powers in parliament, and was, in fact, the very core and heart of parliament. It is, however, to be noted that during our period we do get a few significant assertions of the dignity of parliamentary judicature: a decree of parliament ought not to be revoked save by a parliament;[1] it is 'the highest place in the realm'[2] and the tampering with its endorsement is a serious offence, although the chancellor seems unaware of it.[3] Politically, too, parliament becomes more and more self-conscious and eventually will even oppose the policies of the court and council. We must therefore beware of over-simplifying the constitution of parliament, especially during this period. The growth of the idea of peerage and of the representative principle was certainly changing the political complexion of parliament so that finally parliament could consider itself as not only distinct from, but also as antagonistic to the council to some extent. But even when this development had been accomplished, it was still the council that organized parliament's work, and on many occasions spoke in parliament's name without causing thereby any constitutional scandal. This close intimacy between parliament and council was in fact essential if parliament was to serve any useful purpose. All this, however, must not lead us to the opposite extreme of denying the fact that there are broadly two different institutions. Thus the assertion that 'a meeting only of the king, council and the justices to try *placita* and hear petitions was perfectly a parliament'[4] would be much better expressed in terms of functions rather than of institutions; we should prefer to say that the council, a small group of official experts surrounding the king and forming the heart and core of parliament, would often describe its decisions as

---

(*Year Books 16 Edward III*, Rolls Series, I, 110). In Ireland, however, on one occasion at least the king presented a petition through the justiciar (M.V. Clarke, *Fourteenth Century Studies*, Oxford, 1937, p. 22; *Early Statutes of Ireland*, I, 263 ff.), although not on that sort of subject.

[1] *Rot. Parl.*, II, 7.

[2] *Ibid.*, p. 24, No. 31.

[3] *Ibid.*, p. 45b.

[4] Jolliffe, *Constitutional History of Medieval England*, p. 341.

those of parliament, especially in matters which did not raise important questions of politics. That is by no means the same as the assertion that institutionally council and parliament were one.

Taking all the evidence, we suggest that parliament was nominally, rather than actually, the crown of the judicial edifice, and as the fourteenth century advances, its position was hardly improved. The rise of the present appellate powers of the house of lords dates mainly from post-mediaeval times,[1] when a thin stream of mediaeval authority was rapidly developed. If we seek an answer to the very pertinent question which Mr Richardson and Dr Sayles have posed,[2] we may suggest that one of the principal reasons why our parliament did not go the way of the French *parlements* and become an assembly of jurists and administrators sitting as a court lies in the fact that the council was strong enough to dominate the situation; parliament's judicial powers are as yet indistinguishable from those of the council,[3] and the council never parted with its own, but used them freely out of parliament as well as in. The council, moreover, was continuously available, although parliaments became less frequent soon after our period. The growing prominence of political, peerage, and representative elements in parliament was accompanied by a corresponding decline in the position of the conciliar and official group. These persons, judges and others, were reduced before the end of our century to the position of mere assessors to the peers. This turn of events must have contributed largely to the decline of parliament as a judicial body, and we need hardly be surprised that litigants addressed their complaints to the council, chancery, or exchequer, where they could be sure of their affairs coming before expert officials who were equally competent in administrative and in judicial matters. Above all, the council supervised the working of the common law side of chancery which handled the vast business arising out of the crown's feudal rights, and so parliament was likewise prevented from becoming a true feudal jurisdiction for practical purposes.

It is now time to turn to the petitions, which, as we have remarked, were the principal method by which parties could set in motion and direct the machinery of parliamentary judicature. It was not the primary duty of the commons to present petitions — even from their own constituents; the city of London will therefore send its officers, and not its representatives, to present its petitions.[4] Still less was parliament at this time a body that could be petitioned. The almost universal form

---

[1] W. S. Holdsworth, *History of English Law* (London, 1922), I, 370.

[2] 'The King's Ministers in Parliament,' *E.H.R.*, XLVII (1932), 397.

[3] Jurisdiction in error had become an exception by 1366 (see above, p. 223, n. 5), but after this date such proceedings in parliament are rare.

[4] *Rot. Parl.*, II, 54b; cf. C. H. McIlwain, *High Court of Parliament* (New Haven, 1910), p. 208.

of address is to the king and his council, and generally parliament is not even mentioned.

The evidence from our period as to the procedure governing petitions is somewhat obscure. We do hear, however, of both receivers and triers of petitions in 1333.[1] The receivers for English petitions were Edenestow (the clerk of the parliament), Sir Thomas de Bamburgh, and Sir Thomas de Evesham, while the receivers for petitions from Gascony, Wales, Ireland, and the Isles were Mr John de Blebury and Sir Thomas de Brayton.[2] All of them were senior chancery clerks. In the reign of Edward II it was certainly the duty of receivers to enroll the petitions, leaving spaces for the triers to insert the answers, and to assist the triers,[3] and they may have done so during our period. Several problems are raised by the fewness of these enrollments during our period. It has been suggested[4] that this indicates a diminution in the number of petitions, and that this diminution was due to the competition of the chancellor's equitable jurisdiction.[5] A simpler explanation may perhaps be found in purely procedural changes: thus, it may be that enrolment ceased because the use of the original petitions, suitably endorsed and forwarded to the administrative departments concerned, was found to be more expeditious.[6] There is also the possibility that some of the petitions printed in the *Rotuli Parliamentorum* from Hale's transcripts were originally enrolled.[7]

More important than the receivers were the auditors,[8] as they were

[1] Not 1332, as in Bertie Wilkinson, *The Chancery under Edward III* (Manchester, 1929), pp. 81, n. 2, 82, 150 ff., etc.; *Rot. Parl.*, II, 68.

[2] Biographies of all five will be found in Wilkinson, *op cit.*, pp. 151–5.

[3] Richardson and Sayles in *E.H.R.*, XLVII (1932), 196, n. 5., 380, n. 1; cf. the rolls of petitions mentioned above, p. 93.

[4] By Richardson and Sayles, *ibid.*, pp. 379–380; also Ludwik Ehrlich, 'Proceedings against the Crown 1216–1377,' *Oxford Studies in Social and Legal History*, ed. Paul Vinogradoff (Oxford, 1921), Vol. VI, [No.] xii.

[5] It is very improbable that the chancellor exercised any equitable jurisdiction during our period. Care must be taken to distinguish the casual granting of favors from the settled jurisdiction to administer equity to all comers. This latter cannot be placed with certainty before the reign of Richard II. Similarly, the occasional granting of relief by parliament in circumstances which later were typical of equity (*C.C.R. 1327–1330*, 47; cf. Plucknett, *Concise History of the Common Law*, London, and Rochester, N.Y., 2nd ed., 1936, p. 161, n.) does not show that parliament had equitable jurisdiction. Dr Wilkinson antedates the rise of equity by a whole century (*Chancery under Edward III*, pp. 48 ff.).

[6] As Wilkinson suggests, *op. cit.*, p. 81. It is clear that at this moment extended use was being made of filed writs (much the same as filing cards today) in the exchequer (*Select Cases in the Exchequer of Pleas*, ed. Hilary Jenkinson, Selden Society, London, 1927, p. cxxvii). Cf. below, p. 115, n. 4. As Maitland, (*Memoranda de Parliamento*, p. lxv) says, enrolment was all along something of a luxury.*

[7] This is quite certain in some cases (*Rot. Parl. Inediti*, pp. 104, 141).

[8] Auditor was a word which might imply (as it does here) judicial functions: at this moment there were auditors in the *parlement* of Paris, and the high court of the *Rota* consisted of auditors; cf. McIlwain, *High Court of Parliament*, p. 251.

generally termed, although in 1333 they are styled triers. English petitions were to be tried by three prelates, two 'barons,' and four justices; the rest were assigned to another group of three prelates, two 'barons,' and two justices. The preponderance of magnates clearly shows some distrust of the *curiales* and the rise of the pretensions of the peers. Both groups were empowered to call in the chancellor, treasurer, and the chief justice if they saw fit. The rules laid down for them were simple. Petitions were to be kept by the clerks (possibly the receivers) under the seals of the triers until dealt with. Those which had been tried and determined were to be sent under the triers' seals to chancery.[1] Petitions reserved for the king himself were to be sent to him under seal and tried by him and any assistants he might call in. There is evidently here an attempt to prevent tampering with petitions, which was complained of in 1330.[2]

We have remarked that the commons in parliament were not there primarily to put forward petitions. Certain steps in the development of parliamentary petitioning, however, are to be found during our period[3] in those common petitions[4] which are engaging the attention of constitutional historians. The varying uses of this phrase, and the fluctuating meanings of *la commune, les communes*, and *la communaulte* make the study particularly difficult. It may be that these common petitions at first originated outside of parliament (as petitions regularly did) and that the commons in parliament were induced, by a species of lobbying to take an interest in them.[5] Some of these petitions concerned purely private or sectional interests, but from time to time we find more general matters involved. In either case it is probable that during our period common petitions went direct to the council instead of to receivers and auditors.[6] This procedure was obviously open to abuses, and in 1327 the commons took the precaution of putting the common petitions on an

---

[1] Observe that enrolment is thus unnecessary.

[2] *Rot. Parl.*, ii, 45b.

[3] By 1352 they were formally invited to petition (*Rot. Parl.*, ii, 237, No. 8).

[4] Contemporary terminology is varied and obscure. For a long time occasional petitions had been presented in the name of the community of England, which seems to mean that the promoters regarded their grievance as nation-wide. It is difficult to distinguish this type from another (often beginning *prient les communes*) which implies that the commons in parliament are the petitioning body. A third stage is reached when additional emphasis is conferred upon this type by collecting the petitions of the commons and putting them together on a single roll. By the end of the fourteenth century such a roll may be headed 'common petitions.' It is convenient to use this later expression for those few examples which occur during our period, viz., in 1327 (*Rot. Parl.*, ii, 7, and *Rot. Parl. Inediti*, p. 116), in 1333 (*Rot. Parl. Inediti*, p. 224), and in 1334 (*Rot. Parl. Inediti*, p. 232). See generally H. L. Gray, *Influence of the Commons on Early Legislation* (Cambridge, 1932).*

[5] Thus the commons might 'disavow' (*Rot. Parl.*, ii, 11, No. 38) as well as 'avow' (*Rot. Parl.*, ii, 203, No. 30) as they saw fit.

[6] Richardson and Sayles in *E.H.R.*, xlvii (1932), 388.

indented roll in order to safeguard their authenticity.[1] By the end of the reign, the common petitions come to occupy the most important place on the parliament roll.

This discussion of common petitions naturally leads to the next subject, that is to say, legislation. Here again many questions must be left to the political and constitutional historians, such as the definition of statutes and ordinances, the influences which moulded them, their content, and their legal characteristics.[2] Here we are concerned with only part of the problem, legislation as one of the normal activities of parliament. Parliament now had a large share in stimulating the government to legislate, and, on paper at least, a well-nigh exclusive right of enactment. The common petition was an important element in this development, for it was the origin eventually of most of those statutes which were parliamentary.[3] Whether all statutes during our short period were based on common petitions is hardly provable, for there are serious gaps in the extant collections of parliamentary documents.[4] Two or three propositions, however, can be established. First, although we have only three common petitions surviving during our period, one of them seems to have been wholly ineffectual. This is Chancery, Parliament Roll, No. 4.[5] Although the heading asserts that 'ascuns furent accordez en dit parlement de faire en estatut,' no such statute seems to have been actually made and published; later parliaments had to return to the attack in order to obtain, years later, the legislation desired. This seems to have been often the case, but it is difficult to conclude whether recommendations were kept in mind by the government, or whether they were reiterated in fresh common petitions.[6] In either case, there remains an impression of continuity from year to year in the work of legislation which testifies to the growing position of parliament as a continuous element in national life.

Secondly, it is clear that during our period the petition and the answer

---

[1] *Rot. Parl.*, II, 11, No. 38; the original seems to be Chancery, Parliament Roll, No. 1 (*Bull. nst. Hist. Research*, IX, 1931, 16).

[2] See in general, McIlwain, *High Court of Parliament;* T. F. T. Plucknett, *Statutes and Their Interpretation in the First Half of the Fourteenth Century* (Cambridge, 1922), and Richardson and Sayles, 'The Early Statutes,' *Law Quarterly Review*, L (1934), 201–224, 540–571.

[3] Non-parliamentary legislation is henceforth extremely rare; there is none during our period, or the assembly of 1336 at Nottingham is indistinguishable from a parliament in all but name.

[4] Gray, *Influence of the Commons*, p. 286.

[5] There is an English abstract in *Rot. Parl.*, II, 376–377. The text is now available in *Rot. Parl. Inediti*, pp. 231–239.

[6] The date of the petition is 8 Edw. III, but c. 15 became law only in 9 Edw. III, st. 2; c. 16 in 10 Edw. III, st. 2; c. 3 in 10 Edw. III, st. 1, c. 2; c. 8 had no result until 18 Edw. III, st. 3; c. 2 and c. 9 remained fruitless until 31 Edw. III, st. 1, c. 4. So, too, c. 20 of the petition of 1 Edw. III received the royal assent (*Rot. Parl.*, II, 9, 11) but no statute was made until 5 Edw. III, c. 6. Such instances (which could easily be multiplied) suggest a certain degree of continuous pressure.

to it were only the basis, in a general way, of the resulting statute.   The council, with the expert help of the judges, acted not only as a drafting committee, but also exercised a wide discretion in amending the substance of the demand.   Indeed, there is one chapter of the common petition of 1327 which duly received the royal assent, but failed altogether of enactment.[1]

Thirdly, it is undoubted that many of the parliaments of our period produced no statutes whatever.   Of the twenty-one parliamentary assemblies now under consideration, only seven have left us statutes. Nevertheless, the statute roll during our period is made up with regularity, and (so far as is known) with the omission of only one statute.[2] From 1328 onwards, each statute is followed on the roll by the form of the writ which was directed to every sheriff in England requiring him to proclaim it.   We thus have a systematic method of enrolment and a settled practice of publication.

The one product of parliamentary activity, therefore, which is regularly recorded is its legislation.   If we examine the subject matter of the statutes passed during the ten years of our period, we shall find confirmation of what seems an irresistible conclusion — namely, that the legislative side of parliament's work has by now become its most characteristic and important activity, second only to its general political and administrative supervision of the country.   The particular ten years before us are not conspicuous in the general legislative history of England either for the volume or the importance of their output, but even so the following notes will show that parliamentary statutes had an assured position at the very centre of legal and constitutional life.

On the constitutional side we have the important statutory pronouncement requiring annual parliaments[3]— which during our period was substantially observed — and an impressive statement that the course of justice was not to be diverted by letters under the small seals set up a standard to which practice slowly conformed.[4]   Numerous branches of the royal prerogative were defined and limited; two of these reform seem to have been particularly urgent, those touching purveyance and the prerogative of pardon.

Purveyance included the pre-emption of food at prices fixed conveniently low, against mere promises to pay which seem often to have been forgotten by the crown; it might also comprise the use of horses and cart

---

[1] *Rot. Parl.*, II, 9, No. 19, 11, No. 19.

[2] 9 Edw. III, st. 2 (on the transport of coin) is on the fine roll only. 'The entries on the fir statute roll are contemporary from about the year 1299' (Richardson and Sayles, *Law Quarter Review*, L, 1934, 213).

[3] 4 Edw. III, c. 14 (which London had petitioned for in 1327; *Rot. Parl. Inediti*, p. 134 [27]).

[4] 2 Edw. III, c. 8; for its enforcement see Plucknett, *Statutes and Their Interpretation*, pp. 142-14

and the services of carters. The right to exact these dues was certainly old, and the abuse of them was by no means recent. The great charter, the statute of Westminster the first, and the *Articuli super Cartas* had already stated a few important limitations, but during the reign of Edward II purveyance became a major grievance, constantly appearing in the constitutional documents of the time. In our period a serious attempt was made to deal with the problem by statute. In 1330 it was enacted that the value of goods and services taken should be appraised by sworn valuers, that the quantities should be measured by razed bushels and not by heaped bushels, that cartage should be voluntary, and that purveyance should be made only by the king, the queen, and their children.[1] The very next year, however, a statute declared that the abuse of purveyance was as serious as ever, re-enacted the valuation clause of 1330, and required the making of tallies for goods and services purveyed. The most remarkable of its provisions, however, was the declaration that if any purveyor executed his office otherwise than in the mode prescribed by the statute, he should be arrested and committed to gaol, and, if convicted, he should suffer the pains of larceny.[2] This was a drastic extension of the provision of the *Articuli super Cartas* which in 1300 had made purveyance by persons unauthorized a statutory larceny, and therefore capital; properly commissioned purveyors under the *Articuli* of 1300 who exceeded their powers were merely imprisoned;[3] they, however, were now (1331) put under the shadow of the gallows. This was a remarkable provision, for contemporary law was very loath to extend the scope of larceny beyond the extremely narrow limits which the common law imposed upon it and declined to apply it to persons who took goods under color of right.[4] Whether any purveyors were actually hanged it is impossible to say, but it is equally impossible to believe that the terrors of this statute prevented future abuses. It was in fact re-enacted five years later by a statute which also dealt with a special aspect of purveyance, namely, the taking of 'great horses.' The existing system of sending special keepers of the king's horses for this type of purveyance was replaced (according to the statute) by charging the sheriffs with the task, while commissioners were to be appointed to hear and determine the accusations which hung over the late keepers.[5] No permanent benefit seems to have resulted, and purveyance continued to be a serious grievance throughout the reign of Edward III.* The statutes

---

[1] 4 Edw. III, c. 3; c. 4 confirmed *Articuli super Cartas* (1300) as to purveyance.
[2] 5 Edw. III, c. 2 (1331).
[3] *Articuli super Cartas*, 28 Edw. I, cc. 1 and 2 (1300).
[4] Plucknett, *Concise History of the Common Law*, p. 396 ff.
[5] 10 Edw. III, st. 2, cc. 1–3 (1336).

of 1331 and 1336 both confirm the limitation placed by the *Articuli super Cartas* on the jurisdiction of the court of the steward and marshal of the household, apparently in order to exclude it from dealing with contracts of purveyance.

The legislation on pardons during these ten years is equally voluminous. The importance of the subject is evident when it is remembered that the royal pardon was the only point at which the criminal law became in any degree flexible. For example, the common law treated all sorts of homicide as felony. It knew nothing of the modern distinctions between murder and homicide by misadventure, in self-defense, by negligence, and similar refinements of modern law. If questions of this sort were to be raised at all, it was only in the form of an application for a royal pardon, and, as a matter of legal history, these distinctions only entered the law at last as a result of further statutory regulation of pardons during the reign of Richard II and subsequently.[1] The royal power of pardon therefore fulfilled an important function in rendering the criminal law more just, but it is equally evident that a power so wide, exercised by the monarch without guidance (in many cases) from the judiciary, was open to grave abuses. Moreover, by common law and statute the procedure in several civil actions was conducted under criminal forms, and outlawry might be incurred by the persistent failure of defendants to appear. The serious results of this outlawry were frequently remitted by royal pardons.

On the criminal side, a statute of 1328 recites that malefactors are greatly emboldened by the fact that charters of pardon are so easily obtainable for homicide, robbery, felony, and other trespasses against the peace; wherefore it was enacted that charters should not be granted save in the already well-established cases of homicide in self-defence or by misadventure.[2] This statute undoubtedly went too far in restricting pardons and left many circumstances in which (as criminal law then stood) a pardon was the only available way of doing justice. Nevertheless it was re-enacted in 1330[3] and again in 1336. This last statute made the further requirement that the validity of a pardon should expire unless the grantee should find within three months six mainpernors who would enter into bonds for his good behavior. This was in practice an impossible condition, and the statute was unworkable; it became the custom, in fact, for the crown to insert in charters of pardon a clause

---

[1] The historical importance of pardons is discussed by Stephen, *History of Criminal Law*, II, 38–43. Legislation on benefit of clergy had a similar result; see briefly, Plucknett, *Concise History of the Common Law*, pp. 395–396.

[2] 2 Edw. III, c. 2, 'ou le Roi le poet faire par son serment.'

[3] 4 Edw. III, c. 13.

[4] 10 Edw. III, st. 1, c. 3.

dispensing with this statute.[1]   The real solution to this difficult problem was not found until 1390 when it was enacted[2] that no pardon should
avail for what later statutes called wilful murder; this was a sound distinction which allowed the crown to experiment in the punishment of
those homicides which did not amount to wilful murder.

The problem of pardons of outlawry in civil proceedings was different,
for private as well as public interests were involved. It was therefore
enacted in 1331 that outlawry after judgment[3] should not be pardoned
until the plaintiff was satisfied of the damages he had recovered, and
that no pardon of outlawry incurred before appearance should be effective until the outlaw had actually surrendered to the court.[4]

As for ecclesiastical legislation, the reign opened, as might be expected,
with a gesture of friendliness towards the church and a declaration that
no illegal seizures of episcopal lands and goods should take place[5]— a
promise which the church caused to be reiterated thirteen years later.[6]
The crown likewise promised not to demand more corrodies for its de-
pendents than were due.[7]   Another clause in the same statute, however,
reminds us that relations between church and state could hardly be free
from friction as long as both exercised criminal jurisdiction. It is known
that a large majority of the persons who were indicted were acquitted at
their trial;[8] the statute[9] adds that many persons so acquitted take proceedings in ecclesiastical courts against members of the grand jury for
defamation. It therefore gives the latter remedy by a writ of prohibition. This no doubt helped honest jurors and established the judicial
immunity of the grand jury, but robbed the victims of malicious prose-
cutions of their only effective remedy until the nineteenth century.[10]

Fair promises and the adjustment of jurisdictional details did not ex-
haust Edward III's ecclesiastical policy, and the great crisis in the middle

---

[1] This is explained in the preamble to 5 and 6 Will. and Mary, c. 13 (1694).

[2] 13 Ric. II, st. 2, c. 1.

[3] That is, consequent on defaults after the *capias pro fine.*

[4] 5 Edw. III, c. 12.

[5] 1 Edw. III, st. 2, c. 2.

[6] 14 Edw. III, st. 4 (1340). A very interesting judicial opinion based on this statute is printed by Richardson and Sayles in *Law Quarterly Review*, L (1934), 555, n. 73.

[7] 1 Edw. III, st. 2, c. 10.

[8] In Kent in 1322 out of 64 persons indicted, 57 were acquitted; in Staffordshire in 1597 we still find that 12 trials produced only one conviction (*Kent Keepers of the Peace*, ed. B. H. Putnam, London, 1933, p. xxxvi; *Staffordshire Quarter Sessions*, ed. S. A. H. Burne, William Salt Archaeological Society, London, 1933, III, xxv). Very similar results were obtained in B.H. Putnam, *Select Proceedings before the Justices of the Peace in the Fourteenth and Fifteenth Centuries* (Ames Foundation, London, 1938), p. cxxvii.

[9] 1 Edw. III, st. 2, c. 11.

[10] Where indictments were 'procured,' there was the ineffective writ of conspiracy and a statutory action on the case (8 Hen. VI, c. 10); as to which see P. H. Winfield, *History of Conspiracy and Abuse of Legal Procedure* (Cambridge, 1921), pp. 107, 120–121.

of his reign with its radical legislation on provisors and *praemunire* can
be seen approaching when in 1330, and again in 1331, parliament formally confirmed and re-enacted[1] the most contentious of his grandfather's
statutes, the statute of Carlisle,[2] which in 1307 forbade in sweeping terms
the export of money by ecclesiastical bodies, whether by way of taxation
or by way of contribution to the mother-houses of English priories.

This last measure might be equally well considered as part of the
voluminous economic legislation of the period. In 1335 there was a
general statute of money[3] whereby sterling was not to be melted, bullion
was not to be exported, and the exchanges were to be regulated. In
order to enforce these provisions, tourist traffic (*i.e.*, pilgrims) was all
to pass through the port of Dover.[4] Informers were promised rewards,
searchers were commissioned, and innkeepers were sworn to search their
guests. The same concern to maintain the wealth of the country may
perhaps lie behind the great sumptuary statute[5] of the following year,
1336. If overeating impoverished the individual, did it not thereby impoverish the realm? And so, whereas the rich ruin themselves with
costly viands, and others ruin themselves trying to keep up with the
rich, thus doing great harm as well to the body as to the soul, it was
therefore enacted that the number of courses and messes, and the composition of the sauces, should not exceed the limits set out in the statute.

A commercial experiment of great interest was made in 1328, when all
staples in England and on the continent were abolished.[6] These institutions were the machinery by which trade was brought under the control of the fiscal authorities, since it had to pass through certain ports.
In accordance with mediaeval tradition, the merchants in those ports
were organized for their own self-government, and in practice seem to
have established a monopoly of the trade in foreign goods; it was very
possibly the jealousy of those who were excluded from this monopoly
which prompted the abolition of the staples. Seven years later it became apparent that abolishing the staples had not prevented the traders
in foreign goods from re-establishing their monopoly through informal
arrangements, and so the statute of York (1335)[7] explained in a long
preamble that merchants in ports of entry have prevented foreign im-
porters from selling to anyone except themselves, thus enhancing the
price of foreign wines, victuals and provisions; this (the commons tact-

---

[1] 4 Edw. III, c. 6; 5 Edw. III, c. 3.
[2] 35 Edw. I.
[3] 9 Edw. III, st. 2.
[4] Cross-channel fares were fixed by 4 Edw. III, c. 8 (1330).
[5] 10 Edw. III, st. 3.
[6] 2 Edw. III, c. 9.
[7] 9 Edw. III, st. 1, c. 1.

fully observe) is to the great damage of the king and all the nobility, and the oppression of the people. One is tempted to connect this emphasis on the cost of foreign table-delicacies with the sumptuary statute of this same year just mentioned. If that is so, the problem was attacked from two sides. The sumptuary law tried to reduce unreasonable consumption, while the statute of York proceeded to enact that foreign merchants could sell to anyone, within franchise or without, and that if any town endeavored to restrict this freedom of trade, its franchise should be forfeit. A point of great constitutional interest is contained in a clause which declares that this provision shall override all charters and franchises.[1]

The remaining economic legislation of our period is more normal. Cloth measures were standardized[2] in 1328, while two statutes[3] of 1328 and 1331 deal with the situation when a fair has been continued for a longer time than was permitted by the charter or by custom. The former threatened the lord thereof with the loss of his fair, and the latter imposed on traders the loss of twice the value of all goods sold out of time.

It is in the realm of law reform, however, that the quality of a legislature is best seen, and during our period it is undeniable that parliament seriously endeavored to amend and strengthen the administration of justice.* Powers of trial, as well as of enquiry, were given to justices of the peace[4] in 1328, and in 1330 sheriffs were forbidden to bail persons committed by them save for lawful cause;[5] the commissions of assize were strengthened by restricting them to men 'who know the law,' and only justices of one of the benches were to be put on oyer and terminer.[6] The ordinary justices of gaol delivery were to have jurisdiction over prisoners committed by the justices of the peace;[7] even justices on *nisi prius* were given some criminal duties,[8] and all were required to return their criminal records annually to the exchequer.[9]

Mediaeval law made little provision for what we may loosely call appellate proceedings, including under that head all means of reviewing in superior courts the judgments given and verdicts found in lower courts.

---

[1] It was a difficult question how far a general statute would override local privileges by charter; see Plucknett, *Statutes and Their Interpretation*, pp. 138–139; Richardson and Sayles in *Law Quarterly Review*, L (1934), 552, 554; *Rot. Parl. Inediti*, p. 128, No. 5.

[2] 2 Edw. III, c. 14.

[3] 2 Edw. III, c. 15; 5 Edw. III, c. 5.

[4] 2 Edw. III, c. 6

[5] 4 Edw III, c. 2.

[6] 2 Edw. III, c. 2.

[7] 4 Edw. III, c. 2.

[8] 4 Edw. III, c. 11.

[9] 9 Edw. III, st. 1, c. 5.

The only way of reviewing a jury's verdict was by the writ of attaint, whereby a jury of twenty-four was invited to convict the former jury of perjury. This remedy was originally available only to reverse the recognitions of assizes, but was now extended to verdicts given in actions of trespass, both on the main issue, and on the assessment of damages.[1] The procedure was soon afterwards made very speedy,[2] and further extended to trespass brought without writ if the damages exceeded forty shillings.[3]

'False judgment' was a procedure equivalent to a writ of error where the judgment complained of was given in a seignorial or county court. It frequently happened that the plaintiff denied the accuracy of the lower court's record of its proceedings, and, if so, trial would have to be by battle between the champions of the plaintiff and the court respectively; by 1 Edw. III, st. 1, c. 4, jury trial was substituted. The next chapter of the same statute allows the averment to be tried by a jury when a party disputes the truth of a bailiff's return; this was already possible in respect of returns made by a sheriff.[4] The little known jurisdiction of the steward and marshall of the household was brought into line with other courts of record by enacting that error should lie from it to the king's bench.[5]

One other statute of this nature is principally interesting for the evidence it affords of a changing view of legislation. Its history begins with a petition presented to the king and his council early in the spring of 1328 by Robert Fitzpayn and his wife showing that, in a *scire facias* to execute a fine of lands brought against them by Robert Burnel the sheriff falsely returned that the Fitzpayns had been garnished to appear in the king's bench. In consequence, the Fitzpayns did not appear and judgment went against them. Thereupon the petitioners state that they brought a writ of deceit against Burnel, the sheriff, and the garnishers, and the falseness of the return was duly proved; the court, however, refused to proceed any further without the advice of the council — hence this petition. The reply to the petition was a short sentence granting that a writ of deceit should lie where garnishment had been falsely returned, in the same way as it already lay where summons had been falsely returned.[6] A lengthy writ dated 16 May 1328 ordered the justices of the king's bench to proceed 'as it is agreed by the king and his council in the present parliament at Northampton.'[7]

[1] 1 Edw. III, st. 1, c. 6.
[2] 5 Edw. III, c. 6.   [3] 5 Edw. III, c. 7.
[4] Westminster II, c. 39.   [5] 5 Edw. III, c. 2.
[6] Ancient Petitions, No. 13130, printed in *Rot. Parl.*, II, 26; the earlier stages of the case are in Y.B. 1 Edw. III, fol. 24.
[7] *C.C.R. 1327–1330*, 289.

So far, then, we have a specific case disclosing a specific defect in the existing procedure, followed by a reply to a petition, which in general terms relieved the petitioner and all others who in the future might be in his predicament. Such a situation was not unusual in the years before our period opens, a well known example being the case of Butler *v.* Hapeton which soon acquired the name and character of a 'statute of waste.'[1] That, however, was in the reign of Edward I; in our period more precise views were held, and adjudication could be separated from legislation — at least in an easy case such as this. Consequently we find that the general remedy which was given in answer to the specific grievance of Fitzpayn was carefully separated, re-drafted, and duly published as the statute 2 Edw. III, c. 17.

At least five notable reforms (other than those mentioned above) took place during our period. An improved procedure of indenting indictments was designed to prevent them from being embezzled.[2] The wellnigh impossible task of getting all the executors, who were joined as co-defendants in actions, present in court at the same time was met by allowing cases to proceed against whichever appeared first, without waiting for his fellows[3]— and the Year Books show that this reform was sorely needed, and gratefully appreciated. Another means of indefinitely delaying cases was removed by enacting that deeds made within liberties may be proved (in certain circumstances) before a jury of the county without waiting for the bailiffs of the liberty to secure the presence of the witnesses;[4] it is implied that parties too often took advantage of the delays which could be caused with the connivance of bailiffs of liberties. A further reform of great importance was the right given to defendants in real actions to require that the issue be tried at *nisi prius;* formerly it was at the choice of the demandant only.[5]

The last example we shall mention is not only of interest for the reign of Edward III, but is also a topical question at the present moment. For many centuries there was a principle that personal actions died with the person. This rule, which was doubtless already felt to have its inconveniences, was particularly troublesome in the effort to settle political accounts on the accession of Edward III. A statute[6] therefore allowed a peculiar privilege to the executors of deceased persons who had

---

[1] *Rot. Parl.*, i, 79; Plucknett, *Statutes and Their Interpretation*, pp. 22–23; cf. the interesting case of Lady Stuteville (1307) given in Richardson and Sayles, *Law Quarterly Review*, L (1934), 71. In the course of Edward II's reign the council realized that such an extension of individual relief to all the world was really legislation, and so could be done only in parliament (*Cal. Inq.*, v, 353).

[2] 1 Edw. III, st. 2, c. 17. Cf. the indented common petition of this same year.

[3] 9 Edw. III, st. 1, c. 3.

[4] 9 Edw. III, st. 1, c. 4.

[5] 2 Edw. III, c. 16.   [6] 1 Edw. III, st. 1, c. 3.

suffered loss and damage in their goods and chattels in the quarrel of
the Despensers; executors of these favored persons were to have their
actions of trespass to recover damages in the same way as those members
of the quarrel who were still alive. In 1327 this was perhaps a rash invasion of legal principles by a victorious party, but by 1330 people seem
to have wondered why the whole of the public should not have the benefit
thus accorded to a few, and the result was the really important statute
of 4 Edw. III, c. 7, which converted a party privilege into a general
law reform by enacting that executors may have actions on trespasses
done to the testator's goods and chattels during his lifetime. Once again
we see a trace of continuity from parliament to parliament in the urge
for law reform, resulting in a momentous break with an old established
principle. It is noteworthy that the statute of 4 Edw. III has been re-
enacted as recently as 1925,[1] and that the ravages of the motor car
(added to those of the Despensers and the Mortimers) have finally compelled the abolition of most of the rest of the ancient principle.[2]

An examination of the statutes passed in the first ten years of Edward
III is ample proof of the intrinsic importance of legislation at this period,
and that next to politics, legislation was the most striking attribute of
parliament in the early fourteenth century. Social and legal problems
were attacked skilfully and for the most part successfully and, above all,
in a spirit of practical common sense. Neither parliament nor courts
show the slightest interest in the philosophical problem of the nature
and limits of legislation. No one doubted that parliament was competent to carry out the multifarious changes which we have described; and
no one thought of asking whether parliament was omni-competent. The
common lawyers, whose influence in the council, on the benches, and in
the commons was so powerful, were true to the administrative origins
of their system. The king's court did the work the king assigned to it
in a spirit of marked practicality, for the common law itself grew up
without the aid of political or juridical theory. Indeed, the intrusion of
theory is apt to result in confusion rather than clarity, as may be seen
from the attempts to distinguish between statute and ordinance: those
attempts came to nothing, and as Mr Richardson and Dr Sayles conclude, 'Nomenclature was, in truth, a matter of indifference.'[3] Like
wise intrusive and unpractical is the notion that law cannot be changed
Of this we read but little in the sources, although the modern literature

---

[1] Administration of Estates Act, 1925 (15 and 16 Geo. V, c. 23, sec. 26).

[2] See *Law Revision Committee: First Interim Report*, 1934 (cd. 4540); Plucknett, *Concise History
of the Common Law*, pp. 333–334; Law Reform (Miscellaneous Provisions) Act, 1934 (24 and 25
Geo. V, c. 41).

[3] *Law Quarterly Review*, L (1934), 562.

is considerable. The preceding pages will have shown that parliamentary statutes six hundred years ago did most of the things they are doing
to-day undeterred by fundamental law, and yet without laying claim to
sovereignty.[1]

When we turn to taxation, we find another of the major functions of
parliament which was only intermittently performed. Of our twenty-
one parliaments, only five made grants of supply.* Later, when parliaments kept regular rolls, these grants duly appear on them, but during
our period evidence of them has often to be sought elsewhere — on the
patent rolls (where the taxors' commissions, and sometimes instructions,[2]
are enrolled) and in the financial records. Parliamentary taxation was
not yet the only means of direct taxation, but it was rapidly becoming
so. In 1332 the crown imposed a variety of tallages, but withdrew them
when parliament protested and offered a vote of supply instead.[3] Most
of the grants took the form of a tenth from the towns and a fifteenth
from the counties, but this discrimination was not yet the invariable
rule; in 1327 a twentieth was granted by town and country alike.[4] As
for the clergy, half of a crusading tenth levied by the pope was granted
by him to the king (and it is said that the king got the other half, too),
while in addition the clergy made grants of tenths on most occasions
when parliament voted grants from the laity. The clergy generally
granted theirs in convocation, but there are two occasions when they
seem to have voted grants in parliament.[5] A point of some interest is
that the present form in use in England is not so ancient as it looks.
Grants are now made by the commons alone,[6] but during our period it
is clear that the bishops and magnates joined with the commons in a
united grant.[7]

Such, then, was the work of parliament. As we have several times
suggested, the bulk of it fell upon the council, and so parliamentary sessions were not long. The great resettlement of 1327 required seven
weeks or more,[8] and in 1328 parliaments lasted two, three, and even five
weeks. Thenceforward, we find shorter sessions varying from four days
to a week and a half. Not infrequently the commons were dismissed

---

[1] For the claim that the king may repeal a statute by prerogative, see Plucknett, *Statutes and
Their Interpretation*, p. 144, and *contra*, Richardson and Sayles, *Law Quarterly Review*, L (1934),
549–555.

[2] *Rot. Parl.*, II, 425–427.

[3] *Rot. Parl.*, II, 66.

[4] *Ibid.*, p. 425 (from the patent roll).

[5] Canterbury (March 1336) and York (September 1336); W. Wake, *State of the Church* (London,
1703), p. 285.

[6] E. C. S. Wade and G. G. Phillips, *Constitutional Law* (London, 1931), p. 395.

[7] *Rot. Parl.*, II, 425, 66, 447; it is not suggested that they sat together for this purpose.

[8] Prynne, *Brief Register*, IV, 81.

before the lords, without thereby terminating the parliament; similarly, the commons themselves might not be dismissed all at the same time, for some would be retained longer than others. A parliament might therefore fade away by slow degrees.[1]

Our information of these dates is derived mainly from the enrolled writs *de expensis,* and with these this discussion — like the mediaeval parliament itself — may fitly conclude. There has been some controversy concerning these writs of late, but their nature seems now established. In form a writ *de expensis* is an order to the sheriff (or to the bailiffs of a town) ordering them to 'cause A.B. and C.D. to have' a certain sum by way of expenses for a certain number of days spent in going to, attending at, and returning from a parliament. It was not a draft upon funds already in the hands of the sheriff, but an authority for him to raise the sum from those who were liable to contribute to it. Many of these writs are enrolled on the close rolls and have been printed by Prynne in *The First Part of a Brief Register of Parliamentary Writs* (1659–1664). Why they should have been enrolled at all is not clear, for they are most closely related to such judicial writs of execution as *fieri facias,* which were never enrolled. In fact, the writ might issue, and yet not be enrolled,[2] probably to avoid fees.

The normal payment during our period (subject to few exceptions) was four shillings a day for knights of the shire, and two shillings for citizens and burgesses; these payments were, of course, based on the electoral status of the member and were independent of the actual possession of knighthood by either county or town members. Private arrangements between members and their constituents were, however, ferquent, and this will explain why so many towns do not appear in the enrolled writs *de expensis.* In some cases the rate was much higher; London paid about twenty shillings a day and provided clothes and furs to deck its members. Several towns paid three shillings and fourpence, and some on the other hand bargained for less than the standard rate of two shillings.[3] County members, however, seem generally to have been content with their standard wage, and relied on the writ to collect it. In the earlier part of our period separate writs of expenses were issued for each session if there were two, but in the parliament of 1332–1333 we find the new departure of a combined writ, which, however, gave no wage for the period of the recess.[4]

---

[1] Prynne, *Brief Register,* IV, 81, 83; the dates are tabulated in the *Interim Report.*

[2] McKisack, *Parliamentary Representation of English Boroughs,* p. 76; Wood-Legh, 'Knights' Attendance in the Parliaments of Edward III,' *E.H.R.,* XLVII (1932), 398–401; Prynne suspected this centuries ago (*Brief Register,* IV, 89).

[3] Details are collected in McKisack, *op. cit.,* Ch. V.

[4] Prynne, *Brief Register,* IV, 128.

The payment of parliamentary expenses was a heavy burden, and even London was sometimes hard put to it to find the money. Other towns found it difficult, too, and sometimes paid in kind or by granting privileges. The counties found it harder still, for they had no common fund[1] and so the money had to be raised by direct taxation of individuals. There naturally resulted a scramble to escape liability, and so inevitably there arose a mass of divergent local customs and great obscurity in the law. The tenants of anyone who had personally appeared at the parliament were sufficiently represented by him, and therefore could not be called upon to meet the cost of additional representation; ancient demesne claimed to be quit, and so did gavelkind.[2] Most of these claims appear after our period and embody views upon representation and the nature of parliament of very doubtful validity from a historical point of view. The ingenuity of tax-evaders, then as now, frequently introduced confusion into legal theory.

If the first writ *de expensis* was fruitless, then it could be repeated, like other writs, with the clause *sicut alias*. Possibly there could be a *pluries* as well, and certainly in the last resort the member could sue the sheriff in the court of exchequer upon his account. Examples of such actions have been printed from various reigns by Madox, and one of them actually falls within our period.[3] It was brought by John de Bourne against William de Orlaston, sheriff of Kent. The defendant pleaded that by arrangement with the plaintiff he had commissioned two of the plaintiff's friends to levy the wages and so was quit of any further liability. The plaintiff replied that however this might be, the sheriff had in fact levied the money and received it. On this, issue was joined. We are left with the suspicion that perhaps the sheriff had got the money, and then proceeded to authorize the member's agents to get it a second time.[4]

---

[1] Cambridge took exceptional measures much later by setting up a trust and incorporating its members (Prynne, *Brief Register*, p. 540).

[2] Material can be found through the index to Prynne.

[3] Thomas Madox, *Firma Burgi* (London, 1726), p. 102, n. z.

[4] For a still darker tale of suspicion, involving the member as well as the sheriff, see Putnam, *Select Proceedings before Justices of the Peace*, p. 80, No. 280.

8

PARLIAMENT AND THE
FRENCH WAR, 1336–40*

by E. B. Fryde

In the absence of the rolls of parliament from 1334 to the autumn of 1339, the parliamentary history of those years is regrettably obscure.[1] Yet important proceedings did take place in parliaments and great councils during this period. Representative assemblies were repeatedly consulted about Edward III's dealings with Scotland and France. It will be one of my objectives to show that parliamentary support was carefully secured by Edward for his war with France. The need, after 1336, for continuous and unusually heavy taxation inevitably increased the importance of the commons. When the existing series of parliament rolls does restart in October 1339, the commons appear as leaders in the resistance to a speedy concession of further money grants. A tax-grant offered by the magnates had to be postponed because the members of the commons present on this occasion declared themselves insufficiently qualified to give their assent. They requested the king to summon another parliament. As far as is known, the knights and burgesses had never done this kind of thing before and their action effectively delayed a tax-grant for another six months. Their resentment at the unusually heavy burdens imposed upon the kingdom was coupled with a demand for the redress of a multitude of serious grievances.[2] It was not a sudden and

---

1 There is one exception to this. A common petition of an uncertain date, with a royal reply to it, is edited by H. G. Richardson and G. Sayles, in *Rotuli Parliamentorum Anglie Hactenus Inediti, MCCLXXIX–MCCCLXIII* (Camden 3rd ser. LI, 1935), pp. 268–72. They probably form part of the records of the parliament of March 1337 (see *infra* for a fuller discussion) and would, in this case, have presumably been enrolled on the parliament roll for that assembly. All references to unpublished sources are to documents in the Public Record Office in London, unless otherwise stated. I owe thanks to my wife for much help.

2 *Rotuli Parliamentorum*, II, pp. 104–5.

unexpected storm but the culmination of complaints and protests voiced in a number of earlier assemblies, echoes of which have survived in various classes of records. I shall try to reassemble here this scattered evidence. The piecing together of a fuller record of the parliamentary proceedings during this initial phase of the Hundred Years' War may contribute to a better understanding of the internal crisis in England in 1340–41 on which the writings of Professor Bertie Wilkinson have thrown so much valuable light.[3]

On the eve of the war with France in 1336–37, Edward III and his advisers were well aware of the internal disturbances provoked in England by the earlier Anglo-French conflicts. Among a large collection of memoranda on Anglo-French relations dating from the first decade of his reign, there are several documents drawing attention to such dangers.[4] Not all of this is good history,[5] but they convey clearly the government's anxiety to avoid the errors of the past. The longest of those documents recalls the complaints made to the council of Edward I by his subjects about the burdens imposed upon them and consequent injury done to their ancient franchises and customs. In the opinion of the author of the memorandum, if Edward I had not provided suitable remedies, a civil war might have resulted, such as had occurred in the reign of his father, King Henry.[6]

As England drifted gradually into war with France in 1336–38, there were repeated consultations with parliamentary assemblies at each stage of the slowly developing conflict; the king was trying in this way to anticipate and diminish the internal troubles that had hampered his ancestors in wartime. Edward's capacity to secure adequate financial support for his French venture was bound to depend, to some extent, on the amount of consent he could secure beforehand for that war from both the lords and the commons.

Several reliable texts explicitly record that the actual decision to start the war had been taken by an assembly including both lords and

3 Cf. "The Protest of the Earls of Arundel and Surrey in the Crisis of 1341," *EHR*, XLVI (1931), 181–93; *Studies in the Constitutional History of the Thirteenth and Fourteenth Centuries* (Manchester, 1937), especially section III (pp. 55ff.); *Constitutional History of Medieval England 1216–1399 (1307–1399)*; II, chap. 5, pp. 176ff., "The Crisis of 1341."

4 Chanc. misc., C.47/28/5, nos. 17, 18, 36, 41, 44, 50; C.47/28/9, no. 2; C.47/30/7, no. 9.

5 One memorandum (C.47/28/5, no. 17) links the arbitration of Louis IX in 1264 with the stirring of rebellion that followed in England, which singularly misrepresents that king's motives.

6 C.47/28/5, no. 36.

commons. One very clear statement to this effect occurs in the roll of the parliament of 1343.[7] On 1 May 1343 Bartholomew Burghersh requested on the king's behalf that the lords and the commons debate in their separate assemblies whether negotiations for peace should be started. He explained that it was the king's wish to seek their consent to measures that might end the hostilities as "this war had been undertaken by the common assent of the prelates, magnates and commons."[8] It is not, however, certain which particular assemblies were consulted about the really vital decisions and a patient survey of all the relevant meetings is, therefore, desirable.

Two great councils in the summer and autumn of 1336 were apparently concerned with Anglo-French relations. The first, held at Northampton in June and consisting only of magnates and prelates, sanctioned the sending of a solemn embassy to Philip VI. We learn about this decision from the writs summoning another assembly to Nottingham for 23 September.[9] On this occasion knights and burgesses were also present and the failure of the negotiations with France was presumably one of the main subjects discussed, as the meeting was held some weeks after the return of the royal envoys.[10]

More decisive consultations took place in the parliament of March 1337. Originally summoned for 13 January to York, it was twice prorogued before assembling on 3 March at Westminster, in order, so the royal writs said, to sit nearer the source of the perils that were threatening the kingdom.[11] In the course of its session the king bestowed a dukedom on his eldest son, created six new earldoms, and lavished grants of lands and franchises on numerous magnates. It was the most spectacular of a series of measures taken by Edward III in 1337–38 to enlist the support of the magnates for his policies. About a month after the conclusion of this parliament, the vitally important embassy of Henry Burghersh, bishop of Lincoln, and the earls of Huntingdon and Salisbury left for the Netherlands to procure allies on the continent.[12] It is worth noting that in a subsequent

---

7 *Rot. Parl.*, II, p. 136.
8 For other evidence see below.
9 *Reports from the Lords Committees touching the Dignity of a Peer of the Realm* (1829), IV, pp. 460–1.
10 The embassy, headed by the bishops of Durham and Winchester, was away from late July to the beginning of September: cf. L. Mirot and E. Déprez, *Les ambassades anglaises pendant la Guerre de Cent Ans* (Paris, 1900), p. 14.
11 *Peerage Report*, IV, p. 470.
12 E. Déprez, *Les préliminaires de la Guerre de Cent Ans* (Paris, 1902), pp. 152ff.

letter of privy seal, sent from Antwerp in July 1338, the king asserted
that he had been advised by the lords and the commons to seek these
alliances.[13] He was clearly referring, in part at least, to the deliberations of this very parliament of March 1337. The treaties concluded
by the embassy of bishop Burghersh in the late spring of 1337 were
to determine the pattern of the English strategy on the continent until
1340. The envoys also carried with them instructions for further
negotiations with the king of France "according to a form agreed
upon in parliament,"[14] obviously in March 1337.

When a great council of prelates and magnates met on 30 May at
Stamford it was commanded by the king to continue its deliberations
until news should arrive from the envoys who were abroad.[15] The
preliminary agreement for setting up an English wool company,
which promised to finance the continental war, was concluded in the
course of this session at Stamford.[16] A second great council was summoned for 21 July at Westminster to hear a full report of the achieve-
ments of the bishop of Lincoln and his fellow envoys. On this
occasion the previous agreement with the wool merchants was confirmed by a larger and more representative assembly of English
business men.[17] Yet another great council, attended this time also by
the commons, was ordered to assemble at Westminster at the end
of September to sanction arrangements for the defence and good
government of the realm during the king's projected absence
abroad.[18] It made the unusually generous grant of three fifteenths
and tenths spread over 1337-40,[19] which provided one of the best
securities for the contraction of loans during those years. On 7 October 1337, a few days after the departure of the commons, Edward III
formally asserted his title to the crown of France.[20]

In December the further progress of the war was suspended by
the arrival in England of two cardinals entrusted by the pope with
the mission of securing a truce. They arrived probably at the beginning of that month.[21] The king consulted prelates and magnates.

13 *Ibid.*, p. 418.
14 Gascon roll, C.61/49, m. 22^v: "aut pacis tractatus ... iuxta formam concordie
  in parliamento nostro nuper inde facte" (letter of 24 June 1337).
15 Ancient Correspondence, S.C.1/45, no. 229 (1 June 1337).
16 E. B. Fryde, *The Wool Accounts of William de la Pole* (York, 1964), p. 5, n.16.
17 *Peerage Report*, IV, p. 475; Fryde in *History*, n.s., XXXVII (1952), 11–14.
18 *Peerage Report*, IV, p. 479.
19 See *infra*, p. 257.   20 Déprez, *Préliminaires*, pp. 171–2.
21 On 2 December according to a document in Brit. Mus. ms. Royal 12 D XI,
  f.18. This is a formulary compiled by someone with ready access to the
  register of Archbishop John Stratford and to the records of the chancery.

The cardinals were told, in Edward's presence, that his subjects had previously offered in full parliament to defend his kingdom and seek his rights. Therefore, he and his councillors did not dare to decide upon a truce of any length without consulting with the magnates and the commons of the land. A fresh parliament would have to be summoned for this purpose.[22] In a formal letter to the cardinals, of 24 December, the king informed them of the decision to summon parliament for 3 February 1338 and explained that the need to refer matters of such importance to parliament was a laudable custom of his kingdom. At the same time the cardinals were notified that a temporary truce was to be in operation from 22 December 1337 to 1 March 1338.[23]

Perhaps Edward, in this instance, made such great play with the need to submit the issue of war or peace to parliament because he wanted to gain time for consulting the royal envoys abroad about the wisdom of concluding a prolonged truce. They assured the king that this would destroy the continental grand alliance against France that had been so laboriously created in the course of 1337.[24] Their advice was accepted. We have the king's own version of the proceedings at the February parliament in a letter he addressed to the council on 24 July 1338.[25] We are told that the continuation of the war was upheld and the continental alliances were confirmed by the assent of all the magnates and others present in parliament. The king was urged to hasten his expedition overseas and all those present, unanimously and of their own free will, provided the required financial aid, pledging themselves to give in future other support necessary for the success of the king's venture. This rosy picture of generous financial aid is somewhat at variance with the facts,[26] but the policy of war was undoubtedly upheld by this parliament.

There is thus evidence of consultation about the French war in most of the assemblies held after May 1336. But the real quality of

22 Chanc. misc., C.47/32/18 (a confidential message to the royal envoys in the Netherlands).
23 Rymer, *Foedera* (Record Commission ed., 1821), II, ii, p. 1007. The truce was notified to the seneschal of Gascony on 22 December (Ancient Correspondence, S.C.1/45, no. 232) and the warrant to the chancellor to summon parliament, but without specifying its business, is dated on the same day (Chanc. warrants, C.81/240, no. 10.493).
24 The king's messages to Bishop Burghersh and the other envoys and their replies are copied in Chanc. misc., C.47/32/18.
25 Déprez, *Préliminaires*, p. 418.
26 See *infra*, pp. 260–1.

all these discussions nowhere emerges very clearly. Were the magnates and commons ever allowed to debate seriously the issues of peace and war or did Edward III merely seek from them a purely formal consent for policies already settled beforehand in the narrow circle of the king's closest advisers? It is a pertinent question because all these consultations did not ensure enduring support for the war. By the autumn of 1339, when things were obviously going badly both in the Netherlands and in Scotland, while burdens were mounting at home, it proved impossible to secure quickly fresh supplies from parliament.

To understand better the crisis of October 1339 we must review in some detail the complaints voiced in the earlier assemblies about the financial requirements of the crown and about other burdens imposed upon the country. One basic feature of the financial situation was the fixed yield of the taxes on movables. Since 1334 a fifteenth and tenth assessed on movable property amounted to around £38,000; largely for political reasons it could not be made to produce a bigger sum.[27] The origins of this arrangement only in part went back to 1334, for it was a subject of further debate in 1336 and, perhaps, in 1337 as well. The fifteenth and tenth granted by parliament in 1334 had been assessed in a peculiar way, designed to avoid the flagrant abuses connected with the earlier taxes. An exceptionally reliable group of collectors was appointed and they were instructed to negotiate with particular localities about the amount each village was prepared to pay. The resulting tax charges were thus, for the first time, assessed on localities, not on persons, and apparently each village was then left to collect its quota by methods of its own choice. It could be assumed that a particularly fair assessment had been achieved in 1334.[28]

When a direct tax was next demanded in the parliament of March 1336, the king, in response allegedly to the requests of the magnates, knights, and burgesses, agreed that the new grant should be identical with what had been levied in 1334. If we accept this official version, derived from the preamble to the commissions of the chief taxers,[29] the initiative for perpetuating this change came from parliament.

27 J. F. Willard, "The Taxes upon Movables of the Reign of Edward III," *EHR*, xxx (1915), 69-74. The amounts assessed on each county from 1334 onwards are tabulated on p. 73.
28 *Ibid.* and Willard, *Parliamentary Taxes on Personal Property, 1290 to 1334* (Cambridge, Mass., 1934), pp. 5-6.
29 King's Remembrancer Memoranda roll E.159/112, recorda, Easter, m. 40.

When a fresh grant was secured in September 1336, it was again ordered to be levied on the assessment of 1334.[30]

One feature of the new arrangements was that the old rules about the exemption of the poorer persons disappeared. In 1332 no one possessing less than 10s. worth of taxable goods was to contribute to a fifteenth, while the taxable minimum for the urban taxpayers, paying a tenth, was 6s.[31] From 1334 onwards it was left to the men of each locality to decide who should contribute to the fixed quota for which their village was liable. There was henceforth a possibility that the burden might be spread more widely over most of the inhabitants, including many poorer men who had enjoyed exemption in the past. This certainly happened in Kent in the case of the first wartime taxes of 1338–39.[32] The greater oppressiveness of the new arrangements may help to account for the exceptional difficulties experienced by the collectors of the fifteenths and tenths in 1339–40.[33]

While the idea of a fixed assessment was apparently accepted by parliaments after 1336, on one subsequent occasion, possibly in March 1337, the commons petitioned that the over-all total of the tax should be lowered, so that the sum exacted by the king should correspond to the somewhat lighter tax of 1332.[34] Edward III's reply

30 K.R. Mem. R., E.159/113, m.146 (commissions of the chief taxers of 16 December 1336).
31 Willard, *Parliamentary Taxes*, p. 88.
32 C. W. Chalklin and H. A. Hanley, "The Kent Lay Subsidy of 1334–5," *Kent Archaeological Society, Records Branch*, XVIII (1964), p. 58 (while 11,016 persons contributed in 1334, some 17,000 were taxed in 1338); K.R. Exch. subsidies, E.179/123/14 (extension of the levy in 1339 to taxpayers too poor to pay more than 5d. or 6d., compared with the minimum of 8d. in 1332).
33 See *infra*, p. 264.
34 Richardson and Sayles, *Rot. Parl. Hactenus Inediti*, pp. 269–70. Both a date in March 1337, suggested by me, and a date in February 1339, preferred by Richardson and Sayles, raise some chronological difficulties. The statements that the petition of the commons was presented on the eighth day of the parliament (p. 268) and that it was answered on Thursday in the first week of Lent (p. 270) cannot be reconciled with what is otherwise known of the chronology of either of the two assemblies. The resultant conflicts of evidence are somewhat greater if the hypothesis of Richardson and Sayles is accepted (I owe thanks to Sir Goronwy Edwards for advice on this point). The case for 1337 must rest entirely on the contents of the commons' petition. There is no obvious reference in it to any events after March 1337, while all its statements are compatible with what is known of the happenings up to this date. It is most improbable that a petition presented after 1337 could have treated the hostilities against Scotland as the main war waged by the king (pp. 268–9). The lack of all references to the king's absence from the country and to the council governing in his place also points to 1337 rather than 1339.

was completely evasive.[35] If our dating of this incident is correct, there may be some connection between this request and the negotiations pursued by the government in September 1337 with the individual county courts for separate grants from each shire.[36] It is impossible to offer any other adequate explanation for the adoption of such an exceptional procedure. Some counties are known to have offered sums of money, differing slightly from the amounts that they normally contributed to the fifteenths and tenths and somewhat smaller in most cases.[37] These local grants were superseded soon afterwards by the concession of three fifteenths and tenths by the parliament which met on 26 September 1337. The assessment of 1334 was again adhered to. The levy was intended to be spread over the period from October 1337 to February 1340.[38] Its collection occasioned serious difficulties in several counties in the course of 1339–40.[39]

It was natural for an English king in the first half of the fourteenth century to base his hopes for the financing of a continental coalition on the exploitation of the wool trade. One way of doing it was to increase the duties on exported wool. A heavy subsidy, over and above the traditional "ancient custom" of 6s. 8d. per sack, was bound to be unpopular with the wool producers. They justifiably feared that the merchants might use it as an excuse for purchasing wool in England at lower prices. But the increased duty on wool formed an indispensable part of Edward's plans for financing the war in 1337: it was meant to provide the security for the loans that he wished to contract in the Netherlands from the English Wool Company which he was specially creating for this purpose. It was as a preparatory measure for the wool scheme that a merchant assembly, sitting at Nottingham in September 1336, agreed to an additional subsidy of 20s. per sack.[40] Their meeting coincided with the session of a great

35 *Ibid.*, pp. 271–2.
36 J. F. Willard, "Edward III's Negotiations for a Grant," *EHR*, XXI (1906), 727–31. The difficulties inherent in trying to make local grants by individual county courts binding on everybody are discussed by J. G. Edwards, "Taxation and Consent in the Court of Common Pleas, 1338," *EHR*, LVII (1942), 473–82.
37 For a few figures cf. Willard, "Edward III's Negotiations," 729; L.T.R. enrolled acc. (subsidies), E.359/14, m.27ᵛ (£1,051 received in Northamptonshire).
38 Commissions of the chief taxers dated 6 October 1337 (K.R. Mem. R., E.159/114, m.173).
39 See *infra*, p. 264.
40 As an embargo on wool export had been in operation since 12 August 1336 (*Calendar of Close Rolls, 1333–37*, p. 700), the new rates of duty began to be applied only in the autumn of 1337. They were notified to the collectors of

council at Nottingham, but the granting of the new subsidy was
always attributed in the official records to the merchant assembly
and to no one else.[41] There is nothing to show that the magnates and
commons present at the great council were consulted. Here lay the
seeds of a future conflict between the king and the parliament of
October 1339.[42]

One of the most immediate and effective concessions won by the
parliament of October 1339 concerned purveyance.[43] This royal right
to buy supplies on credit for the king's household became in wartime
a source of ruinous exactions. Its application was then extended to
providing continuously for the needs of a chain of garrisons in
Scotland and it was also employed on several occasions to feed and
equip entire armies and fleets. While ordinary taxation was always
based on some kind of assessment related to the means of each tax-
payer, the seizures of supplies by purveyors tended to be quite arbitrary. They often spared the more influential persons and took instead an excessive proportion of the goods belonging to unimportant
and poorer people. In theory everything was supposed to be paid for
but these promises were often carried out very slowly and, in some
cases, no payment was ever made. Thus purveyance was inherently
oppressive by its very nature, but matters were made far worse by
the abuses to which it gave rise. In the period here studied, it proved
quite impossible to devise some effective means of control over the
royal purveyors or to audit their accounts properly. Between 1336
and 1339 purveyance became apparently the most execrated of all
the burdens thrust upon the population: it could and did seriously
impoverish individuals and might even cause complete ruin of
particular persons.[44]

customs by writs of 26 July 1337 (*Cal. Close R.*, *1337–39*, p. 97). By a subsequent agreement between the king and the English wool merchants, concluded on 4 May 1338 (K.R. Mem. R., E.159/117, recorda, Easter t., m.12),
the subsidy payable by Englishmen was raised to 33s. 4d. per sack. The total
duty, including both the Ancient Custom and the new subsidy, was thus
increased to 40s. per sack. The government also decided that the corresponding aggregate rate for aliens was to be 63s. 4d. per sack. These new rates of
duty came into operation at various harbours "by the order of the council"
in the course of June-July 1338 (L.T.R. enrolled acc., customs, E.356/5, m.4.).

41 E.g. *Cal. Close R.*, *1337–39*, p. 97 (26 July 1337): the grant of the subsidy
    "made by the merchants of the realm at Nottingham."
42 *Rot. Parl.*, II, p. 104.
43 See *infra*, p. 266.
44 This summary of the effects of purveyance is based on a considerable body
    of evidence which I intend to discuss in more detail in a future publication.

The undated commons' petition, which I incline to attribute to March 1337, was much concerned with purveyance. In article one, after requesting the confirmation of the Great Charter and of the other charters and statutes, the petitioners go on to specify in particular the statutes enacted about purveyors.[45] In a subsequent article they affirm that nobody was obliged by law to contribute supplies except of his own free will and demand the cancellation of the current commissions to purveyors "because no free man ought to be assessed or taxed without the common consent of parliament."[46] If our dating of this petition is correct, the commons were especially invoking the observance of a statute of 1331, re-enacted in 1336, under which purveyors guilty of improper conduct were liable to be hanged as thieves.[47] The king's answer was completely evasive. If our petition was indeed presented in March 1337, Edward continued to ignore its main request that purveyance should cease to be used for supplying armies and fleets. On 24 March, a few days after the conclusion of the parliament, his government issued fresh commissions for the purveyance of supplies for the forces destined for Gascony.[48] The government would have to be in a much greater fear of the parliamentary opposition, before it would accept the alternative policy of raising all the needed supplies through purchase by merchants. This happened ultimately only in October 1339.

The same petition also contained requests that the government should bear the cost of equipping the men-at-arms summoned for military service under commissions of array and that it should pay the wages of the arrayed soldiers before they set out to join the king's forces.[49] These were intractable problems and no satisfactory com-

The main sources used are: (1) Accounts of the purveyors in L.T.R. miscellaneous acc., E.358/1 and E.358/2 and the particulars for the same among K.R. exchequer acc. various (E.101), especially the accounts of the two chief receivers William Dunstable and William Wallingford, whose arrest had to be ordered in 1339 (E.101/20/7, E.101/20/13, E.101/21/4, E.101/21/40). (2) Records of inquiries held in 1339-40, especially E.101/21/38, E.101/21/39, E.101/22/1, E.101/22/4 and E.101/35/4. (3) Records of inquiries held in 1341 on assize rolls (Just. Itin. 1), especially the roll for Lincolnshire (no. 521). (4) Numerous records of proceedings before the exchequer on the Memoranda rolls for 1338-41.

45 Richardson and Sayles, *Rot. Parl. Hactenus Inediti*, p. 268.
46 *Ibid.*, p. 269.
47 T. F. T. Plucknett, "Parliament," in *The English Government at Work, 1327-36* (Cambridge, Mass., 1940), I, pp. 117-9.
48 L. T. R. miscellaneous acc., E.358/2, mm. 5, 33v. (appointment of Stephen le Blount on 24 March 1337 and subsidiary commissions to sheriffs).
49 Richardson and Sayles, *Rot. Parl. Hactenus Inediti*, p. 269.

promise solution was found for several more years.[50] The parliament
of March 1337 was perhaps acting in response to this petition when
it tried to settle temporarily one of the issues raised in it: an agreement was reached that the cost of the men-at-arms should be borne
by landowners having property worth annually 40s. or more.[51]

The long-term prospects for financing the war were greatly improved by the grant for three years of fifteenths and tenths by the
great council or parliament[52] that sat from 26 September to 4 October
1337. At that time the English Wool Company also seemed to be
successfully launched. The government may have thought it unlikely
that fresh parliaments would be needed for quite a while. The time
may have seemed ripe for a survey of the prerogative financial rights
of the crown, which was sure to be unpopular with the groups
usually represented in parliament. A few days after the dismissal of
the commons, orders were sent to hold inquiries into the revenue due
from the chattels of felons and fugitives which had been neglected
for several years.[53] The king also bethought himself of his right to
levy a scutage for the Scottish campaign of 1327, as the feudal levy
had been called out on this occasion.[54] All these projects were put in
jeopardy by fresh developments in the course of December. The
papal requests for a truce compelled Edward to convoke a parliament
for 3 February 1338. Worse still, the royal envoys abroad had quarrelled with the leaders of the English Wool Company and the king
found himself in the position of having to seek a fresh parliamentary
grant to compensate him for the collapse of the wool scheme.[55] He
secured the permission to levy a forced loan in wool,[56] but had to
agree to the suspension of inquiries into the chattels of criminals and

50 The most recent discussion is to be found in M. Powicke, *Military Obligation
in Medieval England* (Oxford, 1962), chap. 10, pp. 182ff., and in H. J. Hewitt,
The Organisation of War under Edward III, 1338–62 (Manchester, 1966),
chap. 2, especially pp. 40–2.
51 K.R. Mem. R., E.159/113, m.13.
52 Both terms were used in the official records; cf. *Handbook of British Chronology* (2nd. ed., 1961), p. 520.
53 Writ of 6 October 1337, discussed by G. O. Sayles in *Select Cases in the
Court of King's Bench* (Selden Soc., vol. 74, 1957), IV, p. lxvi; E. 137/216/2.
54 Commissions to levy scutage of 10–12 October 1337; *Calendar of Fine Rolls,
1337–47*, pp. 52–5.
55 E. B. Fryde, "Edward III's Wool Monopoly of 1337," *History*, n.s., XXXVII
(1952), 24.
56 This loan is discussed in chapter 3 of my D.Phil. thesis, "Edward III's War
Finance, 1337–41" (Oxford, 1947, in the Bodleian Library).

to the abandonment of the scutage, before that tax had begun to yield any revenue.[57] The relevant royal mandates, dated on 15 and 16 February, explicitly refer to parliamentary petitions on these matters. The king proclaimed his readiness to renounce these prerogative revenues in view of the grant made to him by parliament.[58] There had obviously been some tough bargaining.

The forced loan in wool, known as the levy of the moiety of wool, soon proved a lamentable failure. It was left to a great council summoned to Northampton for 26 July 1338, ten days after Edward's departure from England, to devise a fresh wool grant. Both magnates and commons were present and they accepted a properly assessed tax in wool, which turned out to be a success.[59] But other financial proposals aroused hostile comments from the magnates. Shortly before his departure overseas Edward III had promulgated at Walton an ordinance regulating the government of the kingdom during his absence.[60] Among other things it inaugurated a policy of financial stringency that challenged many of the established usages. At Northampton the magnates absolutely refused to give their consent to a royal injunction that debts due to the king should henceforth be collected integrally and that all payments of debts by instalments should cease while the current financial difficulties lasted. According to a report sent subsequently to the king by his councillors in England, the magnates had declared that payments by instalments had been allowed since time immemorial and were a part of the custom of the kingdom. Such things could not and should not be changed

---

57 Pipe Roll, E.372/183, m.15 (enrolled accounts for the scutage).
58 K.R. Mem. R., E.159/114, m.68ᵛ. (chattels of criminals); H. M. Chew, "Scutage in the Fourteenth Century," *EHR*, xxxvIII, (1923), 39–40 and the sources there quoted; K.R. Mem. R., E.159/114, mm.49, 130ᵛ (instructions to the exchequer about the scutage and the resultant measures).
59 A writ of 1 August, notifying the exchequer, expressly attributes the grant to the prelates, magnates, and community of the kingdom present in the council at Northampton (K.R. Mem. R., E.159/115, m.18ᵛ). This tax is discussed in chapter 4 of my thesis, *supra*, n.56. Some concessions were secured in return for the grant. The taking of tin by royal agents in Devon and Cornwall was stopped and an order was issued for the restitution of the tin seized since May 1338 (treaty roll, C.76/12, m.17; *Cal. Close R., 1337–39, p.* 449).
60 The best edition of the "Walton ordinances" is in T. F. Tout, *Chapters in the Administrative History of Mediaeval England* (Manchester, 1928), III, pp. 143–50. His discussion of them (pp. 69–80) needs revision and does not supersede the more detailed account in D. Hughes, *A Study of Social and Constitutional Tendencies in the Early Years of Edward III* (London, 1915), chap. 4.

without the assent of the magnates and that had to be given in parliament.[61] The council at home had no desire to take any action in this matter, but was compelled to do so a year later by a royal order issued from Antwerp on 6 May 1339.[62] All existing payments by instalments were cancelled and the king expected to receive abroad the additional funds accruing from the prompt collection of the entire debts due to him. Officials in England were also forbidden to sanction new payments by instalments notwithstanding any custom to the contrary. The royal order was, indeed, unrealistic as his councillors in England pointed out. It was not in practice likely to yield any more revenue since the main beneficiaries of the existing arrangements were magnates whom it was impossible to distrain for debts.[63] On 5 September 1339 Edward at long last gave way and recalled his former orders. He abandoned at the same time several other injunctions contained in the ordinances of Walton and the order of 6 May 1339.[64] He was presumably already aware that another parliament had been summoned by writs dated 25 August and it was becoming impolitic to enforce measures that were arousing so much resistance among influential people.

A parliament held during the first half of February 1339 appears to have been convoked mainly to make provision for the defence of the coastal areas against the French raids or a possible full-scale invasion.[65] It is most improbable that any fresh grant of taxes was requested by the government on this occasion and certainly none was granted. But it gave men a chance to voice their grievances. On 12 February, while parliament was still in session, the exchequer appointed a commission to enquire into the misdoings of William

61 Parl. and council proc., C.49/file 7/7 (a royal message and the council's reply, probably in May, 1339). There is a brief reference to this in Tout, *Chapters*, III, p. 92 and it is discussed by Hughes, *Social and Constitutional Tendencies*, pp. 68–9.

62 Rymer, *Foedera*, pp. 1080–1; K.R. Mem. R., E.159/115, m.267 with a marginal heading "De assignacionibus, respectibus, debitis et atterminacionibus revocatis."

63 There is an useful recent discussion of the prolonged debate between the king abroad and the council at home about fiscal policies in G. L. Harriss, "The Commons' Petitions of 1340," *EHR*, LXXVIII (1963), 631–5.

64 K.R. Mem. R., E.159/116, m.12 (noted by Harriss, "The Commons' Petitions," 635). The message was brought back to England by John Thorp, who was sent to the Netherlands by the council in August 1339 (he was abroad on 1 September, E.404/493/146). The exchequer received these new instructions on 1 October.

65 J. R. Lumby, ed. *Chronicon Henrici Knighton* (Rolls Ser., 1895), II, p. 3; Hewitt, *The Organisation of War*, chap. 1; treaty roll, C.76/14, mm.16–14.

Dunstable "on clamorous information of diverse men of York-shire."[66] It may be significant that one of the commissioners, William Scargill, was sitting as knight of the shire for Yorkshire in that very parliament of February 1339.[67] William Dunstable had been in trouble before. His activities as the chief receiver of victuals north of the Thames since October 1336 were ended on 10 August 1338.[68] The council in England ordered his arrest by a letter dated at North-ampton on 28 July and a more general mandate was sent by the king from Antwerp, dated 3 August, ordering the seizure of William, his brother Thomas, and their deputies, and appointing commissioners who were to receive complaints against them.[69] By February 1339 William and his associates were also facing charges of having con-cealed and sold for their own benefit goods destined for the king, and William was trying to shift all the blame on to his former agents.[70] But other purveyors, guilty of similar malpractices, continued to act until October 1339.

The period of Edward's absence abroad (July 1338 to February 1340) was a time of increasing economic depression in this country. Chroniclers mention several signs of distress and throw light on some of the causes. An anonymous poem, which most probably dates from 1338–39, contains particularly illuminating comments because the author expresses the grievances and bewilderment of the common people.[71] Private estate accounts and various classes of

66 K.R. Mem. R., E.159/115, m.8: "ex informacione clamosa diversorum de predicto comitatu Ebor."
67 A. Gooder, "The Parliamentary Representation of the County of York, 1258–1832," (*Yorkshire Archaeological Soc.*, Record Ser. XCI, 1935) I, pp. 79–81. Scargill had held every kind of office in his native county, though he was never a sheriff.
68 K.R. exch. acc. various, E.101/21/4. For other accounts of Dunstable see references *supra* n.44.
69 *Calendar of Patent Rolls, 1338–40*, p. 145 and chanc. warrants, C.81/248, no. 11274.
70 C.81/251, no. 11516.
71 The best edition is in I. S. T. Aspin, "Anglo-Norman Political Songs," *Anglo-Norman Text Society* (1953), XI, 105–15. She suggested a time between 1337 and 1340, but was unable to date the poem more precisely. It was written during the absence of a *young* king and his army overseas. This rules out the date of 1297–98, formerly suggested by T. Wright (*ibid.*, 105). The references to taxes make it clear that it could have been written only during Edward's first continental expedition: there is mention of the fifteenths year after year and of concurrent wool levies. A poet writing at the time of Edward's second expedition (June–November 1340) would presumably have referred to the very peculiar ninth of 1340. Only a wool levy was being col-lected in 1342–43 (the Breton expedition) and the mention of the collection

exchequer records provide corroborative information about prices
of food. Lastly there is the evidence of the tax records suggesting that
there were excessive delays in payments,[72] which would be readily
intelligible in a time of economic stagnation and mounting popular
anxiety about the worsening situation.

The harvests of 1336, 1337, and 1338 had all been good, the last
two quite outstanding.[73] In normal times this would have been
highly welcome, but in 1338–39 the resultant low prices of food-
stuffs[74] were being depressed still further by heavy taxation and
other royal exactions. The decline in the purchasing power of the
population was so considerable that economic activity was becoming
seriously discouraged. One chronicler speaks of "such plenty of
goods and scarcity of money that a quarter of wheat was fetching at
London [only] two shillings, and a fat ox half a mark.[75] The well-
informed contemporary Adam Murimuth attributed the low prices
not to the special abundance of corn, but to the lack of money.[76] The
poem describes graphically a deflationary situation. "There is a
desperate shortage of cash among the people. At market the buyers
are so few that in fact a man can do no business, although he may
have cloth or corn, pigs or sheep to sell because so many are desti-
tute." The passage occurs in the middle of impassioned complaints
against excessive taxation. The author claimed that because "now
the fifteenth runs in England year after year" men were driven into
much hardship to raise the necessary money "and common people
must sell their cows, their utensils and even clothing."[77] There had

of the fifteenths year after year fits the 1336–40 period better than the time
of Edward's next expedition in 1346–47. There were no further wool levies
after 1347. Nothing in the poem is incompatible with a date of 1338–39. I
owe thanks to Professor E. Miller for first drawing my attention to this poem.

72 K.R. and L.T.R. Mem. R., 13–15 Edward III, views and audits of accounts (the
sections of "visus et status compotorum"), passim; Chanc.misc. C.47/87/4/-
30 and Cal. Close R., 1339–41, pp. 175–6 (July 1339).

73 J. Titov, "Evidence of weather in the account rolls of the bishopric of Winchester," Econ. Hist. R., 2nd. ser., XII (1960), 363, 394–6.

74 J. E. Thorold Rogers, A History of Agriculture and Prices in England, II, pp.
106–9; M. M. Postan and J. Titov, "Heriots and Prices on Winchester
Manors," Econ. Hist. R., 2nd. ser., XI (1959), table facing p. 410; K.R. Exch.
extents and inquisitions, E.143/11/1, nos. 21ff. (inquisitions post mortem on
Thomas, earl of Norfolk in the autumn of 1338). For purveyors' accounts
which contain abundant evidence about prices see supra n.44.

75 J. R. Lumby, ed., Polychronicon Ranulphi Higden (Rolls Series, 1883), VIII,
p. 334 (under 1339).

76 E. M. Thompson, ed., Adae Murimuth Continuatio Chronicarum (Rolls
Series, 1889), p. 89.

77 Aspin, "Anglo-Norman Political Songs," 109, 111, 112–3 [stanzas 3 and 14].

been very heavy rains in the autumn of 1338 followed by intense and prolonged cold so that the ground remained covered with ice for about twelve weeks. By the spring of 1339 it became abundantly clear that the crops sown in the previous autumn had suffered great damage.[78] This was bound to increase the anxiety of the population about the future and presumably increased men's reluctance to spend money. Murimuth implies this when he notes that the bad winter was not followed by a rise in prices.[79] A rise occurred only in the autumn of 1339 when men found themselves short of seed for sowing.[80] The parliament of October 1339 assembled at a time when men were full of bitterness about the current conditions and were filled with even gloomier forebodings about the future.

In preparation for the new meeting of parliament summoned for 13 October, Edward III authorized his representatives in England to offer valuable concessions to his people in return for an expected grant of taxes.[81] Various prerogative rights of the crown could be bargained away in exchange for fines of money. On the proffered list of possible concessions there figured a number of royal claims that had aroused opposition during the preceding years, including the scutage and the revenue from the chattels of felons and fugitives. But nothing was said about the more fundamental grievances of both lords and commons and the inadequacy of royal offers became plain very rapidly.

The magnates demanded the abolition of the higher duties on exported wool and a binding pledge that they would not be levied again. The commons concurred in the demand for a return to the normal pre-war ancient custom of 6s. 8d. per sack and pointed out that the rate of duty had been raised without the assent of either the magnates or of "la Commune."[82] The unsatisfactory state of the wool trade in 1339 may have aggravated the sense of grievance against the high duties. Exemptions from the payment of the customs in favour of the royal creditors were so common in 1338–39 that only those who had them could hope to make appreciable profits. The non-privileged exporters were at a grave disadvantage.[83]

---

78 Murimuth, *Continuatio Chronicarum*, pp. 88–9. The severe winter also mentioned by Higden, *Polychronicon*, p. 334.
79 Murimuth, *Continuatio Chronicarum*, p. 89.
80 *Ibid.*, p. 89, n.3 (an addition found in two of the surviving manuscripts).
81 Rymer, *Foedera*, p. 1091 (26 and 27 September).
82 *Rot. Parl.*, II, pp. 104 (no. 5) and 105 (no. 13).
83 Fryde, *Some Business Transactions of York Merchants 1336–49* (York, 1966), pp. 7–8.

Their plight was made worse by the steady decline in the price of wool abroad, because of the vast stocks thrown on the foreign market by Edward III and the magnates serving with him in the Netherlands. Sales at a loss did not vitally matter to the king and his followers as long as they received enough to maintain themselves abroad, but the prospects of the ordinary exporters were greatly depressed thereby.[84]

The outcry against purveyance came to a head in the October parliament where the commons demanded that unless the purveyors paid for what they took, they should be arrested and treated as breakers of the king's peace. It was subsequently agreed in parliament that the commission of William Wallingford and all the other commissions to purvey victuals should be cancelled forthwith.[85] Wallingford ceased to act on 15 October,[86] two days after the opening of parliament. He was a clerk of the king's household[87] and had been acting since July 1338 as the chief receiver of the supplies for the royal army abroad. He had gone to Brabant, probably in charge of victuals, and on 1 February 1339 he was given a fresh commission at Antwerp. He returned to England immediately afterwards.[88] In the October parliament it was resolved that Wallingford and his deputies as well as other notoriously evil purveyors should be arrested and kept under detention until enquiries into their misdeeds could be completed.[89] Wallingford was arrested on 23 October for alleged failure to account at the exchequer and was lodged in the Fleet prison.[90] Commissions of enquiry were appointed in many counties in late October and November[91] and by early February 1340 Wallingford was being searchingly examined about their findings.[92] Purveyances did not completely cease,[93] but judging by the absence

84 Fryde, *The Wool Accounts of William de la Pole* (York, 1964), p. 12.
85 *Rot. Parl.*, II, pp. 105–6 (nos. 13 and 19).
86 He accounted subsequently for the period up to 15 October (K.R. Exch. acc. various, E.101/21/40).
87 Chanc. warrants, C.81/248, nos. 11262–63 (a list of household clerks deserving ecclesiastical preferment, dated 25 July 1338).
88 Wallingford's enrolled accounts, E.358/2, mm.12 and 27.
89 *Rot. Parl.*, II, pp. 105–6 (no. 19).
90 K.R. Mem. R., E.159/116, m.167.
91 *Ibid.*, m.5ʳ and 5ᵛ.
92 K.R. Exch. acc. various, E.101/21/38 is a record of complaints against Wallingford and of his answers to them. He was being interrogated on 9 February 1340.
93 Stephen le Blount was continuing the purveyances for Gascony until 20 November 1339 (E.358/2, m.7); on 23 December 1339 the king commissioned from abroad Richard Potenhale to purvey fish "a nostre oeps pur noz deniers paiantz" (Chanc. warrants, privy seal no. 12495).

of complaints about Wallingford's successor, there was some improvement in administrative arrangements. On 21 December Thomas Baddeby, another household clerk, was appointed to survey all the purveyances made in the kingdom.[94]

At the opening of the October parliament the assembly was told of the king's immense financial difficulties. Archbishop Stratford and the other royal envoys, who had just returned from the king's camp,[95] declared that he had incurred obligations amounting to £300,000 or more[96] and there was no exaggeration in this.[97] The magnates were willing to give an aid forthwith. The tax grant recommended by them was a levy in kind modelled on the ecclesiastical tithe. It was to apply to the commodities that were the main components of the tithe, comprising all kinds of corn, wool, and lambs. The magnates justified this particular choice of a tax in kind on the ground that there was "a great shortage of money in the land."[98] They were clearly being influenced by the belief that some abnormal economic conditions prevailed in England. The magnates also discussed the possible remedies for this alleged monetary crisis, but no decision could be reached.[99] The commons excused themselves from making a grant by pleading that an exceptionally large sum was required and that there was therefore a need for a more prolonged consultation in the counties. Hence their request for the summoning of another parliament.[100] It may be worth recollecting that in the subsequent common petition presented in the parliament of March 1340 it was claimed that "the community of the land was so impoverished" by previous taxes "that they could survive only with great difficulty."[101]

The second parliament met on 20 January 1340. For a long time the government confidently expected that it would be able to secure a fresh grant of taxes. As late as 11 February Thomas Rokeby, the keeper of the castles of Edinburgh and Stirling, was promised payment "out of the first issues of the new aid that will be granted to

94 Chanc. warrants, privy seal no. 12494.
95 They returned to England on 10 October (K.R. Exch. acc. various, E.101/311, nos. 35 and 36).
96 *Rot. Parl.*, II, p. 101 (no. 4).
97 Cf. my thesis, *supra* n.56, chap. 6 and *Revue Belge de Philologie et d'Histoire*, XL (1962), 1186, n.5; and XLV (1967), 1180–1.
98 *Rot. Parl.*, II, pp. 103–4 (no. 4).
99 *Ibid.*, p. 105 (no. 14).
100 *Ibid.*, p. 104 (no. 8).
101 A. W. Goodman, ed., *Chartulary of Winchester Cathedral* (Winchester, 1927), p. 131.

the king in this parliament."[102] The magnates were willing to repeat their previous proposal and granted a tithe of the produce of their demesne lands for themselves and their peers.[103] The commons departed from their usual procedure and, instead of granting a tax, they merely made a conditional offer of one on 19 February.[104] We have not got the text of the indenture containing their conditions, but the council dared not pronounce on them and referred the whole matter to the king. In view of the scholarly speculations about the significance of this incident[105] one hitherto overlooked feature may be worth noting. The grant offered by the commons may have been thoroughly distasteful to Edward III. The commons were recommending on this occasion a levy of 30,000 sacks of wool. But by the end of 1339 the king appears to have conceived an aversion to wool levies in general. When subsequently a tax of wool was granted by a later parliament, in July 1340, the council informed the king of this decision in terms that were clearly designed to allay his dislike of such a levy.[106] On a still later occasion, in 1347, he referred scathingly to his previous experiences with the wool taxes and he was then presumably recollecting the disappointments suffered in 1337–39.[107] When a fresh parliament met on 29 March 1340, after Edward's return from abroad, the proposal for a tax in wool was discarded in favour of a "tithe" advocated by the magnates.

No *communes petitiones* are mentioned in the roll of the first parliament of 1340 and we can therefore learn nothing about the grievances that may have been aired on this occasion. But the arrangements made in that parliament for the supplying of the English

102 K.R. exch. acc. various, E.101/23/1.
103 *Rot. Parl.*, II, pp. 107–8 (nos. 7–9).
104 J. G. Edwards, *The Commons in Medieval English Parliaments* (London, 1958), p. 24, n.1.
105 The most recent discussion is in Harriss, "The Commons' Petition of 1340"; his account of this parliament is unfortunately marred (652–3), by his failure to note that the entries in the *Cal. Pat. R., 1338–40*, pp. 377–8 (called membrane 29) and pp. 408–9 (called membrane 1) are misplaced in the calendar, though not in the original roll (C.66/201) as repaired today. Hence the mandates of January–February on pp. 408–9 really belong to 1339 and not 1340. These mistakes, which had led Mr. Harriss into error, are corrected in the Public Record Office copy (Literary Search Room) of *Cal. Pat. R., 1338–40*.
106 *Rot. Parl.*, II, p. 122 (no. 29): "l'entente ... est qe cest aide ne soit pas mys en mayns de tielx come vos autres leines ont este mys avant ces houres, ou vous n'avez este serviz de riens."
107 Chanc. warrants, C.81/318, no. 18251, quoted in Fryde, "The last trials of Sir William de la Pole," *Econ. Hist. R.*, 2nd. ser., XV (1962), 19 and n.2.

garrisons in Scotland represented the working of a new policy. Purveyance was being avoided in favour of the making of contracts with important merchants who would not hold any special royal commissions.[108] This anticipated the procedure prescribed by the statute enacted in the next parliament which met on 29 March 1340.[109]

Its assembly must mark the end of the present study. I have tried, in Professor Wilkinson's phrase, "to put parliament back at the center of ... the political life and struggles,"[110] in the obscure period before March 1340 and thus to render more intelligible the concessions that the king was forced to make in April and May of that year. The story told here tries to bring out the importance of the parliamentary sessions for providing opportunities to air the complaints about "the hurts done to *commune poeple*."[111] Government officials must have felt somewhat more insecure whenever a parliament was sitting. An incident in July 1340 provides one unusual illustration of this.[112] Adam de la Mare, the attorney of the sheriff of Somerset and Dorset, had been put in the custody of the marshal of the exchequer because of debts totalling £75. 19s. 2d. which his master had failed to collect. This happened on 20 July and two days later, because the exchequer had been closed for the summer vacation, Adam was consigned to prison. But parliament happened to be in session. The imprisonment of the sheriff's attorney contravened the statute enacted in the previous parliament absolving sheriffs and other local officials from the liability for debts that they had never collected.[113] On 26 July, at the request of the chancellor and other magnates present in parliament, it was agreed by the treasurer, with the assent of the judges and others of the king's council, that Adam should be released on mainprise. One of his two sureties was John de Hungerford, knight of the shire for Somerset in that very same parliament.[114]

---

108 *Rot. Parl.*, II, p. 109 (nos. 25–27). The account of two of these merchants is in K.R. Exch. acc. various, E.101/22/36 and is enrolled on E.358/2, m.12.

109 *Statutes of the Realm* (Record Commission ed.), I, p. 288.

110 Quoted by G. P. Cuttino, "Mediaeval Parliament Reinterpreted," *Speculum*, XLI (1966), 686.

111 Parliament roll of 1352 quoted by D. Rayner, "The forms and machinery of the 'Commune Petition' in the fourteenth century," *EHR*, LVI (1941), 209.

112 L.T.R. Mem. R., E.368/112, m.202.

113 *Statutes of the Realm*, I, p. 291.

114 *Return of the Name of every Member of the Lower House of Parliament, 1213–1874* (House of Commons Parliamentary Papers of 1878), I, p. 133.

K

9

THE THEORY AND PRACTICE OF REPRESENTATION IN MEDIEVAL ENGLAND[1]*

by H. M. Cam

THOUGH REPRESENTATION is an old, not to say, hackneyed subject, we can never get away from it. It is the basis of our Anglo-American assumptions about democracy, though little used by the Greeks who invented the word democracy and repudiated by Rousseau, the prophet of modern democracy. Representative institutions are the background of Stubbs' great book. His design of the growth of the English constitution proceeds from the history of the things represented to that of the series of events by which the principle and practice of representation were incorporated in the national assembly. I use the word *things* (which we are at such pains to eliminate from the undergraduate essay) advisedly, for the problem, as I should like to pose it, is "*What* is represented, and why?"

In the last twenty years the study of this ancient subject has been reinvigorated from two new sources, each of them originating outside England. The first is the one with which I am most intimately concerned, since it is embodied in an international commission of which I have the honour to be president. In 1933, at the International Congress of Historical Sciences held at Warsaw, a Belgian scholar, M. Émile Lousse, whom we are happy to have with us today, propounded to the assembled historians a project for a concerted study of the formation of assemblies of estates. The *Ständestaat*, the *état corporatif*—the realm of estates— had long been a subject of study in Germany; two articles by Otto Hintze, published in the *Historische Zeitschrift* in 1929 and 1931,

---

[1] A paper read at the Anglo-American Conference of Historians, 11 July 1952. Reprinted from *History* i. 1953, pp. 11-26, with some revision of the references to Professor Post's work.

had set forth the theory that the evolution of estates was the clue to the later medieval history not merely of Germany but of all Western Christendom. This view, in tune with the new corporatism which Italy and Germany were translating into fact and which La Tour du Pin had been preaching in France for many years, appeared to the historians at Warsaw worthy of scientific investigation; and in 1935 the international commission for the study of assemblies of estates came into being, with M. Coville as its president and M. Lousse as its secretary and driving force.

Conferences were held year after year, mostly under the auspices of the French *Société d'Histoire du Droit*; volumes of studies by French, Swiss, Belgian, Hungarian, Italian and English scholars were published, on various aspects of the history of estates,[1] and the first volume of Professor Lousse's own book on corporative organization and representation came out in occupied Belgium in 1943.[2] It was followed in 1949 by Signor Marongiu's book, *L'istituto parlamentare in Italia dalle origine al 1500*,[3] and two months ago by Mr. Richardson's and Professor Sayles' book on *The Irish Parliament in the Middle Ages*.[4] Owing largely to Professor Lousse, the commission on estates, unlike some other children of the *Comité International des Sciences Historiques*, justified its existence by its activity and it was reconstituted at the Paris conference two years ago. With representatives of fourteen nations involved, it can fairly claim to be an international undertaking.[5]

This digression is not altogether irrelevant. In our study of English medieval history, we are, perhaps, too ready to stay on our island. Considering the very close relations between England and Rome, and England and France during the greater part of the Middle Ages, our reluctance to look overseas and study parallel developments for enlightenment, is rather less than scientific. If English and American scholars have been roused to protest by some of the statements made about English institutions in the

---

[1] *Études présentées à la Commission Internationale pour l'histoire des assemblées d'états;* I., Paris, 1937; II–VIII, Louvain, 1937, 1939, 1940, 1943, 1949 (henceforth cited as *Études*).*

[2] *La Société d'Ancien Régime*, Louvain, 1943.

[3] Rome, 1949.   [4] Philadelphia, 1952.

[5] By 1962 twenty-four volumes of the *Études* had been published, and the membership included representatives of twenty-one nations.

volumes I have mentioned, the result has, I think, been only beneficial; but I have the impression that considerably more attention has been paid to them in the United States than in England. The outcome should be, I think, first, a stimulus to the use of the comparative method; secondly, a re-examination of our own views. It is attack that compels one to define and justify assumptions that may never have been formulated.

Some of Professor Lousse's criticisms in detail can be answered fairly readily. He does very much less than justice to Stubbs, whose learning stands on a rock, however much his interpretations may be affected by the ebb and flow of circumstance. M. Lousse went so far as to say that Maitland, "who taught at Cambridge", did not think much of Stubbs (an Oxford professor) and published a course of lectures in opposition to him, where he showed his knowledge of Western Christendom (in opposition to Stubbs' insularity), by referring to the idea of the three estates of those who pray, those who fight and those who work. The fact is that Maitland expressly referred his Cambridge students to Stubbs' fifteenth chapter, not only for the phrase he quotes but also for a fuller discussion of the history of estates in France, Germany, Sicily, Aragon, Castile, Naples, and the Netherlands, than he, Maitland, had time to give.

The conception of estates of the realm is indeed not a new one to American and English students of history, for whom McIlwain's chapter in the seventh volume of the Cambridge Medieval History has amplified Stubbs' sketch. The classification of society into those who pray, those who fight, and those who labour, is a medieval commonplace, to be found in Alfred the Great and Aelfric, in Langland and Wyclif, in Gerson and Nicholas of Clamangis; it is familiar in Germany in the three categories of *Lehrstand, Wehrstand, Nährstand*. Dumézil[1] indeed would say that it goes back to the origins of the Indo-European peoples and is one of their basic social and religious conceptions, being reflected in the three Hindu castes of priests, fighters and cultivators—Brahmans, Kshatriyas, Vaisyas; in the Druids, warriors and agriculturists of primitive Celtic society, in the three tribes and

[1] Georges Dumézil, *Jupiter, Mars, Quirinus*. Paris, 1941.

three deities of primitive Rome—Jupiter, Mars, Quirinus; in the three Scandinavian deities, Odin, Thor and Freya. A cruder but more recent expression of it is in the inn-sign of the Four Alls, on which are depicted side by side, the parson saying "I pray for all"; the soldier saying "I fight for all"; the labourer, "I work for all", and the king, "I rule all."[1]

Such a view of society is functional, vocational; it does not of itself indicate the common consciousness or common action that goes with the idea of estates of the realm, or the *Ständestaat*. There may well be division of function in the lord's household or the king's realm; but so long as the functionaries are the tools of their lord, as Alfred called them, and so long as the horizontal principle of the associations of like with like has not yet triumphed over the vertical principle of loyalty to and dependence upon the lord, so long society is still in the feudal stage. It is changing economic conditions, what we used to call "the rise of the middle class", that produces the sense of common interest with one's equals, common aims, common action against one's enemies (often one's superiors), and that leads to the formation of associations and the organization of societies by estates. To take one instance: such a stage is reached when the English bishops begin to regard themselves, and be regarded primarily, as members of the clerical estate, rather than as tenants in chief, owing service at the king's court "like the other barons"—*sicut barones ceteri*, as the Constitutions of Clarendon phrase it. Stubbs notes the corresponding moment in Aragon as occurring in 1301.

For Professor Lousse the process of association is clear cut and deliberate. It follows a regular pattern of mutual oaths—*conjurationes* or *communiones*; of pacts like that of the citizens of London in 1193 or of the community of the baronage of Oxford in 1258. M. Petit-Dutaillis in his last book[2] insisted that it is in this mutual oath that the *sine qua non* of the French commune consists, not in any specific privilege or status. For M. Lousse, however, there is a second stage; the *corporation*, whether urban, mercantile, or noble, that has been constituted by oaths, must secure legal status; it must obtain a charter of privileges from the governmental

[1] Cf. *La société d'Ancien Régime*, p. 103. [2] *Les communes françaises*, Paris, 1947*

authority in order to become an estate and not merely a group. A number of corporations may combine to appeal for privileges and thus establish themselves as an order. He has a rich collection both of pacts and of charters of privileges to bear out his contention. But it is here that the formula begins to look foreign to the student of English institutions.[1]

Confronted with the charge of obstinate insularity and national pride, which M. Lousse hurls against him, the English historian examines the tendencies of English social and constitutional evolution to see how they look in the light of the continental formula. Yes, there are gilds; yes, there is at least one sworn commune; yes, there are charters to boroughs, and charters of liberties to the barons, and to the clergy (though the English historian is a little startled to find the Constitutions of Clarendon and the Statute of Mortmain listed among the concessions of liberties to the English church). Yes, there is—but only for a fleeting moment—a *communitas bachelerie.** But the only lasting associations and corporations that we are aware of in England are the gilds and companies, the universities and colleges, and the religious houses and orders. There is no closed or sworn order or fraternity of nobles, and even less of knights; there are no charters to groups of towns. The associations of magnates for the obtaining of privileges are occasional and ephemeral; they are not part of the permanent order of English society. As with Pirenne's formula for the growth of towns, so with M. Lousse's formula for the corporative state; England is the square peg that will not fit into the round hole.

There are two main reasons for this, as it seems to me—the economic and the political—or rather one that combines the two and is even more basic—the chronological. It is the timing in England that differs from that of the Continent. Owing to the circumstances of the Norman conquest, which wedded military efficiency to the fairly advanced institutions of the Anglo-Saxon monarchy, England had something like 100 years' start of France

[1] In the second edition, however, of *La Société d'Ancien Regime* (1952) M. Lousse refers to the *pays*, which he considers has some points in common with the English shire, and indicates that the local community, as well as the social group, has its part to play.

in the evolution of a royal administrative system. Neither the great feudatories who confronted the Capetian dynasty, nor the imperfectly feudalized regionalisms of the Empire, were present to impede the growth of Anglo-Norman and Angevin authority; the beginnings of the *Beamtenstaat*, the bureaucracy, which, on the Continent, came to be the dominant character of the great monarchies and princedoms of the fourteenth and fifteenth centuries, are traceable in England from the twelfth century onwards.

But if England is administratively and politically ahead of the Continent, she is economically behind. She has her commercial and industrial features—we all know about the tribe of foreign merchants in the port of London in the days of Ethelred—but compared with the ferment in the valleys of the Po, the Rhine and the Scheldt, or even in northern France, her urban and industrial developments are on a small scale. Weaker and less institutionalized central authorities on the Continent are confronted by denser populations, with more urgent economic problems and more substantial resources, which in their turn, it may well be, stimulate the nobles into a more class-conscious solidarity. The pacts, the corporations, and the orders of the Continent are the product of conditions that do not obtain in England.

Nevertheless, this new angle of vision is illuminating, and we need be in no hurry to reject the light it may give us. Certain old commonplaces and recent interests take a fresh colour, for instance, the rise to prominence of the expression *communitas* in the thirteen century, commented on by Stubbs, Jolliffe and Powicke, among many others. Tait in his book *The Medieval English Borough*, as he relates the appearance of the mayor in the English borough to the wave of communal sentiment coming from France, points out that John, who had sanctioned the commune of London on his brother's behalf in 1191, appealed fourteen years later to the commune of the realm, the *communa liberorum hominum*, for the defence of the kingdom against a threatened French invasion in 1205. You will remember how the phrase and possibly the sentiment was turned against John in 1215 when the twenty-five guarantors of Magna Carta were empowered as a last resort to grieve and distrain the king *cum communia totius terrae.* When, under John's son, the expression *communitas regni* or *communitas terrae* recurs more and more frequently, it should have for us now overtones evoked by the continental events to which Lousse and Petit-Dutaillis have been calling our attention. The oath taken by the *comune de la tere* at Oxford in 1258 is absolutely in the continental tradition.*

Or again there is the petitionary process, so intimately bound up with the judicial and legislative activities of early parliaments, so fruitfully studied in recent years by H. L. Gray, H. G. Richardson, G. O. Sayles, G. L. Haskins, D. Rayner and A. R. Myers. This may profitably be examined afresh in relation to the rich material furnished by Lousse in his fourth chapter. We are still very much in the dark as to the genesis of the petitions, whether singular or common, that were presented to the king and his council in the thirteenth and fourteenth centuries. Who drew up the Petition of the Barons of 1258? and how were the *Monstraunces* of 1297 drafted? or the complaints of the rectors of Berkshire in 1240? In the ninth chapter of *Henry III and the Lord Edward,* Powicke has suggested that "the growing coherence of the clergy probably influenced the *communitas* of the barons and made it more conscious"; it seems not improbable that the clerks who drafted the *gravamina* of their own order had the lion's share in moulding the petitionary technique, with its immense potentialities for the future.

In M. Lousse's attack on the *parlementarisme* of Stubbs he was not in 1943 aware of the formidable allies he possessed. He ignored all the undermining of the seventeenth- and eighteenth-century conceptions of primitive democratic institutions by the erection in 1893 of the high court of parliament as a royal and judicial elder brother who had ousted the younger brother, the embryonic house of commons, from the place of honour. But Stubbs' picture —not quite as black and white as some allege—has had to face criticism from a third quarter.

In the same year that M. Lousse's book came out there appeared two important articles by Mr. Gaines Post of the University of Wisconsin on *"Plena Potestas* and Consent" and on "Roman

Law And Early Representation in Spain and Italy",[1] in which he demonstrated, with a wealth of learning; how great was the contribution of Roman and Canon Law to the theory and practice of medieval representation. Medieval representation, he says, was constructed of heterogeneous materials on a foundation of feudal law, local institutions, royal curias, ecclesiastical synods, and the growth of royal and papal authority, but in both ideas and procedure its architects were greatly aided by the revival of Roman Law in the eleventh and twelfth centuries. In his articles on *plena potestas* Mr. Gaines Post has convincingly linked the early summoning of representatives to assemblies in Spain and Italy with the Roman lawyers' device of the plenipotentiary attorney representing his principal in a court of law: a conception that fits in very neatly with the *persona ficta* of M. Lousse's corporations.

In face of all these attacks, are our English knights of the shire and burgesses to retire meekly into the background, saying, as they did to king and lords in 1348, "As to your war and its array, we are so ignorant and simple that we know nothing about it nor can give any counsel in the matter"?

It was a deceptive reply and a pregnant negative; the rolls of parliament show that they took four days of discussion to arrive at it. We also should not be in a hurry to write off the representative element in the English parliaments as irrelevant in the thirteenth and fourteenth centuries. *Sustine modicum*, as the senior clerk said to his junior in the exchequer in 1177 when he asked him a tricky question; *Sustine modicum: ruricolae melius hoc norunt*—"Wait a bit; let us ask the country folk."

There are really two issues: What is represented by the representatives? And what is the origin of the device of representation? M. Lousse alleges that it is a corporation or association that is represented, and one recognized if not created by royal charter, Mr. Gaines Post very rightly emphasizes the authoritarian and legalistic aspects of the device as used by twelfth- and thirteenth-century rulers, and, as Stubbs and other have done before him, points out ecclesiastical precedents. But the earliest reference to representation in England occurs in a slightly old-fashioned record

[1] *Traditio*, i. (1943) pp. 355-408; *Speculum* (1943), pp. 211-232.*

of local custom that can be dated soon after 1110, whilst the earliest instance of political representation outside England is in the year 1136, in Italy. There is no need to deny the influence of the Church; it must have been operative in England at any date after A.D. 600. On the other hand, "representation" is a far from unequivocal expression, as is made clear, for instance, in de Lagarde's brilliant analysis of its various significations in the days of Ockham.[1] But long before jurists and scholastics began examining into the bearing of the word, representation, the thing itself, was already on the scene as an obvious common-sense solution of constantly recurrent problems. If you want to get the opinion of a crowd, whether of children or of adults, you will in effect say, "Don't all talk at once—who will speak for you?" If an agreement on action has been arrived at by a group of people, one man will naturally be empowered to act for them. If a job has to be done for which a body of persons will be held responsible, it is mere common sense for them to arrange among themselves that one or two shall do it and leave the others free to get on with the work of food production, or business, or whatever it may be. These problems, you will note, arise when there is an active community upon which some external demand is made. That is all that is needed to produce some form of representation.[2] The precise nature of the link between community and representative, and between the community and the source of the external demand will be worked out in practice and defined, as becomes necessary, by custom and, in due course, by written law, and last of all, perhaps, in theory.

So we are driven back to our starting point—what is the community that is represented? This is where Stubbs comes into his own and the obstinate insularity of our "nationalist" historians is vindicated. In English sources, the oldest unit to be represented is the vill, in 1110; the next is the shire and hundred, in 1166; the next is the cathedral chapter, in 1226; the next is the diocesan clergy, in 1254; the next is the "community of the land"—

[1] *Bulletin of the International Commission of Historical Sciences*, No. 37 (Paris, 1937), pp. 425-51.

[2] Compare M. V. Clarke, *Medieval Representation and Consent*, pp. 335-47.

otherwise the barons—in 1258; and the next, the borough in 1265.*

The representation of the clergy is clearly inspired by canonist doctrine, and can be associated with Innocent III's enunciation of the principle that links representation with consent—*quod omnes tangit ab omnibus approbetur*. In the case of the borough we have a corporation of Lousse's sort; boroughs owe the privileges which make them boroughs to a royal grant; and the practice of summoning representatives of towns to assemblies had precedents in Italy and Spain from 1162 on, representatives who, from 1214 onwards, come as plenipotentiaries with power to bind those who send them, a device which, as Mr. Post has shown, is directly traceable to papal influence.[1]

But with the earlier instances we are in a different world. The vill, the hundred and the shire are not voluntary associations privileged by royal charter, nor is the community of the barons who, at Oxford, have to elect twelve of their number to attend the parliaments that are to meet thrice a year, to treat of common needs and common business with the king's council. (One of the twelve, it should be noted, is a bishop, who on "functional" principles has no business there.) The twelve are to have power to act on behalf of the community of barons; and the *purpose* of the device is to save the pockets of the barons who cannot afford such frequent journeys to court: *Ceo serra fet pur esparnier le cust del commun***—a sound and practical reason.

It is a reason, moreover, that links up with that given in the *Leges Henrici*, in its account of the attendance of the representatives, of villagers at the shire and hundred moots. In theory, it implies, all the village might be expected to come; but either the lord of the village or his steward can discharge the obligation of the whole vill; failing that, the reeve, the priest and four of the better men of the vill should attend in place of (*pro*) all the village. Again, a common-sense delegation to one or two of a common responsibility. Whether this was a new practice under Henry I, or a recording of ancient custom, as Stubbs assumed, there is nothing

---

[1] Note also the letter of Pope Clement IV to Charles of Anjou in 1267, cited by P. S. Leicht, *Études*, II. (1937), p. 99.

to show; both William the Conqueror and Henry I stressed their preservation of the customs of Edward the Confessor, but we know that they also introduced new practices.

The first reference to representation of the shire, however, does sound like a new practice. In 1166 Henry II provided that if criminals arrested under the new procedure of the jury of indictment could not be brought before a royal justice in their own shire, they should be sent to the nearest royal session in some other shire, and with them, the sheriff was to bring two lawful men of the hundred and township where they had been arrested to bear the record of the shire and the hundred as to why they had been arrested. Neither shire nor hundred court kept a written record of their proceedings; only the oral testimony of "credible men of the court", the ancient "witness of the shire", could be produced to prove what had occurred. And this record, it must be remembered, binds those whom they represent, in the sense that the whole shire may be penalized for the action they report. This is not the same relationship as that of a jury which commits no one beyond itself. Nevertheless, when the jurors give their information to the king's inquisitors in 1086, Domesday Book notes that the "hundred says" so and so, and Stubbs does not seem to be going too far in bringing the jury into his picture of the origins of representation.

We may fully accord to Mr. Edwards* the essential importance of the formula of *plena potestas* that rivets the power of the representatives to bind those who send them,[1] we may fully accept Mr. Post's demonstration that that formula is of Roman origin, like the *plene instructi* of the clerical proctors; but it is clear that the conception in England is older than the adoption of the formula. The burgesses summoned to the council of 1268 had to bring with them letters from their community declaring that they would hold as accepted and established whatever these men should do on their behalf; the community of the barons in 1258 had agreed to hold as established whatever the twelve whom they had elected should do; and men who bore the record of the shire might in fact involve

[1] See also H. Koenigsberger on "The Powers of Deputies in sixteenth-century Assemblies", *Études*, XXIV. (1962), pp. 211-243.

the shire in an amercement if they reported an irregular action of the shire court.

I do not wish to insist on this point; no doubt the barons at Oxford had clerical advisers and colleagues; Bracton, himself a clerk learned in the Roman law, undoubtedly worked with them. But I wish to recur to my point—*what* was represented?—and to insist on the old standing of the communities of shire, hundred and township.

The districts called the shire and the hundred, as they existed in 1166, were not so very ancient, perhaps not more than 200 or 250 years old. But the communities of shire and hundred succeeded to the traditions of the folkmoots; the assemblies in which, as the tenth century hundred ordinance said, men did justice to each other, and folk right, the law of the people, was declared; the *popularia concilia* whose existence, as Stenton reminds us, is attested in the days of Coenwulf of Mercia. The continuity of the twelfth-century shire and hundred courts from those assemblies of the tenth century in which the men of the court had done justice to each other under the presidency of ealdorman or reeve is unbroken down to that thirteenth-century session when the sheriff of Lincolnshire had to give up the attempt to do business and close the court because the country gentlemen went on strike and refused to do their duty as doomsmen. Neither Stubbs' assumption (based on a mangled text) that Henry I was reviving a moribund institution, nor Mr. Jolliffe's that Henry II recreated it, is warranted by any objective evidence. For business, for justice, and for publicity the shire court maintained its vitality, though it may well have been livelier and more active in a county of many small freeholders, like Lincolnshire, than in a county that contained many large liberties, like Dorset.

This is not to deny that the policy of the Norman and Angevin kings helped to keep the shire and hundred alive. They preserved them not merely by edicts that compelled the sheriffs to observe ancient custom, but even more by giving them work to do. The hundreds had had thief-catching duties; William the Conqueror gave them a concern with homicide by the institution of the *murdrum* fine,* besides calling on them for information as to the holding of land, well before 1086. Henry II involved them in the reporting of suspects and Henry III gave them military and police responsibilities, for the keeping of watches and furnishing of armour, and demanded more and more information as to royal rights and private liberties and official misdoing from the hundred juries. The shire found itself involved in the extension of royal justice and the enlargement of the scope of royal revenues: invited by John to send delegates to discuss the affairs of the realm with the king; invited by Henry III to send delegates in 1227 to report on the sheriff's observance of Magna Carta and in 1254 on the willingness of the shire to contribute to the expenses of the king's wars in France.

Who, in fact, ran the shire court? From M. Lousse's angle, it was the *petite-noblesse—de smalre heeren—les seigneurs bassains—the Kleinadel*—though he visualizes them in isolation, each on his own estate, only taking common action in free knightly associations—*Ritterbunde*. The nearest he can get to a shire is a *"localité rurale—une agglomeration plus ou moins dense"*. In the three-fold cord of English traditional institutions, he can distinguish only the royal and feudal, he is not aware of the communal. It is true that, broadly speaking, the thirteenth-century shire is the field of the gentry, the knights, the squirearchy. The magnates have ceased to attend it, probably well before 1259; but, though the knights or gentlemen will undoubtedly take the lead in county doings, they will be working with freemen of ungentle blood, yeomen, *valetti*, who may represent the shire at parliaments if knights are not available. All the freeholders of the shire contribute to the expenses of their representative at a fixed rate. And there are no water-tight class barriers—the burgess may be a squire, the agriculturist may buy a town house, the squire's son may marry a villein's daughter, the same man may represent borough and county by turns. And above all, the locality counts. Devonshire will petition the king to have a Devon-born sheriff; and at Oxford the barons will demand that the sheriffs shall not only be landholders, but residents in the shire they administer.* The *pays*, the *patria*, the *country*, as the county was still called in Jane Austen's days, of the country gentlemen is the dominant *motif*; however he may link up with his fellows in the house of commons as an estate of the realm, it is not an order or estate that he represents, but a locality, and the house of commons, when it finally comes into existence, is not a house of *roturiers*, of the non-noble, but a house of communities, urban and rural.

It is this fact, together with the fluidity of social relations in England, that might lead us to maintain the position that Lousse condemns in Stubbs and in other English historians; to reassert *"le caractère absolument exceptionnel du parlement anglais"*. It is the survival of the shire that is unique; and it is the shire that makes the English parliament absolutely exceptional.

And at the lowest level of all, the community of the vill has still in the thirteenth century a perfectly definite place in the national system as a community that bears joint responsibility, that can and does take common action in its own interests, that is still represented, as it was in 1110, by its priest, reeve, and four men, or something very like it, and that is declared, in a royal document of the year 1255, to be entitled to prosecute its plaints in the courts by three or four of its own men—as the later legal theory of corporations would phrase it, "to sue and be sued".[1] The very fact that this legal status was lost in later days strengthens the case for the antiquity of the tradition of responsibility and representation in the oldest and smallest community.

How far are we justified in maintaining that this relationship of the ancient communities to representation and to the king's court is absolutely unique and peculiar to England?

The latest contributor to the history of the estates strongly disputes the claim of uniqueness. Mr. Russell Major in his book on *The Estates-General of* 1560, published in 1951 by the Princeton University Press, argues that many of the differences alleged between English and continental representative assemblies did not in fact exist. In France, as in England, the different orders co-operated. The same local assemblies gave mandates to the representatives of the different orders, who were not organized as three distinct houses in the estates-general until well on in the sixteenth century. The class antagonism so often insisted on was not, he maintains,

---

[1] See H. M. Cam, *Law-Finders and Law-Makers in Medieval England*, pp. 79-80.

in existence to any degree sufficient to account for the difference in the ultimate fate of the two nations; "the line between noble and non-noble was so vague as almost to defy definition".[1]

> "A deputy to the estates-general was usually elected and empowered by all three estates, but even when named by a single order of society, local ties bound him as strongly to the other orders of his community as his class tie bound him to members of his estate from other parts of France . . . he represented a particular region whose privileges and autonomy he was carefully instructed to maintain."

Further, the men elected were very often men of considerable experience in local government; and they were not only instructed but paid by those who sent them to the national assembly.[2]

For Mr. Major the key to the different history of the national representative institutions of France and England lies in the strength, not the weakness of local feeling—the regionalism which prevented effective common action from being taken in a meeting of the estates-general, or even in the estates of the Languedoil, and made the provincial estates, rather than the estates-general, the source of financial supply for the Crown. The explanation of the greater effectiveness and ultimate survival of the English parliament as against the fading-out of the continental estates is to be found, he maintains, in the policy of the monarchy. Everything turned on the question whether a national representative assembly was or was not of use to the king: if it was, he convoked it; if not, he used the provincial estates in France, the provincial *cortes* in Spain. Mr. Major, whether or not we accept the validity of his arguments, drives us back to look at our facts and our arguments once more, and to ask the question, "What is represented and why?" with renewed determination.

Mr. Chrimes, following on the heels of Maude Clarke, has collected instances to show the emergence of the *term*, "estates of the realm" in England in the fourteenth and fifteenth centuries.[3]

---

[1] This fact is abundantly illustrated in the thirteenth- and fourteenth-century records of Forez, as Professor Perroy has recently demonstrated. See "Social mobility among the French *Noblesse* in the later Middle Ages", *Past and Present*, April 1962.

[2] *The Estates-General of 1560*, pp. 73-5.

[3] S. B. Chrimes, *English Constitutional Ideas in the Fifteenth Century* (Cambridge, 1936), pp. 105-26.

It is most conspicuous in connexion with the depositions of kings —Edward II, Richard II, Edward V. On the occasions when the king's parliament cannot function, the ingredients that go to make a parliament without a king combine to constitute something like a Convention Parliament of the seventeenth century. The lawyers, like Thirning in 1399, see that, legally speaking, a parliament needs a king. The politicians, like the prior of Canterbury in 1326,[1] see that it is desirable to spread the responsibility for revolution as widely as possible, and to involve in the act of changing the succession as many of the elements of society as can be brought in. Preachers will produce texts and similes to underline the conception of a hierarchical order of society; it is a commonplace; but the estates, though they may be a way of thinking, do not seem to be really of outstanding practical significance. Nor can we get away from the fact that the practice of representation does not apply to the two higher estates. However much the Church contributed to the prevalence of the canonist theory, the position of the clergy in parliament does not conform to it. The bishops and abbots are not elected representatives of the clerical order; the diocesan clergy are not in parliament but in convocation. The lay peers of England are not elected by their fellows, they are summoned by the king.

It looks, then, as if we must go back to our traditional formulas, though modified by examination and comparison into something rather different from the Stubbsian pattern. Parliament is both "an assembly of estates and a concentration of local communities", but we couple with this formula the phrase that comes from across the Atlantic: "self-government at the king's command". It was the effective centralization of power under the Angevins that made possible the preservation and utilization of local institutions and local sentiment by the monarchy, which in its turn made possible the growth of the conception of the community of the realm, to which Stubbs directed our attention, and on which Sir Maurice Powicke has so recently insisted. The episode of the villagers of Great Peatling, which Mr. Richardson dug out of the plea rolls

---

[1] M. V. Clarke, *Medieval Representation and Consent* (London, 1936), pp. 177-8.

for us, with its many-sided social, legal and political implications,[1] may be cited once more in this connexion. In 1265 the villagers of this small Leicestershire township could act as a body to meet an emergency; they could, as a community, enter into a contract and be penalized for breaking it; they could sue and be sued, not only by the magnate whose followers they had mishandled, but by individuals of the community itself, and pay damages to them. But Sir Maurice Powicke[2] links up this local episode with political thought on a national scale when he quotes from the record the words by which the men of Peatling Magna justified their attack on the men of a royalist magnate. It was because "they were against the barons and the welfare of the community of the realm" —*contra utilitatem communitatis regni et contra barones*.[3] The fact that in 1265 peasants could speak like this—that the community of the vill was aware of the community of the realm—gives us in a nutshell the clue to the history of representation in England. From such a beginning there could develop what, by Tudor times, was a political commonplace—the conception that all England was represented in the house of commons. A man was there not only for his own locality but for something much more; he was "a publick, a Councellor to the whole State".[4] Though, as Burke was to say long after, the local units were but "inns and resting places", national consciousness had been bred in the "*patria*", the country, the neighbourhood, and it was there that the foundations were laid which preserved the institutions of representation unbrokenly in the countries of Anglo-Saxon tradition when they perished elsewhere.

[1] See Cam, *op. cit.*, pp. 81-82.

[2] *Henry III and the Lord Edward*, pp. 509-10.

[3] As Mr. Post has pointed out (*History*, 1953, pp. 289-90), the phrase *utilitas communitatis regni* indicates the far reaching influence of baronial propaganda, itself reflecting clerical thought. See Powicke, *op. cit.*, p. 387, and cf. above, pp. 157 f.

[4] Quoted by Louise Fargo Brown in "Ideas of Representation from Elizabeth to Charles II", *Journal of Modern History*, xi. (1939), 27.

10

'JUSTICE' IN EARLY ENGLISH PARLIAMENTS*

by J. G. Edwards

A prominent feature of more recent historical study of parliament has been the very strong emphasis placed upon 'justice' in the business of English parliaments during the century or so succeeding the crisis of 1258. This trend began with Maitland's Introduction to his *Memoranda de Parliamento*—the records of the Lent parliament of 1305—published in 1893. Among other things in the course of that illuminating essay, Maitland (i) underlined the fact that the parliament roll which he was editing is mostly occupied by entries which concern the audience of petitions and the hearing of pleas; and (ii) offered the suggestion (in carefully measured terms) that his readers, when more had been discovered about Edward I's parliaments, might come to the opinion 'that a session of the king's council is the core and essence of every *parliamentum*'.[1] The seeds thus sown fell eventually into fertile ground and brought forth fruit manifold. In his *Evolution of Parliament*, published in 1920, Pollard gave to the forceful second chapter the title, 'The High Court of Parliament', and in the course of it wrote:

Mainly, however, the business of Edward I's parliaments is to deal out justice. . . . Primarily a parliament is a high court of justice. . . . There are two reasons against regarding finance as the sole factor in the foundation of the English parliament. In the first place its earliest function was judicial. . . . In most of the parliaments assembled by Edward I and Edward II, if not also by Edward III, no financial supply was asked for, and none was granted. Secondly, the frequent summons of parliaments was a measure required not by the crown so much as by its subjects. It is the barons who in 1258 demand three annual parliaments; it is the Lords Ordainers who insist upon one or more sessions a year; and it is the commons who take up the cry under Edward III. . . . If they desired parliaments at all, it was for the justice therein dispensed, and not for the taxation therein imposed.[2]

A few years later, Mr. Richardson and Professor Sayles contributed to this BULLETIN five important articles, three on the early records of the English parliament and two on the parliaments of Edward III.[3] In the course of those articles they gave considerable space to discussing the question 'what parliament meant to Englishmen living between 1272 and 1327', explaining, however, that they were concerned 'primarily with litigants and suitors and clerks, with

---

[1] *Op. cit.*, p. lxxxviii.**
[2] *Op. cit.* (1st ed.), pp. 35–6, 42–3.
[3] *B.I.H.R.*, v. 129 sqq.; vi. 71 sqq., 129 sqq.; viii. 66 sqq.; ix. 1 sqq. (1928–31).

the notions of those who had occasion to be precise and to have a care for technicalities'.[1] They expressed their conclusion thus:

Is then this parliament the meeting to which the 'estates' are summoned, where legislation is considered, and where taxes are granted? If this question is asked, our answer must be that all these things may indeed happen in the one assembly, but that we should not necessarily expect knights and burgesses to be present at a parliament nor legislation considered nor taxes granted. We would, however, assert that parliaments are of one kind only and that, when we have stripped every non-essential away, the essence of them is the dispensing of justice by the king or by someone who in a very special sense represents the king; these other things, these non-essentials of representation, legislation and taxation may be added to this essence, but they may be and not infrequently are found in other meetings which are not parliaments. . . .

As we have remarked of the parliaments of Edward I, and as these instances [from the reign of Edward II] show, parliaments are of one kind only and the essence of them is the dispensation of justice. . . .

Under Edward III there are reasons why a large proportion of parliamentary time should be given to politics and economics, but it was only a proportion. The dispensation of justice remained in the eyes of the people, if not in the eyes of the king and his ministers, the prime purpose of parliament. . . .[2]

It will be seen that in these passages Mr. Richardson and Dr. Sayles are avowedly looking at parliament through the eyes of 'the people', and especially the 'litigants, suitors and clerks'; and are proceeding on the assumption that the 'essence' of parliament consists in the function which is exercised in every parliament, and that the functions not exercised in every parliament may be 'stripped away' as being 'non-essential'.

All three writers clearly look back to Maitland—particularly Mr. Richardson and Dr. Sayles, who have taken over Maitland's very word 'essence'—but Pollard is the more guarded. It is one thing to say that the dealing out of justice was parliament's function 'mainly' or 'primarily'; it is quite another to say that the dispensing of justice was the 'essence' of parliament. Pollard's statement need be no more than quantitative, but Mr. Richardson's and Dr. Sayles's statement is qualitative, because the 'essence' of a thing is that which constitutes its being, which makes it what it is, which (in the present case) gives parliament its character as parliament.[3] Now in dealing with the 'essence' of an institution like parliament, that 'essence' may be defined by reference either to the make-up or to the function of the institution. When Maitland suggested that 'a session of the king's council is the core and essence of every *parliamentum*', he was thinking of 'essence' in terms of make-up; when Mr. Richardson and Dr. Sayles say that 'the essence of parliaments is the dispensing of justice', they are thinking of

---

[1] *B.I.H.R.*, v. 129.   [2] *Ibid.*, v. 133, vi. 78, ix 2.

[3] It is noticeable that when they deal with Edward III's reign, by which time the relative importance of parliament's 'judicial' function was admittedly waning, Mr. Richardson and Dr. Sayles no longer speak of the dispensation of justice as the 'essence', but as the 'prime purpose', of parliament, and even so only 'in the eyes of the people'.

'essence' in terms of function: Maitland is considering which of the varied elements that may participate in parliaments is 'essential'; Mr. Richardson and Dr. Sayles are considering which of the varied functions that may be performed in parliament are 'essential'. The make-up and the function of an institution are of course closely connected, but they are nevertheless distinct. In the present paper we are concerned with the 'essence' of parliament in terms of function.

In speaking of 'the dispensing of justice' in these early parliaments, it is important to bear in mind how the term 'justice' has been understood in that connection. Judicial business in the strictest sense, of course, is pleas, of which there are frequent examples in early parliaments, as for instance the trial of Nicholas Segrave in the Lent parliament of 1305.[1] Maitland was careful to distinguish between judicial business in this strictest sense and what he called 'the audience of petitions', though noting that the line between them 'is not very sharp'.[2] The audience of petitions in parliament did, in many cases, involve action that was judicial or quasi-judicial, not so much in the direct sense that a decisive judgement on the petition was given in parliament, but in the indirect sense that instructions or rulings were given in parliament which could facilitate the giving of the decisive judgement in some other court.* In that broad sense the audience of petitions in parliament might in many cases rightly be described as a 'judicial' function. There has been a tendency, however, to lump the audience of all petitions in parliament under the general heading of 'justice'. But the audience of petitions by no means always involved judicial action even in the broadest sense. Maitland once more was careful to distinguish between petitions that asked for 'justice' and those that asked for pure favours[3]: the latter were quite numerous, and the answering of them cannot rightly be subsumed under the general heading of 'justice'. Petitioning was not of necessity a 'judicial' or even a quasi-judicial procedure.[4] On the other hand, it seems not unlikely that the greater part of the 'judicial' work done in parliaments was occasioned by petitions.

The scholars who have thus emphasized the 'judicial' aspect of these early parliaments have all had recourse, in varying degrees, to one *locus classicus*. About 1290, an anonymous writer compiled a legal treatise which is usually called *Fleta*,[5] in the course of which he made this remark about parliaments:

Habet enim rex curiam suam in consilio suo in parliamentis suis, presentibus prelatis comitibus baronibus proceribus et aliis viris peritis, ubi terminate sunt dubitationes judiciorum et novis

---

[1] *Mem. de Parliamento*, pp. 255–63.   [2] Above, p. 124.   [3] Above, p. 116.
[4] It should not be necessary to say that the petitions in question in this paper are the 'singular' petitions of individuals, not the 'common petitions' which purported to come from the Commons in parliament.**
[5] Mr. Denholm-Young has suggested that the author may have been Matthew Cheker; see *E.H.R.*, lviii. 1–12, lix. 252–7.†

injuriis emersis nova constituuntur remedia, et unicuique justitia prout meruit retribuetur ibidem.[1]

Fleta does not seem to have had much success as a book, and its author was a compiler with no great originality, but there are many reasons for thinking that he correctly reflected the contemporary legal view of parliament. His words have therefore very naturally been seized upon as the basic original statement of the doctrine of parliament as a 'high court' which is pre-eminently the dispenser of 'justice'. Pollard even went so far as to speak of *Fleta*'s words as 'the earliest definition of an English parliament'.[2] But they are a description rather than a definition, and as a description they are not the earliest: there is an earlier one in 1258. Even so, however, *Fleta*'s words are noteworthy. They are noteworthy as a statement of legal doctrine.

We have seen that one of the arguments advanced by Pollard in support of his view of early parliaments as being primarily 'judicial' was the consideration that the frequent summoning of parliaments was demanded by the king's subjects—by the barons in 1258, by the Ordainers in 1311, and by the Commons under Edward III—and that they desired these frequent parliaments 'for the justice therein dispensed'. A similar argument has been elaborated by Mr. Richardson and Dr. Sayles. The argument has usually been stated in quite general terms, and the evidence deserves to be considered in rather greater detail. The series of recorded demands to which Pollard alludes are scattered over a period of one hundred and twenty years, from 1258 to 1377. It is sometimes said that these demands were 'constant', but that is an illusion produced perhaps by the accident that the last two recorded demands came in the successive years 1376 and 1377. Over the six score years as a whole, the recorded demands for frequent parliaments are very intermittent. Had they been constant, like the frequently repeated demands for confirmation of the charters, they might perhaps be treated as common form. As they are recorded only seven times in six score years their significance, whatever it may be, is at least not the significance of common form. The seven recorded occasions of the demands are in 1258, 1311, 1327, 1330, 1362, 1376 and 1377. 'Demands' is a conveniently comprehensive rather than a strictly accurate term: for four of the occasions— 1327, 1362, 1376 and 1377—the demands are extant in the form of petitions, but for the other three—1258, 1311 and 1330—what we possess are enactments, but these were evidently intended to meet existing demands.

(1) 1258

The earliest extant description of periodically frequent parliaments in

---

[1] *Fleta* (2nd ed. 1685), p. 66.*   [2] *Evolution of Parliament*, p. 24.

England is implicit in two familiar clauses of 'the provisions of Oxford': their substance is summarized in the contemporary memorandum thus:

Il fet a remembrer ke les xxiv unt ordene ke treis parlemenz seient par an: le premerein as utaves de Sein Michel, le secund le demein de la Chandelur, le terz le premer jor de June ceo est a saver treis semeines devant le Seint John. A ces treis parlemenz vendrunt les cunseillers le rei esluz [*i.e.* the council of 15] tut ne seient il pas mandez pur ver le estat del reaume et pur treter les cummuns bosoingnes del reaume et del rei ensement; e autre fez ensement quant mester serra per le mandement le rei.

Si fet a remembre ke le commun eslise xii prodes homes ke vendrunt as parlemenz et autre fez quant mester serra quant le rei u sun cunseil les mandera pur treter de bosoingnes le rei et del reaume, e ke le commun tendra pur estable ceo ke ces xii frunt: e ceo serra fet pur esparnier le cust del commun.[1]

It is of course agreed that in this specific form—the fifteen counsellors afforced by twelve 'prodes homes' on behalf of 'le commun', meeting periodically on three particular dates—the parliaments envisaged by the Provisions of Oxford did not survive the short period during which the Provisions were effectively current. But it is also agreed that the idea of holding parliaments consisting of the king's counsellors afforced by 'prodes homes' of various kinds and meeting periodically several times a year, continued to flourish long after 1258, and was acted upon pretty consistently.[2] Moreover, just as it is quite clear that these periodical parliaments continued to meet long after 1258, so also there are indications suggesting that the same idea had been current and had been acted upon before that date. Mr. Richardson has noted two early references to parliaments in the Close Rolls respectively of 1242 and 1248.[3] Now the former entry speaks of a 'parliamentum regis quod erit Londinii a die Sancte Johannis Baptiste in unum mensem', and the latter mentions a parliament 'quod erit in octabis Purificacionis'.[4] It is a noteworthy coincidence that the two feasts to which the meeting-dates of these very early parliaments in 1242 and 1248 are thus keyed—St. John Baptist and the Purification—appear also as two of the three feasts to which the meeting-dates of the periodical parliaments in the Provisions of Oxford are keyed. These periodical parliaments prescribed in 1258 were therefore no transient phantoms conjured out of the void by the authors of the Provisions of Oxford. So what the Provisions say about the function of those parliaments becomes significant. Their function is described twice, in two distinct sentences of identical import: 'pur ver le estat del reaume et pur treter les cummuns bosoingnes del reaume et del rei ensement', and 'pur

---

[1] Stubbs, *Sel. Charters* (9th ed.), p. 383.*

[2] See the provisional lists of parliaments under Henry III and Edward I appended to Mr. Richardson's article in *Trans. R. Hist. Soc.* (4th ser.) xi. 172–5, and to the joint article by Mr. Richardson and Dr. Sayles, *B.I.H.R.*, v. 151–4.**

[3] *Trans. R. Hist. Soc.* (4th ser.), xi. 154.

[4] *Close Rolls* (1237–42), p. 447; *Ibid.* (1247–51), p. 104.

treter de bosoingnes le rei et del reaume'. Pollard's suggestion that the barons of
1258 demanded frequent parliaments 'for the justice therein dispensed' is thus
shown by the barons' own statements to be quite unconvincing: they describe
the function of parliaments in the widest of terms—terms which doubtless
include, but which also certainly transcend, the dispensing of 'justice'.

During the half-century between the first and the second of our recorded
demands for frequent parliaments there comes a familiar document which is very
relevant to the present discussion. Everyone agrees that the petitions brought
into these early parliaments were sometimes (and perhaps usually) very numerous,
and that it was mainly through these petitions that parliaments became involved
in 'judicial' activities.[1] In the Close Roll of 8 Edward I (1279–80) there is
enrolled an important chancery memorandum of the procedure that was followed
in dealing with these petitions:

Pur ceo ke la gent ke venent al parlement le roy sunt sovent deslaez et desturbez a grant
grevance de eus et de la curt par la multitudine des peticions ke sunt botez devant le rey, de
queus le plus porroient estre espleytez par chanceler e par justices, purveu est ke tutes les
peticions ke tuchent le sel veynent primes al chanceler, e ceus ke tuchent le escheker veynent
al escheker, e ceus ke tuchent justices u ley de terre veinent a justices, e ceus ke tuchent
juerie veynent a justices de la juerie. Et si les bosoigns seent si grantz u si de grace ke le
chanceler e ces autres ne le pussent fere sanz le rey, dunk il les porterunt par lur meins
demeine devant le rey pur saver ent sa volente, ensi qe nule peticion ne veigne devaunt le
roy e son conseil fors par les mains des avauntditz chaunceller e les autres chef ministres,
ensi ke le rey e sun consail pussent sanz charge de autre busoignes entendre a grosses busoignes
de sun reaume e de ses foreines terres.[2]

It will be seen that the *modus operandi* is to reduce to a minimum the number of
petitions that have to be considered in parliament by the king and his council.
The memorandum states that the greater part of the petitions presented could be
disposed of by the chancellor and by the judges, in consultation with the appropriate ministers, and then lays down that no petition shall be brought before the
king and his council unless it involves business that is 'so great or so much of
grace' that 'the chancellor and the others' cannot handle it without the king.
Then comes the final sentence, which is the important passage in the present
connection: only the selected petitions are to be brought before the king and his
council,

ensi ke le rey e sun consail pussent sanz charge de autre busoignes entendre a grosses busoignes
de sun reaume et de ses foreines terres.

[1] It is perhaps well to remember that the large number of petitions presented in the Lent parliament
of 1305—whose roll is one of the best edited and best known of all the early rolls of parliament—is not
necessarily typical: there had been an interval of some two and a half years since the previous parliament,
and there may well have been an accumulation of business.
[2] Stubbs, *Const. Hist.* ii. (4th ed.) p. 276, n. 2.*

The memorandum thus assumes that the king and his council will, during the time of parliament, have 'grosses busoignes de sun reaume e de ses foreines terres', to which they must be able to attend without the distraction of 'autres busoignes'. Now some of these 'grosses busoignes' may well arise out of some of the select petitions that will have been reserved for consideration by the king and his council. But we can hardly suppose that all the 'grosses busoignes' will arise in that way. Quite irrespective of petitions, if the king desires to have any matters whatsoever considered in parliament—not only taxation or legislation or France or Scotland or the papacy, but also any other subject such as we find included in those written 'arrays' of agenda that were commonly drawn up before parliaments met[1]—we may reasonably suppose that the king and his ministers will ensure that such matters shall rank among the 'grosses busoignes'. Naturally such business is bound to be very varied, and no one can expect that taxation, or legislation, or what not, will turn up in every parliament. Nevertheless, the authors of the memorandum of 1280 proceed on the assumption that in every parliament there will always be 'grosses busoignes' of one sort or another over and above the multitude of petitions, and that most of those petitions must therefore be sloughed off and left to 'le chanceler et ces autres'. In other words, the king's officers in 1280 expect as a matter of course to encounter in every parliament two things—petitions (*i.e.* 'justice') and 'grosses busoignes'. Mr. Richardson and Dr. Sayles, on the contrary, maintain that we must not necessarily expect more than one—'justice'. 'Justice' was doubtless the one thing that interested 'the people', 'the litigants and suitors and clerks', the generality of the 'Englishmen living between 1272 and 1327'. But at least some few Englishmen of that period had an equally deep interest in the 'grosses busoignes'. Admittedly those few Englishmen were very few. Yet they were the makers and builders of parliament. They were the king and his officers. These in 1280, like the barons previously in 1258, evidently thought that the function of parliaments always transcended the mere dispensing of 'justice'.

(2) 1311

The subject of frequent parliaments received very emphatic attention in 1311 in chapter 29 of the Ordinances. The great majority of those Ordinances consist of a preamble, which usually specifies some grievance, followed by the enacting clauses, which prescribe the remedy. Some of the remedies prescribed involve the setting up of some definitely new procedure, but others involve only the

---

[1] See the reference to the written 'array' in Edward II's letter of 4 Nov. 1310 to the earl of Lincoln; below, p. 288. For the agenda of the parliament of 1322 see J. Conway Davies, *Baronial Opposition to Ed. II*, p. 583.

stricter or more effective application of a procedure that was already in existence. In Ordinance 29 the preamble runs:

Pur ceo qe moultes gentz sont delaiez en la court le roi de leur demaunde par taunt qe la partie allegge qe les demaundauntz ne deivent estre respounduz saunz le roi et auxint moltz de gentz grevez par les ministres le roi encountre droiture, des queles grevaunces homme ne purra avoir recoverier sanz commune parlement. . . .

This is followed by the enacting clauses, which read:

. . . nous ordeinoms qe le roi tiegne parlement une foiz par an ou deux foiz si mestier soit, et ceo en lieu covenable, et qe en meismes les parlementz soient les pledz qe sont en la dite fourme deslaiez et les pledz la ou les justices sont en diverses opinions recordez et terminez, et en meisme la manere soient les billes terminez qe liverez serront en parlement si avant come lei et reson le demaunde.[1]

It will be seen that while the preamble mentions two specific grievances—(i) pleas delayed in the king's court because the defendant alleges that he ought not to answer without the king; and (ii) grievances illegally inflicted upon men by the king's ministers—the enacting clause mentions three things which are to be dealt with in the annual parliaments: (*a*) pleas delayed in the manner stated in the preamble are to be recorded and determined; (*b*) pleas in which the judges are of diverse opinions are to be recorded and determined; and (*c*) bills delivered into parliament are to be determined as law and reason require. Thus items (*b*) and (*c*) in the enactment are not specifically mentioned in the preamble, while item (ii) in the preamble is not specifically mentioned in the enactment. But since complaints against the misconduct of royal ministers would almost certainly be made by bill (*i.e.* by petition), we may perhaps regard item (ii) of the preamble as covered by item (*c*) in the enactment; and as item (*b*) in the enactment specified another cause of delay in pleas, we may perhaps regard it as *in pari materia* with item (i) of the preamble.

In this ordinance, the emphasis is almost exclusively upon the 'judicial' function of parliament: the determining of delayed pleas and the determining of pleas held up by differences of opinion among the judges were obviously 'judicial'; so also would be the determining of 'bills' which alleged that the petitioner had been 'grevez par les ministres le roi encountre droiture'; so also would be the determining of petitions which asked for 'justice'. Only the determining of those petitions which asked for pure favours would be a non-judicial act. In enacting that the grievances specified should be dealt with in parliaments held once (or if need be twice) a year, the Ordainers were not setting up anything new. We have already seen that the idea of holding parliaments periodically several times a year had been familiar in England for at least half a century, and there is sufficient evidence to show that precisely the kinds of business mentioned

[1] *Rot. Parl.*, i. 285.*

in the ordinance had been dealt with in those parliaments.[1] What then is the significance of Ordinance 29?

No one is likely to suggest that the Ordainers were framing a systematic 'constitutional document', or that they were concerned to provide any 'statement' of constitutional principles for the information of later historians: they aimed at being practical reformers. So we may reasonably suppose that they did not make complaints or enactments about any institutions unless those institutions seemed to them to be working unsatisfactorily. When therefore they prescribed in their 29th Ordinance that the king hold parliaments once a year, or twice if need be, and that petitions and delayed pleas be 'determined' therein, they presumably did so because they believed, either that parliaments were not being held annually, or that the petitions and delayed pleas brought into the parliaments were not being 'determined'—in other words, because they believed that parliaments, for either or both of those reasons, were not adequately fufilling their 'judicial' functions.

The former of these possible explanations—that parliaments before 1311 may not have been occurring annually—can be brought to a test. Some twenty years ago Mr. Richardson and Dr. Sayles contributed to this BULLETIN a provisional but very serviceable list of parliaments held between 1277 and 1377.* If we take the years that would probably be uppermost in men's recollection in 1311, say the twenty years immediately preceding, we find that only two—the years 1303 and 1304, when the king was absent in Scotland—had no parliament, while a substantial number of the other years probably had two or even three parliaments apiece. It would seem, therefore, that during the two decades preceding the Ordinances of 1311, annual parliaments were a well-honoured custom. So it was not any lack of annual parliaments that constituted the Ordainers' grievance. That being so, we are left with the alternative explanation: the Ordainers presumably believed that although parliaments were occurring annually, the petitions and delayed pleas which were brought into them were not being adequately 'determined'. We have already seen that some twenty years earlier the anonymous author of *Fleta* had described parliament as the court

ubi terminate sunt dubitationes judiciorum et novis injuriis emersis nova constituuntur remedia, et unicuique justitia prout meruit retribuetur ibidem.

But while fully recognizing the importance of *Fleta*'s words as a statement of legal doctrine, we should not be misled by his categorical indicatives. While noting that about 1290 one anonymous Englishman is asserting the doctrine that parliament is the court where judicial doubts '*are* determined', new remedies '*are* established' and justice '*is* done', we should also note that by 1311 twenty-one

---

[1] For a case in the parliament of 1305 in which the defendant had pleaded that he could not answer without the king, see *Mem. de Parliamento*, pp. 47–8; for complaints against royal officers, see *ibid.*, pp. 43, 146–7; for petitions generally, see Maitland's useful classified list, *ibid.*, pp. 354–5.

by no means anonymous Englishmen are acting on the belief that the *doctrine* is not being adequately realized in *practice*. Otherwise, why Ordinance 29? Why trouble to ordain that the petitions and the delayed pleas shall be 'determined' in annual parliaments, when this would already have been occurring if the annual parliaments had been adequately living up to *Fleta*'s doctrine? So even thus early in the fourteenth century, parliament as the dispenser of 'justice' is already being weighed in the balances and is being found wanting.

Its shortcomings can be dimly discerned even in the unsystematic and fragmentary records that have come down to us. At best, parliament was an intermittent thing, and its intermissions could delay still further the determining of those pleas which petitioners might wish to bring to it because they were already being delayed in some lower court. Moreover the 'time of parliament' was rarely long and it could be quite short. In November 1309 Edward II wrote to the earl of Lincoln announcing that he had decided to summon his 'great parliament' to be at York on 8 February 1310 'por treter de la busoigne d'Escoce et dautres diverses busoignes', and accordingly ordering Lincoln to call together the treasurer and others of the king's council

et avisez en quele maniere et de quel endreit il nous covendra ceo parlement deliuerer, et soit tut ordeine devaunt vous, et mys en escrit le arrai de nostre parlement, issint qil nous coviegne mye demorrier illosqes por parlementer outre x iours on XII au plus . . .[1]

In the event the meeting-place was changed, and the business transacted was not what the king had envisaged. But his letter to Lincoln is not therefore less significant: it shows that the projected parliament was being planned to last for no more than ten or twelve days at most, and it suggests that any attention that might have been given to 'justice' would have had to be given within the time—if any—remaining after due attention had been given to the Scottish and other business which was to be set down in the 'array'. When, after the venue had been changed, the parliament eventually met on 27 February 1310, it sat indeed for thrice twelve days, but as its proceedings were centred in the all-consuming controversy between king and barons leading to the appointment of the Lords Ordainers, we may reasonably doubt whether the dispensing of 'justice' would occupy—if it occupied at all—anything more than the interstices of time during the session. Parliament was the sort of 'court' where 'justice' could too easily be crowded out by 'grosses busoignes'.[2]

---

[1] J. Conway Davies, *Baronial Opposition to Ed. II*, pp. 548–9.*

[2] In the parliaments of March and September 1332 no petitions were 'received' because of the pressure of other business; nor were any petitions 'received' in the parliament of December 1332, partly because suitable persons were not available to act as auditors, partly because the Christmas feast made it impossible to attend to them; they were 'received' in the next parliament in January 1333; *Rot. Parl.*, ii. 65b, 67a–b, 68a. There were complaints in the Easter parliament of 1309 that Edward II had not appointed receivers of petitions in parliament as his father had done, but the precise significance of this is not clear; see *Rot. Parl.*, 1. 444, and the discussion by Mr. Richardson and Dr. Sayles, *B.I.H.R.*, vi. 75-6.

Moreover the petitionary procedure in parliament had a certain immanent quality of indecisiveness. Maitland pointed out that

the response to the petition seldom gave to the suppliant all that he wanted. He had only, we may say, 'made a *prima facie* case' for relief, and he obtained only a preliminary order. He did not get what he wanted, he was merely put in the way of getting it. [1]

The repeated insistence in Ordinance 29 that delayed and doubtful pleas are to be *determined*, that petitions are to be *determined*, may well be a reference to this fact. The suppliant who was 'put in the way' of getting his remedy could find it a disappointing way. Even if the auditors decided that his petition was important enough to be endorsed 'Coram Rege', and thereby placed among the selected petitions reserved for consideration by the king and his council—even that way was not necessarily a royal road to success. In the parliament of 1362 the Commons made this request:

Pur tant qe cest parlement feust sommons pur redrescer diverses meschiefs et grevances faitz as communes et qe chescun qe se sentroit greve mettreit avant sa bille et serroient les seigneurs et autres assignez de les oier, lesqueux seigneurs issint assignez, si rien touche le roi, font endocer les billes *Coram Rege*, et issint riens est fait ne les meschiefs et grevances de rien redrescez: qe lui plese de sa bone grace ordeiner qe les dites billes soient veues devant les ditz seigneurs et par avis le chanceller, tresorer et autres du conseil le roi responduz et endocez en manere come droit et reson demandent, pur Dieu et en oevre de charite, et ce devant le departir du dit parlement. [2]*

The criticism is significant. A petition endorsed 'coram rege' can evidently remain quite ineffective: 'the mischiefs and grievances are in no wise redressed'. So the Commons ask that petitions be not so endorsed: they ask that petitioners be 'put in the way' not of a *coram rege* but of an *answer*. Even when an 'answer' was given, however, difficulties were by no means necessarily at an end. Thus in the parliament of March 1340 a petition was presented by Geoffrey de Staunton complaining that a plea to which he was party had been delayed in the court of Common Pleas, and asking that a ruling be given in parliament on a technical legal point that was involved. A ruling was duly given and the court of Common Pleas was ordered to proceed to judgement in accordance with it. The court did not do so, and Staunton petitioned again in the next parliament in July 1340. There, when the relevant documents had been considered, 'it was commanded by the prelates, earls, barons and others of the parliament' that Thomas de Drayton, clerk of the parliament, should go to the judges of Common Pleas and tell them to proceed to judgement without further delay, but that if they could not agree 'for difficulty or other cause', they were to come into parliament 'illoeqes a prendre final accord quel juggement se devera faire'.** They chose to come into parliament. There, on 17 July, after diligent debate, the final 'accord' was reached,

[1] *Mem. de Parliamento*, p. lxviii.†   [2] *Rot. Parl.*, ii. 272.

and the judges 'were told in the said parliament' that they were to proceed to judgement accordingly.[1] Whatever might be the legal doctrine about the pre-eminence of parliament as a high court, in practice a ruling given in parliament was evidently not always or immediately effective in overcoming judicial doubts and ending judicial delays.

(3) 1327

The quashing of the Ordinances in 1322 deprived them, for the most part, of legal effect, but evidently left some of their basic ideas still vaguely current.[2] In 1327, the idea of annual parliaments appears in one of a series of petitions put forward by the mayor and citizens of London in Edward III's first parliament. It runs:

Ensement prient qe nostre seigneur le roi teigne son parlement a Westmoustier chescun an taunqe il soit de plenere age. Et qe ceux qi serront assignez destre pres de luy soient remuez au commencement de parlement, et qe chescun qi se sache par reson pleindre de eux soit oi.[3]

This petition in effect amounted to a more precise attempt to meet one of the particular complaints that had been made in the 29th Ordinance of 1311—the complaint that men are aggrieved against law by the king's ministers and can have no recovery without common parliament. But the form of the request was conditioned by the fact that the reigning king in 1327 was under age. The Londoners ask that parliament be held at Westminster each year until the king is of age, and that 'those who have been assigned to be near him', *i.e.* the coun-cillors who will be governing in his name, shall be removed at the beginning of the parliament, and that anyone who has reason to complain against them shall be heard. This automatic 'removal' from office at the beginning of each parlia-ment was presumably suggested in order that no would-be complainant might be deterred from making his complaint by fear of, or regard for, the offender's high position 'near the king'.[4] Apparently the petition came to nothing, for it is 'vacated' and has no *responsio* on the roll, but its concentration upon the single point that defaulting royal ministers should be justiciable in annual parliaments, even though only during the limited period of the king's minority, repeats one of the ideas implicit in Ordinance 29 of 1311.

---

[1] *Rot. Parl.*, ii. 122–5.

[2] A number of the ordinances were salvaged by being reissued in modified form by the king in 1322 (*ibid.*, i. 456–7), but Ordinance 29 was not among these.

[3] *Rot. Parl. Anglie hactenus inediti*, ed. Richardson and Sayles, p. 134.*

[4] Speaking of the dismissal of Bishop Stapledon from the treasurership in 1325 the 'Monk of Malmesbury' remarks: Iccirco amovit eum rex a potestate ut, si contigisset eum aliquos laesisse, necesse haberet querelantibus respondere; et quidem bonum commune foret et consonum juri, ut tanta potestate praedicti annales fierent, ut *qui tempore officii conveniri non possunt*, saltem post annum judicio starent, et non diutina vexatione subjectos opprimerent; *Chron. Ed. I and Ed. II* (Rolls ser.) ed. Stubbs, ii. 283.**

(4) 1330

In 1330 came the first statute prescribing annual parliaments, the statute conventionally cited as '4 Ed. III cap. 14'. It is a laconic measure:

Ensement est accorde qe parlement soit tenu chescun an unefoitz ou plus si mestier soit.[1]

If this statute was made in response to a petition, that petition seems to be no longer extant. Nor is there any preamble to the statute. So we have no specific statement of the function or functions which the annual parliaments were intended by the authors of the statute to fulfil. We can only remark that the statute, whatever its purpose, was at any rate not occasioned by any notable failure to hold annual parliaments: only in three of the preceding twenty years— 1317, 1323 and 1326—did no parliaments meet.[2]

After 1330, a whole generation elapses before there is another recorded demand for annual parliaments.

(5) 1362

When we turn to the fifth recorded demand for annual parliaments in 1362, we fortunately possess not merely (as in 1330) the statute that was made, but also the petition which the statute answered. The statute itself is the tenth in a series of fifteen chapters, and follows closely the wording of the corresponding clause in the petition. It reads:

Item pur meintenance des ditz articles et estatutz et redresser diverses meschiefs et grevances qi veignent de jour en autre, soit parlement tenuz chescun an sicome autrefoitz estoit ordeigne par estatut.[3]

Everyone agrees that the previous statute referred to is that of 1330. But whereas the statute of 1330 does not indicate the functions which were to be performed in the annual parliaments which it prescribes, the statute of 1362 specifies them. Most writers have written as though the statute of 1362 had described the function of the annual parliaments merely in the general terms 'in order that the divers grievances and mischiefs arising from day to day may be redressed'. It will be seen, however, that the actual words of the statute (which reproduces the words of the petition) begin by saying that the function of the annual parliaments was 'pur meintenance des ditz articles et estatutz'. In the context, the said 'articles and statutes' are the nine preceding chapters of the statute of 1362. What was the purport of those preceding 'articles and statutes', and how could annual parliaments 'maintain' them? Of the nine preceding 'articles and statutes', no less than six are directed against the endemic evils of purveyance. The only way in which annual parliaments could 'maintain' those

---

[1] *Stat. of the Realm*, i. 265.*   [2] *B.I.H.R.*, vi. 85–8, viii. 78.
[3] *Stat. of the Realm*, i. 374.** The petition is in *Rot. Parl.*, ii. 271.

statutes would be by annually providing redress of any breaches of them that might occur—and long experience had shown that any regulations for controlling purveyance were apt to be much more honoured in the breach than the observance. The phrase about 'redressing divers mischiefs and grievances that arise from day to day' must therefore be taken in its context: though seemingly general, in its context it would have particular reference to the 'maintenance of the said articles and statutes', and in that connection the 'divers mischiefs and grievances that arise from day to day' would be mischiefs and grievances arising from the breach of 'the said articles and statutes': in the main, they would be mischiefs and grievances connected with purveyance. Now the grievances associated with purveyance were due to the misdoings of royal officers who administered it. So the demand for annual parliaments for the maintenance of statutes concerned mainly with purveyance was but a particular application of the idea that parliament was the pre-eminently appropriate occasion for dealing with complaints against the king's ministers.

(6) 1376

The petition for annual parliaments in the 'Good Parliament' of 1376 runs thus:

Item prie la commune, qe pleise establier par estatut en cest present parlement qe chescun an soit tenuz un parlement de faire corrections en roialme des erroures et fauxtees si nuls y soient trovez.

The response was in these terms :

Endroit du parlement chescun an il y a ent estatuz et ordenances faitz, lesquex soient duement gardez et tenuz.[1]

The statutes referred to in the response were presumably those that had been enacted in 1362 and 1330. The phrase in which the petition describes the function of annual parliaments—'de faire corrections en roialme des erroures et fauxtees si nuls y soient trovez'—is doubtless sufficiently wide to cover almost anything, but if we have regard to the disastrous political events of Edward III's dotage and to the actual proceedings of the parliament of 1376, we can hardly doubt that the 'erroures et fauxtees' more especially in mind were those attributable to the king's ministers. For it was in this very parliament that the novel process of impeachment was first used: it was directed against Latimer and a number of other counsellors and officers of the king. Impeachment was of course a judicial procedure, but as it was an accusation maintained by the Commons in common,[2] it was a more potent weapon against royal ministers

---

[1] *Rot. Parl.*, ii. 355.*
[2] See Professor Plucknett's remarks in *Trans. R. Hist. Soc.* (5th ser.), i. 153–64.

than the traditional complaint by individual petition. It gave a new turn to the old idea that parliament was *par excellence* the occasion for dealing with the defaults of royal ministers: it was indeed judicial in form, but its purpose was 'political' rather than 'judicial'.

Taken in their context, therefore, the four recorded demands for annual parliaments under Edward III emphasize only one aspect of the 'justice' to be dispensed in parliaments—'justice' upon defaulting royal ministers. The 29th Ordinance of 1311, on the other hand, had laid equal emphasis also upon other 'judicial' functions which were to be performed in parliaments—the functions of determining petitions and determining delayed pleas. This broad difference of emphasis reflects a significant change that was coming about during Edward III's long reign—a change in men's attitude towards parliament as a dispenser of 'justice'. This change is exemplified by at least two facts.

(i) In the parliament of March 1340 a statute was made in the following terms. It begins with a preamble:

Item pur ceo qe moultz des meschiefs sont avenuz de ceo qe en diverses places, aussibien en la chauncellerie, en le bank le roi, le commun bank, et lescheqer, les justices assignez, et autres justices a oyer et terminer deputez, les jugementz si ount estre delaiez, ala foitz par difficulte et ascune foitz par diverses oppinions des judges, et ala foitz par autre cause. . . .

Now here we have cases such as had been envisaged in Ordinance 29 of 1311— cases in which judgement had been delayed, whether by 'difficulty', or (and this had been specifically mentioned in the ordinance) by 'diverse opinions of the judges', or by other cause. All this was 'judicial' business in the strict sense. The remedy prescribed in 1311 had been the holding of annual parliaments. But the remedy provided by the statute of 1340 is different. Its enacting clauses proceed:

. . si est assentuz establiz et acordez qe desore en avant a chescun parlement soient esluz un prelat deux contes et deux barons qi eient commission et poair du roi doier, par peticion a eux liveree, les pleintes de touz ceux qi pleindre se vorront de tieux delaies ou grevances faites a eux; et eient poair a faire venir devant eux a Westmoustier ou aillours ou les places serront, ou ascun des places serra, les tenours des recordz et proces de tieux jugementz ensi delaiez, et facent venir devant eux meismes les justices qi serront adonqes presentz, pur oyer lour cause et lour resons de tieux delaiez; queux cause et reson ensi oiez, par bon avis de eux meismes, les chauncellier, tresorer, justices del un bank et del autre, et autres de counseil le roi, taunz et tieux come ils verront qe busoignable serront, aillent avant aprendre bon accord et bon juggement faire; et selonc mesme laccord ensi pris soit remande as justices devant queux le plee pent la tenur du dit record ensemblement ove tieu juggement qe serra acorde, et qe eux illent hastivement a juggement rendre selonc meisme lacord. Et en cas qe lour semble qe la difficulte soit si grande qele ne poet pas bonement estre termine sanz assent du parlement, soit a dit tenour ou tenours portez par les ditz prelat contes et barons a proschein parlement, et illoeqes soit pris final acord queu juggement se devera faire en tieu cas, et solonc cel acord soit mande as justices devant queux le plee pent, qils aillent a jugement rendre sanz delay. Et pur commencier a faire remedie sur cest establissement si est assentuz qe commission et poair soit fait a lercevesqe de Canterbirs les contes darundel et de Huntendon le seignur Wake et monsieur Rauf Basset a durer tanqe au prochein parlement . . .'[1]

There is no evidence that this statute was continuously observed,[2] but that fact does not lessen the significance of the statute's intention. Its intention evidently was to entrust the determining of delayed pleas to the commission of five magnates, who were to consult parliament only if the difficulty of the case were 'so great' that they wished to fortify themselves with the 'assent' of parliament. In other words, the authors of this statute of 1340 were trying to by-pass parliament as much as possible in the 'judicial' business of determining delayed pleas. One of their reasons for wishing to do so is indicated by the provision that the commissioners were to have powers 'lasting until the next parliament'. This meant that the commissioners were to have power to act during the period when no parliament would be in session. In other words, those who framed the statute had grasped the point that the intermittent parliament was a real inconvenience as a court of last resort, because its very intermissions tended to prolong those judicial delays which it was expected to remedy. The authors of the statute of 1340, unlike the authors of the Ordinances of 1311, no longer put their whole trust in parliaments as the resort against the law's delay.

(ii) In the latter half of Edward III's reign there was a marked decline in the numbers of 'singular' petitions presented in parliament by individuals.[3] The reasons for this development have not yet been fully elucidated, and they were probably both complex and cumulative. But unless the indications of the scattered evidence are completely misleading, the fact of the decline seems clear. In the parliaments of the 1360's the 'singular' petitions of individuals seem to loom nothing so large as they do in the parliaments around 1300. By the 1360's parliament is a 'court' which is in course of being deserted by its once multitudinous suitors, the petitioners for 'justice': as 'justice' is being crowded out, the petitioners for 'justice' are no longer crowding in.

(7) 1377

By comparison with the petitions for annual parliaments under Edward III, the petition made in the first parliament of Richard II is surprisingly elaborate.[4]

---

[1] *Stat. of the Realm*, i. 282–3.*

[2] Another commission was appointed in June 1344 which included two members (Huntingdon and Wake) of the original commission nominated in the statute (*Foedera*, III, pt. i. 13–14). The statute, however, was still remembered in 1377 and 1385; see below, p. 295.

[3] See the remarks of Mr. Richardson and Dr. Sayles, *B.I.H.R.*, ix. 3–6.   [4] *Rot. Parl.*, iii. 23.

It begins with a preamble:

Item pur ce qe mayntz gentz sont delaiez en la court du roi de lour demaundes partaunt qe ascun foitz la partie allege qe les demaundantz ne doyvent estre responduz sanz le roi et ascun foitz la partie pleintif allegge en mesme la manere, et auxint moult des gentz grevez par les ministres du roi encountre droiture, desqueux grevances homme ne purra avoir recoverir sanz commune parlement . . .

Then follows the specific petition:

. . . qe plese a nostre dit seignour de tenir parlement un foitz par an au meynz et ceo en lieu covenable, et qen mesmes les parlementz soient les plees qi sont en la dite forme delaiez et les plees la ou les justices sont en diverses opinions recordez et terminez, et qen mesme la manere purrent les billes estre terminez qi serront liverez en parlement si avaunt come raison et ley demaunde.

The response also is worth noticing, for it too is more elaborate than the laconic answers of 1376 and 1362 and the brief statute of 1330. It reads:

Quant a ceo qe parlement serroit tenuz chescun an, soient les estatutz ent faitz tenuz et gardez; mais quant al lieu ou le parlement se tendra, le roi ent ferra sa volentee. Et quant as plees desquelles les justices serroient en diverses opinions il y a estatutz ent faitz queux le roi voet qe soient gardez et fermement tenuz.

Both the petition and the response have certain features which deserve rather more attention than they have usually received.

In the response, the interesting feature is not so much the first clause confirming the existing statutes about annual parliaments, but rather the third clause, which refers separately to some unspecified 'estatutz' dealing with the subject of 'plees desquelles les justices serroient en diverses opinions'—one of the matters which the petitioners wished to refer to annual parliaments. The unspecified 'estatutz', whatever they were, must have prescribed something other than the annual parliaments as the appropriate remedy for determining such pleas, otherwise there would have been no point in referring to them separately. What were these 'estatutz'? The answer seems to be supplied by an actual case.

In 1385—and thus only eight years later than the petition of 1377—one Thomas Lovell complained by petition in parliament of the delaying of judgement in a plea to which he was a party.[1] The king 'by assent of parliament' answered the petition by appointing a number of commissioners who were empowered to deal with Lovell's complaint 'according to the form of a statute' whose terms are recited at some length in the body of the commission. The passages recited show, and indeed the commission itself actually states, that the statute thus recited was made in the parliament held at Westminster in the fourteenth year of Edward III: this was none other than the statute of 1340, already noticed above,[2] which had prescribed the appointment in each parliament

---

[1] *Rot. Parl.*, p. 399.*   [2] *Supra*, p. 294.

of commissioners whose function would be to dispose of pleas in which judgement was delayed by the difficulty of the case, or by disagreement among the judges, or by some other cause. The recourse thus had to the statute in 1385 indicates that the same statute was being referred to when the petitioners of 1377 were told that there were 'estatutz' about the pleas which were delayed by differences of opinion among the judges, and that the king willed that those 'estatutz' be observed. If so, the effect of the response made to the petition of 1377 was this: it granted, indeed, that annual parliaments be held, but with the reservation that the determining of pleas delayed by disagreements among the judges should be achieved, not (as requested by the petition) by recourse to annual parliaments, but by recourse to commissioners appointed under the statute of 1340. It is an interesting answer: for the intention of the statute of 1340 had been to provide a procedure whereby delayed pleas could be determined without necessarily having recourse to parliament at all, and irrespectively even of parliament's being in session.

It is, however, the petition itself rather than the response to it that is the more notable. The petition refers elaborately, not only to the parliamentary function of doing 'justice' on royal ministers, but also to other parliamentary functions that had not been specifically mentioned in the demands of 1327, 1330, 1362 and 1376—the 'judicial' functions of determining petitions and of determining delayed and difficult pleas. This fact so impressed Mr. Richardson and Dr. Sayles that they described the petition of 1377 as 'the fullest statement of the need for annual parliaments'[1]—the fullest statement, that is, of the 'judicial' functions performed in parliament. But they did not point out that the material passages in the petition of 1377 are verbatim repetitions of the 29th Ordinance of 1311.[2] So this 'fullest statement' of the 'judicial' functions performed in parliament belongs originally not to 1377, but to 1311—not to the *last* of the fourteenth-century demands for annual parliaments, but to the *first*. Unless that fact is remembered, the petition of 1377 may easily mislead us. In 1311, men could plausibly believe in the possibility of maintaining parliament as the dispenser of 'justice'. That the men of 1377 appear still to believe in that same possibility is only an illusion—an illusion created by the accident that the drafters of the petition of 1377 chose to frame it by borrowing the idiom of 1311, instead of expressing themselves—as the petitioners of 1376 had done—in their own words. By 1377 the idiom of 1311 was, in this regard, an archaism—an archaism already withering into anachronism.

---

[1] *B.I.H.R.*, ix. 1.

[2] Cf. the passages quoted on p. 295 with those *supra*, p. 286. This petition is one of fourteen which in 1377 were based in varying degrees upon the Ordinances of 1311; the relevant passages are set out in parallel columns, *B.I.H.R.*. xxvi. 200–13.

If we are to reach an adequate view of the ideas underlying the English parliament, the dispensing of 'justice' must be given its due place among the functions performed in the early parliaments. Formerly, historians accorded to 'justice' less than its due place. Latterly, they have given to it more than its due place. The functions performed in these early parliaments cannot be satisfactorily appraised from a single point of view. *Fleta*'s classical description, for instance, forms part of a chapter in which he is giving a list of the various royal tribunals that exercise judicial functions: in such a context, it is very proper that he should mention only the judicial functions that are performed in parliament—the functions other than judicial are irrelevant to his purpose. We shall get equally one-sided views of parliamentary functions if we regard them from the standpoint only of the generality of Englishmen, or from the standpoint only of the king and his counsellors: both parties were concerned in parliament, and the functions performed in it need to be appraised from both points of view. Of the business done in parliament, what specially interested the generality of Englishmen was the dispensing of 'justice'; but what specially interested the king and his counsellors were the 'grosses busoignes'. We must set beside *Fleta* the two other early accounts of parliamentary business contained in the less specialized contexts of the Provisions of Oxford of 1258 and of the chancery memorandum of 1280: both these documents describe parliamentary functions in the widest and most comprehensive terms. Evidently the competence of king in council in parliament was not a 'judicial' competence. It was a general competence. It was an omnicompetence. Parliament was a 'high' court not merely because it was judicially above other courts, but also because it was in itself more than a judicial court: it was an omnicompetent organ of government at the summit of lay affairs in England. Nor can we justly conceive its omnicompetence as something consisting of a basic nucleus of 'judicial' competence, to which king or barons might on occasion 'add' various 'other things'—but only as detachable 'non-essentials' which historians must now 'strip away'. Parliament's robe of omnicompetence was not a thing of shreds and patches: it was a seamless whole.

11

THE ENGLISH PARLIAMENT AND PUBLIC OPINION, 1376-88[1]*

by T. F. Tout

THE twelve years between 1376 and 1388 are recognized as possessing special importance in the history of the English Parliament. They begin and end with the two most striking of parliamentary victories history has recorded before the period of the Lancastrians. Indeed they anticipate practically all that the parliaments of Henry IV were able to claim. Yet in each case the victory of parliament was not lasting. It was followed by a reaction that left things much as they had been before. Nevertheless each victory involved precedents which later ages were not slow to make use of, and secured the permanence of parliament as a form of control, however much parliament had failed when it found executive problems forced upon it.

These twelve years begin with the Good Parliament of 1376 and end with the Merciless Parliament of 1388. It happens that we have better information about these two parliaments than about any other parliaments during the Middle Ages. Recent or forthcoming publications have largely added to that knowledge and enable us to get nearer the mind and work of these assemblies than has been possible until quite recent times. It is not that we do not know a great deal about the composition, acts and influence of the parliaments of the hundred or more years of history that were behind it before our short period begins. We are, however, singularly badly informed as to the procedure, and still worse informed as to the debates of these early parliaments. The reason is that we derive the early history of parliament almost altogether from record evidence. So much the better, says the modern scholar, for its validity. Writs of summons, laws, petitions, rolls of parliament are more likely to tell us the truth than the gossip

[1] [A contribution to the *Mélanges d'Histoire offerts à Henri Pirenne*. 1926.]

of chroniclers.   Yet without the chroniclers and the other literary sources we should only know the dry bones of history.   It is the silence of the chroniclers that leaves us so much in the dark as to the early history of parliament and makes us almost entirely ignorant as to what public opinion thought about it.   It is only when the fourteenth century was well advanced that the chroniclers begin to tell us anything about parliaments.   Before that they had no interest in them.   As they only narrate what seemed interesting to themselves or their readers, we may infer that public opinion was not interested in parliaments.

There was fierce opposition among the nobles and clergy to both Edward I and Edward II.   But it is remarkable how little parliaments came into the story of that opposition.   Thomas of Lancaster, the opposition leader under Edward II, made a point of absenting himself from parliament altogether.   Yet some reference to parliament, and after 1311, some reference to a representative parliament, was thought necessary to ratify all important acts.   The deposition of Edward II was emphatically a parliamentary act*and it was under Edward III, the first king with what we should call a "parliamentary title," that public opinion began to be interested in parliaments.**

The first occasion on which public opinion and parliament were brought into close relation was an accidental result of the quarrels between Edward III and his ministers in 1340.   This story may be briefly told as a good introduction to the events of the next generation which it is our special business to consider.   The early campaigns of the Hundred Years' War in the Netherlands had been costly and disastrous failures.   Edward III and his " secretarii," the clerks and knights of his household, blamed the great officers of state in England, the " officiarii in magnis officiis ministrantes," as having caused this failure by omitting to send the king sufficient support.[1]   Accordingly in November 1340 Edward and his " secretarii " came back suddenly from Flanders and drove the magnate ministers from office.   The ministerial changes were so clumsily and brutally effected that the king's party blundered into attacking both the rights of the magnates and the privileges of the Church. John Stratford, Archbishop of Canterbury, the chief of the incriminated ministers, was therefore able to pose as the champion of the rights of Church and baronage.   He took refuge in the great

[1] Robert of Avesbury, p. 323.

monastery which was his cathedral church and wrote a manifesto in which he formulated the doctrine on which the magnates had long acted. The king was the undoubted ruler of the land, but he could only rule rightly if he took the advice of his natural councillors, the magnates of Church and State. Let the king, therefore, at once summon a parliament to settle the contested issues. Stratford's manifesto was in form a private letter to the king, but it was in substance a party pamphlet, drawn up in French that it might be more generally understood, and widely enough circulated to find its way into some of the chronicles.[1] It was followed by a course of archiepiscopal sermons preached against the king in Canterbury cathedral. Failing to stop the primate's preaching, Edward III issued the so-called "libellus famosus," [2] which, though in form a "letter close," issued from his chancery, was not closed by the seal, the greatest pains being taken to give it extensive publicity. Thus both sides in the quarrel appealed to public opinion.

Parliament was in due course summoned and the courtiers did what they could to prevent Stratford from taking his seat. But the outrageous violence of the controversial methods of the king and his courtiers had overshot the mark, and the indignant magnates at once made common cause against the new ministers. The effect of the controversy on public opinion was such that a contemporary London chronicler, who had given one line to the parliament which deposed Edward II, tells in detail how for a week the Archbishop of Canterbury and two of his suffragans were kept out of parliament by the violence of the king's chief supporters, William Kilsby, keeper of the privy seal, and Sir John Darcy, steward of the household. What follows is worth quoting.

Puisse après, en le secounde semeigne, le counte de Garenne vint au parlement devant le roy, si trova là sire Robert Pervinke, le baroun de Stafforde, sire William Killesby, et sire Johan Darcy, et autres nient covenables de seer en parlement, si comenza sa resoun à dit " sire roy, coment va çeo parlement ? Jadis ne soleit mye ensy estre ; il est tut besturnée en autre manere : car ceux qe deivent estre principals sount forsclos, et autres gentz de mester seent

---

[1] Stratford's letter is in Avesbury, pp. 324–7, and in *Foedera*, ii, 1143.

[2] It is given in Avesbury, pp. 330–5, Birchington in *Anglia Sacra*, i, 23–7, and in *Foedera*, ii, 1147–8. Rumour was busy as to its authorship, but the responsibility was with the king and his new lay chancellor. [See for this Tout, *Chapters in Administrative History*, v, 124.]

icy en parlement qe ne deivent estre à tiel counseil, mès soulement les peres de la tere qe vous, sire roy, puissent eyder et meintener à nostre graunt bosoigne. Et, sire roy, de çeo devez penser." Et meintenaunt coyement sire Johan Darcy se leva, et s'en ala hors, et puisse après sire William de Killesby et touz les autres susnomez saunz nul mot parler.[1]*

In this silent withdrawal of the leaders of the court party from the parliament house, the struggle was abandoned. The field was left open to the expelled prelates and the barons of high degree. Under their leadership parliament forced upon the king a humiliating submission. To the chronicler the magnates are still the important thing : the commons, though present, are not mentioned. The permanent result of the struggle was the establishment of the doctrine of peerage, and of the right of peers to be summoned to parliament. But the constitution of parliament is beside the present point. What matters for us is that proceedings in parliament are important enough to the London annalist for them to be set down at length. Parliament was beginning to interest the man in the street. It was becoming the focus of public opinion. The court party could not even make a decent fight against the storm of public indignation which the controversy had stirred up.

There was the inevitable set-back after the parliament had gone home. There was no executive action possible when the house had been dissolved. Accordingly the king impudently repudiated his chief concessions and the next parliament condoned with barely a protest his arbitrary action. Thirty years were to elapse before so dramatic a situation was repeated, though most annalists record, however briefly, the doings of the numerous parliaments of those days. A larger measure of publicity was given to the parliament of 1371, when there was again an attack, made this time by parliament, on the clerical ministers who were thought to have mismanaged the French war, which had been renewed with disastrous results in 1369. Five years later the failure of the war and the breakdown of the administration had become notorious. The result was the famous Good Parliament, with whose doings we are especially concerned.

The Good Parliament is out and away the best known of mediæval parliaments. In studying its history we have at our disposal not

---

[1] *French Chronicle of London*, p. 90. Camden Soc. [Cf. Dr. Wilkinson's article on this parliament, *Eng. Hist. Rev.*, xlvi, 177 ff., and M. V. Clarke, *Forfeitures and Treason in 1388* (*Trans. R. Hist. Soc.*, 1931).]

only a parliament roll of forty folio pages.[1]   This roll, in print since
the eighteenth century, is supplemented by three long and independent chronicles.   First printed in 1874, came the elaborate, though
prejudiced, account of the St. Albans *Chronicon Angliae*, 1328–
1388." [2]   This enabled Stubbs in 1875 to piece together from it and
the roll his remarkable account of this parliament.[3]   We have later
had John Malvern's continuation of Higden's Polychronicon, published in 1886,[4] and we shall soon have Mr. Galbraith's edition of
the *Chronicle of St. Mary's Abbey, York*," [5] the proofs of which he
has kindly allowed me to use.   A section of this work, containing a
vivid account of the Peasants' Rising of 1381, has been known
since 1898 from an imperfect Elizabethan transcript,[6] but it is not
too much to say that the York chronicler's account of the Good
Parliament is more than equal to this in importance.   Its narrative
of this parliament is the most valuable contribution to mediæval
parliamentary history which has hitherto been discovered.*

How far does this new material modify our general impression
of the Good Parliament ?   Firstly, it enables us to give what
Stubbs said was impossible on the information before him, namely,
a chronological arrangement of all its chief proceedings.   The
careful and accurate dating of the York chronicler [7] will enable the
future historian to tell day by day with reasonable accuracy the
doings of the Good Parliament.   We may even guess that the St.
Albans chronicler's indifference to dates was not always quite
accidental, but inspired by a wish to make as good a case as he
could against his arch-enemy, the duke of Lancaster.   A special
feature of the St. Mary's Chronicle is the new information given
as to the part played by the commons in the parliament's work

---

[1] *Rotuli Parliamentorum*, ii, 321–60.

[2] *Chronicon Angliae*, 1328–1388, auctore monacho Sancti Albani, ed. E. M.
Thompson, Rolls Series. [There is good reason for thinking that the author was
Thomas Walsingham. See V. H. Galbraith, "Th. Walsingham and the St.
Albans Chronicle " (*Eng. Hist. Rev.*, xlvii (1932), 21).]

[3] *Constitutional History of England*, ii, 448–55.

[4] *Polychronicon Ranulphi Higden*, ed. J. R. Lumby, viii, 355–428, Rolls Series.
The further continuation 1377–94 in *ib.*, ix, 1–283, is not Malvern's work, but comes
from an anonymous monk of Westminster (J. Armitage Robinson, *Proceedings of
British Academy*, iii, 61–92.)

[5] [*The Anonimalle Chronicle of St. Mary's Abbey, York.*   Ed. V. H. Galbraith.
Manchester University Press, 1927.]

[6] See for this G. M. Trevelyan's " Account of the Rising in 1381 " in *Eng. Hist.
Rev.*, xiii, 509–22 (1898).

[7] *Anonimalle Chronicle*, pp. 79–94.

and as to the overwhelming influence and initiative of its speaker, Sir Peter de la Mare.   Until now we have been contented to believe that there was a " total absence of any record of the domestic proceedings of the House of Commons in the Chapter House until its *Journals* begin in 1547." [1]   The York chronicler gives something like a diary of these " domestic proceedings " of the knights and burgesses from the time of their first withdrawal from the " parliament house " for their separate deliberations to the last scene of all, when Sir Peter and the knights gave " une tres graunt et excellent fest en lieu et noune de nostre seignour le roy " to the magnates and burgesses of the realm.   We read with interest how at their first assembly the commons swore to be loyal to each other and treat their deliberations as sacred.   Then " un chevaler del south pais " went to the lectern in the midst of the chapter-house, where all might hear him.   His speech was a denunciation of all new taxation.   Another knight succeeded him at the lectern to revile the courtiers who had destroyed the Calais staple in their quest of personal gain.   A third urged the need of seeking the advice of a committee of lords.   But the one speaker mentioned by name was Sir Peter de la Mare, a knight of the March of Wales and steward of the earl of March.   His eloquence and wisdom led the commons at their third session to choose him by acclamation " davoir la sovereinte de pronuncier leur voluntes en le graunt parlement avaunt les ditz seignours."

Not less vividly are the debates of the " great " or " full " parliament described.   Here the commons normally spoke only through their " speaker," and the magnates necessarily took the lead.   Yet here even Sir Peter could hold his own.   On his first appearance he found that the officials had excluded many of the commons from the house.   The duke of Lancaster, who presided as the king's lieutenant, told him that it was enough if some twelve commoners were present.   But Sir Peter refused to say a word until every

---

[1] Pollard, *Evolution of Parliament*, p. 113.   Even Stubbs unduly disparages the parliament's proceedings :—" These debates, if debates they may be called ; " *Const. Hist.*, ii, 450.   Stubbs gets quite wrong in treating the two divisions in which lords and commons commonly sat as if they were meetings of rival factions, the popular party in the Chapter-house at Westminster Abbey and the " court faction under the duke of Lancaster," sitting as " a distinct contracting party, probably at the Savoy."   The duke was not " president of the council " and Sir Peter did not " lay before the council " his grievances.   He put them before a " full parliament " in which Lancaster acted as the king's representative.

knight and burgess had a chance of taking his place. Duke and magnates were kept waiting two hours while enough commoners were collected to make a good show. Then, and only then, Sir Peter expounded the forward policy of the commons. At every stage his quick brain and bold tongue were at work. Every great change made in the parliament was due to the initiative of the commons expressed through their chosen speaker. But other commoners could, when called upon, raise their voices in the full house, notably the two city aldermen, William Walworth and John Pyall, who could stand up against the duke as well as Sir Peter himself.

These stories show that the art of parliamentary reporting had already begun when a Yorkshire monk could learn in such detail of the deliberations both of the commons and of the full parliament. And it was well that it was employed to chronicle the doings of the assembly of which the chronicler said : " Tiel parlement ne fuist unqes oye avaunt." To most men it was the " good parliament."

This story of the Good Parliament is the more remarkable since the mass of the St. Mary's Chronicle is a very ordinary and commonplace example of the humdrum monastic annalist. Only on one other occasion does the monk of York write with the vividness which suggests a real piece of literature. This was when he tells us the tale of the Peasants' Revolt of 1381 by which up to now he has alone been known. Mr. Galbraith refuses to believe that these two pieces of true history could have come from the compiler of the bulk of the chronicle. They were bodily copied, he thinks, from some lost work of exceptional merit. Be this as it may, there is significance in the fact that such narratives could be written, and it is more significant that they should be the passages selected for extraction. It is an accident that they have survived in a single manuscript, lurking in the obscurity of a Yorkshire country house and virtually unknown since the seventeenth century.

Other sources corroborate the monk of St. Mary's account of the Good Parliament. The St. Albans monk is in essential agreement with him, and he may well have got his information from the Bedfordshire knight who was at pains to tell him the wonderful dream that encouraged to persistence both himself and his friends.[1] The testimony of John Malvern, monk of Worcester, is brief but confirmatory. He also speaks of the admiration of all auditors for the eloquence and wisdom of Sir Peter de la Mare and tells us that

---

[1] *Chronicon Angliae*, pp. 70–2.

many poems or songs were composed in his honour : " De quo et factis suis habitis per tempus illud multa metrice valde subtiliter erant composita." [1]* It was always the popular favourite that was commemorated with song. Sir Peter is the first representative of the commons in parliament on whom this honour has been bestowed. It shows that popular opinion was behind the Good Parliament, and that the commons' leader was its hero.

The unanimity of the orders is a special note of the Good Parliament. It is immaterial to be meticulous as to the share which lords and commons took in its acts. It is vital to emphasize the solidarity of the whole parliament in the common cause of restoring order and sound rule. Their common knighthood ensured community of social interest between the lay magnates and the shire representatives. The clerical magnates shared with the lay barons the rights of " peers of the realm," and apart from a few earls of commanding position, there was no clear social or economic line between the various grades. The bishops and abbots were of different social classes, but were as much " peers " as the duke of Lancaster. And apart from a limited circle of grandees whom every king was bound to summon, the lords shaded into the commons by varying social gradations. There were still " lords of parliament " whose summons to parliament was by no means always renewed to their heirs. A note of this period is the prominence of the " bannerets " as lords of parliament. The " baneretes de valeur " are mentioned by the St. Mary's Chronicle as appearing in this parliament,[2] and later we read how the " bannerets " were regularly represented in the councils which supported the minority of Richard II. Some of them became the sources of later hereditary baronies ; others seem to have been what we call in modern phrase " life peers " : sometimes the same person was called at one time " baron," at another time a " banneret." And among the knights were already men who were in the way of becoming peers, and sat alternately with either group.[3] Even the citizens were in wealth, if not in social rank, equated with the magnates, when for instance a poll tax was

---

[1] *Malvern,* p. 385.   [2] *Anon. Chron.,* p. 79.

[3] The parliamentary history of the bannerets is short but needs investigation. Professor Pollard at one time seems to suggest they were a section of the commons, p. 141. The doctrine of Elsynge about bannerets summoned by special writs (*Ib.*, pp. 94–5) is quite sound within limits. They clearly sat among the magnates and were often included in the committees of lords appointed to advise the commons at the opening of most sessions.

soon afterwards assessed on each man according to his means. This solidarity of the landowning and propertied classes, assembled in a common parliament, is one of the chief reasons why the English parliaments escaped the fate of insignificance and extinction that was the lot of the estates of some of her continental neighbours. That same solidarity extended to the substantial part of the nation outside the walls of parliament. Whenever, led by the magnates, public opinion agreed, the Crown was powerless. But the barons invariably broke up into factions as soon as they had gained a victory. Hence the inevitable reaction that always followed the triumph of parliament.

There was no executive agency to carry out the wishes of a parliament after its dissolution. There was indeed a staff of parliamentary clerks, receivers of petitions and the like : but the whole staffing of parliament was done by the chancery, and a chancellor not afraid to oppose the king was the condition precedent of administrative efficiency. John of Gaunt's measures to frustrate the work of the Good Parliament showed that he or his household well understood the manipulation of public opinion. If the lords were independent, fear, flattery or persuasion might move the commons. Afraid at first of the commons, John summoned a great council of barons which undid the Good Parliament's work, impeached William of Wykeham and restored the courtiers to place and power. Master of the government, Lancaster was able to pack the parliament of 1377 with his dependants and to procure the election of one of his stewards as its speaker.[1] The complaisance of the new commons, in which few members of the Good Parliament found seats, turned outside opinion towards the lords. The St. Albans chronicler calls the knights " pussillanimes," " aberrantes a vero," and tells us that the " communis plebs " outside parliament wished to hang Latimer, Lyons and the other culprits whom the commons had restored.[2]

[1] *Chron. Angliae*, p. 112. " Milites vero de comitatibus quos dux pro arbitrio surrogaverat (nam omnes qui in ultimo parliamento viriliter pro communitate steterant procuravit pro viribus amoveri ; ita quod non fuerunt ex illis in hoc parliamento praeter duodecim, quos dux amovere non potuit, eo quod comitatus de quibus electi fuerant alios eligere noluerunt)." * This is accurate but a slight overstatement : only eight knights of 1376 sat in 1377, and three of these were for Leicestershire and Lancashire who were probably returned by his influence on the earlier occasion. [Cf., however, Col. J. C. Wedgewood, " John of Gaunt and the Packing of Parliament," in *Eng. Hist. Rev.*, xlv (1930), 623–5.]

[2] *Ib.*, pp. 130–1. It is unfortunate that a missing leaf of the York Chronicle makes it impossible for us to know its views on this parliament.

The lords saved the situation by their pertinacity and Lancaster dissolved parliament lest worse should happen.

The first years of Richard II's reign gave plenty of scope for parliamentary action. No regent was appointed and a boy of ten was more incompetent to govern than a dotard of seventy. The power of John of Gaunt had been shaken by his recent failures, and supreme control was open to any faction strong enough to combine and take a line. At first it looked as if the policy of the Good Parliament was to be revived, for the first parliament, which met in July 1377, had Sir Peter de la Mare as speaker of the commons and demanded the appointment of ministers in parliament during the minority. But it was again too weak to procure the execution of its wishes and the remedy of a " continual council," as a sort of collective sovereign, proved ineffective, because rival factions balanced each other in the various councils that were appointed. The worst sign of all was the general refusal of everyone to undertake responsibility. Both ministers and continual councillors tried to fortify themselves behind the approval of parliament, so that in the twelve years between 1377 and 1388 the young king convoked fifteen full parliaments. When these proved unmanageable, " great councils " of magnates, summoned by Privy Seal, were brought together, but these gladly turned the responsibility for action on to parliament.

Parliament itself was as blameworthy as those who sought to invoke its authority. It weakly fell in with the desire of the magnates to wage vigorous war against France, but refused adequate supplies to pay for it. There was harmony between magnates and commons in denouncing maladministration : but the only remedies for it that were attempted proved entirely useless. So disgusted were the commons of 1380 with " continual councils " that they demanded their discharge and invited the king to govern through ministers appointed in parliament with the help of a parliamentary commission, which was mainly different from the old council in being parliamentary.

For a moment there seemed peace. A parliament, which met at Northampton in November 1380, passed a handsome vote of confidence in the ministers and granted the fatal poll tax which was the immediate cause of the Peasants' Revolt of 1381. The insurgents showed the existence of a new form of public opinion, which, though unrepresented in parliaments or by writers, was able to express its teaching in letters of blood. But as soon as the rebellion was suppressed, the old game of remonstrance and protest went on as before. The same remedies of councils, commissions of inquiry and ministerial nomination in parliament were tried over again and were as ineffective as ever. None of the governing classes had learnt any wisdom from the revolt.

Public opinion was now becoming increasingly indifferent to parliaments. Let us quote two chroniclers' verdicts on parliaments of these days. First we will hear what the St. Albans chronicler says of one of the parliaments of 1382.[1]

Multa sunt et alia quae statuta sunt ibidem. Sed quid juvat statuta parliamentorum scribere, cum penitus ex post nullum sortiantur effectum? Rex nempe, cum privato concilio, cuncta vel mutare vel delere solebat quae in parliamentis antehabitis tota regni non solum communitas sed et ipsa nobilitas statuebat.*

This was when parliament agreed : but in the years after 1381 parliaments were generally made futile by angry and quarrelsome factions. In the two parliaments of 1384 there was constant dissension. In the Salisbury parliament of the spring the Westminster chronicler tells us how " tam viri ecclesiastici quam domini temporales inter se mirabiliter adversantes effectum parliamenti pæne frustrabant." [2] Of the November parliament he says :

In isto vero parliamento pro commodo regni nihil utile fuit actum quia domini temporales quibus competit loqui pro statu et commodo regni adinvicem adversantes, semper eo tempore discordes fuere, ac eo finito in discordia recesserunt.[3]**

There is no wonder that the young king should develop a contempt for parliaments and that his subjects' faith in them grew slack. When in 1385 parliament sent up its usual demands for a view of the household or for the nomination of ministers, Richard haughtily answered that he would do what he was asked when he pleased.[4] He was now adolescent and had surrounded himself by a group of courtiers, headed by his bosom friend, Robert de Vere, Earl of Oxford, and inspired by his old tutor, Sir Simon Burley, under-chamberlain. The old ministers either gave up office in disgust, like Sir Richard le Scrope, or went over to the court party,

---

[1] *Chron. Angliae*, p. 333.
[2] *Monk of Westminster*, pp. 32-3, in Higden's Polychronicon, vol. ix.
[3] *Ib.*, p. 52.   [4] *Rot. Parl.*, iii, 213.

like Sir Michæl de la Pole, the chancellor, who was made earl of Suffolk. Public opinion now saw that the real danger was in the new court party. Even their wiser acts, such as seeking a reconciliation with France, were looked upon as treasonable.

The only effective opposition to the court party was a league of magnates. In 1386 the departure of John of Gaunt in quest of the Castilian throne removed the most incalculable of personal influences from practical politics. In the face of danger there was then brought about the reconstruction of the aristocratic opposition under the leadership of the king's youngest uncle, Thomas, duke of Gloucester, and with the support of the heir of Lancaster, Henry, earl of Derby, and of bishops like Wykeham of Winchester and Thomas Arundel of Ely.

The effects of this were soon seen in the parliament of 1386. Parliament was once more unanimous and was soon able to reduce the court to impotence. It superseded the royalist ministers by its own nominees, putting the bishop of Ely, brother of the earl of Arundel, into the chancery, impeaching and condemning the former chancellor, the earl of Suffolk, and appointing a commission of eleven magnates to co-operate with the ministers in the overhaul of the whole administration. Richard's resistance was overborne, but as soon as parliament was dissolved he took active steps to upset its decisions.

For the greater part of 1387 Richard wandered about the country, organizing a party of armed opposition to the decrees of parliament. He showed, however, enough respect for public opinion to try and get parliament and the law on his side. A chronicler tells us how he tried to persuade the sheriffs to raise troops and pack a new parliament for him.

Vicecomites convenire fecit ut sciret quantam potentiam possent contrahere contra barones, et ut ipsi nullum militem de pago vel de shira permitterent eligi ad parliamentum, nisi quem rex et ejus consilium eligissent. Ad quem vicecomites dixerunt quod communes faverent dominis, nec esse in potestate illorum ad hanc causam exercitum contrahendi. De militibus ad parliamentum eligendis dixerunt, communes velle tenere usitatas consuetudines quae volunt ut a communibus milites eligantur.[1]*

For us the interest of this is that the king's attempt to influence public opinion entirely failed. He returned to London in Novem-

---

[1] *Monk of Evesham*, p. 85 ; *Chron. Angliae*, p. 379.

ber and surrendered unconditionally to the baronial leaders, who had gathered with a strong force in the suburbs of the capital to oppose him. He allowed the opposition lords, henceforth called the lords appellant, to accuse the five chief courtiers of treason, and summoned a parliament to deal with the accusation against them. It was in vain that the duke of Ireland appealed to arms. He could not find enough followers to make a decent show of resistance. Before the end of the year he and his friends were exiles or fugitives. In the great appeal to public opinion, as in the appeal to arms, the baronage had beaten the court.

The parliament which consummated the baronial triumph sat from 3 February to 4 June 1388 at Westminster. It proscribed the court party with such thoroughness that men called it the Merciless or the Wonderful Parliament.[1] The tragic doings of this ferocious assembly were in themselves enough to ensure the attention of the chroniclers, who are all hotly on the side of the barons and bitterly opposed to the favourites. Their narratives are the more copious since the lengthy articles of accusation against the favourites afforded them useful material for a long account that cost them little trouble. Their personal contributions to the story are not remarkable.[2] For instance, the most elaborate of them, the monk of Westminster, is so careless or hurried that he copies out two different narratives of the doings of parliament, without in the least noticing that the two sometimes differ from each other.

In the widespread currency of the articles of accusation we may see the effectiveness of baronial propaganda. We have more direct evidence that, both at the time and later, there was a deliberate effort to educate public opinion to take up the baronial cause. The most immediate proof of this is the recently discovered history of Thomas Favent, which is clearly strictly contemporary. The persistence with which the propaganda was planned until and after the fall of Richard II can be best studied in the political poetry of John Gower. Let us take these in turn.

---

[1] Knighton, II, 249, Rolls Series: " Et vocabatur parliamentum istud parliamentum sine misericordia; nec alicui misericordiam faceret sine consensu dominorum."* Thomas Favent's little *Historia sive narratio de modo et forma mirabilis parliamenti* dates this " wonderful parliament " in 1386: but the contents show that he really means the parliament of 1388.

[2] [For new evidence from the chronicles see M. V. Clarke and V. H. Galbraith, " Deposition of Richard II," *Bulletin of John Rylands Library*, vol. 14 (1930), pp. 125 ff.]

There survives in a manuscript of the Bodleian library [1] a curious
roll entitled "·Historia sive Narratio de Modo et Forma Mirabilis
Parliamenti apud Westmonasterium, anno Domini millesimo
CCCLXXXVJ, regni vero regis Ricardi post conquestum secundi anno
decimo, per Thomam Fauent clericum indictata." This document
was acquired by Bodley in the early seventeenth century and had
some notoriety in the days of the struggle of Charles I and his
parliament. Then parliamentary pamphleteers, seeing a sufficiently near parallel between Charles I and Richard II, thought
that it was worth while to use the analogy to encourage a strenuous
resistance to the king. Accordingly in 1641, when the Great Civil
War was becoming inevitable, a rude English version was set forth
in a pamphlet, which, however, made no mention of the original
nor of its provenance. This tract has several times been reprinted
in the great collections of pamphlets, but has seldom attracted the
notice of historians of Richard II. Luckily Miss May McKisack
of Somerville College, Oxford, lighted upon the original recently
and is about to publish it in a forthcoming volume of the *Camden
Miscellany* for the Royal Historical Society.[2] I am indebted to her
for a knowledge of it and for the use of the transcript which she
has prepared for the printer.

As to Thomas Favent, or rather Fovant, little can be gathered.
I suspect him to have been a clerk attached to the household of
one of the lords appellant, but the few particulars one can glean
of his personal history throw no light upon his personal position
or political activities. He was, however, certainly a Wiltshire man,
who took his surname from the village of Fovant, half-way between
Salisbury and Shaftesbury. His family held property in Fovant
and its neighbourhood and seems to have been locally important.
A kinswoman, Cicely Fovant, perhaps a sister, became abbess of the
great nunnery of Shaftesbury and founded in 1406 a chantry in
memory of her father Robert and mother Edith, who may well
have also been the parents of Thomas.[3] Thomas himself obtained
in 1393 an indult from Boniface VIII to choose his own confessor [4]
and in 1400 received a " ratification of his estate " in the church of

---

[1] Bodleian Miscellaneous MSS., No. 2963 ; see also *Summary Catalogue of Western
MSS. in the Bodleian Library. Seventeenth Century.* Part I, p. 557.

[2] [*Camden Miscellany*, vol. xiv, 1926.]

[3] *Cal. Patent Rolls 1405–1408*, p. 266.

[4] *Cal. Papal Registers, Letters*, iv, 495.

Dinton, a couple of miles north of Fovant, and a village held by
the abbess of Shaftesbury of the Crown.[1] This last grant suggests
a disturbance of Thomas in the quiet holding of his benefice, such
as would naturally result in the later years of Richard II's reign in
the case of a violent Lancastrian partisan.

Favent wrote so soon after the victory of the Merciless Parliament, that he was ignorant of the shortness of its triumph. He
clearly had not even cognizance of the miserable deaths of the chief
Ricardian partisans in their exile. His " history " is on the face
of it a political pamphlet, written in Latin, and therefore addressed
to clerical and educated circles, and aiming at glorifying rather than
apologizing for the work of the lords appellant.. Despite its one-
sidedness, it is well informed and not inaccurate. After the York
chronicler's account of the debates of the Good Parliament, I am
inclined to place Favent's pamphlet next in importance, as giving
us a vivid picture of the procedure of a fourteenth-century parliament. It is the more instructive since the nature of the case compels him to stress the deliberations of the " full parliament " before
which were brought most of the judicial acts with which the parliament was chiefly concerned. Though giving few new facts of
great moment, it paints in turgid colour scenes that are hard to
imagine from the cold records.

Particularly instructive is Favent's description of the opening
scenes in the White Hall of Westminster Palace. The young king
is seated on his throne. On his right sit the dignitaries of the
Church ; on his left the lay magnates " secundum antiquam parliamenti consuetudinem." To them, attended by a numerous train,
the five lords appellant " una secta, vestibus aureis, alterius amplexis
brachiis, aulam intrarunt, intuentes autem unanimiter genuflectando
salutarunt regem." * The hall was now packed : " una vero
hominum congluvies inibi fuerat usque in angulos." There were
" omnes utriusque status proceres et egregii hujus regni " ; there
were also, of course, the commons at the Bar.[2] Then the chancellor,
standing behind the king, expounded the reasons for the summoning
of parliament. After this was heard the mouthpiece of the appel-

[1] *Cal. Patent Rolls 1399–1401*, p. 138 ; *Feudal Aids*, v, 212.
[2] I interpret Favent in the light of Monk of Westminster, p. 157. " Le roy seant
en plein parlement et touz les seignurs temporelx et espirituelx steant entour luy,
et les communes esteantz a le barre. . . ."**Compare Pollard, *Evolution of Parliament*, and especially his interesting prints of parliaments in session at much
later dates.

lants, Sir Robert Pleasington, smarting from his dismissal as chief baron of the Exchequer, and soon Geoffrey Martin, clerk of the Crown,[1] read rapidly, for two hours on end, the lengthy articles of the appeal. The auditors listened with emotion : " Quorundam vero corda concussa sunt mesticia propter inhorribilia in dictis articulis contenta. Et plures vultus turgidos dederunt cum lacrimis in maxillis." It was a striking scene, rivalling in vividness the York chronicler's narrative of the debates of the commons in 1376.

In due time the culprits were sentenced, and bloody reprisals atoned for the royalists' war against the parliament of 1386. The only debates were as to the extent to which mercy was to be shown. That some of the culprits got off lightly was due to divisions among the appellants. The commons were on the side of severity.

The poets were pressed into the service of publicity. But not the greatest of them all. Geoffrey Chaucer was a household official and therefore exposed to popular condemnation. As knight of the shire for Kent, he had sat with the commons of 1386 and, as a powerless member of a court minority, had been one of the silent victims of its policy of retrenchment. But the permanent official generally went on his way without much regard to politics. Chaucer was too prudent to be a politician and perhaps prided himself on his aloofness. It was otherwise with his friend John Gower, whose more pedestrian muse was largely attuned to the politics of the hour. His earliest long poem deals with the Peasants' Revolt, and his longest Latin poem, written at the king's request, shows the gradual decay of his faith in Richard and his growing devotion to Henry of Derby and the appellants, a devotion expressed in the later version by its change of dedication from the king to the earl and culminating in the *Chronica Tripartita* which is a poetical party pamphlet against the favourites. Langland, again, in his " Richard the Redeless," is equally angry

---

[1] I have spoken of the control of parliamentary procedure by the chancery whose clerks received and classified all petitions, drafted its official records and had the larger share in the composition of the statutes which embodied the final conclusions of parliament. The clerk of parliament was an important personage, was always a senior chancery clerk, and another chancery clerk assisted him as clerk of the commons. The " clerks of the Crown " had also an important position in parliament and they also were chancery clerks. The popular sympathies of the chancery clerks who managed Richard II's parliaments are well marked. To the name of Martin himself may be added those of John Waltham and John Scarle. [For Martin see also Tout, *Collected Papers*, II (*cit. supra*), p. 163.]

with the king and his policy. Though none of these writers has much to say about parliaments, they are at one in upholding the policy of the barons which secured parliament's support.

We must turn to another quarter for clear literary evidence of the growing interest in parliament. But there is certainly a proof of this in the remarkable vogue of the strange tract called *Modus tenendi Parliamentum*, of which the extremely large number of surviving manuscripts attest how eagerly it was studied. The oldest of those manuscripts belong to the age of Richard. Much has been written about this tract, but the fundamental problem of its date is difficult and is not likely to be authoritatively settled. Yet it is impossible to imagine an author so possessed of the gift of prophecy as to have written it before the crisis of 1340–1. It is more likely that it emerged from the struggles of the period with which we are concerned.* Even at that date the ascription of the title " peers " to all of the " six grades " of parliament and the assumption that the lower clergy participated in the normal sessions suggest a somewhat archaic doctrine. However that may be, its popularity adds to the testimony that men's faith in parliament was then high.

That faith was soon to be rudely shattered. Powerful as was parliament as an expression of public opinion, the whole history of these years shows it incapable of government because it had no means of executing its decisions. The happy accident which drove Richard II from Westminster in 1387, leaving the administration in the hands of a popularly elected chancellor, treasurer, and keeper of the Privy Seal, did allow the constitutionalists the control of the executive for a brief period and so made easy the bloodthirsty victory of the Merciless Parliament in 1388. Yet victory as usual split up the baronial ranks and it needed but an easy exercise of the royal will to remove the baronially appointed ministers in 1389. These ministers had done so little that a reasonable amount of prudence might well have ensured for Richard II the control of the state for the rest of his life. It was only because of his mad excesses in despotism in 1397, that he provoked the reaction which in 1399 cost him his throne and his life. Thus without even the exception of 1387–8, the parliamentary attempts at the control of the administration were invariably failures, not only between 1376 and 1381, but even after 1399, when the leader of the appellants had become king by a parliamentary title.   As instruments of a united baronage, or as backers of a popular king, parliaments could do much ; save that in times of deep political feeling they were often liable to be manipulated or coerced.   Mediæval life was too rude and primitive for there to be any real anticipation of modern parliamentary conditions. " Governance " was what England needed and that was exactly what parliament could not give it.   It suggests the real vitality of English parliaments that, with all their faults, they seemed to make a clear appeal to English public opinion.   If the evidence available to demonstrate this point is not always very convincing, some of it is quite new, and it is at least better than what we generally have when we attempt to show the relations of opinion to political action during the later Middle Ages.

12

THE PARLIAMENTARY COMMITTEE
1398*

by J. G. Edwards

IN the constitutional history of the last two puzzling years
of Richard II's reign there is nothing which has attracted so
much attention as the committee of eighteen set up in the parliament of Shrewsbury in January 1398, the committee whose
appointment led Stubbs to stigmatize the Shrewsbury assembly
as a ' suicidal parliament '.[1] Yet none of the current accounts of
the committee is altogether clear about either its powers or its
purpose, and both points are of sufficient interest to warrant
further investigation. There has always been some doubt about
the terms of its appointment. As is well known, one of the
accusations made against Richard II at his deposition was that

in parliamento ultimo celebrato apud Salop., idem rex proponens opprimere
populum suum procuravit subtiliter et fecit concedi, quod potestas parliamenti de consensu omnium statuum regni sui remaneret apud quasdam
certas personas, ad terminandum dissoluto parliamento certas petitiones
in eodem parliamento porrectas protunc minime expeditas. Cuius concessionis colore persone sic deputate processerunt ad alia generaliter
parliamentum illud tangentia, et hoc de voluntate regis, in derogationem
status parliamenti et in magnum incommodum totius regni et perniciosum
exemplum. Et ut super factis eorum huiusmodi aliquem colorem et auc-
toritatem viderentur hàbere, rex fecit rotulos parliamenti pro voto suo
mutari et deleri, contra effectum concessionis predicte.[2] **

Hallam[3] and Stubbs,[4] while noting this accusation, did not
definitely accept it as true. Dr. Tait, however, subsequently
pointed out in his article on Richard II in the *Dictionary of
National Biography* that the roll of the parliament of 1397–8
survives in three manuscript copies, two of which express the

---

[1] *Const. Hist.* (4th ed.), ii. 522.   [2] *Rot. Parl.* iii. 418.
[3] *Middle Ages* (12th ed.), iii. 78.   [4] *Loc. cit.*

committee's powers in narrower terms than the third copy, from which the printed version of the roll was taken ; this fact, he argued, ' raises a strong presumption in favour of the charge of interpolation afterwards brought against Richard '. As Dr. Tait only touched the point in this brief fashion, a few additional particulars may be given here.

The available information about the committee is contained chiefly in three separate records. Firstly, there is the parliament roll of 1397–8, which survives in the Public Record Office in three copies, catalogued as Parliament Rolls nos. 57, 58, and 59. Then there is the roll of pleas of the Crown in the same parliament, of which there are two copies, catalogued in the Record Office as Parliament Rolls nos. 60 and 61. Lastly there is the statute roll, of which there are two copies, numbered 3 and 4, in the Public Record Office. The three copies of the parliament roll are worth comparing in more detail. Two of them, nos. 58 and 59, are for all practical purposes duplicates, and they differ in several material points from no. 57, which is evidently the original from which the printed version was taken. One difference is that nos. 58 and 59 stop with a record of certain events which occurred on 19 March 1398, whereas no. 57 goes further and adds an account of some business transacted on 18 March 1399. Another difference is that nos. 58 and 59 give the committee much narrower powers than no. 57 purports to give. It will be remembered that when the eighteen persons were constituted into a committee in January 1398 they were entrusted with two distinct tasks. On the one hand they were instructed to ' terminate and finally discuss ' the accusations brought by Hereford against Norfolk ; their powers in this matter are stated in identical terms by all three copies of the parliament roll and also by the two copies of the roll of pleas of the Crown in parliament.[1] But the committee was also entrusted with other business as well : they were to deal with certain petitions left unanswered by parliament owing to shortness of time. It is here that the terms of reference as stated by rolls 58 and 59 differ from the version given by no. 57. In roll 58 (and also in roll 59, except for differences of spelling) the record is as follows :

[Margin.] Poair commis pur terminer peticions.[2]

Item mesme le Jeody le darrein iour de parlement les communes prierent au roy qe come ils eient deuers eux diuerses peticions sibien pur especiales persons come autres nient luz et responduz et queux pur briftee du temps ne purront bonement estre terminez a cest foiz durant le temps de cest present parlement, qe plerroit au roy commetter pleine poair as certeins seignurs et autres persons qe luy plerra de examiner respondre et

[1] *Rot. Parl.* iii. 360 (54), 382 (11).

[2] In no. 59 the marginal entry reads, ' Poair pur terminer peticions apres le parlement '.

terminer les ditz peticions et les matiers contenuz en ycelles. Sur quoy
nostre seignur le roy par auctorite et assent du parlement ad ordeine
et assigne . . . [18 persons named] . . . de examiner, respondre et pleinement
terminer touz les ditz peticions et les matiers contenuz en ycelles come
lour meux semblera par lour bon advys et discrecion en celle partie par
auctorite du parlement susdit.

In roll 57 the corresponding entry reads thus [1] (words which
do not appear in rolls 58 and 59 are here italicized) :

[Margin.] Poair commys pur terminer petitions *et autres choses*.
Item mesme le Joefdy les communes prierent au roi qe come ils aient
deuers eux diuerses petitions, si bien pur especials persones come autres
nient luez ne responduz, *et auxi pleuseurs autres matiers et choses aient
estee moevez en presence du roy, lesqueux* pur briefte du temps ne purront
bonement estre terminez *a present*, qe plerroit au roy commettre plein
poair as certeines seignurs et autres persones queux luy plerra dexaminer
respondre et terminer les ditz petitions et les matiers *et choses suis ditz
et toutes les dependences dicelles. A quel prier le roy sassenti. Et sur ceo*, par
auctorite et assent du parlement ad ordine et assigne . . . [18 persons
named] . . . de examiner, respondre et pleinement terminer *si bien* toutz
les ditz petitions et les matiers *comprisez* en ycelles *come toutes autres
matiers et choses moevez en presence du roy et toutes les dependences dicelles
nient determinez solonc ceo qe* meulx lour semblera par lour bon advys et
discretion en celle partie par auctorite du parlement suis dit. *

This entry in roll 57 is made without any interlineations or alterations. At a slightly later stage in the parliament roll of 1397–8
the committee's powers for dealing with petitions are once more
recited by way of preamble to a record of the petitions which
the committee, in pursuance of their powers, examined and
answered after the dissolution of parliament. Here again precisely the same variations appear in the terms of reference.
Roll 58 (and roll 59, except for differences of spelling) reads thus :

Fait a remembrer qe come nostre seignur le roy a la requeste des communes de mesme le parlement eantz deuers eux diuerses peticions si bien
pur especialx persones come autres nient luez ne responduz et queux pur
briefte du temps ne purront bonement estre terminez durant le temps
du parlement, eit ordeine et assigne par auctorite et assent du dit parlement . . . [18 persons named] . . . de examiner respoundre et pleinement
terminer touz les ditz peticions et les matiers contenues en ycelles come
lour meulx semblera par lour bone advis et discrecion en celle partie
par auctoritee du dit parlement come plus pleinement appiert desus en
le rolle du parlement etc. etc.

Roll 57, on the other hand, reads as follows [2] (words which do not
appear in rolls 58 and 59 are italicized as before) :

Fait a remembrer qe come nostre seignur le roy, a la request des communes de mesme le parlement aiantz deuers eux diuerses petitions si bien

---

[1] Printed in *Rot. Parl.* iii. 368 (74).   [2] Printed *ibid.* p. 369 (80).

pur especiales persones come autres nient luez ne responduz, *et auxi pleuseurs autres matires et choses aient este moeuez en presence du roy lesqueux* pur briefte de temps ne purroient *alors* estre terminez, ait ordinez et assignez par auctorite du parlement . . . [18 persons named] . . . dexaminer, respondre et pleinement terminer *si bien* toutes les ditz petitions et les matirs *comprises* en ycelles *come toutes autres matires et choses moeuez en presence du roy et toutes les dependences dicelles nient determinez solonc ceo qe* meulx lour semblera par lour bon advys et discretion [en] celle partie par auctorite du dit parlement, come plus pleinement appiert etc. etc.

This passage appears in roll 57 without any interlineations or alterations. It fortunately happens that this record of the petitions examined and answered by the committee after the dissolution of parliament is also entered on the statute roll.[1] The version there given—in both copies of the statute roll in the Public Record Office—agrees verbatim with that of Parliament Rolls 58 and 59, thereby establishing their authenticity as against roll 57. Other evidence shows, too, that rolls 58 and 59 are earlier in date, as well as more authoritative in form, than roll 57. Thus rolls 58 and 59 end, as already noticed, with certain business transacted in March 1398, whereas roll 57, which is written throughout in the same hand, mentions events which happened a year later. On several occasions, moreover, words and passages which appear in rolls 58 and 59 as additions or alterations come in roll 57 in the body of the text. Taken together, these various facts—that roll 57 is subsequent to rolls 58 and 59, and that it purports to give the committee wider powers than are given by the other two rolls—all point to the same conclusion. There can be little doubt that roll 57, from which the printed version was taken, is not an original roll. The authentic record of the parliament of 1397–8 is represented by rolls 58 and 59. Roll 57 is an altered version drawn up at some date after (probably soon after) 18 March 1399.

It is worth noticing that the differences between roll 57 and the other two rolls are in number but few. Beyond the variations in the terms of the committee's powers only two differences are of any interest. In its account of the first session of the parliament in September 1397, roll 57 records the following as one of the decisions made :

Auxint nostre seignur le roy par lassent suis dit ad ordeinez et establiz qe toutz les juggementz, ordenances, declarations et establissementz faitz en cest present parlement soient tenuz et declarez pur estatutz et tiegnent force et uigour destatut en toutz pointz.[2] *

This passage duly appears in the other two rolls, but in roll 58 it is quite clearly, and in roll 59 less clearly, an insertion in different

---

[1] *Statutes of the Realm*, ii. 107.   [2] Printed in *Rot. Parl.* iii. 354 (32).

ink. It does not appear at all in the corresponding portion of
the statute roll.[1] Again, in its account of the session at Shrewsbury,
after recording the oaths taken by the lords spiritual and temporal
and affirmed by the proctors of the clergy and a great part of the
commons, to maintain the judgements and ordinances of that
parliament for ever, roll 57 has these words :

> Et puis apres proclamation feust fait en audience de tout le pœple pur
> sauoir sils uorroient consentir a ceste manere de seuretee; a quel ils respon-
> derent, adresceantz en haut leur maines dextres et criantz oue hautes
> uoices qil lour plest bien et qils sont a ceo pleinement assentuz.[2]*

This passage does not appear in rolls 58 and 59. But with these
two exceptions, the only important differences between the
altered roll 57 and the authentic rolls 58 and 59 are those which
concern the powers of the committee. The charge made against
Richard II of falsifying the parliament roll in order to give the
committee a semblance of wider powers is therefore substantially
justified by the facts. It follows that the parliament of 1398, in
setting up the committee, did not really intend to be 'suicidal';
the powers which were actually granted to the committee were,
as Hume long ago remarked, 'limited in the object'.[3]

The question now arises, What use did Richard propose to make
of the committee with its ostensibly widened powers? Did he
intend it as a permanent substitute for parliament? This
question has been variously answered. Hallam asserts roundly
that 'these eighteen commissioners, or some of them . . . usurped
the full rights of the legislature'.[4] Other writers, however, like
Wallon[5] and Dr. Tait,[6] speak with more reserve. It may help
to clear the ground if we endeavour to determine what use Richard
is known to have actually made of the committee during the period
of its existence. Definite accounts of its doings appear to survive
only in the parliament roll of 1397–8, the roll of pleas of the Crown
in the same parliament, and the statute roll of 21 Richard II.
From these sources one learns something of its proceedings on
five separate occasions. The first occasion is on 19 March 1398,
when the king and the committee sat at Bristol. At this meeting
two items of business are recorded to have been transacted.
Five petitions left undetermined by the late parliament were
examined and answered.[7] The first was a petition from the merchants complaining of the inconveniences of certain regulations
made in 1397 with the intention of maintaining good coinage.

---

[1] See *Stats. of the Realm*, ii. 101.
[2] Printed in *Rot. Parl.* iii. 360.   [3] *History of England* (ed. 1770), iii. 37.
[4] *Loc. cit.*   [5] *Richard II*, ii. 204.
[6] *Dict. Nat. Biog.* xlviii. 153.
[7] *Rot. Parl.* iii. 369–72. The text, though printed from roll 57, is quite authentic
except for the version of the committee's powers given in the preamble.

The second was a petition from the commons complaining that shoemakers were tanning leather contrary to a statute of 1390.[1] The third was from the commons complaining of the royal licences which enabled merchants to evade the regulations of the staple. The fourth was from the treasurer of Calais, stating that certain repairs and improvements were required in the harbour there, and asking that the cost might be met by levying various dues on ships using the harbour. The fifth was from the commons, complaining that the rivers of England were being obstructed by weirs and similar erections, so that boats could not freely ply for purposes of trade. To the first petition about the coinage regulations answer was made that the king would put things right by communicating with his officers at Calais. The other four petitions were met by drawing up ' certain ordinances and statutes ', five in number, which are duly enrolled in the statute roll.[2] So far as is known, these five ' statutes and ordinances ' are the only legislation made by the king with the assent of the committee. Four of them answer to the four petitions just mentioned : one forbids shoemakers to tan leather ; the second prohibits any one from breaking the staple regulations unless he have the special licence of the king himself ; the third makes provision for the repair and maintenance of Calais harbour ; the fourth provides for the clearing of obstructions from rivers.

All these were quite minor matters, and obviously cannot be regarded as exceeding the powers that had really been given to the committee by parliament. The fifth of these ' statutes and ordinances ', however, is at first sight more serious. The king, ' by the same assent of the said lords and knights of shires so assigned by the said authority of the parliament ', willed and ordained that if any person should endeavour to procure the repeal of the said statutes or ordinances made by the king with the assent of the said lords and knights (i.e. the four ' statutes and ordinances ' already mentioned), and the fact be duly proved in parliament, then that person should be punished as a traitor, in the same manner as those who should endeavour to procure the repeal of the statutes and ordinances made while the parliament was actually sitting. This fifth statute is in form rather a startling assumption of power by the committee. In substance, however, it was no more than an affirmation of the statute already made by the parliament itself, that any one who should endeavour to repeal any statutes or ordinances made in that parliament, or any part of them in any manner, should be adjudged a traitor.[3] With the exception of this fifth statute, which was objectionable, however, rather in form than in substance, the statutes and

---

[1] See *Stats. of the Realm*, ii. 65. [2] *Ibid*. pp. 107–10.
[3] *Ibid*. p. 99.

ordinances known to have been made by the king and the committee seem to have been quite harmless and well within the
powers really granted to the committee by parliament. To say
with Hallam that the committee ' usurped the full rights of the
legislature ' is an exaggeration. The second piece of business
transacted by the committee at Bristol on 19 March 1398 was
to consider the accusations of Hereford against Norfolk. The
king, ' by the advice of those who had authority of the parliament ', decided that if sufficient proofs were not found, the matter
should be settled by battle.[1]

The second occasion on which we hear of the committee at
work is at Windsor on 29 April 1398. On that day Hereford
and Norfolk appeared, and as no sufficient proofs of Hereford's
accusations had been found in the meantime, it was decided,
' both by the advice of the dukes, earls, barons, bannerets and
chivalry of England in great number assembled for this same
cause, and also of those who had authority of the parliament ',
that the two should join battle.[2]

The third occasion on which the committee appears in the
records is at Coventry on 16 September 1398, when Hereford
and Norfolk met to do battle. As is well known, the fight was
prevented by the king, who ' willed, ordained and adjudged '
that Hereford should leave the realm for ten years, Norfolk for
life. This decision is described in the roll of the pleas of the Crown
in parliament as made ' by full advice, authority and assent of
the parliament ', which means, presumably, the assent of the
committee.[3]

The fourth occasion on which the committee is found at work
is at Westminster on 18 March 1399. On that day it is recorded
to have transacted two items of business. Permission had been
given by letters patent to both Hereford and Norfolk, before they
went overseas, to appoint attorneys to act for them during their
absence, and in particular to receive on their behalf any inheritance that might fall to them. The king now decided to recall
this concession, and on 18 March 1399 the letters patent issued to
Hereford and Norfolk were revoked, on the grounds that they had
been granted ' by inadvertence ' and that they were contrary
to the judgements given at Coventry. This revocation is stated
to have been ' adjudged ' by the king and the committee ' aiantz
a ceo poair par vertue et auctorite du parlement '.[4] On the
same occasion the king and the committee considered the case of a
certain Sir Robert Plesyngton. This gentleman had been a partisan

---

[1] *Rot. Parl.* iii. 383.   [2] *Ibid.*

[3] *Ibid.* According to the *Chronicque de la Traïson* (pp. 21-2), the decision was
announced by Sir John Bussy as ' le jugement du roy et de son conseil '.

[4] *Rot. Parl.* iii. 372.

of Gloucester, and had acted with him in 1386–7, but had died in 1393.[1]* The king nevertheless desired that he should be formally branded as a traitor. This was accordingly done on 18 March 1399

par assent de les seignurs et chivalers des countees, aientz poair de tout le parlement dexaminer respoundre et pleinement terminer si bien diverses petitions et les matiers comprises en ycelles come toutz autres matiers et choses moevez en le presence du roy et nient terminez, ovesque toutz les dependences dicelles, come piert par le record ent fait en mesme le parlement.[2]**

The fifth and last occasion on which the committee seems to have acted was at Windsor on 23 April 1399.† On that day a clerk named Henry Bowet, who had assisted Hereford in drawing up the petition whereby he had asked to be allowed to receive inheritances by attorney, was brought before the king and adjudged to be a traitor by the assent of the committee, whose powers are expressed in exactly the same words as in the record of Plesyngton's condemnation.[3]

Only on these five occasions, apparently, can one learn anything definite about the committee's doings. On the first two of the five occasions the committee can scarcely be said to have exceeded its real powers. The four statutes and ordinances made at Bristol concerning the tanning of leather, &c., were clearly within its competence, as was also the decision that in default of sufficient proofs Hereford's charges against Norfolk should be settled by battle ; the only doubtful point in the Bristol proceedings is the ordinance which made it treason to attempt any alteration of the four statutes and ordinances then made. The proceedings at Windsor in April 1398, when the committee, along with the chivalry of England, advised that Hereford and Norfolk should join battle, were likewise clearly within its powers, since it had been authorized by parliament to ' terminate and finally discuss ' the charges which Hereford had made. The proceedings of the committee on the third occasion—at Coventry in September 1398—are not easy to defend on moral grounds, and the partisans of Lancaster evidently regarded them as being ' contra omnem iusticiam et leges et consuetudines regni sui ac iura militaria in hac parte'.[4]†† The record in the roll of the pleas of the Crown in parliament states, as already seen, that the judgements at Coventry were given ' par pleyn avys, auctorite et assent du Parlement':§ this may have been intended to imply that the authority and assent of parliament, as the highest court of the realm, would validate the unusual course that was taken.[5]

[1] *Dict. of Nat. Biog., s. n.*
[2] *Rot. Parl.* iii. 384.   [3] *Ibid.* p. 385.   [4] *Ibid.* p. 419.
[5] Richard may very well have remembered that the lords of the parliament of 1388, in dealing with the appeal against the king's friends, had declared that ' lour

Moreover, the powers given to the committee by parliament were general powers to 'terminate and finally discuss' the Hereford-Norfolk case. From the narrowly legal point of view, therefore, it might be argued that the proceedings at Coventry were justifiable. But morally they did involve some stretching of the committee's powers. It is on the fourth and fifth occasions, however, in connexion with the condemnation of Plesyngton and Bowet in March and April 1399, that the committee's proceedings become specially interesting for our present purpose. The record gives a version of the committee's powers which is not recited in the records of its proceedings on any other occasion, except in the account of its Bristol session given by parliament roll no. 57; and that account, as has been seen, is a demonstrably falsified account. On the evidence at present available it seems clear, therefore, that the phrase 'toutz autres matiers et choses moevez en le presence du roy et nient terminez, ovesque toutz les dependences dicelles' was not inserted into the committee's powers till March or April 1399; that it was then introduced in order to give the committee some colour of authority for handling the cases of Plesyngton and Bowet; and that thereupon a fresh copy of the parliament roll—roll no. 57—was written out with the spurious phrase interpolated in the earlier places so as to agree with the powers of the committee as recited in the record of the condemnations of Plesyngton and Bowet. This examination of the committee's activities suggests that the use to which it was ultimately put may have been no more than an ingenious afterthought, and need not have been in the king's mind when the committee was set up in January 1398. But however that may be, there is one noteworthy fact that stands out clearly. So far as the evidence goes, the committee, when it did exceed its powers either morally or legally, always seems to have done so in one connexion: it only seems to have stretched or overstepped its real powers in the process of wreaking vengeance upon the king's remaining enemies of 1386-8 and those who had then or subsequently aided and abetted them in any way.

This last fact indicates that Richard II may not necessarily have intended to use the committee as a means of dispensing with parliament altogether. That this was his intention is indeed suggested by some of the chroniclers,[1] but there are various

entent n'est pas de reuler ou governer si haute cause come cest appel est, que ne serra aillours trie ne termine q'en parlement come dit est, par cours processe et ordre use en ascune court ou place plus bas deinz mesme le roialme; queux courtes et places ne sont que executours d'anciens leys et custumes du roialme et ordinances et establisementz de parl' ment' (*ibid.* p. 236).*

[1] 'Fecitque parliamentum hoc compromittere in xii personas, quae continuando parliamentum ubicunque et quandocunque regi placeret statuta sibi placita secum ordinarent'** (*Eulogium Historiarum* (Rolls Series), iii. 377-8). Adam of Usk (*Chronicon*, p. 24) says much the same thing.

pieces of evidence which do not altogether square with the suggestion. In the parliament of January 1398, in which the committee was appointed, the king, in return for a grant of the subsidy on wool, wool-fells, and leather for life, and of fifteenths and tenths for a limited period, granted a general pardon to his subjects, but in doing so he made a declaration ' with his own mouth . . . that if the lords or commons of the realm who should come to the parliaments in the future ' should impede or disturb the grant made to him for life, then the pardon should be void.[1] It may also be worth noticing that in the ordinance made by the king and the committee at Bristol in March 1398 it is ordained that if any one attempt to reverse any of the four statutes and ordinances then made ' and this be duly proved in parliament ', he shall be executed as a traitor.[2] These two facts seem to show that in the early months of 1398, at any rate, the king did not contemplate using the committee as a means of completely superseding parliament.

If the scheme occurred to him, it must have been later. The evidence even for this is ambiguous. In his will, dated 16 April 1399, Richard made various bequests to his successor, with this condition :

dum tamen omnia et singula statuta et ordinationes et stabilimenta et iudicia in parliamento nostro xvii die mensis Septembris anno regni nostri xxi apud Westmonasterium inchoato, et in eodem parliamento usque Salopiam continuato et ibidem tento, facta lata et reddita, necnon omnes ordinationes et iudicia quae auctoritate eiusdem parliamenti in futuro contigerit fieri, approbet ratificet et confirmet teneat et teneri faciat ac firmiter observari.[3]*

This at first sight looks as though the king by that time intended the committee to be permanent, and therefore, presumably, to supersede parliament altogether. But it may only imply that he meant to continue, if necessary, using the committee as he had used it already, i. e. mainly as an instrument of vengeance. At any rate it should be noted that apparently the only ordinance or judgement made by the committee after the date of the will was the condemnation of Bowet on 23 April, and this was an item in the king's exhaustive vengeance ; indeed the close proximity of dates suggests that the passage in the will about future ordinances and judgements may quite conceivably have been inserted mainly with a view to the coming condemnation of Bowet. Again if the king by 1399 had conceived the idea of superseding parliament altogether by using the committee ' ubi

---

[1] *Rot. Parl.* iii. 369.   [2] *Stats. of the Realm*, ii. 110.
[3] *Foedera* (1st ed.), viii. 77. This passage in the will was subsequently made the basis of one of the articles of deposition (*Rot. Parl.* iii. 421).

et quando sibi placeret ',[1]*one would have expected him to take the committee, or at any rate a quorum of it, with him to Ireland : Wallon, indeed, asserts that he did so.[2] Now the committee consisted of eighteen persons, twelve lords and six commoners ; but the quorum differed slightly according to the business in hand. For dealing with petitions the quorum was to be at least six of the twelve lords and at least three of the six commoners.[3] For dealing with the Hereford-Norfolk case the quorum was as follows : one of the two lords (the earls of Wiltshire and Worcester) who were the proctors of the estate of the clergy ; six of the other ten lords ; and three or four of the six commoners.[4] Now on the two occasions when the attendance at sessions of the committee is stated, there was undoubtedly a proper quorum present : for dealing with petitions at Bristol in March 1398 there were eight lords and three commoners, but neither of the earls of Wiltshire and Worcester ; [5] for quashing Hereford's and Norfolk's patents in March 1399, on the other hand, there were seven lords and four commoners and also the earls of Wiltshire and Worcester.[6] This shows that Richard probably paid some attention to the technical requirements of a formal quorum when using the committee. If so, then it is important to observe that when he went to Ireland, although he certainly had six of the twelve lords there with him,[7] he did not take the requisite minimum of three commoners : of the six commoners only Robert Teye seems to have accompanied him ; [8] Bussy, Grene, and Russell were left behind in England ; [9] Chelmeswyk and Golafre were by this time dead.[10] It is thus clear that Richard did not take a quorum of the committee to Ireland as Wallon supposed.   Moreover, there seems to be no record that the committee ever acted while the king was in Ireland. The two facts combined throw some doubt upon the assertion that Richard meant to use the committee as a substitute for parliament ' ubi

---

[1] Adam of Usk, *Chronicon*, p. 24.   [2] *Richard II*, ii. 237.
[3] *Rot. Parl.* iii. 368 ; *Stats. of the Realm*, ii. 107. The printed version of the parliament roll, though taken from roll 57, gives the quorum quite correctly.
[4] *Rot. Parl.* iii. 360, 382-3.
[5] *Ibid.* p. 369 ; *Stats. of the Realm*, ii. 107. The record does not give the names of the members of the committee who were present when Hereford's accusations were considered on this occasion at Bristol ; it merely enumerates the full committee, and then says that the decision was made by the king ' and the above-mentioned lords and knights ', as though they were all present (*Rot. Parl.* iii. 382-3).
[6] *Ibid.* p. 372.
[7] The dukes of Aumarle, Surrey, and Exeter, and the earls of Salisbury, Gloucester, and Worcester.
[8] *Cal. of Patent Rolls, 1396-9*, p. 554.
[9] *Annales Ricardi Secundi* (Rolls Series), pp. 243-4.
[10] Chelmeswyk is referred to as ' deceased ' in September 1398 (*Cal. of Patent Rolls, 1396-9*, p. 410 ; see also *ibid. 1391-6*, p. 684). Golafre is said to be ' now deceased ', in February 1399 (*ibid. 1396-9*, p. 508).

et quando sibi placeret '. That Richard intended to free himself
from the need of frequently summoning parliament is proved by
his obtaining a grant of the subsidy on wool, wool-fells, and leather
for life. That he intended to dispense with parliament altogether
by means of the committee is not proven. And it is of some
importance to bear in mind that the very way in which Richard
used the committee—especially his alteration of the parliament
roll—was a formal recognition of the existence of parliament as
part of the constitution.

These considerations suggest that the importance of the
parliamentary committee of 1398 in Richard's schemes may
easily be overrated. It was not necessarily a permanent or
essential feature of those schemes. The clue to the essence of his
plan may perhaps be found in the speech delivered by the
chancellor at the opening of the Shrewsbury parliament, a speech
which practically repeats what he had said at the beginning of the
previous session at Westminster in September 1397. The cause
of the summoning of the parliament, according to the chancellor,
was ' for the honour of God, and that Holy Church should have
all its liberties and franchises, and that all the lords spiritual and
temporal, citizens and burgesses [1] should have and enjoy all
their liberties and franchises as they had reasonably had and used
them in the times of the king's noble progenitors and in his own
time ; also, that there should not be several rulers in the realm,
but one '.[2] This sums up Richard's scheme quite briefly. He
does not deny his subjects their liberties and franchises ; they
may have and enjoy them—but only ' reasonably ', in accordance
with established usage. Then comes the vital point—that there
should not be several rulers in the realm, but one. That is a reference to the commission of 1386. That commission involved, for
all practical purposes, the vesting of the king's powers in a council
chosen from among the lords of parliament. The king's main
concern in the years 1397-9 was probably not so much to supersede parliament as to prevent any possibility of a revival of the
hated commission of 1386. His purpose was to keep power
in his own hands, where by law it ought to be and where in
fact it generally had been under his predecessors : he desired
to have as his council a body of ministers who were there to
conduct, not a number of barons who were there to control, his
government. He set himself against constitutional government
as that term had been understood by the baronial opposition under
Gloucester's lead. Even during the so-called ' constitutional '
period of the reign from 1389 to 1397, there seems to have been

---

[1] At Westminster in September 1397 he said ' lords spiritual and temporal and also
cities, boroughs and other communities ' (*Rot. Parl.* iii. 347). ' Other communities '
would include the shires.   [2] *Ibid.* pp. 356–7.

a consistent tendency on the king's part to increase the influence of the curialist or bureaucratic element in the council. During the years 1397–9 this tendency appears to have been still stronger : Professor Baldwin is of opinion that ' the council had never before been so clearly outlined as a staff of expert men ', of whom the earls of Wiltshire and Worcester, and the three knights, Bussy, Grene, and Russell, are typical.[1] This was the natural result of the king's determination ' that there should not be several rulers in the realm, but one '. It seems likely that this uncontrolled, curialist council was much more essentially important to Richard's plans in the last two years of his reign than the committee of parliament. For the curialist council was an organ of government, and therefore a permanent necessity. The parliamentary committee, on the other hand, seems to have been little more than an instrument of vengeance, and therefore quite possibly a temporary expedient.

[1] *The King's Council*, pp. 132–42.

13

THE DEPOSITION OF RICHARD II AND THE ACCESSION OF HENRY IV*

by B. Wilkinson

THE Lords' *Report on the Dignity of a Peer*, dated 25 May 1820, stated that Henry IV, obtaining the throne against the prevailing opinion of hereditary right, depended for his title ' wholly on the authority of the Lords and Commons, summoned in the name of Richard to attend his Parliament, assuming the character of representatives of the three estates of the realm, accepting in that character the forced resignation of Richard and then assuming the power to pronounce his deposition, and the vacancy of the throne, and to advance Henry to the throne so vacant '.[1] Stubbs went further, and believed that Henry became king by authority of parliament : he ' made the validity of a parliamentary title indispensable to royalty '.[2] Recently Mr. Lapsley has withdrawn from the position taken up by Stubbs, though he has not gone back entirely to the position of the *Reports*.[3] He believes that there was some question of a parliamentary title for Henry, but that the latter refused this because of its constitutional implications ; and that he was elected by authority, not of the estates of parliament alone, but by authority of the estates and others who had been invited to be present on 30 September, the day of Richard's deposition. The record of these proceedings was so worded, however, as to give the impression that parliament had actually given its consent and authorization to the events of the day.

None of these views, we shall venture to suggest, can be accepted as it stands. The Lords' *Reports* made an important contribution in emphasizing the non-parliamentary nature of the assembly in which Richard II's deposition took place. Stubbs unwisely ignored this, and Mr. Lapsley had both to restore and amplify their interpretation, and to examine more scientifically

---

[1] *Op. cit.* i. 348. [2] *Const. Hist.* ii. 533.
[3] 'The Parliamentary Title of Henry IV', *E.H.R.*, xlix, 423 *seqq.*, 577 *seqq.*; 'Richard II's "Last Parliament" ', *ibid.* liii. 53–79.** Comments on the views expressed in these articles were offered by Mr. H. G. Richardson in ' Richard II's Last Parliament ', *ibid.* lii. 39–47.

the evidence on which it was based. He showed conclusively the
need for some explanation of the wording adopted in the official
account of the transactions of 30 September, the ' record and
process ', incorporated in the Rolls of Parliament, and widely
copied by contemporary chroniclers. All previous attempts to
understand the procedure of 1399 had been vitiated by an acceptance of this ' record and process ' as being an accurate and fair
report, whereas Mr. Lapsley, following up the important lead
given by Professor Galbraith and Miss Clarke,[1] was able to argue
convincingly that it had been drawn up deliberately to deceive.
But his further view of the meaning and intention of the ' record
and process ' is not so easy to accept. It seems probable that,
to understand this document aright, the reaction against Stubbs
must be carried further still. It must extend to a re-examination
of the whole political and constitutional background of the crisis
of 1399.

Engrossed in the constitutional aspect of the deposition,
Stubbs failed to nótice, or at least to bring out, the fact that
the political problems which confronted Henry of Lancaster in
1399 were far more urgent and important than the constitutional ones. In this he has been followed by every modern
writer on the subject. Yet, in this respect, his conclusions seem
to be almost exactly the reverse of the truth. It will be suggested below that the constitutional issues presented in the procedure of Richard's deposition were comparatively unimportant
to Henry IV, because he was faced with the problem of a serious
and menacing political opposition to the whole design, and because
he attached little value to the precise formalities which attended
its execution, so long as they did not give the opposition a chance
of making itself too plainly felt. The nature of this opposition
to Henry is the first problem which must be dealt with below.

The constitutional background presents questions almost
equally important ; but they are not simply concerned with the
events of 1399. They are concerned, more generally, with the
nature of parliament and the relations, in parliament, of the
monarch and the estates. A conception of this relationship was
established by Stubbs, and has been accepted since his time, on
which alone the theory of a ' parliamentary title ' of Henry IV
could be based, and this, we may now suspect, is at variance with
the weight of evidence available as to the nature of the parliamentary assembly from the days of Edward I at least to those of
Henry VIII. If the suggestions made below are correct, it was
never possible, even in a revolution, for parliament to judge and
depose a monarch who had summoned it, who was an integral
and necessary element in its assembly and who dissolved it by

---

[1] ' The Deposition of Richard II ', in *Bull. of John Rylands Library*, xiv. 125–81.*

his abdication or death. It is evident that our second urgent problem will be the nature of the conception of parliament which would permit Henry IV even to have contemplated a parliamentary authorization for the revolution of 1399.

A third problem deserves, and has not yet obtained, serious consideration specifically for the light that it might shed on the procedure of Richard's deposition. This is the deposition of Edward II. Though Mr. Lapsley rightly argued strongly as to its importance, he did not subject it to the same careful scrutiny which he bestowed on the records for 1399. Yet it has an importance for us far greater than that simply of the only precedent available for Richard's deposition. It has not been suggested, and there is in fact no proof, that any misrepresentation occurred in 1327 comparable with that which we now know to have taken place at the later date. If we are in doubt as to the meaning of the records of Richard II's deposition, or as to the nature of the facts, surely an obvious precaution is to examine the existing precedent with every care. Perhaps neither Stubbs nor even Mr. Lapsley adequately appreciated the fact that, in the last analysis, the approach to an understanding of the procedure adopted in the revolution of 1399 is through the only existing precedent, that of the deposition of Edward II.

II

The question of the political background turns largely on the relations between Henry and the northern magnates. Here, recent research has tended to attach much more weight to the Percy tradition, expressed strongly by Hardyng, that the Percies opposed Henry's design on the throne up to the very last. It now seems likely that, in the first place, though Richard II was betrayed at Conway,[1] Henry Percy, at least, had negotiated with him in good faith. Henry of Lancaster's design to claim the throne was only subsequently disclosed.*

This is the impression given by a scrutiny both of the chronicles long accessible, and of the fragments recently printed by Professor Galbraith and Miss Clarke. According to the later *Davies Chronicle*, it was Lancaster and Thomas Arundel (not Percy) who told Richard at Flint that ' he sholde no lenger regne '.[2] The continuation of the *Polychronicon* preserved at Whalley [3] and the

---

[1] Cf. the Dieulacres Chronicle, *Bull. of John Rylands Library*, xiv. 173.

[2] Ed. J. S. Davies (Camden Soc.), p. 16.

[3] *Bull. J.R. Lib.* xiv. 144. ' Postmodum prefatus dux cum complicibus suis ivit Cestriam ubi dominus Ricardus rex securitate sibi facta per sacramentum domini Thome Arundel et comitis Northumbrie venit Cestriam ad colloquium, sed prefatus dux Herefordie contra juramentum predictum cepit ibidem eundem Ricardum regem et ducens London posuit in turri London' in custodia.'**

Kirkstall Chronicle [1] both throw the onus of the decision to regard Richard as a captive at Flint, pointedly on to Henry himself. This is, of course, a northern tradition, and though it agrees perfectly with Hardyng,[2] it might be difficult to accept if there were anything directly contradicting it from the south. But that is not the case. All that we can place against it is the version of Creton,[3] followed by the *Traïson et Mort*. And even Creton, convinced though he was of Northumberland's treacherous intentions, represents Lancaster as acting without Percy, once Richard was safely in his hands.[4]

The weight of evidence, even if we allow for the untrustworthiness of Hardyng, is against Northumberland's having agreed, already before the interview at Conway, to any plan by Henry of Lancaster of claiming the throne. We may perhaps conclude that he still regarded as binding Lancaster's oath, taken at Doncaster, that he would not do this. If so, he might well be opposed to the whole project which unfolded itself after Richard's captivity began at Flint. There is in fact a strong Percy tradition, expressed in Hardyng,[5] and in the manifesto of 1403,[6] and perhaps hinted at in that of Archbishop Srope in 1405,[7] that he was. And there is the strong, independent evidence of the *Dieulacres Chronicle*: 'sed probabile signum erat quod Henricus Percy ad hoc non consenciit quia in die coronacionis ad festum non incedit quia pro certo ipso invito coronacio facta fuit quia Henricus dux iuravit aliis duobus Henricis super reliquas de Bridlynton quod coronam nunquam affectaret'.[8]*

---

[1] *Kirkstall Chronicle, ibid.* xv. 134 : ' Cumque dominus dux Lancastrie certitudinaliter sciret dominum regem Walliam intrasse, festinavit illuc ire, et cumque non multum distarent, misit ad regem comitem Northumbrorum cuius verbis et persuasionibus multiphariis dominus rex assensem prebuit dieque sequente convenerunt dominus rex et dux Lancastrie et ex diffinito consilio domini ducis et aliorum dominorum ductus est rex ad civitatem Londoniarum.'**

[2] According to the version published by Webb in the *Archaeologia*, xx. 240 : the two envoys, Hardyng here says, brought Richard to the duke ' withouten felony ', but Henry, after at first treating Richard with the deference due to a prince, ' than forthe to London ledde in Septembre, in strong and myghty warde '.

[3] *Ibid.* xx. 360. Creton believed simply that Northumberland was lying when he swore that there was no deceit in the agreement with Richard at Conway. The *Traïson et Mort* (p. 50) agrees. This was a natural conclusion as to his motives, by hostile witnesses who saw what happened at Flint and Chester.

[4] Percy is not mentioned after the arrival at Flint, when he and Lancaster ' parlerent assez longuement ensemble ' (p. 372). Creton says he was an eye-witness of the events (p. 374).

[5] *Chronicle*, p. 353 : ' And tho two declared in the counsell and in the parlement at Westmynster, on the morowe of Seynt Michell thanne next followynge, what of his myght and his wilfulness, and what be certeyne lordes and strenght of the commons, he wase crounde ayenst his oth made in the White ffreres at Doncastre to the seid erle of Northumberlonde and other lordes, ayenst the wille and counsell of the seide erle and of his sonne '. Cf. *ibid.* p. 351.   [6] *Ibid.* pp. 352–3.

[7] Discussed by Mr. Lapsley, *E.H.R.*, xlix. 443. See also *Historians of the Church of York and its Archbishops*, edited by J. Raine (R.S.), ii. 294–6.

[8] *Bull, J. R. Lib.* xiv. 179; *E.H.R.*, xlix. 442.

The only evidence to place against these comes from the tainted ' record and process ' of 1399, which shows Henry Percy as acting on two prominent occasions amongst the supporters of the coronation. The ' record and process ' was copied by a number of chronicles favourable to the Lancastrians, but there seems to be no clear, independent support of its version in any other source.

The first occasion was when Henry Percy was amongst the leaders of the delegation which visited Richard in the Tower on 29 September. It is by no means certain, however, that this deputation ever functioned, in the form recorded in the Rolls : [1] it is certainly hard to understand why, if it did, it did not figure in the assembly of 30 September as well,[2] and why it was superseded by another committee, elected in this assembly to convey the news of his deposition to Richard II. It can hardly be without significance that Henry Percy was omitted from this second committee. It is possible that Bishop Merks, in the assembly of 30 September, actually questioned whether Richard had freely resigned his throne on the 29th,[3] but yet no member of the deputation which is supposed to have visited him rose to confirm the official account.

On 23 October Northumberland is also recorded as asking the Lords what should be ordained for Richard ' pur luy mettre en saufe garde ; sauvant sa vie, quele le Roy voet qe luy soit sauvez en toutes maneres',[4*] but this is by no means irreconcilable with the Percy tradition. On the whole, we may conclude, it may be argued that, after the recent research on the ' record and process ', the weight of evidence as to the attitude of the Percies now favours the tradition set forth by Hardyng, suspect though he rightly is. In approaching the events of Richard II's deposition, we have

[1] The account of the deputation is copied by the chronicles which give the Lancastrian version, but not by others (*Rot. Parl.* iii. 416 ; Adam of Usk, p. 184 ; *Annales Ricardi*, pp. 252–3 ; Walsingham in *Hist. Ang.* ii. 234 ; *Eulogium Historiarum*, iii. 382). The *Traïson et Mort* omits it altogether. The *Dieulacres Chronicle* has an account which makes it unlikely that Richard surrendered his throne to any deputation ; *Bull. J.R. Lib.* xiv. 173. According to Creton only bishops and abbots witnessed the surrender, *Archaeologia*, xx. 197. The nearest to the official account, in the chronicles which did not simply copy the ' record and process ', is in the *Davies Chronicle* (p. 17) which talks of a deputation of ' bishoppis, erlis, barons, knyʒtis and notarieʒ '.

[2] Adam of Usk says that it did ; but his version at this point is almost certainly wrong ; *Chronicle*, p. 185. Perhaps he thought that it *ought* to have appeared and acted in the assembly of the 30th. There was certainly an urgent need of the testimony of the committee which had visited Richard on the 29th, to reply to the suggestions of Bishop Merks that Richard might still be unwilling to relinquish his crown.

[3] *Bull. J.R. Lib.* xiv. 153–4. It seems probable, from William of Feriby's material printed by the same authors, that Bishop Merks was supported by some of the magnates,—' cui idem archiepiscopus et *quam plures alii domini* affirmant illam renunciacionem et cessionem fore utile et expediens';** *ibid.* p. 147.

[4] *Rot. Parl.* iii. 426. On the previous day the commons had asked, rather ominously, ' what Juggement he [Richard] shall have, and that hit be so done and ordeyned ffor hym that the Rewme be not trouble by hym ' ; Kingsford, *Chronicles of London*, p. 56.

at least to allow for the possibility of a very serious opposition
to Henry of Lancaster's designs, including some of the leading
magnates of the north.   This would, incidentally, provide a much
more satisfactory explanation of the rising of the Percies in 1403.
We shall not go far astray, perhaps, if we assume that the supreme
consideration of Henry of Lancaster in arranging for Richard's
deposition, was not the constitutional significance of the procedure
to be adopted,[1] or the opposition of certain of his own followers,
but the open or anticipated hostility of a strong section of the
nation, exactly as in the deposition of Edward II in 1326 and 1327.

III

The second general problem affecting our interpretation of
the 'record and process', and of the procedure of Richard II's
deposition, that of the nature of parliament, is of the utmost
importance.   On this point, the opinion of historians has moved
considerably away from the views of Stubbs.   Probably they have
not yet moved far enough.   Three aspects of our conception of
parliament are, in this connexion, outstanding.   The first is that
of its general relations to the monarch; the second is that of
its powers ; and the third is that of the relative position and
functions of commons and lords.

The first is fundamental.   The idea of a parliamentary deposition involves a conception of Crown and parliament as two
distinct entities which is contrary to all that we know of their
constitutional relations in the fourteenth century or for long
after.   We cannot, in this connexion, ponder too deeply on the
words of Henry VIII : ' We be informed by our judges that we at
no time stand so highly in our estate royal as in time of parliament,
wherein we as head and you as members are conjoined and knit
together in one body politic '.[2]   The king was at least as much
an integral part of parliament as the commons or the lords.
Properly understood, it is probable that *Fleta's* ' Habet enim rex
curiam suam in consilio suo in parliamentis suis'* is not more
indicative of the existence of parliament apart from the king,
than is the assertion of the *Modus Tenendi Parliamentum* that
' Rex est caput, principium, et finis parliamenti'**.   There is,
perhaps, no great need to stress the point here.   Professor Pollard

[1] It is very significant, in this connexion, that Henry departed from the precedent
of 1327 by extorting Richard's abdication from him before the ' parliament' of 30
September had assembled.   He was able to confront the members with the decisive
fact that Richard had already ' freely' resigned his throne.   But to do this he sacri-
ficed any real chance of obtaining ' parliamentary' sanction for any of the procedure
of deposition even if the constitutional difficulty of parliament's deposing a monarch,
discussed above, could be ignored.   We may suspect that it was the political advantage to be derived from Richard's abdication on the 29th which was uppermost
in Henry's mind.

[2] Cited in my *Studies in the Constitutional History of the Thirteenth and Fourteenth
Centuries*, p. 14.

has warned us long ago that 'The conception of crown and
parliament as two distinct entities confuses much of the interpretation of our constitutional history '.[1] Parliament was, in
1399 as throughout the later fourteenth century, the king discussing, treating, and judging, together with the commons and the
lords.   There was no place for the constitutional idea that parliament could judge or depose the king.   It may even be asserted,
without much possibility of error, that nobody in 1399 would,
or could, contemplate, even as an extra-legal and revolutionary
procedure, an attempt to distort the traditions of parliament so
far as to assert that the actions of commons and lords remained
parliamentary even after Richard II ceased to be king,—after
the abdication of 29 September or at least after this had been
published on the following day.

The functions as well as the nature of parliament in the
fourteenth century are in danger of being misunderstood.   It is
being credited at more than one point with functions which it
almost certainly did not possess.   Some historians still believe
that the coronation oath of Edward II had shown the growing
power of parliament, a power even of demanding the king's agreement to legislation which it was to make.[2]   Miss M. V. Clarke
perhaps helped in the over-valuation of parliament's position as
against the king, in her treatment of the deposition of Edward II.
The growth of the claims of parliament, after this, was discerned
not only in the legislation of 1341 but also in the impeachments of
1376, the latter the work of lords and commons, in which the
theory of the responsibility of ministers to the nation was established ; [3] and finally the declaration of the lords in parliament
in 1388 has been construed as an enunciation of the conception of
the ultimate sovereignty of parliament.   Thus, by the end of the
fourteenth century, it is believed, parliament was able to dethrone
the monarch himself.

But this conception of the growth of the powers of parliament
in the fourteenth century can be, and indeed has been, questioned
at nearly every point.   The famous declaration of the lords in
parliament in 1388 should perhaps be discussed at some length.
According to Mr. Lapsley's view, its significance can hardly be
over-stressed : 'If the law is made by parliament and can be
altered by it so that no one parliament can bind its successors,
then the doctrine of the sovereignty of the law taught by Bracton
falls and the king will not be under God and the law but under

---

[1] *Evolution of Parliament* (2nd edition), p. 258.
[2] On this subject see my ' Coronation Oath of Edward II ', in *Essays in Honour of
James Tait* ; cf. H. G. Richardson and G. O. Sayles, ' Early Coronation Records ',
in *Bull. Inst. Hist. Res.* xiii. 129–45 and xiv. 1–9.
[3] This is discussed in my *Studies*, pp. 82–107.

God and the parliament that is superior to the law since it can make and unmake it '.[1] But it is possible that here the implications of the famous assertion have been carried too far. All that the lords asserted in 1388 was that crimes touching the king and the realm, perpetrated by peers of the realm, should be tried in parliament by the 'Ley et Cours du Parlement',* and the judges should be the lords in parliament. They would not try this case anywhere but in parliament, for other courts were only the executors of the ancient laws and customs of the realm, and of the ordinances and ' establishments ' of parliament.[2]

The lords were asserting the superiority of the court of parliament over other courts ; but this does not mean that they were formally maintaining its supremacy over the Crown. Indeed, considering that in effect they were coercing the monarch, the moderation of their theoretical position is a notable fact. The Lords Appellant were indeed—and probably they were fully conscious of the fact—treading revolutionary paths. Their actions need not necessarily, and would not probably, provide precedents for constitutional procedure at a later time. These actions showed the possibilities of using parliament as an instrument for coercing the monarch ; but they did not, nevertheless, serve to raise parliament to be constitutionally superior to the Crown in the sense that parliament could, as a normal constitutional procedure, pass judgement on the king. Indeed, the magnates did not attempt anything so revolutionary in 1388. All they did was to attack and judge the king's servants in the king's name : what they invoked was only the traditionally accepted notion of trial by peers.

When we talk of their asserting ' the ultimate sovereignty of parliament ',[3] we must be very clear as to what we really mean. Whatever powers they claimed for parliament in 1388, as far as constitutional precedent was concerned, they claimed for the king in his ' estates '. As far as the king himself was concerned, the declaration of the barons still left him subject to God and the law. But he and his subjects had long been in the habit of defining and declaring the law ; in this sense, every monarch since Aethelbert and Ine had been superior to the law, and every witenagemót which, of its knowledge declared what was the law, had been superior to the king.

Legally and constitutionally the acts of parliament were the acts of the king ; the precedent of 1388, however much, in

[1] E.H.R., xlix. 584; Tout, Chapters, iii. 432. Miss Clarke in 'Forfeitures and Treason in 1388', in Transactions of the Royal Historical Society (4th series), xiv. 65–94,** does not go so far as this.
[2] Rot. Parl. iii. 236 ; cited Stubbs, ii. 503. n. 3 ; cf. Tout, Chapters, iii. 432 ; Stubbs, ii. 503, saw no special significance in their claims.
[3] Tout, Chapters, iii. 432.

reality, directed against Richard, could offer no precedent for a ' parliamentary ' deposition of the monarch.   Such a procedure was, and remained, outside the realm of fourteenth-century experience and ideas.   Nor, if we refuse to distinguish between the inseparable elements of which parliament was composed, did the assertion of the magnates in 1388 add very much to the sum total of its powers.   It was, and remained, the supreme court and legislature in the land ; it was and remained the assembly of estates petitioning, ' treating ' with, and advising the king.

Nor, in this assembly, is it easy to imagine a deposition of Richard II by the commons equally with the lords.   Deposition involved judgement ;   and the commons, as they themselves vigorously protested in the first parliament of Henry IV, were not, and did not wish to be, judges in parliament.   Their function, it was truly said, was petitioning and consenting.   Nor is it probable that they would be willing to play a rôle, in an assembly of the *universitas regni* without parliamentary organisation and traditions, which they were unwilling to perform within parliament itself.   All the traditions of the commons in the fourteenth century, and all precedents such as impeachment which were remotely parallel to the deposition of a monarch, warn us not to expect the decisive actions in the assembly of 1399 to come from the commons.   A somewhat exaggerated conception of the rôle and importance of the commons, even in parliament in the fourteenth century, is apt to be obtained by a too great concentration on questions of finance.   In law and in politics the commons were still not nearly so important.   Judgement of their peers was a matter for the lords.   So, we should expect was the ' judgement ' by which a king was deposed.   All this has an important bearing on our interpretation of the ' record and process ', the official version of Richard's deposition in 1399.

IV

The third general problem, that of the precedent of 1327, must be considered at some length   Valuable work was done by Miss Clarke in working out the details of the procedure adopted at Edward II's deposition, but Miss Clarke certainly gave the impression that the deposition was the work of parliament,[1] that the deputation which visited Edward at Kenilworth was a deputation of parliamentary estates.   Mr. Lapsley seems to have

[1] ' Committees of Estates and the Deposition of Edward II ', in *Historical Essays in Honour of James Tait*, pp. 27–45 ; e.g. (p. 36), ' the conclusion is that Parliament deposed Edward II and appointed delegates to go to Kenilworth on the previous day '.*

regarded the precedent of 1327 as suggesting a procedure of parliamentary deposition in 1399. In view of what has been said about parliament above, it would be very surprising if this were the case. A detailed examination will suggest that it was not. It was a precedent for exactly what the committee, set up to consider the matter, suggested in 1399—deposition *by authority of* clergy and people. Not even, we must notice, deposition *by* clergy and people. It was rather their authorization, their acclamation, their consent which was provided in 1327, and probably envisaged by the committee of 1399. The nation had been called upon to participate in the deposition of Edward II ; but it was rather by accepting acts which were performed by the magnates, or a section of them, in its name, than by itself, either directly or through a representative committee, deposing the king.

It is doubtful indeed, if there was any general agreement that a parliament was in being when Edward was deposed. The *Chronicle of Lanercost* shows how important the attendance of Edward II himself was considered : one of the first acts was to send a deputation ' ex parte dominae reginae et filii sui ducis Aquitaniae, et omnium comitum et baronum et communitatis totius terrae Londonias congregatae',[1*] to ask him to come. When Edward refused, the writer goes on to talk of the ' clerus et populus ' rather than of parliament.[2] The *Historia Roffensis* gets over the difficulty by making the parliament assemble by the authority of the queen—' ad Parliamentum Reginae regnantis convenerunt'.[3**] So does the canon of Bridlington.[4] But to the *Lichfield Chronicle* it was only a ' concilium generale tocius cleri et populi Anglie '.[5†]

The fact that other writers are not so meticulous [6] does not destroy the significance of instances like these. From the official point of view, the situation could hardly be better described than by Mr. Lapsley himself :[7] ' The leaders of the rebellion which made Edward III king during his father's lifetime refused to throw any official responsibility upon parliament or to attribute to it any share in the transaction. The rolls of parliament contain no account of the proceedings between 7 and 25

---

[1] *Op. cit.* p. 257.

[2] The committee sent to interview Edward, to ask him to attend parliament, reported in the great hall at Westminster ' ubi tenebatur parliamentum predictum ', before all the clergy and people. After this event, parliament is not mentioned.

[3] *Anglia Sacra*, i. 367.

[4] *Chronicles of Edward I and Edward II*, ii. 90. ' Regina igitur et filius ejus primogenitus, convocatis Angliae proceribus, parliamentum Londoniis tenuerunt.'

[5] Cited by Miss Clarke, *loc. cit.* p. 36.

[6] *The Vita et Mors Edwardi Secundi* (p. 313) calls the assembly a *parliamentum.* So does the *Pipewell Chronicle* (Miss Clarke, *loc. cit.* p. 35) and the monk of Malmesbury *Chronicles Edward I and Edward II*, ii. 289) and the *Annales Paulini* (*ibid.* i. 322).

[7] *E.H.R.*, xlix. 581; cf. *Foedera*, ii. pt. 2, 683.

January.[1] When the new king's peace was proclaimed on the 24th it was announced that Edward, formerly king of England, had, of his own free will, and by the advice and assent of the prelates, nobles, and the whole community of the kingdom, retired from the government and intimated that it should pass to his eldest son and heir.'

It is well known that no attempt was made to confine the proceedings against Edward to the official members of the assembly which had been summoned in his name.[2] According to the *Lichfield Chronicle*, Edward was deposed ' ad clamorem tocius populi unanimiter in ipso clamore perserverantis*. . .'[3] The most detailed account, however, comes from the *Lanercost Chronicle*. The description given here of what occurred between 13 and 15 January 1327 has been variously interpreted, and has given rise to considerable doubt, but it seems to be beyond question that the writer was well informed.[4] He describes, in

---

[1] Mr. Lapsley asks the highly relevant question, ' Why should not the acceptance of the abdication have been entered on the parliament roll ? ' More than one answer is possible. Lapsley suggests ' that people were still very uncertain about the legal position of parliament and were very reluctant, particularly in so grave a matter as this, to create a precedent '. The precedent created was, as Maitland suggested, one for revolution rather than legal action. Yet it could not be destroyed simply by omitting it from the Rolls. There remains a clear possibility that it was omitted simply from doubt as to the nature of the assembly.

[2] See e.g. Lapsley, *E.H.R.*, xlix. 581.   [3] Miss M. V. Clarke, *loc. cit.* p. 36, n. 3.

[4] The difficulties have been pointed out by Miss Clarke, *loc cit.* p. 36 ; but it is possible that the description is substantially correct. There is little doubt that the agreement to depose Edward was reached on 13 January, but the Lanercost writer has stated this quite clearly : ' et respondit omnis populus una voce " Nolumus hunc amplius regnare super nos "'. The rest of the proceedings he describes after this date were merely establishing the popular approval. The repeated rejections of Edward on these later days were not judicial sentences, but expressions of the nation's agreement. Miss Clarke has argued that the deputation to visit Richard at Kenilworth to declare his deposition must already have left Westminster on Wednesday 14 January, before these appeals to the populace had been made (*op. cit.* p. 36), since it reached its destination on the 20th (*Pipewell Chronicle*, cited by Miss Clarke, *loc. cit.* p. 44), and ' the unwieldy cavalcade of lords and commons can hardly have ridden much more than a dozen miles a day '. Thus ' we must suppose that they left Westminster on Wednesday, January 14th '. But the time seems to be excessive ; it seems possible that the deputation left on the morning of the 16th, in which case it could have been finally appointed on the evening of the 15th, after the Archbishop of Canterbury's speech recorded by the Lanercost scribe. The decision to dethrone Edward, at least, we must conclude, was probably arrived at on 13 January ; the deputation to depose him chosen some time after, when public opinion had been carefully prepared. There may have been an earlier deposition on the very first day of parliament, as described by the *Historia Roffensis*, but this must remain very doubtful. It sounds very unlikely—medieval parliaments were seldom entirely assembled on the very first day. Nor could this supremely important matter be rushed. On the other hand, the king's absence would have to be explained, and some general indication may have been made that Edward's refusal to attend need not hold up all business, because the supreme matter for discussion would be his own deposition from the throne. The question of deposition may have been seriously discussed in the more restricted assembly of the lords. But that the whole matter was rushed through parliament in this and the following day is very hard to believe. The assertion that Edward was led into the great Hall at Westminster and homage done to him on the 8th is

those days, what, as Miss Clarke pointed out, amounts to a skilful and deliberate working up of popular enthusiasm in favour of the deposition. The bishop of Hereford addressed the assembly on the 13th on the theme 'Rex insipiens perdet populum suum',* recounting all the evils of Edward's rule ; and *omnis populus* replied 'nolumus hunc amplius regnare super nos'.** The following day the bishop of Winchester preached on the theme ' Caput meum doleo'.† On the last day the archbishop on the theme 'Vox populi vox Dei',†† and at the end he announced to all that with the unanimous consent of all the earls, barons, archbishops and bishops, and of all the clergy and people, Edward had been deposed ; adding that all the aforesaid, as well people as clergy, unanimously consented that Edward the son should succeed. Which done, the magnates, with the assent of all the people, appointed solemn messengers to go to Kenilworth, to declare his deposition to the king.

Miss Clarke was apparently so impressed by the emphasis on the *populus* as the object of these exhortations, and by the popular nature of the appeal, that she transferred all these important episodes from parliament to ' the city ', thus dissociating them from the formal procedure of deposition, and even from the formal election of the committee to proceed to Kenilworth— from the activities, according to her interpretation, of parliament properly so called. But the *Lanercost Chronicle* at least offers no suggestion that the sermons of the bishops and archbishop occurred anywhere but in the ' parliament ', which elected the committee to declare Edward's deposition. Failing evidence to the contrary, we must surely conclude that here we have the assembly which was passing as parliament to some chronicles, as a ' concilium generale tocius cleri et populi ' to another—and which elected the famous ' parliamentary committee of estates '.

Nor does the composition of the committee accord ill with such a suggestion. There is copious evidence as to both its election and its composition, which suggests that it was the outcome and representation of just such a ' popular ' assembly as the narrative of the *Lanercost Chronicle* seems to describe. The decision to send the deputation was taken on 13 January, at the great Hall at Westminster, in an assembly of ' the archbishops and bishops, earls and barons, abbots and priors, and all others from the cities and boroughs, together with the whole commonalty of the land '.[1] It was elected to go ' ex parte totius

very hard to reconcile with the procedure of 13–20 January, both at Westminster and at Kenilworth. Whatever the value of this story of Edward's deposition on 8 January, we can hardly allow it as it stands to invalidate the much more probable details of the *Lanercost Chronicle*.

[1] Miss M. V. Clarke, *loc. cit.* p. 35, from a hitherto unpublished chronicle of Pipe-well.

regni '.[1] It may have contained at least three citizens of London, two preaching friars and two Carmelites, as well as representatives of the normal *gradus* of a parliament.[2] Its chief spokesman, William Trussell, may not even have been a knight of the shire.[3] He was variously described, and his own description of himself is reported in different ways. He was procurator ' of all in the land of England and of the whole parliament '.[4] He spoke, it was said, in the name of all the earls and barons of the realm of England.[5] He acted, the Malmesbury chronicle records ' vice omnium de terra Angliae et totius parliamenti procurator'.[6]* He stood, according to another authority ' ex parte totius regni '.[7] The only description of him which could be taken to indicate clearly that he represented the estates of parliament comes from a Winchester chronicle roll [8]—Edward ' tanquam regni delapidator ab omnibus in Parliamento diffidatus est per Willelmum Trussel, militem, in cuius ore universitas Parliamenti sua verba posuerat'.** As a matter of fact, all these more popular descriptions of Trussell's office must give way to that which he applied to himself, reported by the canon of Bridlington, a chronicler whose general accuracy for events of this period is high. He was, Trussell said, ' procurator praelatorum comitum, et baronum, et aliorum in procuratorio meo nominatorum'.[9]† Whether this is incomplete or not, the fact remains that these important words make no reference to parliament at all, and only in a very general way to the commons who were undoubtedly there.

On the other hand, the actual decision or ' judgement ' to depose Edward did not come from the general assembly, which was only called upon to ratify and approve an action which had been already determined by a comparatively small body of prelates and lords. When this occurred, we do not know ; if the writer of the *Historia Roffensis* is right, it probably occurred at the very beginning of the assembly, perhaps in the first two days. Most writers, who give no details, are content to point to 13 January, the day when the *populus* was invited to approve. That there was some serious consultation of the magnates alone can hardly be in doubt. According to the *Historia*, the bishops

---

[1] *Vita et Mors Edwardi Secundi*, in *Chronicles of Edward I and Edward II*, ii. 313.
[2] Miss M. V. Clarke, *loc. cit.* pp. 37–41.   [3] *Ibid.* p. 42.
[4] From Cotton MS. Nero D. 11, fo. 204b, cited by Miss Clarke, *ibid.* p. 37.
[5] *Annales Paulini*, in *Chronicles of Edward I and Edward II*, i. 323.
[6] *Ibid.* ii. 290. He was, the writer says, ' procurator totius parliamenti ', who spoke ' vice omnium '. The words quoted above are supposed to be those actually used by William, but they are not nearly so authentic as those given by the canon of Bridlington quoted below. They are a paraphrase—and coloured, we may suspect, by the writer's own ideas.
[7] *Vita et Mors Edwardi Secundi*, in *ibid.* ii. 314.
[8] Cited by Miss Clarke, *loc. cit.* p. 42.
[9] *Chronicles of Edward I and Edward II*, ii. 90.

refused, at first, to answer the bishop of Hereford's question as
to whether they wished the father or the son to reign over them,
but at length 'una voce omnium Filius in Regem sublimatur'.[1*]
There was strong opposition from the archbishop of York, the
bishops of London, Rochester, and Carlisle. The propaganda
before the *populus*, described by the *Lanercost Chronicle*, probably came after this. All it was intended to do was to obtain
the consent of the ' commons ' for a course which had been
decided upon already by the lords. The sermons and the popular
replies were not in any sense, and have never been claimed to
be, ' judgements ' of parliament or of the nation. Such judgement
as is to be discovered in the proceedings was provided by the
lords, the peers.

Probably few knew or cared to know exactly who ' adjudged '
Edward to be deposed. The *Annales Paulini* were perhaps expressing the process as formally and exactly as it could generally
be expressed : ' Et ibidem dominus Rex Edwardus per processum
contra ipsum factum fuit depositus'.[2**] The chronicler of Pipe-
well wrote that ' by common assent of all ', the archbishop of
Canterbury declared that Edward had failed in his duties as king ;
therefore ' it was agreed by all that he ought not to reign ' : [3]
the *Lichfield Chronicle*, that ' in quo concilio ad clamorem tocius
populi unanimiter in ipso clamore perseverantis ut rex Edwardus
. . . deponeretur . . . Sicque Waltero Cantuariensi archiepis-
copo huiusmodi articulos pronunciante, assensu et consensu
omnium rex Edwardus . . . depositus est'.[4†] Edward, they are
content to say, was deposed with the consent of all.

But the well-informed canon of Bridlington ventures to be
more precise, and he shows us how essentially the deposition was
a matter for the magnates. According to him the *proceres* (and
apparently the *proceres* alone) held a parliament ; ' Deinde tract-
antibus illis de regni regimine, rationibus hinc inde propositis,
compertum est regem inconsulte plurima perpetrasse, ipsumque
minus sufficientem ad officium regium reputabant ', or again, ' et
statim diffinitum et approbatum est ab omnibus et singulis regni
nobilibus ibidem tunc praesentibus, quod filius pro patre ad regni
regimen admittatur'.[5††] There was no formal judgement ; the
magnates simply determined that Edward was unfit to rule.

There would be little question of a parliamentary deposition.
Neither the attributes of that assembly nor the circumstances of
the moment made it possible, even if it had been practicable, to
ignore the purely constitutional difficulty created by the absence
of the king. The *universitas regni* did indeed, in the end, reject

[1] *Anglia Sacra*, i. 367.   [2] *Chronicles of Edward I and Edward II*, i. 322.
[3] M. V. Clarke, *loc. cit.* p. 35.   [4] *Ibid.* p. 36, n. 3.
[5] *Gesta*, in *Chronicles of Edward I and Edward II*, ii. 90, 91.

Edward II, but it was a *universitas* different from and more comprehensive than that which had been summoned in Edward's name to parliament. The precedent of 1327 was not only not a precedent for ' parliamentary ' deposition ; it was not even a precedent for deposition by the parliamentary ' estates '. It was a precedent for deposition by the magnates, with the co-operation, agreement and acclamation of the people.

There were, in 1399, no other precedents of practical importance for deposition, but there were for election. Every monarch was ' elected ' in the sense that he was accepted by the nation. The *collaudatio* of the assembled people was a feature of royal elections in Germany and France from the tenth and eleventh centuries.[1] For two hundred years in England, possibly from the accession of Henry I, it appears in the *ordo* for the English coronation : ' His expletis, unus episcoporum alloquatur populum si tali principi ac rectori se subicere et iussonibus eius obtemperare velint. Tunc a circumstante clero et populo respondeatur : *Volumus et concedimus.'*. Stephen's accession provides a remarkable antecedent to that of Edward III and Henry IV. On reaching London after his landing he was elected king by an assembly of the citizens, who declared it to be their right and special privilege to appoint another king on the vacancy of the throne.[2] Even if the claim was ' a grotesque exaggeration ',[3] nevertheless, ever since the ' election ' of Edmund Ironside and of Cnut, Londoners had played an important part in elections.

Henry II was elected by all, received the acclamation of all, and this acclamation was echoed throughout England. The *collaudatio* was inconspicuous at the accession of Richard I,[4] perhaps due to the increasing respect for simple hereditary right. But at the accession of John, Hubert Walter expanded the *collaudatio* into a speech recalling how previous kings had only been recognised if they had been unanimously elected by the whole people. John was the king ' quem . . . unanimiter elegimus universi '. No sooner had the hereditary principle triumphed in 1272 and 1308 (when the coronation *ordo* was modified to give less place to the idea of election) than the crisis of 1327 drove men back once more to the idea of the importance of election by the *universitas*.

The idea was probably familiar throughout the reign of Edward III and his successor.[5] It was not and could not be election or acclamation by *parliament ;* it was election by magnates and acclamation by *populus*. The Lytlington *ordo* of about 1377 makes

[1] P. E. Schramm, *A History of the English Coronation*, p. 143 : cf. F. Liebermann, *National Assembly in the Anglo-Saxon Period*, p. 38.

[2] *Gesta Stephani*, p. 5, cited Stubbs, *Sel. Charters*, p. 136.

[3] Schramm, *op. cit.* p. 157.   [4] *Ibid.* p. 160.   [5] *Ibid.* p. 171.

this quite clear—'Summo mane conveniant *prelati et nobiles in palatio regio apud Westmonasterium*, tractaturi de novi regis consecratione et electione et de legibus et consuetudinibus regni confirmandis et firmiter statuendis. *Hiis sub universorum concordia peractis*.* . .' [1] This is the ancient tradition as it existed in the *ordo* of 1308, and as we can actually see it operating in the memorable events attending Edward II's coronation.[2] Parliament had grown vastly in importance and in its actual position in the state since the beginning of the fourteenth century, but it may be questioned how far it had as yet absorbed the representation of magnates and people in the time-honoured act of electing a new king.

V

These general considerations must govern our approach to the deposition of Richard II. If the above conclusions are correct, all talk of a parliamentary deposition of Richard will probably be wide of the mark. Such a procedure would have been contrary to all that we know of the nature, the composition, and functions of parliament in the fourteenth century; contrary to the only existing precedent, that of 1327; and contrary to what we may legitimately suspect concerning the intentions and preoccupations of Henry himself.[3] Even the idea of a deliberate rejection by Henry of the authority of parliament, in the procedure he ultimately adopted, can have little to commend it. In point of fact the only definite evidence which has been advanced in favour of such a theory is the description by Adam Usk of the conclusions of the committee of which he was a member, which had been appointed to study the matter of setting King Richard aside, and of choosing Henry in his stead; [4] the committee finding that there were reasons enough for setting Richard aside on account of his crimes, and concluding that although Richard was ready himself to yield up the Crown, 'yet for better security was it determined, for the aforesaid reasons, that he should be deposed by the authority of the clergy and people; for which purpose they were then summoned'.[5] Mr. Lapsley's comment on this is: 'It is hard to see how the commission expected the authority of the clergy and people to be obtained except through parliament, and this would appear to have been Adam of Usk's meaning when he says that

[1] Schramm, *op. cit.* p. 174.

[2] See my 'Coronation Oath of Edward II', in *Historical Essays in Honour of James Tait*, pp. 405–16, and especially p. 408; *Ann. Paulini*, in *Chronicles of Edward I and Edward II*, i. 260.

[3] He may have *desired* the approval of parliament: there is no evidence that he thought it practicable; but he might have claimed it, as part of the Lancastrian propaganda after the event, if the commons had not been so opposed to the idea.

[4] Mr. Lapsley, *ante*, xlix. 586, regards it as 'what very nearly amounts to direct evidence that the Lancastrians in September 1399 intended to proceed by way of parliamentary deposition'.　　　　　　　　　　[5] Adam of Usk, pp. 30, 182.

they were summoned for that purpose '.[1]   But, remembering that
we are dealing here with a lawyer and an actual member of the
commission, surely the whole point of this presumably accurate
and technically worded report is that it does *not* suggest deposition
by authority of parliament, but only by that of the clergy and
people—exactly as in the precedent of 1327.

Nor is the idea of a compromise between Henry and his more
constitutionally minded supporters itself easy to accept. It is
true that Henry at one time contemplated claiming the throne
by right of conquest alone. But this did not affect the question
of the procedure of Richard's deposition ; nor is it clear that
this claim would have been incompatible with parliamentary
' election '—or at least that it would have been more incompatible than the basis Henry ultimately adopted. The terms
of Thirning's objection to the original project are very significant.
The essence of his argument against the claim was simply that it
would upset the people, through the insecurity it would create.
The idea was certainly dropped ; but Henry did, in fact, adopt
as the real basis of his appeal for the Crown in the assembly of
30 September the idea of divine elevation which would have been
every bit as destructive of any theory of election by parliament
(if such had existed) as the claim by conquest would have been.
When Henry said that he was sent by God's grace to ' recover '
the realm which was in point of being undone for lack of governance,[2] he was only refining upon his more brutal and direct claim
by the power of the sword ; he avoided the suggestion that by
violence he had destroyed the security of law, but he nevertheless
did not open the door very much wider to admit the action of
election by the ' parliament ' to which he appealed. In either
case there was no place for election in any real sense of the word
as implying a freedom of choice. The successor had already been
chosen, either by victory or by God or by both.

In any case the conception of Henry lending support to the
idea of an ' elective ' monarchy seems to have been carried too far.
It is doubtful if he would ever have admitted that he was elected
by parliament or by the nation or by anybody else in the modern
sense of the term. If he could not establish a claim by hereditary
right or conquest, he still would not accept election by the people.
He based his claim on designation by God. He did not wish—
indeed he could not afford—to have any doubts in the minds of
the assembly as to who Richard's successor was. He ' challenged '
the realm because it was his, because he was of the royal stock
(from Henry III) and appointed by God. It is difficult indeed to
see in this procedure a concession to those who wished to see a

---

[1] *Loc. cit.* p. 586.   [2] *Rot. Parl.* iii. 423.

' parliamentary ' election. There is no reason whatever to think that Henry and his supporters did not agree on these points. There is no reason to believe that any of them would have objected to the support of a parliamentary acceptance of Henry's claims ; but on the other hand there is no reason to believe that, if this had been possible, either Henry or his supporters would have regarded it as imposing any real constitutional limitations on the king. It would have been simply, like the acceptance of the magnates and the acclamations of the people, the recognition, not the creation, of an overwhelming claim.

Rejecting the theory of constitutional struggle and compromise, we are driven back on what seems to be a more straightforward and obvious interpretation of the procedure adopted in 1399. With one very significant exception, noticed above,[1] this seems to have followed very closely indeed that of 1327. This was natural. Broadly speaking, the political situation in both crises was the same : we have an aristocratic opposition overthrowing the monarch through a movement which began as an attempt to redress a private wrong, strongly supported in London, but confronted with a considerable hostility in other parts of the land. There is no reason whatever to imagine that the procedure of Richard's deposition was not taken directly and naturally from the general political traditions of the period, and the specific precedent of 1327. Both have been examined above, and both leave little doubt that the procedure to be adopted was trial and judgement by the magnates, supported by as general an acclamation by the ' nation ' as it was possible to obtain. Everything suggests that the meeting of parliament would provide the necessary concentration of people ; but the deposition was not an act which could be either authorized or performed by parliament itself.

This is, in fact, what the available evidence suggests. Mr. Lapsley has been well justified, we may venture to suggest, in arguing that neither Stubbs nor his successors [2] gave due attention to the insistence of the ' record and process ' that Richard was deposed, not in parliament, nor even in a convention of the parliamentary estates, but in an assembly of *status et populus*. Unfortunately, he has obscured the real identity of procedure in 1327 and 1399 by an interpretation of *status et populus* which conceals effectively the parts played relatively, on the latter occasion, by the ' nation ' or ' people ' and the lords.

Mr. Lapsley believes that the *status* were the estates who had been summoned to parliament, what, indeed, the Lords' *Reports* called the ' convention of estates ' ; the *populus* was composed of

[1] P. 334, . n. 1,
[2] E.g. S. B. Chrimes, *English Constitutional Ideas in the Fifteenth Century*, p. 114.

the 'outsiders' who were invited by Henry in addition.[1] According to this view, there is, and can be, no distinction in the 'record and process' between the parts played by the commons and the lords. It hardly seems preferable to the earlier suggestion of the authors of the *Reports*, that the 'estates' were the magnates, while the *populus* was the elected and non-elected commons. The natural line of division in a non-parliamentary assembly was between noble and common.[2] It corresponds to an important division of function in the process of deposition already visible in 1327.[3] Moreover, if parliament, as such, did not enter into the proceedings of 30 September, if, indeed it could not with certainty be said to exist, the distinction between elected and non-elected member of the 'commons' became an irrational one. If objection be raised that, in spite of these considerations, we have to face the fact that the authors of the 'record and process' deliberately employed a term 'estates' for the magnates which they knew might easily suggest the elected commons as well, some explanation of this fact will be attempted later on. We may agree that they may have intended deliberately to mislead. At the same time they did afford the reader a clear and careful indication of the real meaning of the language they employed.

Almost at the outset of their account of the assembly of 30 September, they recorded how Richard's resignation was conveyed to all the lords spiritual and temporal and to the *populus* of the realm—'dictis Archiepiscopis Cant' et Ebor', ac Duce Lancastrie, aliisque Ducibus ac Dominis tam Spiritualibus quam Temporalibus. . . . Populoque dicti Regni tunc ibidem propter factum Parliamenti in maxima multitudine congregato presentibus.'[4]* Though we have here the phrase *populus regni* and not *populus* alone, this passage is of the utmost significance as suggesting where the commons of parliament found a place in a formal enumeration of the exceptional assembly which deposed

---

[1] It should be noticed that, as they are used here, *status* and *populus* are complementary. Hence *status* will probably not signify *all* the estates of the land. It is something which we should perhaps distinguish from *status totius regni*. The meaning of *coram omnibus statibus regni*, therefore, discussed by Mr. Richardson in *E.H.R.* lii. 44, and by Mr. Lapsley in *ibid.* liii. 62–3, cannot entirely settle the problem of *status* used in conjunction with *populus*.

[2] We may recall *Piers Plowman*, B. Prologue, l. 116 :

> 'The kyng and knyȝthode and clergye bothe
> Casten that the comune shulde hem-self fynde.
> The comune contreued of kynde witte craftes,
> And for profit of alle the poeple plowman ordeygned.'

The distinction between noble and non-noble was the deepest social distinction of the age.

[3] Cf. the remarks in the Lords' *Reports*, i. 350–1.

[4] *Rot. Parl.* iii. 417. They are, it is said, the lords, spiritual and temporal who are enumerated ' below '. Does this refer to the names given in the *Rot. Parl.* on p. 427 ?

Richard II.[1] Similarly (though this instance is not so clear), the committee appointed to declare Richard's deposition was elected ' per Pares et Proceres Regni . . . et ejusdem Regni Communitates omnes Status ejusdem Regni representantes '.[2*] Its members were ' procurators of all the estates and people ' ; they renounced homage on behalf of the ' estates and people ' ; in the specific enumeration of the grades represented by these proctors [3] the same distinction occurs,—the dukes and earls, barons and bannerets are represented on the one hand, the bachelors and commons on the other. It is surely impossible to imagine the elected commons coming anywhere but in this last group, with the general *populus ;* no satisfactory argument has been advanced to justify our rejection of the conclusion in the Lords' *Reports,* that ' in these proceedings also appears the division of the laymen of the kingdom in two classes, under the description of two distinct estates . . . the Lay Lords of Parliament seem to have been generally considered as forming by themselves, one estate '.[4] The authors of the *Reports* perhaps went too far in insisting that the distinction was essentially a parliamentary one ; but, however we account for it, the distinction remains. Still another variation is given in Henry's words to the assembly of 30 September : ' Sires, I thank God and zowe Spirituel and Temporel and all the Astates of the lond.' [5] There is the same line of division here, between lords and others ; there is also an illustration of the meaning of ' estates of the land ', signifying *all* the social classes. This is, indeed, so much the natural meaning of ' estates ', that the use of the term in the ' record and process ' to signify only the lords is not, despite the lack of comment on the point in the lords' *Reports,* easy to explain. That problem will be discussed below. Whatever our solution, it cannot affect the evidence of the language of the ' record and process ' itself.

This language, thus interpreted, records, carefully and precisely, a deposition of Richard II, not by parliament and not by the estates of the land, but, as we should expect, in the first

---

[1] Mr. Richardson also finds it hard to believe that *populus* means merely the mob, additional to the summoned representatives at Westminster, *E.H.R.* liii. 60. Of course the above enumeration may not have been intended to be exhaustive. Still, the commons were undoubtedly present. By inference, at least, we must have been intended to understand them as being among the *populus,* since they cannot have been enumerated amongst the dukes and lords. This view is strengthened by the addition of the phrase *propter factum parliamenti.* It is not easy to exclude the commons summoned by writ, when thinking of the *populus* present *propter factum parliamenti.* This instance of the use of *populus* is the most important of all. In it the authors of the ' record and process ', so to speak, establish their terminology. They do it, it is suggested, so as to safeguard themselves from all claim that they have misrepresented the function of the commons in Richard's deposition—they clearly include the commons in the term *populus,* but confuse the issue later by their use of the term ' estates '.

[2] *Rot. Parl.* iii. 422. [3] Given by Thirning, *ibid.* iii. 424.
[4] *Reports,* i. 350–1. [5] *Rot. Parl.* iii. 423.

instance by the assembly of lords, with the *collaudatio* and approval of the *populus*, the commonality of all the land.   It brings our interpretation of the crisis into conformity with the precedent of 1327 and the general political traditions concerning parliament which have been already discussed.   Richard's resignation was read, in the assembly of 30 September, before the *status et populus* ; [1] judgement on him was that of the *siatus* alone. [2] On the other hand, the committee which declared this judgement spoke in the name of all and was, as in 1327, chosen by all. [3] Though the committee, declaring the sentence in parliament before the interview with Richard, did not make the distinction clear, [4] they were not concerned to elucidate this particular point so much as to clothe their declaration in sonorous and imposing terms. [5] Similarly, only the lords were asked, in the first place, what they thought of Henry's claim to be king ; [6] whilst both lords and commons agreed to their reply. [7]   The same distinctions appear in Thirning's speech to Richard (incorporated, of course, in the ' record and process '), [8] and in the informed chronicles of all shades

---

[1] *Rot. Parl.* iii. 417.

[2] *Ibid.* p. 422.   ' Et quoniam videbatur omnibus Statibus illis . . . omnes Status predicti unanimiter consenserunt.'   Thirning agrees exactly, in his speech to Richard II (*ibid.* p. 424) : ' tho wele herd and pleinelich understonden to all the States forsaide . . . hem thoght it was resonable and Cause for to depose zowe '.

[3] *Ibid.* iii. 422.   ' Unde Status et Communitates predicti certos Commissarios . . . unanimiter et concorditer constituerunt.'* According to Thirning (p. 424), by ' all the States of the Reaume '.   This is more comprehensive than *states* used as the complement of *people*.

[4] On the other hand, the ' record and process ' made it fairly clear (p. 422) : the committee was elected by, and represented, the *status et communitates*, but it was elected to pronounce judgement in the name only of the *status*, that is, the lords : ' vice, nomine et auctoritate omnium statuum predictorum '.

[5] *Rot. Parl.* iii. 422 : ' prehabita super hiis et omnibus in ipso negotio actitatis coram Statibus antedictis, et nobis deliberatione diligenti, vice, nomine, et auctoritate nobis in hac parte commissa, ipsum Ricardum . . . ab omni Dignitate et Honore Regiis . . . merito deponendum Pronunciamus, Decernimus et Declaramus, et ipsum simili cautela Deponimus per nostram diffinitivam Sententiam '.**

[6] *Ibid.* p. 423 : ' tam Domini Spirituales quam Temporales, et omnes Status ibidem presentes, singillatim et comuniter interrogati '.

[7] *Ibid.* : ' iidem Status, *cum toto Populo* . . . unanimiter consenserunt '.

[8] Thirning was most meticulous in his choice of words.   He began (p. 424) by saying that a parliament had been summoned ' Of all the States of the Reaume ', and he continued ' by cause of the whiche sommons all the States of this Londe were ther gadyrd '. This was all perfectly correct and precise, but Thirning was disguising the fact (probably deliberately) that others besides the normal members had entered this assembly in considerable numbers.   He tried to represent it as a perfectly normal gathering, which it was certainly not.   Thirning then recounted how all the estates of the land had elected the proctors who visited Richard, but he did not describe all these estates as judging.   Richard's defaults had been read at the instance of ' all the States and People ', but judgement was only by the ' States ' : ' And over this, Sire, at the instance of *all thes States and Poeple*, ther ware certein articles of Defautes . . . redde there : and tho wele herd and pleinelich understonden to *all the States forsaide*, hem thoght hem so trewe and so notorie and knowen, that by the Causes and by mo other, os thei sayd, . . . hem thoght that was resonable and Cause for to depose zowe, and her Commissaries *that thei made* and

of opinion,[1] excepting Adam of Usk.[2]   But Adam of Usk's version
of a *parliamentary* deposition is not the question.[3]   We may perhaps agree that the evidence, as interpreted above, is fairly consistent in pointing towards a judgement on Richard II by the
lords, with the approval and concurrence of the commonalty,
including both elected commons and others as well.

Nevertheless the language of the 'record and process', although precise and not unnatural, could have been chosen with
greater clarity and precision.   Mr. Lapsley was almost certainly
correct in suggesting that it was drawn up with some intention to
deceive.   On the other hand, Mr. Richardson was equally correct
in observing that the deception was clumsy and half-hearted.   We
have still to attempt an explanation and reconciliation of these
facts.

Partly, the terminology of the 'record and process' may
have been due to a natural hesitation to define too closely the
part played by the various elements present on 30 September,
united in what was, at bottom, an unconstitutional act.   Yet
this is not, probably, the whole truth.   The whole problem of the
'record and process' lies, not in the use of the general term
'estates' but in its use to signify only the estates of the lords.

ordeined, os it is of record ther, declared and decreed and adjugged zowe for to be
deposed'. Thus, strictly speaking, the committee to declare judgement had been
elected by, and spoke in the name of, the lords alone. On the other hand, the same
commission, renouncing homage, was properly represented as doing so in the name of
both estates and people : 'And we, Procuratours to all these *States and People*' renounce
homage on behalf of all the people and estates.

[1] E.g. the *Continuatio Eulogii Historiarum* (iii 384). This writer in the main
follows the official account, but at this point he has condensed it into the following
words : 'ad quod [Henry's claim] omnes domini singillatim assenserunt, et communitas
communiter hoc clamabat'. This is exactly the interpretation of the 'record and
process' suggested above. It even agrees to the extent of making the lords approve
singly. Cf. also the *Historia Vitae et Regni Regis Ricardi* (edited Thos. Hearne,
Oxford, 1729, p. 159 : cf. *Davies Chronicle*, pp. 17–8) : 'Post quam quidem renuncia-
tionem publice lectam, et per dominos et per plebeios unanimiter admissam, dictoque
Rege Ricardo deposito, et sic Trono regio vacante cum tractaretur inter Dominos
de Rege futuro, populus totus acclamavit Dominum Henricum Ducem Lancastriae,
ipsumque in Regem elegerunt'.[*] Unfortunately Creton is of no value at this point
(*Archaeologia*, xx. 192–9), and Hardyng gives no details (*Chronicle*, p. 352), though
he says that Henry 'was electe by ye hole parliament'. We can hardly attach any
importance to the version given in the *Traïson et Mort* (pp. 218–20) on technical
details such as these, though we can perhaps see in it the distinction suggested above
between commons and lords.

[2] *Chronicon*, pp. 32, 33, 186.

[3] It is hard, remembering Adam's relations with the advisers of Henry IV, not to
regard his version as a piece of deliberate and extreme misrepresentation. He makes
the report of the committee which had interviewed Richard on the 29th take the
place of the judgement of the lords recorded in other sources. We have no grounds
whatever for accepting this version. Its merit in Adam's eyes may have been largely
due to the fact that it evaded the awkward question of judgement altogether. Adam
represents the procedure as being authorised by 'the consent of all and every in parliament', and 'by consent and authority of the whole parliament'. He neither distinguishes between lords and commons nor refers to the *populus* additional to both.

That this is a natural meaning for the word, used in conjunction with *populus*, is hardly an excuse for the authors of the ' record and process ', accustomed as they must have been to a precise and careful use of words.   The ' record and process ' was intended for the public as well as for the lawyer and official ; and it is hard to believe that those who compiled it did not consider the interpretation which the public would frequently give to ' estates '. To the public, the assembly óf 30 September might seem to have met as a parliament ; the estates would be, to many, its members, commons and lords.   The distinction between *status* as the complement of *populus* and *status totius regni* was over-subtle ; it has eluded even the elaborate analysis of Mr. Chrimes.[1]

The aim of the compilers must be deduced from the purpose they achieved.   This has been written plainly on the pages of history ever since.   Even the authors of the Lords' *Reports* (unaccountably neglected by Mr. Chrimes), who appreciated the distinction between magnates and others, failed to disentangle the parts played by commons and lords.   It is, of course, the action of the commons, not of the lords, which has been misunderstood.   The object achieved by the ' record and process ', whether deliberately or not, was to suggest the commons as judges of Richard II along with the lords.   However shocking such an idea was to all sense of political decency and fitness, it had this much to recommend it, that it was not so obviously incompatible with the situation as it existed after the abdication of Richard II on 29 September as judgement by parliament was.   It did not quite so hopelessly conflict with parliamentary tradition.   If Henry could not have the judgement of parliament in his favour, he might still hope for that of the ' estates '.[2]

There was, indeed, a quite particular reason for such a desire. Ever since the events of Conway and Flint, men had looked to this assembly to settle the issues between Henry and Richard II. Henry himself had accepted, and partly created, the situation. Parliament, Henry had said, loosely (and perhaps optimistically) in the early days of his triumph, will decide between us ; and the general run of Englishmen, somewhat naïvely, expected it to decide.   Neither they nor Henry had reckoned with the niceties of tradition and procedure, which made it impossible for parliament as a body to judge.

---

[1] *English Constitutional Ideas in the Fifteenth Century*, pp. 83–115.   Mr. Chrimes came very near to the view put forward above, in his remarks on p. 109 : ' So far it might possibly be said that the word " estate " was being used only to mean " persons of estate " ; and no doubt that may be true.'

[2] Not, it should be added, an actual judgement by all the estates.   What we are here concerned with is not the actual procedure, but the representation of this procedure to the world at large.   It is hardly conceivable that the commons should actually have participated in judgement.

Failing a parliamentary title, the wording of the 'record and process' suggests that Henry wished to represent his succession as resting on the judgement of the 'estates' of all the land, commons as well as lords. Nor does this evidence stand quite alone. There are grounds for believing that his intention had been discovered by, and was unwelcome to, the parliamentary commons themselves. A petition of the commons in the first parliament of Henry IV was in all probability directed against the very project of representing them as participating in the judgement on Richard II : [1] ' Les Communes firent leur Protestation en manere come ils firent au commencement du Parlement ; et outre ceo monstrerent au Roy, qe come les Juggementz du Parlement appertiegnent soulement au Roy et as Seigneurs, et nient as Communes sinoun en cas qe s'il plest au Roy de sa grace especiale lour monstrer les ditz Juggementz, pur ease de eux, qe nul Record soit fait en Parlement encontre les ditz Communes q'ils sont ou serront parties as ascunes Juggementz donez ou a doners en apres en Parlement. A qoi leur feust responduz par l'Ercevesqe de Canterbirs, de comandement du Roy, Coment mesmes les Communes sont petitioners et demandours, et qe le Roy et les Seigneurs de tout temps ont eues, et aueront de droit, les Jugementz en Parlement.'* The pledge which Henry gave the commons in his reply would explain perfectly the restraint under which the authors of the 'record and process' worked. They were not prohibited from expressing bluntly the commons' judgement on Richard by any constitutional preoccupations of the new monarch, but by the inconvenient inhibition of Henry's solemnly pledged word.

It is surely legitimate to suggest that we have here an explanation, and perhaps the only possible explanation, of the peculiar wording of the 'record and process'. This document was deliberately vague and possibly misleading ; but it was not intended either to suggest or avoid a parliamentary title for Henry IV. In so far as it confused the functions of lords and commons, it merely attempted to identify the knights and burgesses entirely with the procedure which inaugurated the new régime. Its wording was the outcome, not of the constitutional

---

[1] *Rot. Parl.* iii. 427. Mr. Lapsley relates this to the proceedings against Richard's appellants in 1397. The commons, he believes, did not wish to be represented as having taken part, as judges, against the appellants. But it is not easy to accept this view. The proceedings against the appellants were already a matter of record, not seriously in doubt. Judgement had, as Mr. Lapsley points out, been given, very properly, by the king and the lords. It is not easy to believe that the commons were afraid of a falsification of this record, which they themselves had requested should be produced. On the other hand, we know that at this very moment Henry was contemplating, or had put into effect, a design of misrepresenting the events of 29 and 30 September. The commons had not, we have seen, participated, on the 30th, in the actual judgement on Richard II ; if Henry had contemplated representing them as so doing, this would explain entirely their anxiety to disclaim such a rôle.

preoccupations, but of the political weakness, of Henry IV.   Its
origins must be sought in the obscure episodes at Doncaster and in
the March of Wales, when Henry began to play a double game and
destroy the unity of the movement which first gave him support.
It breathes the same main political and constitutional traditions as
had already found expression in the deposition of Edward II.   In it
we may perhaps discern the increased importance of the commons
in parliament by 1399 ;   perhaps also of parliament itself.   But
it does not reflect Henry IV himself as either dependent on, or
hostile to, a parliamentary title to the throne.   Perhaps the most
important conclusion which a study of it suggests is that a parliamentary title to the throne was outside the practical possibilities
offered to a successful rebel by the constitution of 1399.

EDITORIAL NOTES

I. Some Factors in the Beginnings of Parliament

p. 31* Reprinted from *T.R.H.S.*, 4th Ser. XXII (1940), 101–39.

p. 33* 'He should sue before the justices of the bench of the king and he should be heard there and let justice be done'; 'they should go to the chancery and the king's will is that justice should be done'; 'he should show the charter before the treasurer and barons of the exchequer and let justice be done.'

p. 33** Translated on p. 34.

p. 34* For the word *querela* (plaint) and the legal processes to which plaints gave rise, see. F. M. Powicke, *The Thirteenth Century*, pp. 351–3 and the references cited there.

p. 34** For *quo warranto* procedures, see T. F. T. Plucknett, *Legislation of Edward I*, pp. 35–48.

p. 36* See p. 135.

p. 37* See p. 117.

p. 37** See p. 117.

p. 39* '. . . before us and our council in our next parliament . . . to do and receive justice.'

p. 39** '. . . until the king's parliament three weeks after the Purification of the Blessed Mary in order that it may be discussed before the barons of the exchequer and themselves.'

p. 39† '. . . to the forthcoming parliament. And the sheriff should inform them that on that day they should appear before the said justiciar to receive justice thereon.'

p. 39†† '. . . so that on that day full justice may be done them thereon before our barons of the exchequer'; '. . . in order that it may then be discussed before the king's barons of the exchequer.'

p. 40* '. . . to the parliament next coming . . . so that on that day they should be before the justiciar . . . to receive justice thereon.'

p. 40** The 'quindene of Easter' is the next Monday but one following Easter Monday.

p. 40† 'The barons of the exchequer are commanded that the demands they are making of the abbot of St Edmund's in regard to certain liberties, which the said abbot says belong to him, should be respited to the quindene of Easter because the king cannot at present manage a discussion of this matter on account of his plan to go overseas.'

p. 42* 'John Balliol comes before ... the king's council and seeks the consideration of the barons of the exchequer ... and the barons of the exchequer are commanded to see that justice is done to him thereon.' The doubtful assize in 1252 is postponed to the quindene of Michaelmas 'in order that then we may ensure that complete justice is done by the advice of discreet men'.

p. 42** '... so that on that day, with the impartial advice of the said barons [of the exchequer] and of other men faithful to the king, the king's right and the abbot's right in the said liberties may be discussed.'

p. 51* In fact, an intended parliament is mentioned *eo nomine* in 1242: *Close Rolls*, 1237–42, p. 447; and in November 1236 parties before the king's bench were given a day 'at Westminster at the parliament' to be held in January 1237: H. G. Richardson and G. O. Sayles, *E.H.R.* LXXXII (1967), 747–50 (there is a translation of the text in P. Spufford, *Origins of the English Parliament*, p. 28).

p. 52* 'The king greets his justices itinerant in the county of Kent ... All the demands which have been brought before us whereby men claim franchises, i.e. those which the lord archbishop of Canterbury, G. Earl of Clare and others lay claim to, should be respited until the quindene of Hilary to come before our council at Westminster.'

p. 53* 'Regalian rights pertaining solely to the king.'

p. 54* 'Regarding rights and liberties and other things touching the said king.'

p. 54** 'Now letters of this sort were scattered about in all directions which included this detestable additional clause: notwithstanding any ancient liberty, this matter should proceed.'

p. 55* 'And if a prelate is compelled to appear and show the charter of a donor, and whether it is contained therein that the donor gave such and such liberties, ... it will avail him nothing unless express mention is made of the said liberty in that charter' (see H. R. Luard's edition, Rolls Series VI, pp. 363–4). Royal proceedings in regard to franchises in the thirteenth century are discussed by H. M. Cam, *Liberties and Communities in Medieval England*, pp. 173–82; Plucknett, *op. cit.*, pp. 35 ff.; and D. W. Sutherland, *Quo Warranto Proceedings in the Reign of Edward I*.

p. 56* 'Speak with the king.'

p. 56** 'If that debt is evident, they should proceed to a judgement on the matter; if, however, they discover any sort of ambiguity therein they should have the said plea brought before the king on a fixed day so that it may be determined.'

p. 59* 'Regarding many liberties. All those who claim to possess liberties by charters should have a day appointed for them to hear their judgement regarding the said liberties . . . on the quindene of Michaelmas.'

p. 63* 'The demand which they have made upon him for 20 marks by summons of the exchequer . . . which 20 marks have now remained in demand for 15 years past.'

p. 66* 'Because we wish to have discussion of the aforesaid matters by our council in our presence and that of certain of the said men.'

p. 68* For the *nisi prius* system, see W. S. Holdsworth, *History of English Law* (7th ed.) I, 278–83.

2. The Nature of Parliament in the Reign of Henry III

p. 70* Reprinted from *E.H.R.* LXXIV (1959), 590–610.

p. 71* In the second, revised edition (1965), the earliest noted occurrence is dated *c.* 1210.

p. 71** For the early significance of the word on the Continent see also A. Marongiu, *Medieval Parliaments; a Comparative Study*, trans. S. J. Woolf (London, 1968), pp. 23, 48.

p. 72* 'All the nobility of the English kingdom assembled in London at a most general parliament convoked by the king's order, that is the prelates, including bishops, abbots and priors, together with the earls and the barons, in order to discuss effectively the disturbed state of the realm, as urgent necessity demanded.'

p. 73* The earliest known use of the word *parliamentum* in an official document occurs in a *curia regis* roll in November 1236: H. G. Richardson and G. O. Sayles, *E.H.R.* LXXXII (1967), 747–50.

p. 73** For a critique, which is not necessarily conclusive, of this method, see H. G. Richardson and G. O. Sayles, *L.Q.R.* LXXII (1961), 424–6.

p. 73† The statistics that follow do not include the four instances listed in the addenum, below, p. 90.

p. 73†† ' "The parliament at Runemed" between King John, our father, and his barons of England.'

p. 75* See above, pp. 31–69.

N

3. Introduction to 'Memoranda de Parliamento' 1305

p. 91* Reprinted from *Selected Historical Essays of F. W. Maitland*, ed. Helen M. Cam (Cambridge University Press and Selden Society, 1957), pp. 52–96. For a recent critical assessment of this essay, see H. E. Bell, *Maitland; a Critical Examination* (London, 1965). An earlier attempt to set it in the context of developing views about the history of medieval parliaments was made by G. Templeman, 'The History of Parliament to 1400 in the Light of Modern Research', *Birmingham University Historical Journal* I (1948), reprinted in *The Making of English History*, ed. R. L. Schuyler and H. Ausubel (New York, 1952), pp. 114–15.

p. 91** 'Because we understand that the said archbishop and others of the clergy may perchance wish to make representations at our coming parliament about certain matters touching their estate.'

p. 92* Writs authorizing the knights and burgesses to receive their expenses from their local communities were dated 20 March: *Parl. Writs* I, 156–7.

p. 92** For another view of these events, see B. Wilkinson, *Studies in the Constitutional History of the Thirteenth and Fourteenth Centuries*, 7–14.

p. 94* The independent role and the importance of the second secretariat based on the privy seal has been more fully revealed by the recent rediscovery of a large range of its records: see P. Chaplais, 'Privy Seal Drafts, Rolls and Registers (Edward I—Edward II)', *E.H.R.* LXXIII (1958), 270–3.

p. 98* John Bush was an official of the king's household, but he cannot be shown to have been a chancery clerk: H. G. Richardson and G. O. Sayles, *E.H.R.* XLVI (1931), 545, note 2.

p. 98** John was probably also an illegitimate son of Edward I: *Handbook of British Chronology*, ed. F. M. Powicke and E. B. Fryde (2nd ed., 1961), p. 35.

p. 100* *Cal. Close Rolls*, 1302–7, p. 321.

p. 100** *Cal. Patent Rolls*, 1301–7, p. 317.

p. 106* For the circumstances which gave rise to the ordinance of trailbaston, see also *Select Cases in the Court of King's Bench under Edward II*, ed. G. O. Sayles (Selden Society, vol. 74), LV–LVI.

p. 108* 'To the petition of A. de B., seeking that etc., answer is made as follows, that etc.'

p. 108** This letter is printed in translation in B. Wilkinson, *Constitutional History of England, 1215–1399* III, 144.

p. 109* Translated *ibid.*, pp. 144–5.

p. 117* Printed below, ch. 7.

p. 117** Langlois's comment is: 'parliament, that vague word, a barbarous synonym initially both for an assembly and a discussion, attained a precise meaning both in England and in France at about the same time'.

p. 123* For the later distinction between 'common' and 'singular' petitions, see above, pp. 15–17 and the references quoted there.

p. 134* The passage in French reads: 'saving the bishops, earls and barons, justices and others who are of the council of our lord the king'.

p. 134** The published *curia regis* rolls now extend to 1230; and the Pipe Roll Society has published the memoranda rolls of the exchequer for 1208 (New Ser. XXXI, 1955) and 1230–1 (New Ser. XI, 1933).

p. 135* 'To the petition of the university of Cambridge seeking the lord king's aid, that he should be willing to become the founder of a house which the said university has ordained for the maintenance of poor scholars dwelling in the said university; and that the said house may be endowed with lands and rents to the amount of £40 or more or less as the king wishes:

Answer is given as follows: that the king wishes to be informed by the sheriff whether this would be to his advantage or his damage.
Ancient Petition, 13758.

The chancellor, masters and clerks of the university of Cambridge show to our lord the king, whom God keep, that they have provided, for the well-being of holy Church and with God's help for the profit of the land, a college for poor scholars who need to be maintained in the said university by means of your aid, dear lord, if you are willing to give it, and of other alms from clerks and layfolk who wish, for God's sake, to help them and to further their intention; we beseech you for the love of God, and for the souls of your father, mother, consort and ancestors, that you will be willing to be the founder of that house, that it will be under your protection and that it may be endowed by the purchase in free alms, from those willing to proffer them, of lands and rents to the value of £40, or of more or less as you wish, notwithstanding your statute regarding lands and tenements alienated in mortmain, whereby the scholars dwelling therein may be maintained; and so that those scholars shall be chosen and accepted and shall be resident and governed by the chancellor and according to the franchise of the said university in the same manner as other scholars studying there.

(*Endorsement*) The king wishes to be informed by the sheriff whether this would be to his advantage or damage.

To the chancellor.'

4. The Plena Potestas of English Parliamentary Representatives

p. 136* Reprinted from *Oxford Essays in Medieval History presented to Herbert Edward Salter* (Oxford, 1934), pp. 141–54. Gaines Post has made a general study of the concept of *plena potestas* in an essay reprinted in his *Studies in Medieval Legal Thought* (Princeton, 1964), pp. 91–162.

p. 136** 'On behalf of all and sundry.' The writ of 1254 is translated in B. Wilkinson, *Constitutional History of Medieval England, 1216–1399* III, 302–3.

p. 136† 'For the whole county.' The writ of 1264 is translated in Wilkinson, *op. cit.*, p. 304.

p. 136†† 'For the community of the county' and 'on behalf of the communities of the counties.'

p. 137* The record of 1268 is translated in C. Stephenson and F. G. Marcham, *Sources of English Constitutional History*, pp. 152–3.

p. 137** 'For the community of the said county.' The writ for the parliament of October 1275 is translated in Wilkinson, *op. cit.*, pp. 306–7.

p. 137† 'Having full power on behalf of the communities of the same counties.' The writ for the two assemblies of representatives in 1283 is translated in Stephenson and Marcham, *op. cit.*, pp. 155–6.

p. 137†† 'And we shall hold as established and accepted whatever those men do on our behalf in the aforesaid matters' (*ibid.*, p. 153).

p. 138* 'With full powers for themselves and for all the community of the county.' The writ for 1290 is translated in Wilkinson, *op. cit.*, p. 307.

p. 138** The writ for 1294 is translated in part *supra.*, p. 136.

p. 139* 'To hear and to do what we shall then and there more fully require of them.'

p. 139** 'For wine drunk by the mayor, by John de Stodle, and others at the time of the sealing of the commission of the said mayor and John as parliamentary burgesses.'

p. 140* 'In the same year were summoned four knights from each county of England, who were to have the power of binding the county and doing what would be ordered to them by the king's council. They were to appear before the aforesaid council on the morrow of St Martin in November and it was then ordained that a tenth should be granted to the lord king in the form that follows.'

p. 142* Stephenson's essay is reprinted in his *Mediaeval Institutions; Selected Essays*, ed. B. D. Lyon (Ithaca, N.Y., 1954), ch. III.

p. 142** See an English translation by K. L. Wood-Legh under the title of *History of English Electoral Law in the Middle Ages* (Cambridge, 1940), pp. 10–15.

p. 145* 'Full power . . . to hear and do what on our part we shall cause to be explained to them.' Cf. Stephenson and Marcham, *op. cit.*, p. 156.

p. 145** 'With full power for themselves and for all the community of the shire to counsel, and to consent, for themselves and for that community, to those things which the earls, barons and magnates aforesaid shall be led to agree upon.' *Cf.* Wilkinson, *op. cit.*, p. 307.

p. 146* 'To do what shall then be ordained by common counsel.' The writ of 1295 is translated in Wilkinson, *op. cit.*, p. 308.

p. 147* 'What touches all should be approved by all.' For a study of the currency and significance of this notion, especially in England, see Gaines Post, *op. cit.*, pp. 163–238.

5. The Personnel of the Commons in Parliament under Edward I and Edward II

p. 150* Reprinted from *Essays in Medieval History presented to Thomas Frederick Tout* (Manchester, 1925), pp. 197–214. See also Edwards's defence of his method and conclusions, 'Re-election and the Medieval Parliament', *History* XI (1926), 204–10 against the critical appraisal of his original essay by A. F. Pollard, 'History, English and Statistics', *ibid.*, pp. 15–24. Pollard accepted the validity of this reply.

There are similar studies of the membership of the House of Commons in the reigns of Edward III and Richard II by K. L. Wood-Legh in *E.H.R.* XLVII (1932) and by N. B. Lewis, *ibid.* XLVIII (1933).

p. 150** Pasquet's *Essay* appeared in an English translation by R. G. D. Laffan (Cambridge, 1925) and Lapsley's article is reprinted in his *Crown, Community and Parliament in the Later Middle Ages* (Oxford, 1951), ch. IV.

p. 159* 'Failed to answer' or 'sent no answer'.

p. 159** Riess's study appeared in an English translation by K. L. Wood-Legh under the title *The History of the English Electoral Law in the Middle Ages* (Cambridge, 1940).

p. 160* 'And irrespective of whether the said sheriff had certified the court of the said return or not, we certify you, sir, that by our common assent we have elected our fellow burgesses Geffrei Stace and Cristophe del Boys, for we are ready, as far as we can, to obey the mandates of our liege lord as we are obliged to do in law.'

6. The Legislators of Medieval England

p. 168* Reprinted from H. M. Cam, *Law-Finders and Law-Makers in Medieval England* (London, 1962).

p. 174* Ottobuono was papal legate in England; for his part in the political settlement of England after the baronial rebellion see F. M. Powicke, *Henry III and the Lord Edward*, pp. 526 ff.

p. 176* Extracts from the record on the parliament roll are translated in Stephenson and Marcham, *op. cit.*, pp. 228–30.

p. 178* For this relationship see H. M. Cam, *The Hundred and the Hundred Rolls*, pp. 225 ff.

p. 178** Reprinted with some revisions in Gaines Post, *Studies in Medieval Legal Thought*, pp. 61–162.

p. 179* The references will be found below, pp. 181–4 and in the bibliography.

p. 181* Translated B. Wilkinson, *Constitutional History of England* III, 315–16.

p. 183* The suggestion that Edward I inspired the Statute of Carlisle is very debatable: Wilkinson, *op. cit.* III, 382–3.

p. 185* Translated Stephenson and Marcham, *op. cit.*, p. 265.

p. 187* Extracts translated *ibid.*, p. 275.

p. 188* For the thirteenth-century background of measures to keep the peace see A. Harding, 'Origins and Early History of the Keeper of the Peace', *T.R.H.S.*, 5th Ser. X (1960), 85 ff.

p. 190* 'The king will think about it'; as Maitland says, this was 'a civil form of saying No, but a form not unfrequently used': *Constitutional History of England*, 189.

7. Parliament, 1327–36

p. 195* Reprinted from J. F. Willard and W. A. Morris, *The English Government at Work, 1327–36* (Cambridge, Mass., 1940), I, 82–128.

p. 196* Some distinction did, however, exist between parliaments and councils in the minds of government officials, though modern scholars have been unable hitherto to define it. A memorandum of decisions taken by the king's council in January 1325 provides 'qe les grantz soient somouns dy estre pur conseiller etc. et noun pas pur parlement' (the magnates are to be summoned to assemble [at Winchester] to counsel etc. and not for a parliament). *Cf.* P. Chaplais, *The War of St. Sardos*, Camden 3rd Ser. LXXXVII (1954), 134, arts. VI and VII.

p. 196** H. G. Richardson and G. O. Sayles have tried to reply to Plucknett's critique of their position in *L.Q.R.* LXXVII (1961), 215–20.

It should also be observed that from 1327 onwards no assembly is ever called a parliament in the writs of summons unless elected representatives were summoned to it, though not all the assemblies containing representatives were termed parliaments.

p. 202* 'The Commons request that all the petitions presented by the Commons in diverse parliaments of the present king and never answered, should be duly answered and executed in this parliament.'

p. 203* See pp. 126–8.

p. 203** A new edition of *Fleta* is being prepared for the Selden Society by H. G. Richardson and G. O. Sayles. One volume has been published so far (vol. II, as vol. 72 of Selden Society for 1953).

p. 208* The most recent study, J. Enoch Powell and K. Wallis, *The House of Lords in the Middle Ages* (1968), does not consistently adopt the historian's viewpoint for the first half of the fourteenth century.

p. 211* Lists of the king's serjeants have been published by G. O. Sayles in *Select Cases in the Court of King's Bench*, V, 1958 (vol. 76 of Selden Society), pp. CVII–CXVI (1278–1340) and VI, 1965 (vol. 82 of Selden Society), pp. XCIII–CVI (1341–1422).

p. 212* The taxation of the clergy in the years 1327–36 has been subsequently discussed by W. E. Lunt in *The English Government at Work, 1327–36* (1947), II, 227–80. See also Lunt, *Financial Relations of the Papacy with England, 1327–1534* (1962).

p. 214* See pp. 136–49.

p. 216* The evidence has subsequently been published in M. Bassett, *Knights of the Shire for Bedfordshire* (Bedfordshire Historical Record Society, XXIX, 1949).

p. 219* *Cf.* J. S. Roskell, 'The problem of the attendance of the Lords in medieval parliaments', *B.I.H.R.* XXIX (1956).

p. 220* See pp. 150–67.

p. 221* For the subsequent discussion of this term see H. M. Cam, 'From witness of the shire to full parliament' in her *Law-Finders and Law-Makers in Medieval England* (1962).

p. 222* See also M. H. Keen, 'Treason trials under the Law of Arms', *T.R.H.S.*, 5th Ser. XII (1962).

p. 227* See p. 116.

p. 228* See especially D. Rayner, 'The forms and machinery of the 'Commune Petition' in the fourteenth century', *E.H.R.* LVI (1941), for a more definitive study, which supersedes all earlier publications.

p. 231* For abuses in the period immediately after 1336 see *infra*, chapter 8.

p. 235* Subsequent publications on the experiments to improve the machinery of justice in the decade 1327–36 include the following: G. O. Sayles, *The Court of King's Bench in Law and History* (Selden Society lecture, 1959); E. L. G. Stones, 'Sir Geoffrey le Scrope (*c*. 1285–1340), Chief Justice of the King's Bench', *E.H.R.* LXIX (1954) and 'The Folvilles of Ashby-Folville, Leicestershire, and their associates in crime', *T.R.H.S.*, 5th Ser. VII (1957); G. O. Sayles, introductions to *Select Cases in the Court of King's Bench, cit. supra*, IV (1957) and VI (1965); J. G. Bellamy 'The Coterel gang', *E.H.R.* LXXIX (1964).

p. 239* The taxation of the laity in the years 1327–36 has been subsequently discussed by C. Johnson in *The English Government at Work* (*cit. supra*), II, 201–26. See also *infra*, ch. 8.

8. *Parliament and the French War, 1336–40*

p. 242* Reprinted from *Essays in Medieval History Presented to Bertie Wilkinson* (Toronto, 1969), pp. 250–69.

All references to unpublished sources are to documents in the Public Record Office in London, unless otherwise stated.

9. *The Theory and Practice of Representation in Medieval England*

p. 262* Reprinted from H. M. Cam, *Law-Finders and Law-Makers in Medieval England.*

p. 263* The International Commission has continued to publish annual volumes of *Etudes*.

p. 265* The International Commission has recently published a new study of the urban movement in France during the eleventh and twelfth centuries: A. Vermeesch, *Essai sur les origines et la signification de la commune dans le nord de la France* (Heule, 1966).

p. 266* For the 'community of bachelors' in 1259 see F. M. Powicke, *Henry III and the Lord Edward*, p. 407.

p. 268* The texts referring to 'community of the whole land' in 1215 and to 'the community of the land' in 1258 are translated in Stephenson and Marcham, *op. cit.*, pp. 125, 144, 146.

p. 269* Reprinted with revisions in Gaines Post, *Studies in Medieval Legal Thought*, pp. 61–162.

p. 271* See Stephenson and Marcham, *op. cit.*, pp. 54–5 (1110), 77 (1166), 144–6 (1258), 151–2 (1265).

p. 271** 'This should be done to save expense to the community.'

p. 272* The principal reference is to J. G. Edwards's essay printed above, ch. 4.

p. 273* For the 'murder fine' see F. Pollock and F. W. Maitland, *History of English Law* I, 89: II, 487.

p. 274* For the regulations regarding sheriffs in 1258, see Stephenson and Marcham, *op. cit.*, p. 145.

10. 'Justice' in Early English Parliaments

p. 279* Reprinted from *B.I.H.R.* XXVII (1954). There is a critical review of some of the views expressed here by H. G. Richardson and G. O. Sayles in their *Parliaments and Great Councils in Medieval England* (reprinted from *L.Q.R.* LXXVII (1961), esp. pp. 410–20).

p. 279** See p. 133.

p. 281* On the way in which petitions were dealt with in parliament see also Jolliffe's discussion above, pp. 31–69.

p. 281** On 'singular' and 'common' petitions, see above, pp. 15–17.

p. 281† H. G. Richardson suggests that *Fleta* 'did not acquire its present form until some date between 1296 and 1300': *Bracton; The Problem of his Text*, pp. 31–2.

p. 282* See also *Fleta*, ed. H. G. Richardson and G. O. Sayles (Selden Society, LXXII, 1955), II, 109 and the translation in B. Wilkinson, *Constitutional History of Medieval England* III, 170.

p. 283* Translated in C. Stephenson and F. G. Marcham, *Sources of English Constitutional History*, p. 146.

p. 283** There is a more recent list of medieval parliaments and other related assemblies in *Handbook of British Chronology*, ed. F. M. Powicke and E. B. Fryde (2nd ed., 1961), pp. 492 ff.

p. 284* Translated Wilkinson, *op. cit.*, III, 144.

p. 286* Translated Stephenson and Marcham, *op. cit.*, p. 197.

p. 287* See also the *Handbook of British Chronology* referred to above.

p. 288* 'To treat of the business of Scotland and divers other matters ... and to consider in what manner and fashion it will be suitable for us to despatch the business of this parliament; and have everything settled before you and the agenda of the parliament set out in writing, since it suits us to stay there for the parliament not more than ten days or twelve at the most.'

p. 289* 'Because this parliament was summoned to redress divers mischiefs and injuries done to the commons, and anyone who felt himself aggrieved should put forward his bill and there should be lords and others assigned to hear them; but the lords so assigned, if anything touches the king, have the bills endorsed *coram rege*, for which reason nothing is done thereon and the mischiefs and grievances are in no wise redressed. Therefore may it please him of his good grace to ordain that the said bills should be scrutinized before the said lords and, by the advice of the chancellor, treasurer and others of the king's council, answered and endorsed in the manner which right and reason demand, for God's sake and as a work of charity; and that this be done before this parliament disperses.'

p. 289** 'There to come to a final agreement what judgement should be given.'

p. 289† See p. 118.

p. 290* 'Further, they pray that our lord the king will hold his parliament at Westminster each year until he is of age; and that at the beginning of each parliament those appointed to be near him should be removed and that anyone who has reason to plead regarding them should be heard.'

p. 290** 'Therefore the king removed him from power so that, if he had harmed anyone, he would be obliged to answer the complainant; and, indeed, it would be to the common good and in accordance with right if offices conferring so much power were made annual, in order that those who cannot be summoned while in office should at least be brought to judgement at the end of the year and not oppress those subject to them with prolonged hardship.'

p. 291* 'Further it is agreed that parliament shall be held on one occasion each year, or more often if there be business.'

p. 291** 'Item, for the maintenance of the said articles and statutes and to redress divers grievances and mischiefs which arise from day to day parliament shall be held each year as was previously ordained by statute.'

p. 292* 'Item, the *commune* prays that it will please him to ordain by statute in this present parliament that each year a parliament will be held to correct errors and falsities in the realm should any be found . . . In regard to annual parliaments there are statutes and ordinances which have been made, and which should be duly kept and observed.'

p. 294* 'Item, since many mischiefs have arisen from the fact that in divers places (as well in chancery, the king's bench, common pleas and the exchequer as before justices of assize and of oyer and terminer) judgements have been delayed: sometimes because of the difficulty of the case, sometimes because of differing opinions amongst the judges and sometimes for some other reason . . . It is conceded, established and agreed that in future, at each parliament, there will be chosen one prelate, two earls and two barons who will be commissioned and empowered by the king to hear, on petition delivered to them, the complaints of all who wish to complain regarding such delays or such grievances done to them; and they will have power to cause to come before them at Westminster (or at whatever other place they may be) the texts of the records and process of judgements so delayed, and to cause to come before them the said justices, who shall then be present, to hear what cause and reasons they give for such delays. When they have heard cause and reasons, after taking good advice amongst themselves, the chancellor, treasurer, justices of both benches and others of the king's council, as many and such as they deem necessary, they will proceed to a good agreement and a good judgement; and in accordance with the agreement so reached the text of the said record, together with such judgement as they have agreed on, shall be remitted to the judges before whom the plea is pending, which latter should proceed speedily to a judgement in accordance with the said agreement. And in case it seems to them that the difficulty is so great that it cannot properly be determined without the consent of parliament, let the text or texts [of the record] be brought by the said prelate, earls and barons to the next parliament and there let final agreement be reached about what judgement ought to be given in such a case; and in accordance with that agreement the justices before whom the plea is pending should be ordered to proceed to judgement without delay. And to make a start in providing remedy under this ordinance it is agreed that a commission and power be granted to the archbishop of Canterbury, the earls of Arundel and Huntingdon, Lord Wake and Sir Ralph Basset, to last until the next parliament.' For a summary account of the competence of the various courts referred to at the beginning of this statute, see T. F. T .Plucknett, *Concise History of the Common Law* (ed. of 1940), pp. 142, 148–9.

p. 295* 'Item, because many people are delayed in their pleas before the king's court, sometimes because a party alleges that the plaintiff ought not to be answered without the king [being consulted] and at other times the plaintiff himself makes the same allegation; and therefore many people are grieved by the king's ministers against right and cannot have recovery for such grievances without a common parliament . . . May it please our

said lord to hold parliament once yearly at the least and that in a convenient place; and that in these same parliaments pleas which are delayed in
this manner, and pleas whereon the judges are of divers opinions, may be
recorded and determined, and that in the same way bills delivered in
parliament should be determined as reason and law demand . . . In so far
as it is asked that parliaments should be held annually, let the statutes
made thereon be held and kept. And in the matter of pleas whereon the
judges are of divers opinions, there are statutes made thereon which the
king desires should be kept and firmly held.'

11. The English Parliament and Public Opinion, 1376–1388

p. 298* Reprinted from *The Collected Papers of Thomas Frederick Tout*
(Manchester, 1934), II, 173–90.

p. 299* The assembly that deposed Edward II in 1327 is discussed in
ch. 13, *infra.*

p. 299** For the background of this crisis *cf. supra,* ch. 8 and *Revue
belge de Philologie et d'Histoire* XLV (1967).

p. 301* Translated in B. Wilkinson, *Constitutional History of Medieval
England, 1216–1399* II, 193.

p. 302* For suggestions about the authorship of this chronicle see J. G.
Edwards, *E.H.R.* XLIII (1928), 103–9 and A. F. Pollard, *ibid.,* LIII (1938),
577–605.

p. 305* 'Many very fine verses were composed about him and his deeds at
this time.'

p. 306* 'The duke substituted at his will knights of the shire for others
(for he procured the removal of all who in the last parliament boldly
stood up for the community, so that only twelve of them were left in this
parliament, whom the duke could not remove, because the counties who
had elected them would not elect any others).'

p. 308* 'Many other things were enacted there. But who is going to relish
writing down parliamentary statutes, which were later entirely of no effect?
For the king with his privy council used either to alter or to annul all that
in previous parliaments had been enacted not only by the community of
the whole kingdom but by the nobility as well.'

p. 308** 'In this parliament nothing useful was done for the realm's
advantage because the lay lords, who should speak out for the welfare
and advantage of the realm, were opposed to each other and throughout
this time remained in discord. After the parliament had ended they parted
in discord.'

p. 309* 'He convened the sheriffs to find out what forces they could assemble against the barons and whether they would permit the election to parliament of only such knights of the shire as the king and his council had selected. To which the sheriffs replied that the commons supported the lords [opposed to the king] and for this reason they could not assemble an army for him. Concerning the election of the knights of the shire to parliament, they said that the communities wished to retain the accustomed procedures by which the knights were chosen by the communities.'

p. 310* 'This parliament was called merciless and it did not show mercy to anyone without the permission of the lords.'

p. 312* 'They entered the hall arm-in-arm, dressed in golden coats, and simultaneously bending their knees saluted the king.'

p. 312** 'The king sitting in full parliament and all the temporal and spiritual lords standing around him and the Commons being present at the bar [of the parliament hall].'

p. 313* This poem is not now considered to have been written by Langland. *Cf.* H. Cam, *Liberties and Communities in Medieval England* (1944), p. 229.

p. 314* A date in the second half of the reign of Edward II now seems very probable to most scholars. See especially M. V. Clarke, *Medieval Representation and Consent* (1936), V. H. Galbraith, *Journal of the Warburg Institute* XVI (1953), 81–99 and J. Taylor, *E.H.R.* LXXXIII (1968), 673–88.

12. The Parliamentary Committee of 1398

p. 316* Reprinted from *E.H.R.* XL (1925), 321–33.

p. 316** Translated in C. Stephenson and F. G. Marcham, *Sources of English Constitutional History* (1938), p. 252.

p. 318* Translated in B. Wilkinson, *Constitutional History of Medieval England, 1216–1399* II (1952), 308–9.

p. 319* 'Also our sovereign lord by the aforesaid assent has ordered and established that all the judgements, ordinances, declarations and establishments made in this present parliament should be held for statutes and declared as such and should have the force and vigour of a statute at every point.'

p. 320* 'And afterwards proclamation was made within the hearing of all the people to know whether they wished to consent to this kind of safeguard; to which they answered, raising high their right hands and shouting with loud voices, that it pleased them well and that they fully assented to this.'

p. 323* The subsequent publication in 1926 of the narrative ascribed to Thomas Favent showed that he was the chief spokesman of the Lords Appellants (*cf.* Wilkinson, *op. cit.*, p. 271).

p. 323** 'By assent of the lords and the knights of the shires, having the power of all the parliament to examine, answer and fully terminate both diverse petitions and the matters contained in them and all other matters and business moved in the presence of the king and never determined, with all that arises from them, as appears by the record of these things made in the same parliament.' *Cf.* Wilkinson, *op. cit.*, pp. 308–9.

p. 323† The commission may have met again on the following day, 24 April 1399. *Cf.* C. M. Barron, 'The Tyranny of Richard II', *B.I.H.R.* XLI (1968), 15, n. 5 (continued on p. 16).

p. 323†† 'Against all justice and against the laws and customs of his realm and contrary to the law of arms.'

p. 323§ 'By full advice, authority and assent of parliament.'

p. 324* Translated in Wilkinson, *op. cit.*, p. 280.

p. 324** Translated in Wilkinson, *op. cit.*, p. 290.

p. 325* 'Provided, however, that he approves, ratifies, confirms, observes and assures the firm observance of all and single statutes, ordinances, establishments and judgements made, given and rendered in our parliament which began on 17 September in the 21st year of our reign at Westminster and in the same parliament prorogued to and held at Shrewsbury, and also all the ordinances and judgements that may have to be made by the authority of the same parliament.'

p. 326* 'When and where he pleased.'

13. The Deposition of Richard II and the Accession of Henry IV

p. 329* Reprinted from *E.H.R.* LIV (1939), 215–39.

p. 329** Lapsley's two articles are reprinted in his *Crown, Community and Parliament* (Oxford, 1951), ch. 7 and 8.

p. 330* M. V. Clarke's contribution to this joint work is reprinted in her *Fourteenth Century Studies* (Oxford, 1937), ch. III.

p. 331* Wilkinson's views, as summarized here and discussed in detail in what follows, still remain controversial. They have been criticized by J. M. W. Bean in *History* XLIV (1959), 215–21. Wilkinson restated his case in *Constitutional History of England in the Fifteenth Century, 1399–1485* (1964), pp. 2–4, but the controversy continues. *Cf.* H. M. Cam in *Speculum* XLI (1966), 194 with Wilkinson's rejoinder, *ibid.*, XLII (1967),

675, n. 11 and R. H. Jones, *The Royal Policy of Richard II* (1968), p. 103, n. 6, who agrees with Bean.

Wilkinson's fundamental contention is that at the end of September 1399 Henry of Lancaster was facing serious political dangers and that this, rather than any 'constitutional' ideas, shaped most of his acts. Wilkinson appears to be making a valid point here and the controversy concerns only the precise nature and extent of these political dangers (*cf.* Jones, *op. cit.*, pp. 106-7).

p. 331** 'Afterwards the said duke went with his accomplices to Chester where king Richard went for a parley, having received assurance of security by the oath of lord Thomas Arundel and the earl of Northumberland. But the said duke of Hereford, seized king Richard there in breach of this oath and, taking him to London, put him in prison in the Tower of London.'

p. 332* Translated in Bean, *History* XLIV (1959), 217-18.

p. 332** 'When the duke of Lancaster knew for certain that the king had entered Wales, he hurried there and when they were not far from each other [the duke] sent the earl of Northumberland to the king. The latter was won over by the earl's words and multiple persuasions. The next day the king and the duke met and by a definite decision of the duke and the other lords the king was conducted to London.'

p. 333* 'To put him under secure custody, safeguarding his life, which the king wishes to be preserved most certainly.'

p. 333** 'In reply to him, the archbishop and very many other lords affirmed that such a renunciation and cession [of the crown] would be very useful and expedient.'

p. 334* 'The king has his court in his council in his parliaments.'

p. 334** 'The king is the head, the beginning and the end of parliament.'

p. 336* 'Law and Court of Parliament.'

p. 336** Reprinted in her *Fourteenth-Century Studies* (*cit. supra*), ch. v.

p. 337* There is a slightly fuller version of this article in M. V. Clarke, *Medieval Representation and Consent* (1936), ch. IX, quoted hereafter as Clarke (1936).

p. 338* 'On behalf of the queen, her son, the duke of Aquitaine and of all the earls, barons and community of the whole land assembled in London.'

p. 338** 'They came to the Parliament of the ruling queen.'

p. 338† 'General council of all the clergy and people of England.'

p. 339* 'Amidst the clamour of all the people unanimously persisting in this clamour.'

p. 340* Ecclesiastes x, 16, 'Woe to thee, O land, when thy king is a child.' (Clarke, 1936, p. 184, n. 5.)

p. 340** 'And all the people answered with one voice: we do not wish him to reign any more over us.'

p. 340† 2 Kings IV, 19, 'My head, my head.' (Clarke, 1936, p. 184, n. 6.)

p. 340†† 'The voice of the people [is] the voice of God.'

p. 341* 'Proctor of all in the land of England and of the whole parliament.'

p. 341** 'Allegiance was renounced to him, as a waster of the kingdom, by William Trussel, knight, into whose mouth the universality of parliament have put their words.'

p. 341† 'Proctor of the prelates, earls and barons and of the others named in my letter of procuration.'

p. 342* 'By one voice of all the son was raised to be king.'

p. 342** 'And there King Edward was deposed by the process conducted against him.'

p. 342† 'In this council, amidst the clamour of all the people unanimously persisting in their clamour that king Edward should be deposed ... Walter, archbishop of Canterbury declared these articles and king Edward was deposed by the assent and consent of all.'

p. 342†† 'The ruling of the kingdom was discussed and various proposals were made about it. It was revealed that the king, without seeking counsel, had perpetrated various [evils] and he was declared unfit for the kingly office.' ... 'and immediately it was decided and approved by all the nobles of the kingdom there present that the son should succeed the father in the rule of the kingdom.'

p. 343* 'After these things had been completed, one of the bishops shall ask the people whether they wanted to submit themselves to that prince and ruler and to obey his commands. Then the clergy and people there present would answer: we will and grant it.'

p. 344* Translated in Wilkinson, *Constitutional History of Medieval England, 1216–1399* III (1958), 99.

p. 347* 'Because of the assembly of Parliament there were present there the said archibishops of Canterbury and York, the duke of Lancaster and other dukes and lords both spiritual and temporal ... and the people of the said kingdom assembled in great multitudes.'

p. 348* Translated in Wilkinson, *op. cit.*, II (1952), 316.

p. 349* Translated *ibid.*

p. 349** Translated *ibid.*, p. 317.

p. 350* 'After this renunciation had been read publicly and unanimously accepted by the lords and the lesser people, king Richard was deposed and his royal throne was vacant. While the lords treated among themselves about [the choice of] a future king, the people acclaimed lord Henry, duke of Lancaster, and elected him king.'

p. 352* Translated in Wilkinson, *Constitutional History of the Fifteenth Century* (*cit. supra*), p. 299 and also in part in the introduction, *supra*, pp. 29–30.

SELECT BIBLIOGRAPHY

I HANDBOOKS AND SOURCES

(a) *Lists of Parliaments and Related Assemblies*
   Handbook of British Chronology, ed. Powicke, F. M. and Fryde, E. B. (2nd ed., London, 1961).

(b) *Collections of Sources in Translation*
   Stephenson, C. and Marcham, F. G. (eds.). *Sources of English Constitutional History* (New York, 1937).
   Wilkinson, B. *Constitutional History of Medieval England, 1216–1399*, 3 vols. (London, 1950–58).

(c) *Major Collections of Original Sources*
   Parliamentary Writs and Writs of Military Summons, ed. Palgrave, F. 2 vols. (London, 1827–34).
   Powicke, F. M. and Cheney, C. R. *Councils and Synods with other Documents relating to the English Church, 1205–1313*, II (1964).
   Rotuli Parliamentorum, I–III (London, 1783).
   Rotuli Parliamentorum Anglie Hactenus Inediti, 1279–1373. ed. Richardson, H. G. and Sayles, G. O. (Camden Society, 3rd Ser. LI, 1935).
   Statutes of the Realm, I–II (London, 1810–16).

(d) *Bibliographical Studies.*
   Cuttino, G. P. 'Medieval Parliament Reinterpreted', *Speculum*, XLI (1966).
   Edwards, J. G. *Historians and the Medieval English Parliament* (Glasgow, 1960).
   Hoyt, R. S. 'Recent Publications in the United States and Canada on the History of Representative Institutions', *Speculum*, XXIX (1954).
   Powicke F. M. 'Recent Work on the Origin of the English Parliament, *S.I.C.*, III (1939).
   Templeman G. 'The History of Parliament to 1400 in the Light of Recent Research', *University of Birmingham Historical Journal* I (1948); repr. *The Making of English History*, ed. Schuyler, R. L. and Ausubel, H. (New York, 1952).

II GENERAL STUDIES

(a) *General, Constitutional and Legal Histories*
   Clarke, M. V. *Fourteenth Century Studies* (Oxford, 1937).
   Holdsworth, W. S. *History of English Law*, vols. I—V, (London, various editions; vol. I, 7th ed. revised by Chrimes, S. B., 1956; vols. II—V, 1936–45).
   Jolliffe, J. E. A. *Constitutional History of Medieval England* (3rd ed., London 1954).
   Lyon, B. *Constitutional and Legal History of Medieval England* (New York, 1960).
   McKisack, M. *The Fourteenth Century, 1307–1399* (Oxford, 1959).

374

Petit-Dutaillis, C. and Lefebvre, G. *Studies and Notes Supplementary to Stubbs' Constitutional History*, III, trans. Robertson, M. I. E. and Treharne, R. F. (Manchester, 1929).

Plucknett, T. F. T. *Concise History of the Common Law* (5th ed., London, 1956).

Powicke, F. M. *The Thirteenth Century* (Oxford, 1953).

Stubbs, W. *Constitutional History of England*, 3 vols. (5th ed., Oxford, 1891–1903).

Wilkinson, B. 'The Political Revolution of the Thirteenth and Fourteenth Centuries in England', *Speculum*, XXIV (1949).

(b) *Comparative Studies of Representative Institutions*

Cam, H. M., Marongiu, A. and Stökl, G. 'Recent Work and Present Views on the Origins and Development of Representative Assemblies', *Relazioni del X Congresso di Scienze Storiche*, I (Florence, 1955).

McIlwain, C. H. 'Medieval Estates', *Cambridge Medieval History*, VII (Cambridge, 1958).

Marongiu, A. *Medieval Parliaments: a Comparative Study*, trans. Woolf, S. J. (London, 1968).

Myers, A. R. 'The English Parliament and the French Estates-General in the Middle Ages', *S.I.C.*, XXIV (1961).

Richardson, H. G. and Sayles, G. O. *The Irish Parliament in the Middle Ages* (Philadelphia and London, 1952).

(c) *General Studies of English Parliamentary History*

Cam, H. M. 'From Witness of the Shire to Full Parliament', *T.R.H.S.*, 4th Ser., XXVI (1944); repr. *Law-Finders and Law-Makers in Medieval England* (London, 1962).

Clarke, M. V. *Medieval Representation and Consent* (London, 1936).

Haskins, G. L. *The Growth of English Representative Government* (London, 1948).

Lapsley, G. *Crown, Community and Parliament in the Middle Ages*, ed. Cam, H. M. and Barraclough, G. (Oxford, 1951).

McFarlane, K. B. 'Parliament and Bastard Feudalism', *T.R.H.S.*, 4th Ser., XXVI (1944).

McIlwain, C. H. *The High Court of Parliament and its Supremacy* (New Haven, 1910).

Pollard, A. F. 'Plenum Parliamentum', *E.H.R.*, XXX (1915).

Pollard, A. F. *The Evolution of Parliament* (2nd ed., London, 1926).

Richardson, H. G. and Sayles, G. O. 'Parliaments and Great Councils in Medieval England', *L.Q.R.*, LXXVII (1961).

Richardson, H. G. and Sayles, G. O. 'The Early Records of the English Parliaments', *B.I.H.R.*, V–VI (1927–9).

Richardson, H. G. and Sayles, G. O. 'The Parliaments of Edward III', *B.I.H.R.*, VIII–IX (1930–2).

Thompson, F. *A Short History of Parliament, 1295–1642* (Minneapolis, 1953).

Thorgrimson, J. 'Plenum Parliamentum', *B.I.H.R.*, XXXII (1959).

Wilkinson, B. *Studies in the Constitutional History of England in the 13th and 14th Centuries* (Manchester, 1937).

(d) *Political Theories*

Carlyle, R. W. and A. J. *History of Medieval Political Thought in the West,* v (Edinburgh, 1928).

McIlwain, C. H. *Constitutionalism Ancient and Modern* (Ithaca, N.Y., 1947).

Post, G. *Studies in Medieval Legal Thought: Public Law and the State, 1100–1322* (Princeton, 1964).

Ullman,, W. *Principles of Government and Politics in the Middle Ages* (London, 1961).

(e) *Taxation and Representation*

Harriss, G. L. 'Parliament and Taxation: The Middle Ages', *S.I.C.*, xxxi (1966).

Harriss, G. L. 'Parliamentary taxation and the origins of appropriation of supply in England (1207–1340)', *Recueils de la Société Jean Bodin*, xxiv; *Gouvernés et Gouvernants* (1966).

Hoyt, R. S. 'Royal Demesne, Parliamentary Taxation and the Realm, 1294–1322', *Speculum*, xxiii (1948).

Hoyt, R. S. 'Royal Taxation and the Growth of the Realm in Medieval England', *Speculum*, xxv (1950).

Power, E. *The Wool Trade in English Medieval History* (Oxford, 1941).

Stephenson, C. *Medieval Institutions: Selected Essays*, ed. Lyon, B. D. (Ithaca, N.Y., 1954).

(f) *The Lords in Parliament*

Chew, H. M. *Ecclesiastical Tenants-in-Chief* (Oxford, 1932).

Pike, L. O. *Constitutional History of the House of Lords* (London, 1894).

Powell, J. E. and Wallis, K. *The House of Lords in the Middle Ages* (London, 1968).

Reich, A. M. *The Parliamentary Abbots to 1470* (Berkeley, 1941).

Roskell, J. S. 'The Problem of the Attendance of the Lords in Medieval Parliaments', *B.I.H.R.*, xxix (1956).

(g) *The Commons in Parliament*

Bassett, M. *Knights of the Shire for Bedfordshire during the Middle Ages* (Bedfordshire Historical Record Society, xxix, 1949).

Cam, H. M. 'Medieval Representation in Theory and Practice', *Speculum*, xxix (1954).

Cam, H. M. 'The Community of the Shire and the Payment of its Representatives in Parliament', *Liberties and Communities in Medieval England* (Cambridge, 1944).

Cam, H. M. 'Theory and Practice of Representation in Medieval England', *History*, xxxviii (1953); repr. *Law-Finders and Law-Makers in Medieval England* (London, 1962).

Cam, H. M. 'The Relation of English Members of Parliament to their Constituencies in the Fourteenth Century', *S.I.C.*, iii (1939); repr. *Liberties and Communities in Medieval England* (Cambridge, 1944).

Gooder, A. *Parliamentary Representation of Yorkshire*, i (Yorkshire Arch. Society, Record Series, xci, 1935).

Hornyold-Strickland, H. *Biographical Sketches of the Members of Parliament of Lancashire, 1290–1550* (Chetham Society, xciii: Manchester, 1935).

Latham, L. C. 'Collection of the Wages of the Knights of the Shire in the Fourteenth and Fifteenth Centuries', *E.H.R.*, XLVIII (1933).

McKisack, M. *The Parliamentary Representation of the English Boroughs during the Middle Ages* (Oxford, 1932).

Richardson, H. G. 'The Commons and Medieval Politics', *T.R.H.S.*, 4th Ser., XXVIII (1946).

Riess, L. *History of English Electoral Law in the Middle Ages*, trans. Wood-Legh, K. L. (Cambridge, 1940).

Roskell, J. S. *Knights of the Shire for the County Palatine of Lancaster, 1377–1460* (Chetham Society, XCVI: Manchester, 1937).

Roskell, J. S. 'Parliamentary Representation of Lincolnshire', *Nottingham Medieval Studies*, III (1959).

Roskell, J. S. *The Commons and their Speakers in the English Parliament* (Manchester, 1965).

Roskell, J. S. 'The Medieval Speakers for the Commons in Parliament', *B.I.H.R.*, XXIII (1950).

Willard, J. F. *Parliamentary Taxes on Personal Property, 1290–1334* (Cambridge, Mass., 1934).

Willard, J. F. 'Taxation Boroughs and Parliamentary Boroughs, 1294–1336', *Historical Essays in Honour of James Tait* (Manchester, 1933).

(h) *The Organization of Parliament*

Baldwin, J. F. *The King's Council in England during the Middle Ages* (Oxford, 1913).

Chrimes, S. B. *Introduction to the Administrative History of Medieval England* (Oxford, 1952).

Cuttino, G. P. 'King's Clerks and the Community of the Realm', *Speculum*, XXIX (1954).

Pollard, A. F. 'Receivers of Petitions and Clerks of Parliament', *E.H.R.*, LVII (1942).

Pollard, A. F. 'The Clerical Organization of Parliament', *E.H.R.*, LVII (1942).

Richardson, H. G. and Sayles, G. O. 'The King's Ministers in Parliament, 1272–1377', *E.H.R.*, XLVI–XLVII (1931–2).

Tout, T. F. *Chapters in Medieval Administrative History*, vols. I–IV (Manchester, 1910–28).

(i) *Parliament, Leglislation and the Courts of Law*

Gray, H. L. *The Influence of the Commons on Early Legislation: a Study of the Fourteenth and Fifteenth Centuries* (Cambridge, Mass., 1932).

Richardson, H. G. and Sayles, G. O. 'The Early Statutes', *L.Q.R.*, L (1934),

Sayles, G. O. (ed.). *Select Cases in the Court of King's Bench*, 6 vols. (Selden Society, 1936–65).

(j) *Representation of the Clergy*

Barker, E. *The Dominican Order and Convocation* (Oxford, 1913).

Kemp, E. W. *Counsel and Consent: Aspects of the Government of the Church as exemplified in the History of the English Provincial Synods* (London, 1961).

Lowry, E. C. 'Clerical Proctors in Parliament and Knights of the Shire', *E.H.R.*, XLVIII (1933).

Lunt, W. E. *Financial Relations of the Papacy with England to 1327* (Cambridge, Mass., 1939).

Lunt, W. E. *Financial Relations of the Papacy with England, 1327–1534* (Cambridge, Mass., 1962).

Weske, D. B. *Convocation of the Clergy* (London, 1937).

III WORKS PRINCIPALLY RELATING TO SPECIFIC PERIODS

(a) *Parliamentary Origins to 1307*

Cam, H. M. *The Hundred and the Hundred Rolls* (London, 1930).

Cam, H. M. 'The Quo Warranto Proceedings under Edward I', *History*, XI (1926); repr. *Liberties and Communities in Medieval England* (Cambridge, 1944).

Chaplais, P. 'Privy Seal Drafts, Rolls and Registers (Edward I—Edward II)', *E.H.R.*, LXXIII (1958).

Edwards, J. G. 'Confirmatio Cartarum and Baronial Grievances in 1297', *E.H.R.*, LVIII (1943).

Langmuir, G. I. 'Politics and Parliaments in the Early Thirteenth Century', *S.I.C.*, XXIX (1966).

Lunt, W. E. 'The Consent of the English Lower Clergy to Taxation during the Reign of Henry III', *Persecution and Liberty: Essays in Honor of George Lincoln Burr* (New York, 1931).

Lunt, W. E. 'William Testa and the Parliament of Carlisle', *E.H.R.*, XLI (1926).

Miller, E. *The Origins of Parliament* (Historical Association, London, 1960).

Plucknett, T. F. T. *Legislation of Edward I* (Oxford, 1949).

Powicke, F. M. *Henry III and the Lord Edward.* 2 vols. (Oxford, 1947).

Richardson, H. G. 'The Origins of Parliament', *T.R.H.S.*, 4th Ser., XI (1928).

Richardson, H. G. and Sayles, G. O. 'The Parliament of Carlisle, 1307', *E.H.R.*, LIII (1938).

Richardson, H. G. and Sayles, G. O. 'The Earliest known Official use of the Term "Parliament"', *E.H.R.*, LXXXII (1967).

Rothwell, H. 'Edward I and the Struggle for the Charters', *Studies in Medieval History presented to F. M. Powicke* (Oxford, 1948).

Rothwell, H. 'The Confirmation of the Charters, 1297', *E.H.R.*, LX (1945).

Sayles, G. O. *Medieval Foundations of England* (London, 1948).

Spufford, P. *Origins of the English Parliament* (London, 1967).

Sutherland, D. W. *Quo Warranto Proceedings in the Reign of Edward I* (Oxford, 1963).

Treharne, R. F. *The Baronial Plan of Reform, 1258–1263* (Manchester, 1932).

(b) *The Beginnings of Representation to 1307*

Deighton, H. S. 'Clerical Taxation by Consent', *E.H.R.*, LXVIII (1953).

Haskins, G. L. 'Les Fonctions des Représentants aux Parlements du Roi Edouard Ier d'Angleterre', *S.I.C.*, XXXI (1966).

Haskins, G. L. 'Petitions of Representatives in the Parliaments of Edward I', *E.H.R.*, LIII (1938).

Jenkinson, C. H. 'The First Parliament of Edward I', *E.H.R.*, XXV (1910).

Pasquet, D., *Essay on the Origins of the House of Commons*, trans. Laffan, R. G. D. (Cambridge, 1925).

Sayles, G. O. 'Representation of Cities and Boroughs in 1268', *E.H.R.*, XL (1925).

(c) *The Reign of Edward II and the Early Years of Edward III* (1307–36)

Clarke, M. V. 'Committees of Estates and the Deposition of Edward II', *Historical Essays in Honour of James Tait* (Manchester, 1933).

Clementi, D. 'That the statute of York is no longer ambiguous', *S.I.C.*, XXIV (1961).

Cuttino, G. P., 'A Reconsideration of the "Modus tenendi parliamentum" ', in Utley, F. L., *The Forward Movement of the Fourteenth Century* (Columbus, Ohio, 1961).

Davies, J. C. *Baronial Opposition to Edward II: its Character and Policy* (Cambridge, 1918).

Galbraith, V. H. 'The *Modus Tenendi Parliamentum*', *Journal of the Warburg and Courtauld Institutes*, XVI (1953).

Haskins, G. L. *The Statute of York and the Interest of the Commons* (Cambridge, Mass., 1935).

Hughes, A. 'The Parliament of Lincoln, 1316', *T.R.H.S.*, N.S., x (1896).

Johnstone, H. 'The Parliament of Lincoln of 1316', *E.H.R.*, XXXVI (1921).

Morris, W. A. 'Magnates and Community of the Realm in Parliament', *Medievalia et Humanistica*, I (1943).

Morris, W. A. 'The Date of the "Modus Tenendi Parliamentum" ', *E.H.R.*, XLIV (1934).

Roskell, J. S. 'A Consideration of Certain Aspects and Problems of the English *Modus Tenendi Parliamentum*', *Bulletin of the John Rylands Library*, L (1968).

Strayer, J. R. 'The Statute of York, and the Community of the Realm', *A.H.R.*, XLVII (1942).

Tout, T. F. *The Place of the Reign of Edward II in English History* (2nd ed., Manchester, 1936).

Trueman, J. H. 'The Statute of York and the Ordinances of 1311' *Medievalia et Humanistica*, x (1956).

Wilkinson, B. 'The Coronation Oath of Edward II and the Statute of York', *Speculum*, XIX (1944).

Wilkinson, B. 'The Negotiations preceding the Treaty of Leake, August 1318', *Studies in Medieval History presented to F. M. Powicke* (Oxford, 1948).

(d) *Beginnings of the Hundred Years War*

Edwards, J. G. 'Taxation and Consent in the Court of Common Pleas, 1338', *E.H.R.*, LVII (1942).

Fryde, E. B. 'Edward III's Wool Monopoly of 1337: a Fourteenth Century Royal Trading Venture', *History*, XXXVII (1952).

Fryde, E. B. 'Financial Resources of Edward I in the Netherlands in 1294–98 . . . and some comparisons with Edward III in 1337–40', *Revue Belge de Philologie et d'Histoire*, XL (1962) and XLV (1967).

Fryde, E. B. 'The English Farmers of the Customs, 1343–51', *T.R.H.S.*, 5th Ser., IX (1959).

Harriss, G. L. 'The Commons' Petitions of 1340', *E.H.R.*, LXXVIII (1963).

Hughes, D. *A Study of Social and Constitutional Tendencies in the Early Years of Edward III* (London, 1915).

Plucknett, T. F. T. *Statutes and their Interpretation in the First Half of the Fourteenth Century* (Cambridge, 1922).

Putnam, B. H. *The Place in Legal History of Sir William Shareshull* (Cambridge, 1950).

Rayner, D. 'Forms and Machinery of the "Commune Petition" in the Fourteenth Century', *E.H.R.*, LVI (1941).

Unwin, G., *Finance and Trade under Edward III* (Manchester, 1918).

Wilkinson, B. 'The Protest of the Earls of Arundel and Surrey in the Crisis of 1341', *E.H.R.*, XLVI (1931).

(e) *The Later Years of Edward III*

Bailey, C. C. 'The Campaign of 1375 and the Good Parliament', *E.H.R.*, LV (1940).

Edwards, J. G. *The Commons in Medieval English Parliaments* (London, 1957).

McFarlane, K. B. 'Parliament and Bastard Feudalism', *T.R.H.S.*, 4th Ser., XXVI (1944).

Plucknett, T. F. T. 'The Impeachments of 1376', *T.R.H.S.*, 5th Ser., I (1951).

Plucknett, T. F. T. 'The Origins of Impeachment', *T.R.H.S.*, 4th Ser., XXIV (1942).

Plucknett, T. F. T. 'Impeachment and Attainder', *T.R.H.S.*, 5th Ser., III (1953).

Rezneck, S. 'Early History of the Parliamentary Declaration of Treason', *E.H.R.*, XLII (1927).

Richardson, H. G. 'John of Gaunt and the Parliamentary Representation of Lancashire', *Bulletin of the John Rylands Library*, XXII (1938).

Roskell, J. S. 'Sir Peter de la Mare, Speaker for the Commons in Parliament in 1376 and 1377', *Nottingham Medieval Studies*, II (1958).

Wood-Legh, K. L. 'Sheriffs, Lawyers, and Belted Knights in the Parliaments of Edward III', *E.H.R.*, XLVI (1931).

Wood-Legh, K. L. 'The Knights' Attendance in the Parliaments of Edward III', *E.H.R.*, XLVII (1932).

(f) *The Reign of Richard II*

Chrimes, S. B. 'Richard II's Questions to the Judges, 1387', *L.Q.R.*, LXXII (1956).

Edwards, J. G. 'Some Common Petitions in Richard II's First Parliament', *B.I.H.R.*, XXVI (1953).

Jones, R. H. *The Royal Policy of Richard II: Absolutism in the Later Middle Ages* (Oxford, 1968).

Lewis, N. B. 'Re-election to Parliament in the Reign of Richard II', *E.H.R.*, XLVIII (1933).

McKisack, M. 'Borough Representation in Richard II's Reign', *E.H.R.*, XXXIX (1924).

Mathew, G. *The Court of Richard II* (London, 1968).

Plucknett, T. F. T. 'State Trials under Richard II', *T.R.H.S.*, 5th Ser., II (1952).

Rogers, A. 'Parliamentary Appeals for Treason in the Reign of Richard II', *American Journal of Legal History*, VIII (1964).

Roskell, J. S. 'Sir Richard de Waldegrave of Bures St. Mary, Speaker in the Parliament of 1381–2', *Proc. of Suffolk Institute of Archaeology*, XXVII (1957).

Ross, C. D. 'Forfeiture for Treason in the Reign of Richard II', *E.H.R.*, LXXI (1956).

Steel, A. *Richard II* (Cambridge, 1941).

(g) *The Lancastrian Revolution*

Barron, C. M. 'The Tyranny of Richard II', *B.I.H.R.*, XLI (1968)

Bean, J. M. W. 'Henry IV and the Percies', *History*, LIV (1959).

Richardson, H. G. 'Richard II's Last Parliament', *E.H.R.*, LII (1937).

Richardson, H. G. 'The Elections to the October Parliament of 1399', *B.I.H.R.*, XVI (1938).

INDEX

Aids, 143
Alexander IV, pope, 77
Amercements, 41, 51n, 53-4, 65
Anonimalle Chronicle, 302ff, 369
Articuli super cartas, 231
Arundel, Richard earl of, 26, 309
Arundel, Thomas, bishop of Ely and
    archbishop of York and Canter-
    bury, 23-4, 29-30, 187, 309, 331
Assize of Arms, 169
Assize of Measures, 41, 65

Bannerets, 305, 322, 348
Baronage
    and legislation, 187-8
    character of under Edward I, 132-3
Baronies, 208-9
Bedfordshire, knights of the shire for,
    215-16
Bek, Anthony, bishop of Durham,
    95ff, 112, 119
Bill containing the form of an act,
    185-6, 190
Black Death, 177
Bolingbroke, Henry of, *see* Henry IV
Boroughs, parliamentary, 217-18
Brabazon, Roger, 96-8, 133
Bracton, Henry de, 49, 128, 174, 179,
    203, 273, 335-6
Braybrook, Gerard de, 158, 215
Brittany, John of, 95-8, 110, 112
Bruce, Robert, 102-3
Burley, Simon, 308
Bussy, John, 26, 326, 328

Calais, 321
Cambridge, University of, 118, 135,
    359-60
Chancellor, 93-4, 108, 110, 112, 119,
    284, 309, 312, 327
Chancery, 17, 33ff, 93-4, 101, 108,
    113-15, 119-20, 138, 186, 224, 293,
    355, 367-8
    clerks of, 227
    jurisdiction of, 227
    masters in, 93

records of, 72-3, 113-15
    warrants, 119
Channel Islands, petitions from, 111,
    112, 227
Chaucer, Geoffrey, 313
Chester, justiciar of, 66
Clarendon, constitutions of, 265-6
Clement V, pope, 6, 104n
Clergy
    and idea of representation, 269-71,
    277
    and legislation, 187
Clerks, the king's 93-4, 98
Commissions of array, 251-2
Common law, 171, 173, 223, 231, 232,
    238
Common lawyers and legislation, 186-7
Common Pleas, court of, 49, 101, 127ff,
    203, 289-90, 293, 367-8
Commons, 6ff, 13ff, 26, 29-30, 79-80,
    88, 123-4, 178ff, 198, 200, 214-18,
    221, 224, 242ff, 262ff, 301ff, 337,
    347ff
    attendance of, 13-14, 150, 160ff,
    217-18, 219-20, 361-2
    elections to, 15, 217-18
    endorsement of petitions, 182ff
    expenses paid to, 80, 150, 160ff, 217n,
    219-20, 240-1, 358
    'full power' of, 7, 13, 30, 136ff, 178,
    268-9, 272-3, 360-1
    intercommuning with lords, 21-2, 23,
    177, 303
    re-election to, 14, 19-20, 150ff
    speakers of, 21, 26, 28n, 303ff
    See also Bussy, Hungerford, Mare,
    Tiptoft
Communitas bachelerie, 266, 365
Community, concept of, 267-8
    of the borough, 146-9
    of the county, 70, 144ff, 173, 273ff,
    360
    of the hundred, 273
    of the realm, 146-9, 181, 193-4,
    270-1, 278, 365
    of the vill, 273, 275, 277-8

382